Prayer: God's Prescription For Total Breakthrough

By the author of the Wonders of Fasting

Victor I. Iruobe

Discovering the incredible and limitless power of prevailing Prayer

Copyright 2016 © Victor I. Iruobe

All rights reserved. No part of this publication may be produced, distributed, or transmitted in any form or by any means, including photocopying, recording, or other electronic or mechanical methods, without the prior written permision of the publisher, except in the case of brief quotations embodied in critical reviews and certain other noncommercial uses permitted by copyright law.

For permission requests, write to the publisher, addressed "Attention: Permissions Coordinator" at the email address below:

Life and Success Media Ltd

e-mail: info@abookinsideyou.com

www.abookinsideyou.com

Unless otherwise stated, all scripture quotations are taken from the Holy Bible, New King James Version. Quotations marked NKJV are taken from the HOLY BIBLE, NEW KING JAMES VERSION. Copyright © 1973, 1978, 1984 by International Bible Society. Used by permission of Hodder and Stoughton Ltd, a member of the Hodder Headline Plc Group. All rights reserved. "NKJV" is a registered trademark of International Bible Society. UK trademark number 1448790.

Quotations marked KJV are from the Holy Bible,

King James Version.

ISBN Number: 978-1-907402-81-4

Cover Design: **MIA**design.com

DEDICATION

To all the 'Generals' of prayer: past and present who have paved the way for the glory of the LORD to invade the earth through their much praying.

For those that are still alive, may we continue to occupy till He comes!

CONTENTS

Foreword 11
Prologue 13

Part 1: the Bible and Prayer   19

Chapter 1: the Bible Perspective to Prayer 21
Chapter 2: Prayer Defined 35
Chapter 3: Man In Union With God Through Prayer 47
Chapter 4: Prayer Is the Connection Between Heaven and Earth 61

Part 2: the Purpose of Prayer   67

Chapter 5: Understanding the Purpose of Prayer 69
Chapter 6: Prayer Helps Us to Conform to Christ's Image 85
Chapter 7: Prayer Makes Tremendous Power Available 95
Chapter 8: Prayer – A Sure Place of Supernatural
    Protection and Rest 107
Chapter 9: Prayer Reveals the Will of God 123
Chapter 10: Prayer Has Power to Change the Plans of God 129
Chapter 11: Prayer - the Battlefield of the Believer 143

Part 3: Biblical Perspective to Prayer   159

Chapter 12: Principles of A Bible-Centred Prayer 161
Chapter 13: Putting First Thing First 185
Chapter 14: Prayer Must Be Effectual and Fervent 193
Chapter 15: Prayer Must Be Consistent with God's Word 203

Part 4: Common Misconceptions about Prayer   211

Chapter 16: Prayer: Not an Activity But A Lifestyle 213

Part 5: Understanding the Potency of Prayer   225

Chapter 17: Prayer: A Prerequisite for Breakthrough In Life............ 227
Chapter 18: Hannah - A Woman In Need... 245
Chapter 19: King Hezekiah... 255

Part 6: Prayer Enforcers   267

Chapter 20: the Word of God – Key Prayer Enforcer......................... 269
Chapter 21: Reasons Why the Word of God Is Vital In Prayer 285
Chapter 22: Prayer - Thanksgiving, Praise and Worship 301
Chapter 23: A Church In Constant Prayer Without Faith 313
Chapter 24: Prayer and Boldness (Confidence).................................. 331
Chapter 25: the Power of Importunity In Prayer 347
Chapter 26: the Parable of the Importunate Friend 367
Chapter 27: the Persistent Widow and the Canaanite Woman......... 375
Chapter 28: Vital Lessons In the School of Importunity................... 385

Part 7: Common Blockades to Prayer   407

Chapter 29: Hindrances to Prayer 409
Chapter 30: Selfish Motives 423
Chapter 31: Idols In the Heart 437
Chapter 32: Doubt and Unbelief 451
Chapter 33: the Ministry of the Holy Spirit in Prayer 463

Part 8: Categories of Prayer   481

Chapter 34: Personal Prayer 483
Chapter 35: Corporate or United Prayer 493

Chapter 36: All Kinds of Prayer 509
Chapter 37: Prayer of Faith 523
Chapter 38: Prayer of Agreement 535
Chapter 39: Prayer of Dedication or Consecration............................. 539
Chapter 40: the Prayer of Praise, Worship and Thanksgiving 543
Chapter 41: the Prayer of Binding and Loosing 551

Part 9: Understanding the Purpose and Potency of Biblical Fasting   555

Chapter 42: When Prayer Is Not Enough 557
Chapter 43: God's Purpose for Fasting 575

Epilogue... 593
Bibliography 597

My deepest appreciation to...

My wife, Pastor Ann Iruobe - my pearl and treasure. Thank you for your unwavering encouragement, weeks of prayer, editing and personal opinion you contributed to this book. I deeply love and appreciate you, sweetheart!

My four children (mighty men and women of valour). You are individually a treasure! All of you have brought tremendous joy to my life. Thank you for sharing in the call of God on my life.

The staff of Hope of Glory International Ministries. Thank you for your unflinching support and faithfulness. My wife and I love each of you dearly.

Most significantly, my sincere gratitude to the Almighty God for His unspeakable gift. Thank you Lord for your inspiration, great grace and for entrusting your people to me. I love you LORD.

JESUS IS LORD.

Foreword

Prayer is the staff the Christian pilgrims leans upon as he walks with God. It is the believer's opportunity to verbalise the needs of the heart. Prayer is the breath of the spirit. The food necessary for the spiritual man. Socialisation is necessary for the mind, prayer is a necessity for the spirit.

For us who live in this period, we need to learn the importance of praying and the most supreme argument for prayer is the Lord Jesus Christ himself.

He prayed at the grave of a dead man, the gate of a lost city, the Garden of Eden. He prayed in the morning. He took time alone apart from his disciples and sometimes all night - Luke 22:44

Prayer is important because God anticipated that human needs will arise. God created us to be people who look up to him. The Greek word for man Anthropos means he who is always looking up. He created us to look up to him, to call on him.

The true test of our Christian faith is revealed by the prevalence of prayer. The true proof of grace is confirmed by a life of prayer. We have a mandate to pray, if we don't we are in trouble.

The church must pray for its strength lies in its capacity to pray. The church must pray because we are under attack. The hungry soul of man shows that nothing else can be sufficient unless we pray.

In this book on prayer, Pastor Iruobe has done a most comprehensive work covering almost every remit and challenging us to this great lofty exercise. In this season when we see battles raging against the church, secularism and Darwinism eating the power of the church in the West. False doctrine and charlatanism destroying the power of the church in Africa and third world nation. Only prayer can become the major instrument to salvage the situation. The church must pray to push back this satanic encroachment which we have noticed.

It is my conviction that this classical work on prayer will become a major reference point for several decades to come. I believe it will become a tool for training in bible colleges and a major source for running prayer cells, prayer groups and raising praying churches.

Pastor Matthew Ashimolowo

Senior Pastor, KICC GLOBAL

PROLOGUE

Throughout history mankind has been filled with probing questions, which have invariably culminated in man searching for answers. Such seeming expenditure has left man searching for anything that would satisfy his desperate longing for solutions. His exploration in this sense has caused man to seek for knowledge in various fields, diligently and desperately searching for clues to a better life. There has also been an age-long quest for inner peace and for understanding the real purpose for man's existence on earth.

Out of this quest comes one of the greatest searches: the one to know and experience the power of God. There is an undeniable instinct inside the human heart that craves for communion with God. There is an undying appetite in man to relate and fellowship with the Almighty as the true source of life. God's promises to mankind to seek Him through prayer only serve as potent stimulus for man to find meaning to life through unflinching and selfless devotion to knowing Him.

Paramount, in my opinion, is God's invitation to mankind to call unto Him, with the unqualified promise to answer and unveil to him a world of limitless possibilities.

"Call unto me, and I will answer thee, and show thee great and mighty things, which thou knowest not" (Jer. 33:3).

The key to living in such a world is, undoubtedly, prayer! Destiny is not a matter of chance, it is a matter of choice, it is not a thing to be waited for, it is a thing to be pursued and achieved. The greatest power God has given to mankind is the power of prayer, and the greatest secret of prayer is secret prayer! R. A. Torrey could not be more correct when he said, "All that God is, and all that God has, is at the disposal of prayer. Prayer can do anything that God can do, and as God can do everything, prayer is omnipotent." Prayer is the connector between heaven and earth. The resources, treasures and blessings of heaven find residence on earth only through prayer. The only key that unlocks heaven-gates and causes an outpouring of His divine presence and blessings on man is none other than Holy Ghost inspired prayer.

A more thorough examination of Jeremiah 33:3 leaves us with a somewhat frightening insight: Whatever God promises to unveil or reveal to mankind through his prayer has already been provided for and made ready for him, waiting to be released if and when he calls on God. Paul gives a fascinating insight in his letter to the Ephesians on the matter:

"Blessed be the God and Father of our Lord Jesus Christ, who hath blessed us with all spiritual blessings in heavenly places in Christ (Eph. 1:3). Note the phrase *"Who hath Blessed us..."* In the same token, Peter teaches, *"... as his divine power* **hath given unto us all** *things that pertain unto life and godliness, through the knowledge of him that hath called us to glory and virtue: Whereby are given unto us exceeding great and precious promises: that by these ye might be partakers of the divine nature, having escaped the corruption that is in the world through lust."* (2 Pet. 1:3-4, emphasis added). Things pertaining to life and godliness are already ours, ready to be dispatched and appropriated only through prayer.

If man calls on 'his' maker, according to Jeremiah 33:3, he is given a legal right to God's blessings. But if he fails or refuses to call on God, he is denied those things forever. This is the reality that surrounds prayer. Prayer is effective and hugely beneficial to mankind as the only source of involving God in the affairs of man. The position is made categorically clear in the following scriptures:

"And Asa did that which was good and right in the eyes of the Lord his God...Therefore he said unto Judah, Let us build these cities, and make about them walls, and towers, gates, and bars, while the land is yet before us; because we have sought the Lord our God, we have sought him,

and he hath given us rest on every side. So they built and prospered" (2 Chr. 14:2, 7).

"And the Spirit of God came upon Azariah the son of Oded: And he went out to meet Asa, and said unto him, Hear ye me, Asa, and all Judah and Benjamin; The LORD is with you, while ye be with him; and if ye seek him, he will be found of you; but if ye forsake him, he will forsake you" (2 Chr. 15:1-2).

Verse 2 of the last scripture shows reciprocity, a principle we must understand. The Bible shows clearly that God deals with us as we deal with Him, and if we are seeking Him and applying His ways, He will respond in far greater measure to us in blessing. Nobody out-gives God! The principle of reciprocity, part of the much broader principle of "whatever one sows, one reaps," (Gal. 6:7) brings it down to a finer point and makes it very personal. We need to realise that this principle is at work in our relationship with God.

In describing God's love and desire to bless His people, Prophet Azariah declared a truth that is staggering in its implications: *"For the eyes of the Lord run to and fro throughout the whole earth, to shew himself strong in the behalf of them whose heart is perfect toward him…"* (2 Chr. 16:9). Since God is unchanging, what was true in Asa's days applies to us today. God is still on the search. He is searching for a man that will seek Him with the degree of intensity that is required to *upload* His blessings from heaven. The Bible says that God

"*...is a rewarder of them that **diligently** seek him*" (Heb. 11:6, emphasis added).

A good number of people have encountered God through prayer. Lives have been significantly changed and transformed through an encounter with God. The story of every great Christian achievement or a momentous change of circumstances on earth is the history of answered prayer.

Experiencing total breakthrough in life invariably requires God's significant input. Breakthrough in life is not an accident. It is a product of much sacrifice, self-discipline, warfare, and a habitual seeking of the help of the Almighty. No matter how grand and splendid a man's plans are, without the involvement of God, they are but exercise in futility. Remember, "*...Not by might, nor by power, but by my Spirit, saith the Lord of hosts*" (Zech. 4:6).

The Bible teaches, "*Except the Lord build the house, they labour in vain that build it: except the Lord keep the city, the watchman waketh but in vain. It is vain for you to rise up early, to sit up late, to eat the bread of sorrows: for so he giveth his beloved sleep*" (Psalm 127:1-2).

Man's greatest effort is doomed without God. Paul teaches, "*Not that we are sufficient of ourselves to think any thing as of ourselves; but our sufficiency is of God*" (2 Cor. 3:5). Further, in Phil. 4:13, he affirms, "*I can do all things through Christ which strengtheneth me.*"

It is an irrefutable fact that total breakthrough in life comes as a result of selfless and diligent seeking of God. The Scripture is replete with incredible examples of holy men and women whose lives had been radically and miraculously transformed, having discovered the secret of sheer dependence on God through revolutionary prayer.

I trust that the reading of this book will impact and ignite you with the fire of passionate seeking of the glory of God and its ultimate manifestation among mankind. Such longing and avid pursuit will, no doubt, impel you to a life of ardent prayer and service that will exemplify, propagate and celebrate the reign of Christ among His people even as we eagerly anticipate His glorious return to rapture His Church.

PART 1
THE BIBLE AND PRAYER

Chapter 1

THE BIBLE PERSPECTIVE TO PRAYER

GENERAL OVERVIEW

> *Forasmuch as many have taken in hand to set forth in order a declaration of those things which are most surely believed among us… It seemed good to me also, having had perfect understanding of all things from the very first, to write…* (Luke 1:1-3).

I find the above scripture a solid platform to start the noble journey of a 'chronicle' that unravels the incredible potency of the greatest force God has endowed humanity with. Many had, indeed, taken it upon themselves from the beginning of time to open great minds, through their writings on this all-important subject. Indeed, a plethora of books, articles, workshop sand conferences give credence to the renewed and overwhelming interests in the all-important topic of biblical prayer, and its relevance in bridging the two worlds of the celestial powers and the terrestrial world.

In spite of such volume of publications in this regard, the subject of prayer in all its ramifications, specifically the various ingredients of prevailing prayer remain an area of great interest in the body of Christ. I have, amongst those honoured with the onerous task of looking into this sacred calling, also decided, by the leading of the Holy Spirit, to contribute my heaven-inspired understanding and revelation to the vast work that has already been published in this field.

This book covers a wide range of topics including: several definitions of what prayer is from a biblical perspective, common misconceptions about prayer, things that must accompany prayer, common blockades to prayer, and the power of importunity in prayer, different kinds of prayer; biblical fasting and a host of other soul-inspiring topics.

As a committed Christian, I must confess that my views of the value and effectiveness of prayer has evolved over time, through the help of the Holy Ghost and the impactful teachings of the great men and women of God I have, over the years, been exposed to.

Prayer is God's royal invitation to man to ascend to the privileged position the death and resurrection of His son-Jesus has offered mankind.

Prayer is the highest honour God has bestowed on man. Prayer is God's royal invitation to man to ascend to the privileged position the death and resurrection of His son-Jesus has offered mankind. Prayer is man and his creator having something in common. Prayer takes place when man, therefore, accepts the "undeserved"

invitation of God and allows his creator to lavish His unconditional love on him. Prophet Isaiah expressed deep amazement at God's unmerited love for mankind when he said:

> *I will mention the lovingkindnesses of the Lord, and the praises of the Lord, according to all that the Lord hath bestowed on us, and the great goodness toward the house of Israel, which he hath bestowed on them according to his mercies, and according to the multitude of his lovingkindnesses* (Isaiah 63:7).

God, by His divine nature, seeks fellowship with man. The Bible tells us that *"The LORD looked down from heaven upon the children of men, to see if there were any that did understand, and seek God"* (Psalm 14:2). Right from the beginning of time, when God established relationship with man, He left him in no doubt of His intense crave for fellowship with him. This was vividly demonstrated in the Garden of Eden, where God constantly and habitually left His glory to seek intimacy with man, *"They heard the sound of the LORD God walking in the garden in the cool of the day..."* (Gen. 3:8). Interestingly, 2 Chronicles 16:9 tells us that the eyes of the LORD run to and fro throughout the whole earth, *"to shew himself strong in the behalf of them whose heart is perfect toward him..."*

The Bible teaches that when God created man, He breathed into man the breath of life, and man became a living soul (Gen. 2:7). By this singular act, man became quickened and brought to life with burning desire to seek God. In other words, man was created to seek communion with God. There is, indeed a void that cannot be filled by anything but genuine communion with God. No matter what man acquires, it cannot replace the fellowship that fulfils the very essence of man's being – giving purpose to life, nourishing the core of his soul.

John puts the position succinctly:

> *After this I looked, and, behold, a door was opened in heaven: and the first voice which I heard was as it were of a trumpet talking with me; which said, Come up hither, and I will shew thee things which must be hereafter* (Rev. 4:1).

The above scripture contains the incredible opportunities that are opened to the believer as he gives himself to prayer. We shall summarise these as follows:

As the believer diligently gazes at his maker in prayer (Psalm 34:5), the following takes place:

A DOOR IS OPENED UNTO HIM BEFORE THE THRONE OF GRACE:

"After this I looked, and, behold, a door was opened in heaven: and the first voice which I heard was as it were of a trumpet talking with me; which said, Come up hither, and I will shew thee things which must be hereafter...And they heard a loud voice from heaven saying to them, "Come up here." And they ascended to heaven in a cloud, and their

enemies saw them. And immediately I was in the spirit: and, behold, a throne was set in heaven, and one sat on the throne...And the temple of God was opened in heaven, and there was seen in his temple the ark of his testament: and there were lightnings, and voices, and thunderings, and an earthquake, and great hail." (Rev. 4: 1-2, 11:12, 19).

God yearns for a fervent relationship with man; consequently the door of unrestricted intimate fellowship is always opened unto man. God says to man: *"Call unto me, and I will answer thee, and shew thee great and mighty things, which thou knowest not"* (Jer. 33:3, emphasis added). Prayer is the door for an intimate relationship with God.

HE HEARS GOD'S SWEET VOICE.

Prayer is not rhetoric, or a religious ritual of *throwing* words at God. Prayer is a platform of bonding with God – becoming one with Him.

In essence, this further defines what prayer is; a dialogue, not a monologue. As we pray, we must be keen to hear God's voice in response. That is true biblical prayer! Prayer is not rhetoric, or a religious ritual of *throwing* words at God. Neither, is prayer so much of what we say as in being a platform of bonding with God - becoming one with Him. Prayer therefore, is not an activity but a lifestyle. When Solomon prayed, as recorded in 2 Chronicles 6:12-42, the Bible tells us that God appeared to him in the nigh (2 Chr. 7:12). Solomon's encounter with God carried on as we see in the following verses:

> *If I shut up heaven that there be no rain, or if I command the locusts to devour the land, or if I send pestilence among my people; If my people, which are called by my name, shall humble themselves, and pray, and seek my face, and turn from their wicked ways; then will I hear from heaven, and will forgive their sin, and will heal their land. Now mine eyes shall be open, and mine ears attent unto the prayer that is made in this place. For now have I chosen and sanctified this house, that my name may be there for ever: and mine eyes and mine heart shall be there perpetually.* (2 Chr. 7:13-16).

In Isaiah 38: 1-2, we have an account of Hezekiah's illness. The Bible says he *"was sick unto death…"* (Isaiah 38:1). Then the event that immediately followed was practically unexpected by him. We have a sense of this in the flow of emotion that was generated by the said event: right in the heat of his ordeal, Hezekiah had an unexpected guest in the person of Prophet Isaiah – a prophet of great renown, no doubt, a man of unquestionable character and repute. Quite naturally, Hezekiah, like any believer going through a dark moment in life would have expected this outstanding prophet to bring a message of hope from the Lord; but the opposite was, in fact, the case. Isaiah came, as it were, to proclaim a message of 'doom', *"…And Isaiah the prophet, the son of Amoz, went to him and said to him, "Thus says the Lord: 'Set your house in order, for you shall die and not live"* (Isaiah 38:1).

Upon receiving this rather unexpected message, what Hezekiah did in response remains an invaluable lesson for believers of all time: *"Then Hezekiah turned his face toward the wall, and **prayed** unto the Lord"* (Isaiah 38:2, emphasis added). Why? Because prayer is the answer to every problem there is. Every situation on earth has a solution waiting in the presence of the Lord!

In a dramatic twist of events, God spontaneously moved in response to the prayer of Hezekiah:

Verse 4 opens with a significant word *"then"*, indicative of the fact that what followed was precipitated upon a previous or prior event; in this case, the prayer of Hezekiah. The full text of that verse says, *"Then came the word of the Lord to Isaiah, saying..."* In other words, Hezekiah prayed and God responded! This is a master-piece of a Bible-based prayer.

What did God say in response?

> *Go, and say to Hezekiah, Thus saith the Lord, the God of David thy father, I have heard thy prayer, I have seen thy tears: behold, I will add unto thy days fifteen years. And I will deliver thee and this city out of the hand of the king of Assyria: and I will defend this city. And this shall be a sign unto thee from the Lord, that the Lord will do this thing that he hath spoken; Behold, I will bring again the shadow of the degrees, which is gone down in the sun dial of Ahaz, ten degrees backward. So the sun returned ten degrees, by which degrees it was gone down* (Isaiah 38:5-8).

INVITATION IS ISSUED FOR GREATER INTIMACY

Prayer connects the praying believer to God. Prayer leads to intimacy with God which, in turns leads to greater prayer, which further causes the saint to conform to God's image. The Bible teaches that as we bask in His divine presence, a process of transformation ensues which causes the praying believer to become less of himself and less of the world, to become more divine, and therefore, more of God.

> But we all, with open face beholding as in a glass the glory of the Lord, are changed into the same image from glory to glory, even as by the Spirit of the Lord (2 Cor. 3:18).

Notice that the process of divine transformation, while not the main object of seeking the Lord, results as a by-product of intimacy with God, through prayer.

A FLOODGATE OF REVELATION IS IMPACTED ON THE PRAYING SAINT.

> Prayer opens the eyes of God's children to the spirit world. Instead of just intuition, the believer flows in discernment.

God Himself takes the believer on a journey. Revelation of things to come is unveiled to the praying saint. Prayer opens the eyes of God's children to the spirit-world. Instead of just intuition, the believer flows in discernment. While the carnal man or the less matured believer says *"something told me"*, the praying saint is surer and far more accurate about the source of his revelation. God unveils things to His children that seek Him. The Bible tells us clearly that, *"Surely the Lord GOD will do nothing, but he reveals his secret to his servants the..."* (Amos 3:7). His secret—namely, His will and purposes that are hidden from man, His determinate counsel, which would never be known otherwise, is revealed to the praying believer. Very clearly, the Bible stipulates, *"The secret things belong unto the LORD our God: but those things which are revealed belong unto us and to our children for ever, that we may do all the words of this law."* (Deut. 29:29).

For instance, in Genesis 18:17, God puts Himself under obligation to reveal His plans about Sodom and Gomorrah to Abraham. In a wider sense, God's will is revealed to all who love and seek Him. The offer of God's deep secret is not to the world. Psalm 25: 14 says, *"The secret of the Lord is with them that fear him; and he will shew them his* covenant." Further in John 15:15, Jesus affirms,

"Henceforth I call you not servants; for the servant knoweth not what his lord doeth: but I have called you friends; for all things that I have heard of my Father I have made known unto you."

Paul was succinct when he said:

"But as it is written, Eye has not seen, nor ear heard, neither have entered into the heart of man, the things which God

has prepared for them that love him" (1 Cor. 2:9). Thank God it does not stop there. The subsequent verse lends so much weight to our discussion. It says, "**But God hath revealed them unto us by his Spirit**: *for the Spirit searcheth all things, yea, the deep things of God*" (1 Cor. 2:10, emphasis added). God's divine provisions – "*the things which God has prepared* "for man" (1 Cor. 2:9) are not locked away somewhere inaccessible. The Bible says, "*they are revealed …*" (1 Cor. 2:9), not to the world, or the generality of Christians necessarily, but to "*…them that love him*" (1 Cor. 2:9). I believe this is in reference to the praying saints, because it takes deep love for God to spend time with Him in prayer. Recall the calibre of men the Bible generally refers to as the "*friend of God*". The only criteria that qualified them for such accolade was their intimate relationship with God. These men were affectionately in-tune with God through prayer. Profiling these men showed a common trend: they were ordinary men that achieved the extra-ordinary for God and their generations through the power of fierce, intense and prevailing prayer. They were not without flaws, but men who, through their personate pursuit of His presence, were able to subdue and overcome their weaknesses, faults, and imperfections; against all odds did astonishing exploits for God.

The depth of the revelation we receive from God is in direct proportion to the level of intimacy we maintain with Him. As a matter of fact, God promises an unfolding of divine revelation specifically to those that are intimate with Him in prayer. God says, "*Call unto me, and I will answer thee, and* **show thee great and mighty things, which thou knowest not**" (Jer. 33:3, emphasis added).

I am profoundly amazed at the incredible depth of revelation the word of God credits to Apostle Paul, a man that did not have any human contact with the Lord Jesus when He walked the earth. He writes in 1 Cor. 11:23, "*For I have received of the Lord that which also I delivered unto you...*"

According to the Pulpit Commentary, the above statement refers to some immediate revelation from Christ. Many saints of God, in Bible time, were visited with profound, eventful, and sometimes, destiny-altering revelations through prayer. This was particularly the case with Jacob, the son of Isaac and grandson of Abraham.

In Gen. 28:10-22, Jacob was fleeing from his twin brother Esau, who had vowed to kill him because Jacob had stolen the latter's birth-right, according to the Jewish claim to inheritance and blessing. His destination was Haran where both Jacob and Esau had a relative. However, in a place near Luz, Jacob lay down for the night, and had a dream. In the process, Jacob had a vision of a ladder, or stairway, between heaven and earth. God's angels were on it, ascending and descending.

Jacob saw God standing above the ladder. God repeated the promise of support he had made to Abraham and Isaac. God then made the following pronouncement:

"And, behold, I am with thee, and will keep thee in all places whither thou goest, and will bring thee again into this land; for I will not leave thee, until I have done that which I have spoken to thee of" (Gen. 28:15).

When Jacob awoke, he believed that God was present in the place. He took the stone he had been using to rest his head, poured oil on it and consecrated it to God. Then Jacob made a vow, saying,

> *If God will be with me and will keep me in this way that I go, and will give me bread to eat and clothing to wear, so that I come again to my father's house in peace, then the LORD shall be my God, and this stone, which I have set up for a pillar, shall be God's house. And of all that you give me I will give a full tenth to you* (Gen. 28:20-22, ESV).

Jacob called the place Bethel, meaning "House of God."

What God is looking for is yielding vessels to partner with. When Prophet Isaiah said *"Here I am, send me..."* (Isaiah 6:8), in response to God's diligent search for a man, he had in God's assessment and estimation, become *"a vessel set apart and useful for honourable and noble purposes, consecrated and profitable to the Master, fit and ready for any good work"* (2 Tim. 2:21 Amp.), hence God flooded his heart with the profound revelation of

His plan for the redemption of man. There was no iota of doubt, in his heart about the clarity and vividness of the revelation he had received from God. He was so sure and certain of the revelation that took another 400 years to materialise, that he coded it as though the event had already taken place.

He said:

*"**For unto us a child is born**, unto us a son is given: and the government shall be upon his shoulder: and his name shall be called Wonderful, Counsellor, The mighty God, The everlasting Father, The Prince of Peace"* (Isaiah 9:6, emphasis added).

There is no limit to what God can reveal to any willing vessel, deemed qualified by God. Like Deborah, God's heart is towards [those] that have *"offered themselves willingly..."* to Him (Judges 5:9).

Chapter 2

PRAYER DEFINED

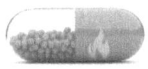

In its simplest definition, prayer is fellowship with God. It is God and man sharing communion through a life-transforming dialogue. Prayer, in the true biblical sense, therefore, is the whole spectrum of man's expression to God. To use Bob Sorge's phrase, "Prayer is the all-encompassing title to describe the entire gamut of expressing we offer up to God. Therefore, prayer", he affirms, " includes praise, thanksgiving, adoration, intercession, worship, supplication, shouts of joy, lifting of hands…spiritual warfare…"

Myles Munroe, on the other hand, defines prayer as, "…man giving God the legal right and permission to interfere in earth's affairs." He affirms that prayer is, "…man exercising his legal authority on earth to invoke heaven's influence on the planet."

Prayer is the most powerful force on the earth; the most thrilling and fulfilling privilege of the Christian world. Prayer is entirely a personal and spontaneous expression of the attitude of the soul toward the Almighty. It is the communion of sonship and the expression of fellowship with the father. True praying is the sincere attitude of reaching heavenward for the attainment of His likeness and holiness. It is the expression of man's dependency upon God for all things.

There is a profound longing, indeed cry, in the heart of man for a heart connection with his maker. As a matter of fact, man was created to abide in God's presence. There is to be an abiding-relationship between God and man for the latter's inextinguishable hunger for his maker to be satisfied. This was the case in the Garden of Eden, we earlier referred to. The Garden of Eden was a place of magnificent beauty and glory, an epitome of God's spiritual paradise - where God, in all His majesty, longing for fellowship with man, would visit and share union with Adam and Eve – his wife, who also craved for His majesty's presence and intimacy.

"...And they heard the voice of the Lord God walking in the garden in the cool of the day" (Gen. 3:8).

Note that this process went on for such a considerable time that Adam and Eve lived in anticipation of a flamboyant and robust fellowship with God. They expected God to be walking with them in the garden. Had they not sinned, they would have been in fellowship with God forever.

From the beginning of time, God had demonstrated to us His intense desire to bond with man in glowing fellowship.

JESUS – THE CONNECTOR

Jesus is the link between God and humanity. All of God's resources, indeed, everything man ever desires: in health, prosperity, restoration, progress and breakthrough in life is in Christ Jesus. Without a shadow of doubt, Paul was emphatic when he said, we *"are complete in Him"* (Col. 2:10). He who has the son – Jesus, therefore, has everything that God has made available for humanity.

> *Philip said to Him, "Lord, show us the Father, and it is sufficient for us." Jesus said to him, "Have I been with you so long, and yet you have not known Me, Philip?* **He who has seen Me has seen the Father**; *so how can you say, 'Show us the Father?* (John 14:8-9, emphasis added).

In John 10:30, Jesus said, "I and my Father are one." Also in Phil. 2:6-9, Paul writes, *"Who, being in the form of God, thought it not robbery to be equal with God: But made himself of no reputation, and took upon him the form of a servant, and was made in the likeness of men: And being found in fashion as a man, he humbled himself, and became obedient unto death, even the death of the cross. Wherefore God also hath highly exalted him, and given him a name which is above every name."*

In an amazing fashion, Jesus laid bare this truth without hesitation:

"...I am the way, the truth, and the life: no man cometh unto the Father, but by me" (John 14:6).

Jesus came to make us one with God. In other words, He came to reconcile us to God. The word "redeem" which is susceptible to several meanings, but in particular, indicates a state of *'being bought back'*, gives a vivid illustration of the process of the reconciliation Jesus undertook on our behalf. This brings greater illumination into such Jesus' teachings as in John 23:16, "*Verily, verily, I say unto you, whatsoever you shall ask the Father in my name, he will give it to you.*" That means there is no access to the father without Jesus. He is the way, the only way to the father!

In John 17:12-23 Jesus explains, "*That they all may be one; as thou, Father, art in me, and I in thee, that they also may be one in us: that the world may believe that thou hast sent me. And the glory which thou gavest me I have given them; that they may be one, even as we are one: I in them, and thou in me, that they may be made perfect in one; and that the world may know that thou hast sent me, and hast loved them, as thou hast loved me.*"

As stated, at creation, the Bible says God breathed into Adam the breath of life, and Adam became a living soul. Adam was a physical being before he became a spiritual being. Adam's spiritual dimension gave him the capacity for communion and fellowship with God. Even though man lost fellowship with God through sin, God still desired to have constant, uninterrupted fellowship with man, so God took the initiative with Abraham – the father of the faithful who would have the opportunity to fellowship with God.

In sum, prayer is the all – encompassing concept that describes the totality of human expressions to and communion with God. Without prayer any relationship with God is futile; as a matter of fact, impoverished because life is at its wit's-end without communication with God. For a better understanding, it is imperative for us to explore some of other various ramifications of biblical prayer at a definitional threshold.

PRAYER IS COMMUNION

Prayer is a means of engaging in deep communion with God – rendered *Koinonia* in Greek; which identifies the deep state of fellowship and bond that should exist between man and his maker.

In the profession of faith, everything rises and falls on relationship. Relationship with God is crucial! It is the pivotal ingredient of the Christian faith.

In the profession of faith, everything rises and falls on relationship. Relationship with God is crucial! It is the pivotal ingredient of the Christian faith. You are either in a healthy relationship with God, and therefore, have a common ground to commune with and express your desires to Him or you are not, and consequently rob yourself of the tremendous benefits that such relationship offers. What qualifies your communication with God as prayer is your communion with Him. Without communion, your seeming communications with the father are, but empty words.

Relationship with God is further strengthened by constant fellowship with Him. In the course of such fellowship, the believer goes through stages of transformation that nothing else, but unceasing and deep fellowship with God orchestrates. The Bible says, *"But we all, with open face beholding as in a glass the glory of the Lord,* **are changed into the same image from glory to glory***, even as by the Spirit of the Lord"* (2 Cor. 3:18, emphasis added).

Notice according to the above scripture, the believer constantly goes through a transforming process as he spends time with God. He is "...*changed into* **the same image**..." (2 Cor. 3:18, emphasis added) - the image of the one he beholds. What a privilege! In the process, the Lord reveals Himself further to the believer; which gives the believer greater burden to seek God deeper. Prayer produces spiritual understanding that motivates us to seek Him with tremendous burden and intensity.

David vows, *"My voice shalt thou hear in the morning, O LORD; in the morning will I direct my prayer unto thee, and will look up"* (Psalms 5:3). A degree of understanding brought David to this level of intimacy with God. He did not attain such height of desperate pursuit of the Lord overnight. He had discovered that there was no meaning to life without God's involvement in the affairs of man, through prayer. Indeed, prayer makes the difference! The same David affirms, *"I will bless the LORD who has counseled me; Indeed, my mind instructs me in the night. I have set the LORD continually before me; Because He is at my right hand, I will not be shaken. Therefore my heart is glad and my glory rejoices; My flesh also will dwell securely…"* (Psalm 16:8, NIV).

This is the level of fellowship that moves God to lavish His treasures upon the believer.

For Abraham, God was not ashamed to be seen consulting with a mortal man on the vital issues He had absolute prerogative to decide upon, in the first place:

> *And the LORD said, Shall I hide from Abraham that thing which I do; Seeing that Abraham shall surely become a great and mighty nation, and all the nations of the earth shall be blessed in him? For I know him, that he will command his children and his household after him, and they shall keep the way of the LORD, to do justice and judgment; that the LORD may bring upon Abraham that which he hath spoken of him* (Gen. 18: 17-19).

What an endorsement! Why was God so certain of Abraham's disposition? Where did it all begin with them? Where could God have known Abraham? The answer is at the place of the altar.

At the place of the altar, Abraham had sold out his heart to God, holding nothing, absolutely nothing back. So, God could say, *"For I know him…"*, putting His integrity on the line. This is a 'knowing' of a deeper sense. It speaks of a level of intimacy with God that makes man indispensable in the unfolding of God's program on earth.

PRAYER IS TRANSLATING MAN'S HELPLESSNESS INTO A MONUMENT OF NEED BEFORE GOD.

Often when man is in a dire situation, he does everything but the only thing he should do – run to God. However, there comes a stage where his best effort proves abortive, his best ideas only but remind him of his frailty as human. Usually when man gets to his wits' end – a place of helplessness and hopelessness, he, without hesitation, always seeks the Lord's intervention. Isaiah declares, *"LORD, in trouble have they visited thee, **they poured out a prayer** when thy chastening was upon them"* (Isaiah 26:16, emphasis added).

At such times, without fail, he comes face to face with the reality of God being man's refuge in times of trouble. He builds confidence in God as a tower of refuge (Pro. 18:10).

David affirms:

> *God is our refuge and strength, a very present help in trouble. Therefore will not we fear, though the earth be removed, and though the mountains be carried into the midst of the sea; Though the waters thereof roar and be troubled, though the mountains shake with the swelling thereof. There is a river, the streams whereof shall make glad the city of God, the holy place of the tabernacles of the most High. God is in the midst of her; she shall not be moved: God shall help her, and that*

> *right early....Be still, and know that I am God: I will be exalted among the heathen, I will be exalted in the earth. apparently, and not in dark speeches; and the similitude of the LORD shall he with us; the God of Jacob is our refuge* (Psalm 46: 1-5, 10-11).

The work of the Lord is adorable! The reason we should be comforted in the Lord in the face of, even the greatest challenges of life, according to this scripture, is God's *presence* with the believer in tribulations and His *ability* to deliver him in adverse situations. This revelation helps us, according to Paul, to "*...glory in tribulations ...*" (Rom. 5:3), and he adds, "*...knowing that tribulation works patience; And patience, experience; and experience, hope: And hope maketh not ashamed; because the love of God is shed abroad in our hearts by the Holy Ghost which is given unto us*" (verses 4-5). Hope has the ability to help us see the final outcome in a positive way, even while the situation is still ongoing.

The overall strength of the entire chapter lies in the weight of the very first verse:

"God is our refuge and strength, A very present help in trouble."

Verses two and three are anchored on three fundamental attributes offered in verse one : refuge, strength and present help; which are repeated in verses seven and eleven:

"The Lord of hosts is with us; The God of Jacob is our refuge. The Lord of hosts is with us; The God of Jacob is our refuge" (verses 7, 11).

This does not suggest, in any way, that man should have recourse to prayer only when he is faced with seemingly insurmountable situations. The fact remains, however, that people usually do not see the need to pray until they are faced with the challenges of life.

GOD'S INTERVENTION WITHOUT MAN'S IMPUTE

In extreme cases, however, God in His sovereignty intervenes in situations without any spiritual impute from the person needing such intervention. A very splendid example is found in Ezekiel 37:1:

"The hand of the LORD was upon me,[God grabbed me. God's Spirit took me up and sat me down in the middle of an open plain strewn with bones] and carried me out in the spirit of the LORD, and set me down in the midst of the valley which [was] full of bones" (The Message Bible).

The whole process was initiated by God, not man. This is consistent with the view held by Matthew Henry who postulates that:

"No created power could restore human bones to life. God alone could cause them to live. Skin and flesh covered them, and the wind was then told to blow upon these bodies; and they were restored to life. The wind was an emblem of the Spirit of God, and represented his quickening powers."

Also in Zechariah chapter 3:1-4, we find another vivid example of God's intervention in a situation where the recipient had no impute whatsoever, at least, at the instigation of the event:

> And he shewed me Joshua the high priest standing before the angel of the Lord, and Satan standing at his right hand to resist him. And the Lord said unto Satan, The Lord rebuke thee, O Satan; even the Lord that hath chosen Jerusalem rebuke thee: is not this a brand plucked out of the fire? Now Joshua was clothed with filthy garments, and stood before the angel. And he answered and spake unto those that stood before him, saying, Take away the filthy garments from him. And unto him he said, Behold, I have caused thine iniquity to pass from thee, and I will clothe thee with change of raiment.

It is no doubt, beyond the scope of this book to canvass the possible scenarios that necessitated the events detailed in the two scriptural passages explained above. The golden rule remains that for God to be involved in the affair of man in any significant way, He has to be consciously brought into it through prayer.

Chapter 3

MAN IN UNION WITH GOD THROUGH PRAYER

There is a point in spiritual growth and spiritual union with God that the needs of God and the needs of man become indivisible. When a person attains that level of growth and union he will find that he cannot pray for God's holiness without being concerned about his own holiness ;that he cannot pray about the kingdom of God coming without praying that his own kingdom might be caused to disappear... - Zacharias Fomum.

The life of Abraham fits this description quite accurately. His life was in union with God. In perhaps, one of the most remarkable examples of intercessory prayer in the entire Bible, Abraham was undoubtedly, concerned about his nephew -Lot and all the people he had rescued from the four kings who lived in Sodom. Although he was well aware of their spiritual condition, he hoped that they would repent and turn to the Lord:

In Genesis 18:16-33, Abraham appeals to God's righteousness to intercede for Sodom and Gomorrah.

Abraham, in a desperate attempt to spare the destruction of the righteous in Sodom and Gomorrah, appealed to God quite passionately:

> *And Abraham drew near, and said, Wilt thou also destroy the righteous with the wicked? Peradventure there be fifty righteous within the city: wilt thou also destroy and not spare the place for the fifty righteous that are therein? That be far from thee to do after this manner, to slay the righteous with the wicked: and that the righteous should be as the wicked, that be far from thee: Shall not the Judge of all the earth do right?* (verses 18: 23-25).

According to Abraham, the righteous should not die with the wicked; instead, God should spare the cities for the sake of the righteous. Abraham asked God if the cities would be spared for the sake of certain quotas of righteous people. He began with 50 people, lowers the number to 45, then to 40, 30, 20, and ends, apparently satisfied, at 10. God agrees to each request.

Why was Abraham so bold in his conversation with God?

The answer is 'intimacy'. A relationship had developed between God and Abraham that made God relate with Abraham as a friend.

Concerning Moses, God said,

> **With him will I speak mouth to mouth**, *even apparently, and not in dark speeches; and the similitude of the* LORD *shall he behold: wherefore then were ye not afraid to speak against my servant Moses? (Num. 12:8, emphasis added).*

This statement is one of the most compelling declarations in the Bible that substantiates the position of honour God places man in His heart. On its basis, it is apt to conclude, first; that there are different levels of relationship one could maintain with God. Second, that man determines the degree of relationship that exists between him and his maker. James 4:8 goes to the heart of the matter, *"Draw nigh to God, and he will draw nigh to you..."* Man must, of necessity, desire and instigate intimacy with God to earn God's friendship.

PRAYER- THE RAIL OF BLESSING AND POWER

> *I never saw a man get anything from God who prayed on the earth. If you get anything from God you will have to pray into heaven for it is all there* -**Smith Wigglesworth**.

Prayer is the rail through which God conveys His blessing and power.

James 1:17 declares:

"Every good gift, and every perfect gift is from above, & cometh down from the Father of lights, with whom is no variableness, neither shadow of turning".

In the words of Richard Newton, "The principal cause of my leanness and unfruitfulness is owing to an unaccountable backwardness to pray. I can write or read or converse or hear with a ready heart; but prayer is more spiritual and inward than any of these, and the more spiritual any duty is, the more my carnal heart is apt to start from it."

The more we pray, the more God is in a position to release blessings into our lives. As a matter of fact, the believer determines the measure of God's blessings that flow in his life, because the more of the rails of prayer that the believers make available, the more God's vehicle of blessings and power moves in his life. God will never crash into or interfere in the affairs of man. He is either invited through the believers' prayer or He's disregarded and He steers clear. The Bible says, "…*ye have not, because ye ask not...*" (James 4:2). This truth is illustrated perfectly in John's Gospel chapter 2: 1-11.

> *And the third day there was a marriage in Cana of Galilee; and the mother of Jesus was there: And both Jesus was called, and his disciples, to the marriage. And when they wanted wine, the mother of Jesus saith unto him, They have no wine. Jesus saith unto her, Woman, what have I to do with thee? mine hour is not yet come. His mother saith unto the servants, Whatsoever he saith unto you, do it. And there were set there six waterpots of stone, after the manner of the purifying of the Jews, containing two or three firkins apiece. Jesus saith unto them, Fill the waterpots with water. And they filled them up to the brim. And he saith unto them, Draw out now, and bear unto the governor of the feast. And they bare it. When the ruler of the feast had tasted the water that was made wine, and knew not whence it was: (but the servants which drew the water knew;) the governor of the feast called the bridegroom, And saith unto him, Every man*

at the beginning doth set forth good wine; and when men have well drunk, then that which is worse: but thou hast kept the good wine until now. This beginning of miracles did Jesus in Cana of Galilee, and manifested forth his glory; and his disciples believed on him.

Notice that Jesus was at this very special occasion only for one reason: He was *invited*. One can insinuate that had He not been invited, He would not have been at the event. We have a striking elucidation of this principle all through the Bible. Jesus steps into the affairs of man only by invitation through prayer! A wedding ceremony of any type is nearly always a special event, let alone the one that warranted the presence of the King of Glory! The fact that the organisers of the wedding deemed it fit to invite not only Jesus, but His mother and the disciples to this grand occasion has huge implications, not least, the fact that this was an occasion to be attended only by dignitaries. As such, it is fitting to assume that great preparation had gone into the planning of the said occasion, leaving no stone unturned! As meticulous as they could have been with the planning for the wedding, disaster, we are told, struck at the very core of the ceremony - the people had ran out of wine. *"When the wine was gone, Jesus' mother said to him, "They have no more wine"* (verse 3, NIV).

The situation must have caused pandemonium of great magnitude for, not only the organisers of the notable event, but for the wedding couple, their family members and the entire company of well-wishers present. But, thank God Jesus was present! If He had not been, just take a moment to imagine the degree of embarrassment this would have caused everyone connected one way or another, with the wedding ceremony. Notice the immediate reaction of Mary - the mother of Jesus *"They have no more wine"* (verse 3).This statement meant far more than just an erratic passing of information to Jesus that something had gone terribly wrong. I take the view that Mary passed this information expecting Jesus to fix the problem. This could have only been possible because Jesus had been invited to the occasion long before disaster struck.

Then in verse 5, the *status* of Jesus at the occasion suddenly changed from that of an invited guest to a far more serious position. What position? The Bible says, *"His mother saith unto the servants, Whatsoever he saith unto you, do it"*(verse 5). The situation at hand which only Jesus could deal with meant that He was at this stage now in control entire event. Right away, He knew what to do to bring the rather embarrassing situation under control.

> *Jesus saith unto them, Fill the waterpots with water. And they filled them up to the brim. And he saith unto them, Draw out now, and bear unto the governor of the feast. And they bare it* (vv 7-8).

And what was the outcome?

"When the ruler of the feast had tasted the water that was made wine, and knew not whence it was: (but the servants which drew the water knew;) the governor of the feast called the bridegroom, And saith unto him, Every man at the beginning doth set forth good wine; and when men have well drunk, then that which is worse: but thou hast kept the good wine until now" (vv 9-10).

It is to be noted that the whole of the narrative above was summed up in just one word in verse 11: Miracle!

"This beginning of miracles did Jesus in Cana of Galilee, and manifested forth his glory; and his disciples believed on him." How awesome!

It must be stressed, however, that Jesus had, as it were, been given a place (invited) in this event before the people ran into a problem, and not the other way round as is often the case with many believers today. Many have little or no relationship, whatsoever, with the Lord until they are faced with grave problems, a situation perfectly illustrated by the following words of Prophet Isaiah:

*"Lord, in **trouble** have they visited thee, **they poured out a prayer when thy chastening was upon them**"* (Isaiah 26: 16, emphasis added).

Heaven backs the believer that prays. God is committed to blessing the 'pray-er', hence prayer remains God's prescription and irreplaceable key for breakthrough in life. However, God has to be honourably brought into the scene. There is no other way through which God can deposit His power and blessings into the life of the believer, except through intimate, heart-felt communion with Him. The lesson is driven home in the following passage:

> *And this is the confidence (the assurance, the privilege of boldness) which we have in Him: [we are sure] that if we ask anything (make any request) according to His will (in agreement with His own plan), He listens to and hears us. And if (since) we [positively] know that He listens to us in whatever we ask, we also know [with settled and absolute knowledge] that we have [granted us as our present possessions] the requests made of Him* (1 John 5:14-15, Amplified).

Jesus presented prayer to the believer as a means of receiving from God.

In Matthew 7:7-8, Jesus says:

> *Ask, and it will be given to you; seek, and you will find; knock, and it will be opened to you. For everyone who asks receives, and he who seeks finds, and to him who knocks it will be opened...*

In Luke's Gospel chapter 11:9-10 (Amplified), we see an interesting dimension given to the teachings of Jesus on the degree of intensity the believer must observe in his approach to God: *asking, seeking and knocking.*

According to the Amplified Version of the Bible on Luke 11: 9-10, it is not enough for the believer to just ask, seek or knock, he must do so importunately (repeatedly):

> So I say to you, Ask and keep on asking and it shall be given you; seek and keep on seeking and you shall find; knock and keep on knocking and the door shall be opened to you. For everyone who asks and keeps on asking receives; and he who seeks and keeps on seeking finds; and to him who knocks and keeps on knocking, the door shall be opened.

Consequently, God cannot bless a prayerless life, neither can He anoint a prayerless Church. An individual or church that is void of prayer is cut off from the power source and the source of blessing.

God cannot bless a prayerless life. He cannot anoint a prayerless Church. An individual or church that is void of prayer is cut off from the power source and the source of blessing.

In the word of Matthew Henry:

"Prayer is the appointed means for obtaining what we need. Pray; pray often; make a business of prayer, and be serious and earnest in it. Ask, as a beggar asks alms. Ask, as a traveller asks the way. Seek, as for a thing of value that we have lost; or as the merchantman that seeks goodly pearls. Knock, as he that desires to enter into the house knocks at the door. Sin has shut and barred the door against us; by prayer we knock. Whatever you pray for, according to the promise, shall be given you, if God see it fit for you, and

what would you have more? This is made to apply to all that pray aright; every one that asketh receiveth, whether Jew or Gentile, young or old, rich or poor, high or low, master or servant, learned or unlearned, all are alike welcome to the throne of grace, if they come in faith... Let us never suppose our heavenly Father would bid us pray, and then refuse to hear, or give us what would be hurtful".

LIFE OFFERS NOT WHAT YOU DESERVE BUT WHAT YOU DEMAND

Prayer is the pen that re-writes life's greatest stories; an age-long tool that re-shapes destinies, from utter defeat to victory.

Life's greatest resources are available only to those who can move the hand that rules the world. Prayer is the pen that re-writes life's greatest stories; an age-long tool that re-shapes destinies, from utter defeat to victory. Prayer is the force that swings the hand of success your way like a pendulum. It therefore, does not matter how you were born, by whom you were born or where you were born, or the circumstances that surrounded your birth; prayer generates unlimited power that changes your past. Why? Because prayer alters history; an ugly past becomes a celebrated story of the present when prayer is employed. Having read this, begin to pound the gate of heaven with explosive, destiny-altering prayer, and expect the extraordinary in your life. Forget the past; stop bemoaning your yesterday! Your tomorrow is a product of your investment today. Invest in prayer, and your life will never remain the same. As a Shepherd over God's people, I have witnessed with amazement over the years, the profound transformation and breakthrough prayer has delivered to lives.

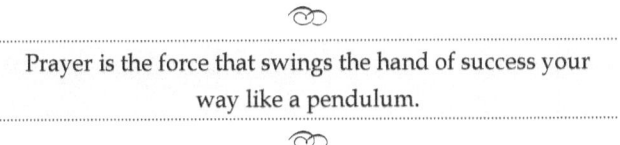

> Prayer is the force that swings the hand of success your way like a pendulum.

I have seen several cases that had defiled the best of medical efforts, astonishingly bowing to the incredible power of prayer. The case of a couple, whom I shall rename Jane and Johnson John to preserve anonymity, who had gone through a difficult time in their marriage, stands out among many. Family members on both sides had given up hope of any possible resolution of the crises that had engulfed the marriage of the Johns. However, the breakthrough came when Mrs John attended a Sunday service in my church for the first time. The message of the day was: "Marriage without tears".

According to her, she felt she had been set up by God to worship in my church that Sunday morning. Every word preached addressed her situation, yet, I had not met her before. After the service, she obtained a CD copy of the message which she listened to now and again. In the process of time, she sought audience with me. In the subsequent meetings that followed, I took her through the word of God and we prayed fervently together. As a result of the protracted prayer, her heart got touched by God to forgive her husband his wrongs, and the marriage was restored to the glory of God!

A man's situation, no matter the intensity or duration is subject to change. Have you discovered by the way, that success does not mind who has it? Success is gender blind, race blind, and colour blind. Prayer is a vehicle that delivers success in the life of the "pray-er". Your breakthrough in life cannot be achieved through man-made or self-help programs that ignore God. There is no success in any other than in Jesus Christ.

In 1 Chronicles 4:9-10, we see the astonishing impact of prayer in the life of a young man. The Bible says, *"Jabez was more honourable than his brothers. His mother had named him Jabez, saying, 'I gave birth to him in pain.' Jabez cried out to the God of Israel, 'Oh, that you would bless me and enlarge my territory! Let your hand be with me, and keep me from harm so that I will be free from pain.' And God granted his request."*

Forget the past; stop bemoaning your yesterday! Your tomorrow is a product of your investment today. **<u>Invest in prayer, and your life will never remain the same.</u>**

Jabez had one of the shortest narratives in the Bible. Very little was known of Jabez, other than the fact that he was a descendant of Judah. Looking at the genealogy of Jabez where the Bible account of his life started from, we are told in very clear terms that Jabez had ancestors, and then we have a full list of their names in Chapter 4:1-8. The first striking feature of this Bible story is that a great deal of attention is drawn to Jabez's name and its meaning. We are told his mother named him "Jabez" (meaning "sorrowful" or "sorrow-maker") because he had been a painful birth; yet, between verses one and eight of the said scripture, we have a plethora of names said to be those of Jabez's descendants, none of which was deemed important enough to deserve the special place of honour given to Jabez in the narrative. We do not know the meaning of any of the names, not even one of them!

However, verses nine and ten, devoted to Jabez contained a detailed analysis of his life. Verse nine opens with an incredible public declaration of Jabez's position in contract to that of his brothers. We are told:

"Jabez was more honourable than his brethren…" (1Chr. 4:9). However, verse 10 records a remarkable twist in the narrative – this being an event that turned the young man's fortune from dust to fame: *"And Jabez called on the God of Israel, saying, Oh that you would bless me indeed, and enlarge my border, and that your hand might be with me, and that you would keep me from*

evil, that it may not grieve me! And God granted him that which he requested" (v. 10). The prayer of Jabez was no doubt, a major transitional event, which incredibly uttered his position in life from shame to fame, from disgrace to greatness. Suddenly, the rather shame and reproach-ridden man became 'honourable Jabez'. He had used the God given tool for breakthrough in life – prayer! If it worked for Jabez, be rest assured, it will work for you.

Jabez's goal in his prayer was to live free from sorrow, and the last thing we read about him was that God heard and answered his prayer. Like Solomon's humble prayer for wisdom (1 Kings 3:5-14), Jabez's devout prayer for blessing was answered; and like Hannah whose prayer broke the yoke of barrenness from her life, Jabez's prayer shattered the reproach of shame off his life. He became, through the instrumentality of prevailing prayer, 'honourable', meaning, 'one deserving honour, respect, a person of high repute, a significant and notable figure'. The success Jabez enjoyed outweighed the sorrow of his beginning. The prayer of Jabez overcame the meaning of his name. Jabez had enough fortitude to face the reality of his failures, limitations and impediments in life. You see, heroes are men who act in a moment of time on a need greater than themselves. Jabez was able to overturn a world of sorrow in his life through God's ordained instrument of effecting change in life, prayer!

Chapter 4

PRAYER IS THE CONNECTION BETWEEN HEAVEN AND EARTH

Prayer is God's established procedure or process that connects heaven to earth. Prayer is the cord that binds earth and heaven's affairs. It is what causes heaven to invade the earth. A life is held to ransom until a connection between heaven and earth is established as with the ladder in the case of Jacob.

"And he lighted upon a certain place, and tarried there all night, because the sun was set; and he took of the stones of that place, and put them for his pillows, and lay down in that place to sleep. And he dreamed, and behold a ladder set up on the earth, and the top of it reached to heaven: and behold the angels of God ascending and descending on it. And, behold, the LORD stood above it, and said, I am the LORD God of Abraham thy father, and the God of Isaac: the land whereon thou liest, to thee will I give it, and to thy seed..." (Gen. 28:11-13).

New Testament teachings present Jesus as the only way to the father. In John 14:6 He said of Himself:

> *Jesus saith unto him, I am the way, the truth, and the life: no man cometh unto the Father, but by me* (John 14:6).

In the words of Myles Munroe,

"Prayer is man giving heaven earthly license to influence earth…prayer is man exercising his legal authority on earth to invoke heaven's influence on the earth."

Although God has all the power to rule and govern the earth without any "input" whatsoever from man, in His sovereignty, however, He has decided, that unless He finds people who co-operate with Him through diligent investment in prayer, He will temporarily let His will go unaccomplished.

Detailed examination of scriptures reveals that God has bestowed on man the power to govern the affairs of heaven through prayer.

Let us examine some of those scriptures:

"If my people, which are called by my name, shall humble themselves, and pray, and seek my face, and turn from their wicked ways; then will I hear from heaven, and will forgive their sin, and will heal their land" (2 Chr. 7:14).

"Let the priests, the ministers of the LORD, weep between the porch and the altar, and let them say, Spare thy people, O LORD, and give not thine heritage to reproach, that the heathen should rule over them: wherefore should they say among the people, Where is their God?" (Joel 2:17).

"Thus saith the LORD of hosts, Consider ye, and call for the mourning women, that they may come; and send

for cunning women, that they may come: And let them make haste, and take up a wailing for us, that our eyes may run down with tears, and our eyelids gush out with waters. For a voice of wailing is heard out of Zion, How are we spoiled! we are greatly confounded, because we have forsaken the land, because our dwellings have cast us out" (Jer. 9: 17-19).

First addressed to Peter, Jesus says,

"And I will give unto thee the keys of the kingdom of heaven: and whatsoever thou shalt bind on earth shall be bound in heaven: and whatsoever thou shalt loose on earth shall be loosed in heaven" (Matt. 16:19).

Then later addressed to all the disciples, He said:

"Verily I say unto you, Whatsoever ye shall bind on earth shall be bound in heaven: and whatsoever ye shall loose on earth shall be loosed in heaven. Again I say unto you, That if two of you shall agree on earth as touching any thing that they shall ask, it shall be done for them of my Father which is in heaven" (Matt. 18:18-19).

> The whole of heaven will stay silent until earth takes action; consequently, earth must bind and earth must loose for there to be corresponding action in heaven

The whole of heaven will stay silent until earth takes action; consequently, earth must bind and earth must loose for there to be corresponding action in heaven.

Accordingly, heaven binds what earth binds, and heaven looses what earth has loosed. Heaven needs our permission to impact and invade the earth.

In the same vein God says:

> *I have set watchmen on your walls, O Jerusalem; They shall never hold their peace day or night. You who make mention of the Lord, do not keep silent,* **And give Him norest** *till He establishes And till He makes Jerusalem a praise in the earth (Isaiah 62:6-7 emphasis added).*

Every program of God on earth requires the involvement of man. As argued, man is indispensable in the program of God. No agenda of God on earth is ever established without man taking his rightful position in ordering and causing things to line up with God's plans. If the "watchmen on the walls" (Isaiah 62:6), would exercise their legal authority on earth in prayer, God's program on earth would be established.

Watch God's mandate or charge to the "Watchmen":

"I have set watchmen upon thy walls, O Jerusalem, **which shall never hold their peace day nor night: ye that make mention of the LORD, keep not silence,** *And give him no rest, till he establish, and till he make Jerusalem a praise in the earth"* (Isaiah 62: 6-7, emphasis added). Notice the phrase: *'And give him no rest, till he establishes'*. The prayer of the saints is God's energy booster to establish things on the earth, as nothing on earth is established without prayer. Interestingly, notice that so long as the "Watchmen" fulfil the Master's charge,

He will, on His part, fulfil the side of the 'contract' which He authenticated by an oath:

"The LORD hath sworn by his right hand, and by the arm of his strength, *Surely I will no more give thy corn to be meat for thine enemies; and the sons of the stranger shall not drink thy wine, for the which thou hast laboured: But they that have gathered it shall eat it, and praise the LORD; and they that have brought it together shall drink it in the courts of my holiness"* (Isaiah 62:8-9, emphasis added).

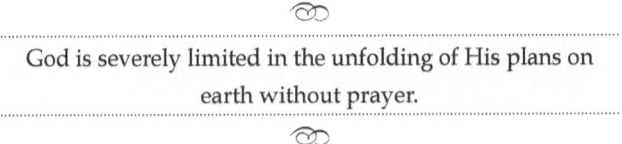

God is severely limited in the unfolding of His plans on earth without prayer.

God is severely limited in the unfolding of His plans on earth without prayer. Prayer therefore, is not an option for mankind but a necessity. If we do not pray, heaven cannot interfere in earth's affairs.

It appears that God will go as far as temporarily allowing the devil to have his way until He finds a "man" or people who would give Him the legal right to intervene in any given situation. God will never "crash" into the affairs of man. He is always to be invited through prayer. Take for instance the often quoted scripture on intercession:

> *And I sought for a man among them that should make up the hedge, and stand in the gap before me for the land, that I should not destroy it: but I found none. Therefore have I poured out mine indignation upon them; I have*

> *consumed them with the fire of my wrath: their own way have I recompensed upon their heads, saith the Lord Go*d (Eze. 22:30 -31).

Only the exercise of man's legal right on earth through prayer could have averted God's judgement according to this scripture. Had God found praying people to co-operate with Him and intercede for the land, God's mercy would have overruled His judgement. There is a principle to be expanded on later which best explains the point. It is the principle that says, 'when man repents of his sins, God repents of His judgment'.

S. D. Gordon remarked, "Prayer surely does influence God. It does not influence His purpose. It does influence His action. Everything that has ever been prayed for, of course I mean every right thing, God has already purposed to do. **But He does nothing without our consent. He has been hindered in His purposes by our lack of willingness**. When we learnt His purpose and make them our prayers we are giving Him the opportunity to act" (emphasis added).The co-operation of man is, therefore, crucial to the fulfilment of God's assignment on planet earth. God can only engage man in this noble task by getting man into a covenant relationship with Him. God has no business with a 'foreigner.' Concerning Abraham, God said, "*for I know him...*" (Gen. 18:19). God uses the vessels He 'knows', and intimate relationship through prayer is the connection.

PART 2
THE PURPOSE OF PRAYER

Chapter 5

UNDERSTANDING THE PURPOSE OF PRAYER

The Bible leaves us in no doubt as to the huge significance of prayer in the life of the believer in Christ Jesus. The need and significance of prayer in the lives of God's children form an integral part of the word of God right from the Old Testament, all through the New Testament, down to the Epistles and beyond. God is limited to the degree to which the believers pray.

For Jabez, the Bible says, "...*God granted him **that which he requested**"* (1 Chr. 4:10, emphasis added).

According to God's Word Translation, "...***God gave him what he prayed* for**" (1 Chr. 4:10, emphasis added). God stopped 'granting' where Jabez stopped asking. If Jabez had asked for more, God would, no doubt, have granted him more. A man whose name meant "sorrow" became 'honourable' because he chose to partner and do business with God. Child of God, the key to your receiving is in your asking; that key is in your hands; use it!

The following quote credited to John Wesley sums it up accurately, "It seems God is limited by our prayer life – that He can do nothing for humanity unless someone asks Him."

Kenneth Hagin Sr. capsules it this way:

"...Adam had dominion upon this earth and in this world. He was originally, in a sense, god of this world. But Satan came and lied to Adam. Adam committed high treason and sold out to Satan. Then Satan became the god of this world. Second Corinthians 4:4 calls Satan 'the god of this world.' As such, he has dominion. Where? In this world. He will have that dominion; he will be god of this world, until Adam's lease runs out. God cannot legally and justly move in and take away that dominion from the devil. The devil has dominion here. He has a legal right because he has Adam's lease. ***And God cannot do anything unless somebody down here asks him"*** (emphasis added).

God delights in the prayer of the saints. God has time to listen to us if we have time to spend in His presence. Your prayer time is the most important hour of the day. We are challenged by the word of God:

> *The fire on the altar shall be kept burning on it. It shall not go out, but the priest shall burn wood on it every morning; and he shall lay out the burnt offering on it, and offer up in smoke the fat portions of the peace offerings on it. 'Fire shall be kept burning continually on the altar; it is not to go out (Leviticus 6:12-13)*

The busier Jesus was, the more He prayed.

According to Bob Sorge, the secret place of the believer is the "womb of the morning…" It should not be put off. Never be deceived in believing that you are too busy to pray. Do not let the jet speed pace of our modern world encroach into and corrode your prayer life. A day with the Lord is worth far more than a decade without Him.

Martin Luther, asked what his plans were for the following day, answered, "Work, work, and more work from early until late. In fact, I have so much to do that I shall spend the first three hours in prayer." We see this vividly exemplified by Jesus. The busier Jesus was, the more He prayed.

"And in the morning, rising up a great while before day, he went out, and departed into a solitary place, and there prayed" (Mark 1:35).

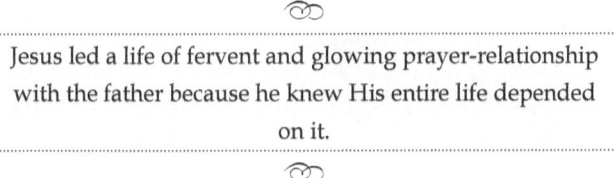

Jesus led a life of fervent and glowing prayer-relationship with the father because he knew His entire life depended on it.

For Jesus, a fresh encounter with God was the key to everything He came to accomplish on earth. If Jesus could have accomplished His mission on earth without prayer, why would He have bothered to pray? Jesus led a life of fervent and glowing prayer-relationship with the father because He knew His entire life depended on it. In His earthly ministry, Jesus did not assume that miracles were phenomenal or sheer coincidence; neither did He assume that success in life endeavours was a matter of luck. Jesus did not take the Father-hood of God for granted either.

In my earlier book, '*The Wonders of Fasting: Unravelling the Astonishing Mystery of Biblical Fasting*', I argued extensively that the notion of "working for God" was the greatest deception the enemy has sold to our generation. Jesus, in His entire earthly ministry did not work for God, He worked **with** God; there is a big difference. Quite succinctly the Bible says in Acts 10:38:

"*How God anointed Jesus of Nazareth with the Holy Ghost and with power: who went about doing good, and healing all that were oppressed of the devil;* **for God was with him**"(emphasis added). He did all kingdom exploits in partnership with the father. It was a lesson of incredible value that Jesus had learnt from His father.

In John 10:30, Jesus says "I and my Father are one", and John 5:19, "*Then answered Jesus and said unto them, Verily, verily, I say unto you, The Son can do nothing of himself, but what he seeth the Father do: for what things soever he doeth, these also doeth the Son likewise*".

In these scriptures, we see Jesus working in close partnership with the one that sent Him. Many believers, and indeed, ministers of God may have started out working with God, but today, are "doing their own thing", all in the guise of working 'for' God.

After Jesus gave His disciples the great commission, the Bible says:

> And they went forth, and preached everywhere, **the Lord working with them, and confirming the word with signs following**... (Mark 16:20, emphasis added).

We are not called to discharge kingdom exploits in isolation, solitude in or detachment from the one that sent us.

Did you see that even after Jesus had relinquished power to the disciples to carry out the great commission, He still worked with them, *"confirming the word with signs following"* (verse 20). Just as His father did with Him, He did with the disciples. Here is a vital lesson. We are not called to discharge kingdom exploits in isolation, solitude in or detachment from the One that had sent us. We are to ensure that intimacy with the One that commissioned us is in place, and vital communication with Him is maintained. The problem, of cause, sterns from the fact that many are not sent!

THE "GOD" MAN USES

Long before I had the opportunity of reading Oswald J. Smith book, "The Man God Uses", I was conversant with teachings along those lines, especially in my undergraduate days as a young Christian. One could not but be challenged by such teachings, almost impatiently waiting for an opportunity to be used by the God of all universe. But as years passed by, I noticed with disgust, the emergence of a twist in this regard: the "God that Man Uses".

This is the God that the contemporary Christian has invented for himself, that is totally different from the King of Glory. This is the God man has relationship with only when he is in need, or in trouble, the God man uses like a bank cash machine. A God who, like an artist springs to the stage as of when occasion demands. So we then have a performing God, whom man tries so hard to manipulate to do his self-centred will, and sought on the basis of what He has to offer, not on the basis of who He is. The consequence of this misconception in the end-time church is dire. The fear of God is at its lowest ebb. Remember, this "god" man has invented for himself is no better than a robot; he lives his life to please man, not the other way round. He does not bother how the believer lives his life. As a matter of fact, He winks at ungodliness and unrighteousness, why? Because He must be seen to be 'politically correct'. Needless to say 'this man-invented' God is not the creator of the heaven and the earth. This is "another god".

This accounts so much for reasons why many are rather working *for* God instead of working *with* Him. In the process, man has lost contact, relationship and intimacy with the true God. What is the result? *Icabod* (the glory has departed 1 Sam. 14:3 and 4:21). How sad!

Part of the clear instructions given to the priests of old was never to profane the sanctuary of God. Reason? *"...for the crown of the anointing oil of his God is upon him..."* (Lev. 21:12).

The sad reality is that the sanctuary of God today is profaned. The contemporary Church has lost the due order, which was what distinguished the Church centuries ago. So the intriguing question for the modern day ministers and believers alike is, whose crown are you wearing? Whose anointing are you operating with? Unless the crown is that of the true and living God, and the anointing flows directly from Him and not from another source, you are likely to perpetually profane the sanctuary of God.

In his book "The Power of Prayer" Reuben A. Torrey, one-time President of Moody Bible Institute, contends "We do not live in a praying age. We live in an age of hustle and bustle, of man's efforts and man's determination, of man's confidence in himself and in his own power to achieve things, an age of human organization and human machinery, and human push, and human scheming, and human achievement; which in the things of God means no real achievement at all... What we need is not so much some new organization, some new wheel but the Spirit of the living creature in the wheels we already possess."

The Psalmist realising the importance of prayer vows:

> *My voice shalt thou hear in the morning, O Lord; in the morning will I direct my prayer unto thee, and will look up* (Psalms 3:5).

Personal time with God in prayer was an indispensable practice in the lives of great men and women, throughout church history that did astonishing exploits for God in their generations. They were successful in spite of all odds, accomplishing the seemingly impossible tasks for God.

Let us examine some of the significance of prayers in the life of the believer.

PRAYER SECURES INTIMACY WITH GOD

This is one of the most fundamental significance of prayer. Prayer is a vehicle that takes us to the throne of grace, and establishes intimate relationship between the believer and God. In the words of Oswald Chambers, "Our ordinary views of prayer are not found in the New Testament. We look upon prayer as a means for getting something for ourselves; the Bible idea of prayer is that we may get to know God Himself."

Apostle Paul perfectly expresses the most earnest desire of every true follower of Christ: *"That I may know him"*(Phil. 3:10).

"Knowing Christ," from Paul's perspective is not the sort of mystical relationship many people imagine.

How can we pursue knowing Christ the way Paul had in mind?

The answer is a life that is addicted to and interwoven with God through intimacy. This was distinctly demonstrated in the life of a young King who habitually and devotedly sought God, and became successful in all his endeavours:

"Then all the people of Judah took Uzziah, who was sixteen years old, and made him king in the room of his father Amaziah. He built Eloth, and restored it to Judah, after that the king slept with his fathers. Sixteen years old was Uzziah when he began to reign, and he reigned fifty and two years in Jerusalem. His mother's name also was Jecoliah of Jerusalem. And he did that which was right in the sight of the LORD, *according to all that his father Amaziah did.* **And he sought God in the days of Zechariah,** *who had understanding in the visions of God:* **and as long as he sought the** LORD**, God made him to prosper"**(2 Chr.26:1-5, emphasis added).

As seen, prayer is one of the proven ways the Bible offers the believer to pursue intimacy with God. The *secret place* is the believer's platform for attaining and enhancing relationship and fellowship with God. God longs and seeks true audience with His saints. In Rev. 4:1-2 John writes, *"After these things I looked, and behold, a door standing open in heaven, and the first voice which I had heard, like the sound of a trumpet speaking with me, said, "Come up here, and I will show you what must take place after these things." Immediately I was in the Spirit; and behold, a throne was standing in heaven, and One sitting on the throne...*" The affectionate, passionate heart of God 'swells' with incredible delight for our fellowship with Him. If we understand what a tremendous privilege and huge honour it is to be invited to the throne of grace, we would surely spend more time there, pouring out our most intimate thoughts, fears, desires, and expressions of love to Him.

I agree with David Macintyre, "*...the habit of prayerfulness produces a singular serenity of spirit… when one looks into the quiet eyes of him that sitteth upon the throne; the tremors of the spirit are stilled. Pharaoh, king of Egypt, is but a noise; and the valley of the shadow of death is tuneful with songs of praise. Storms may rave beneath our feet, but the sky above is blue. We take our station with Christ in heavenly places; we dwell in the Sabbath of God.*"

Isaac Newton was profound when he said, "I can take my telescope and look millions of miles into space; but I can lay my telescope aside, get down on my knees in earnest prayer, and I can see more of heaven and get closer to God than I can when assisted by all the telescopes and material agencies on earth."

Through prayer, the believer is acquainted with the ways of God, he is impacted with the knowledge of God, and he is infused with the power of God. Through prayer our whole being becomes more sensitive to spiritual reality. Abraham became a friend of God through intimate relationship and fellowship with Him.

> Through prayer the believer is acquainted with the ways of God, he is impacted with the knowledge of God, and he is infused with the power of God.

"And the scripture was fulfilled which saith, Abraham believed God, and it was imputed unto him for righteousness: and he was called the Friend of God" (James 2:23).

Notice how James draws attention to the fact that Abraham was called the friend of God. The term "friend" conveys a sense of closeness, trust, and sharing. What is remarkable is that this was not Abraham's assessment of his relationship with God, nor how he thought about God. It was a statement that God made about Abraham, as recorded in Isaiah 41. 8:

"But you, Israel, my servant, Jacob, whom I have chosen, the offspring of Abraham, my friend…"

To understand the Father heart of God, we need to pray. To lead a life of intimacy with God, we need to pray.

In John 15:15, Jesus says He no longer calls us His servants, but calls us His friends.

The prophet Amos posed the rhetorical question:

Amos 3:3 *"Can two walk together, except they be agreed?"*

The sense of the Hebrew text here is interesting. The word "agreed" is from the Hebrew *ya`ad* which means to fix, appoint, assemble, meet, set, betroth; to meet, to meet by appointment. The sense is not simply two walking in a common direction because they agree to it, but rather two agreeing to and making an appointment to come together and from there set out on a journey to a destination together.

This raises some interesting questions:

1. How was such a relationship possible?
2. What constitutes that kind of friendship?

The relationship Abraham enjoyed with God was a remarkable one by human standard and tremendously encouraging for us. We see the extreme extent of this relationship in the test of faith Abraham endured. As we will soon come to see, Abraham was not accorded this robust accolade without paying a heavy price for it.

Abraham had been tested and obeyed God many times in his walk with Him, but no test could have been more severe than the one in Genesis 22. How did Abraham respond to God's command to sacrifice Isaac? With immediate obedience; early the next morning, Abraham started on his journey with two servants, a donkey and his beloved son Isaac, with firewood for the offering. His swift obedience to God's command gave God the glory He deserves and is an example to us of how to glorify God. When we obey God as Abraham did, trusting that God's plan is best, we exalt His attributes and praise Him. Abraham's obedience in the face of this crushing command extolled God's sovereign love, His trustworthiness, and His goodness, and it provided an example for us to follow. His faith in the God he had come to know and love placed Abraham in the pantheon of faithful heroes in Hebrews 11

Abraham's faith was such that, even if he had sacrificed Isaac, he believed the Lord would keep His word and raise Isaac from the dead (Hebrews 11:17-19). God uses Abraham's faith as an example of the type of faith required for salvation. Genesis 15:6 says, *"Abram believed the LORD, and he credited it to him as righteousness."* This truth is the basis of the Christian faith, as reiterated in Romans 4:3 and James 2:23. The righteousness that was credited to Abraham is the same righteousness credited to us when we receive by faith the sacrifice God provided for our sins — Jesus Christ. *"God made him who had no sin to be sin for us, so that in him we might become the righteousness of God"* (2 Cor. 5:21). The Old Testament story of Abraham is the basis of the New Testament teaching of the atonement, the sacrificial offering of the Lord Jesus on the cross for the sin of mankind. Jesus said, many centuries later, "Your father Abraham rejoiced at the thought of seeing my day; he saw it and was glad" (John 8:56).

God is not a partial God. He is not a respecter of persons. He extends the hand of friendship to all those who seek Him. If we follow the example of Abraham by being in agreement with God, displaying loyalty and dependability towards God, and freely confiding in Him in all matters, then we too will be called the friends of God.

PRAYER SECURES HEALTHY RELATIONSHIPS IN THE CHURCH

Prayer does not only build relationship between God and His saints, prayer has been found to be a formidable force that orchestrates and enhances healthy relationships among believers, even among couples. The old saying: "the family that prays together stays together" could not be truer. It is expected that as couples express their deep affection for and dependence on God together in prayer, their love for each other deepens and flourishes.

Healthy churches are marked by healthy relationships – among the members on one hand, and between the members and their leaders, on the other. A church is a relational network. We are sheep in a fold, branches on the vine, and members of a family. We must learn to live and work together. The quality of a church is greatly determined by the quality of its inter-personal relationships.

What makes such bond possible within the church community is the refining work of prevailing prayer.

There is something about unity in prayer that causes hearts to flow in the same direction. There lies the strength of corporate or united prayer. The prayer of the saints in an environment of unity is a formidable weapon of warfare, "mighty through God to the pulling down of stronghold" (2 Cor. 10:4). Deuteronomy 32:30 alludes to the strength of such prayer: "*How should one chase a thousand, and two put ten thousand to flight, except their Rock had sold them, and the **Lord had shut them up**"*? What makes the collective prayer of the church quite distinct is the power of unity it incorporates. The principle being explored has its full application in many of the corporate prayers recorded in scriptures. It was the thrust and pith of Jesus' teaching on prayer in Matthew 18:19: "*...I say unto you, That if two of you shall agree on earth as touching anything that they shall ask, it shall be done for them of my Father which is in heaven.*" It was the force that made the early church prayer explode in heaven like a raging inferno (Acts 12), causing the miraculous release of Peter from the prison.

It is to be noted that the prayer of unity, as taught by Jesus is answered on the basis of the agreement that exists among God's children. It is agreement, which sterns from relationship and fellowship that gives such prayer the necessary boost, causing it to have such tremendous impact.

Paul's admonition to the Church on the subject was explicit:

"I therefore, the prisoner of the Lord, beseech you that ye walk worthy of the vocation wherewith ye are called, With all lowliness and meekness, with longsuffering, forbearing one another in love; Endeavouring to keep the unity of the Spirit in the bond of peace [eager to maintain the unity of the Spirit in the bond of peace–ESV]. There is one body, and one Spirit, even as ye are called in one hope of your calling; One Lord, one faith, one baptism, One God and Father of all, who is above all, and through all, and in you all" (Eph. 4:1-6). Also in Romans 12:10, Paul enjoins the Church to, *"Be kindly affectioned one to another with brotherly love; in honour preferring one another"*

Notice that in Ephesians 4:1-6, we are told that the household of faith – the church – is called into the vocation of *"... Endeavouring to keep the unity of the Spirit in the bond of peace"* (verse 3).

Lowliness, meekness, longsuffering, forbearing one another in love; unity of the Spirit in the bond of peace, affection, and brotherly love are all possible only in an environment of healthy relationship which emanates from a culture of prayer.

Chapter 6

PRAYER HELPS US TO CONFORM TO CHRIST'S IMAGE

> *But we all, with unveiled face, beholding as in a mirror the glory of the Lord, are being transformed into the same image from glory to glory, just as from the Lord, the Spirit* (2 Cor. 3:18).

According to the above scripture, we are transformed into the image of the *one* we behold. Prayer brings the divine omnipotence into our life. Mike Bickle affirms that, "no one can ever come face to face with what God is like and ever [remain] the same. Seeing His true image touches the depths of our temperament, bringing us to spiritual wholeness and maturity. Beholding the glory of who He is and what He has done renews our minds, strengthens us and transforms us." When we go before the Lord in prayer, we are caught up with the glowing warmth of God's divine consciousness. Our hearts are opened to the Holy Spirit- we yield to the divine impulse – and His divine power takes over. Often our plans are set aside, and substituted for His supreme plans. E. M. Bounds affirms that prayer makes a godly man, and puts within him the mind of Christ, the mind of humility, of self-surrender, of service, of pity, and of prayer. If we really pray, we will become more like God, or else we will quit praying.

Conforming to His divine image was in the mind of God when He created man in His image and likeness and breathed into him the breath of life. Consequently, there was transference of God's nature, character and personality to man. Man began to reason and act like his maker. God's authority and dominion were also legally given to man:

> *And God said, Let us make man in our image, after our likeness: and let them have dominion over the fish of the sea, and over the fowl of the air, and over the cattle, and over all the earth, and over every creeping thing that creepeth upon the earth. So God created man in his own image, in the image of God created he him; male and female created he them* (Gen. 1:26-27).

Ephesians 2:10 says, *"For we are his workmanship, created in Christ Jesus unto good works, which God hath before ordained that we should walk in them. You were created in Christ Jesus when the Father raised Him from the dead and sat Him in heaven on His throne with Him."*

You must constantly renew your mind to be able to walk in this divine truth, appreciating your privileged identity and position in Christ.

Paul affirms in Ephesians 2:6-7, *"And hath raised us up together, and made us sit together in heavenly places in Christ Jesus. That in the ages to come he might shew the exceeding riches of his grace in his kindness toward us through Christ Jesus."* This is our true identity, and we are to continually renew our minds to live as such. The Bible teaches, *"Let this mind be in you which was also in Christ Jesus…"* (Phil. 2:5). Paul goes even further to explain the process of conforming to the image of Jesus Christ.

> *And that, knowing the time, that now it is high time to awake out of sleep: for now is our salvation nearer than when we believed. The night is far spent, the day is at hand: let us therefore cast off the works of darkness, and let us put on the armour of light. Let us walk honestly, as in the day; not in rioting and drunkenness, not in chambering and wantonness, not in strife and envying.* **But put ye on the Lord Jesus Christ***, and make not provision for the flesh, to fulfil the lusts thereof* (Rom. 13:11-14, emphasis added).

Prayer is the means and method God has designed to achieve the process of putting on the Lord Jesus.

Romans 13:14 contains one of the most practical, and direct exhortations in all of Scriptures: the first half of the verse, *"Put on the Lord Jesus Christ"* is an indication of what the Christian life truly is. Even the ancient rabbis used to talk about the true worshiper of God putting on the cloak of the *Shekinah*. In other words, becoming like the one he worshiped.

A process – a three phase dispensation – is, however, involved. The initial phase takes place when the believer puts off the old man and puts on the new man: The Bible teaches that, *"… if any man be in Christ, he is a new creature:* **old things are passed away; behold, all things are become new**" (2 Cor.5:17, emphasis added). A divine transformation takes place the moment we are born into the family of God. It is like throwing off an old cloak and putting on a brand new one, so you are clothed in an entirely new way from head to foot. This imperfectly illustrated in another of Paul's letter. In Ephesians 4: 22-24 Paul says,"*...you have put off concerning the former manner of life the old man which is corrupt according to the deceitful lust, and be renewed in the spirit of your mind so that you have put on the new man which after God is created in righteousness and true holiness.*"

Accordingly, at salvation we put on the Lord Jesus Christ in the sense of taking on His righteousness and holiness. In Romans 3:22 we read, "*The righteousness of God which is by faith in Jesus Christ unto all and upon all them that believe.*"

There is, of course, another dimension. It is one thing to possess the personal gift of the righteousness of Jesus Christ, and it is quite another to live up to it. It is all about becoming what you are. The process is again illustrated in Colossians 3: 12-14:

> *Put on therefore, as the elect of God, holy and beloved, bowels of mercies, kindness, humbleness of mind, meekness, longsuffering; Forbearing one another, and forgiving one another, if any man have a quarrel against any: even as Christ forgave you, so also do ye. And above all these things put on charity, which is the bond of perfectness.*

What Paul is saying to the believer in essence is, 'put off the old so that the new can stay'. God is not in the business of *mixture*. If for anything, in Leviticus 19:19 God warns, "*thou shalt not sow thy field with mingled seed: neither shall a garment mingled of linen and woollen come upon thee.*" The old and new cannot co-exist! There must be a circumcision of the heart as a prerequisite for God's involvement with man, before any significant accord can exist between the two parties. According to Paul, "*Circumcision is that of the heart, in the spirit, and not in the letter*" (Rom. 2:29). John Wesley postulates that the distinguishing mark of a true follower of Christ, of one who is in a state of acceptance with God, is not either outward circumcision, or baptism, or any other outward form, but a right state of soul, mind and spirit, renewed after the image of Him that created it.

The difference between the two dimensions is that one is positional and the other is practical. In yet another letter, Paul uses another thrilling illustration to buttress this position: "*And beside this, giving all diligence, add to your faith virtue; and to virtue knowledge; and to knowledge, self-control; and to self-control, perseverance; and to perseverance, godliness; and to godliness, brotherly kindness; and to brotherly kindness, love*" (2 Pet.1:5-7). I call this scripture 'true evidence of salvation.' This agrees with Paul's notion or estimation of the invaluable lessons contained in the said scripture:

"For if these things be in you, and abound, they make you that ye shall neither be barren nor unfruitful in the knowledge of our Lord Jesus Christ. But he that lacketh these things is blind, and cannot see afar off, and hath forgotten that he was purged from his old sins" (2 Pet. 1: 8-9). Galatians 5:16 says, *"Walk in the Spirit and you will not fulfil the lusts of the flesh."* Walking in the Spirit simply means obeying the Scripture. As we gaze at the glory of the Lord and meditate on His person, His beauty and His wonder, we find ourselves being clothed with Christ, and the lust of the flesh with its concomitant effect is crowded out. We are no longer enslaved to the demands of the flesh, and sin tendencies are subdued.

There is yet a third dimension. There is a purpose for God creating man in His image, after His likeness. God is to facilitate conformity of this divine process throughout His dealings with mankind. Consequently, God accommodates evil to bring forth godly character in the believer; the sole purpose being to best act as the salt and light of the earth. This process is to continue *"Till **we all come** in the unity of the faith, and of the knowledge of the Son of God, **unto a perfect man, unto the measure of the stature of the fullness of Christ"*** (Eph. 4:13, emphasis added).

According to Francis Frangipane, we would never ascend to the heights of Christ-like love, which loves even one's adversary, without there being actual enemies to perfect our love. God cannot establish within us a pure heart and a steadfast spirit without allowing genuine temptations and obstacles that must be refused and overcome. The reason the Lord even tolerates evil in the world is to produce a righteousness within us that not only withstands the assault of evil, but grows stronger and brighter in the midst of it. God uses our struggles, afflictions, adversities and mishap to work out His eternal purpose and His divine nature in our lives. Paul admonishes, *"...that by these ye might be partakers of the divine nature, having escaped the corruption that is in the world through lust"* (2 Pet.1:4).It is one thing to escape the corruption that is in the world through lust, as stated in this scripture, it is yet another to work out our salvation in a way as to daily conform to His image by being partakers of His divine nature. A key scripture that highlights the exceptional lessons on the subject is Psalm 84. It says:

"Blessed is the man whose strength is in thee; in whose heart are the ways of them. Who passing through the valley of Baca make it a well; the rain also filleth the pools. ***They go from strength to strength, every one of them in Zion appeareth before God"*** (verses 5-7, emphasis added).

For better understanding, let us read the above passage in the Amplified version of the Bible: *"Blessed (happy, fortunate, to be envied) is the man whose strength is in You, in whose heart are the highways to Zion. Passing through the Valley of Weeping (Baca), they make it a place of springs; the early rain also fills [the pools] with blessings. They go from strength to strength [increasing in victorious power]; each of them appears before God in Zion".*

Notice the people spoken of in this scripture have the Lord as the basis of their strength, and have totally yielded their hearts to the Lord, yet, as often the case with everyone of us, in their hour of trial and challenges, they went through a period of weeping and great ordeal. Verse 6 says, they went through "*the valley of Baca...*" which, according to the Amplified Bible, is "*the valley of **weeping**.*" However, notice the astonishing outcome of the apparent appalling situation: the Bible testifies, "*They go from strength to strength [increasing in victorious power]; each of them appears before God in Zion*" (verse 7). What an amazing outcome! The narrative, from human perspective, does lead to some sort of paradoxes – a negative and seemingly hopeless situation producing for us an absolutely incomparable eternal weight of glory. Paul affirms that the process of conforming to Christ's image does often entails some unwelcome and painful experiences at the beginning, but the overall outcome leaves us increasing in victorious power, from glory to glory, as seen in Psalm 84.

In 2 Cor. 4:16-18, he writes:

> *For which cause we faint not;* **but though our outward man perish, yet the inward man is renewed day by day. For our light affliction, which is but for a moment, worketh for us a far more exceeding and eternal weight of glory;** *While we look not at the things which are seen, but at the things which are not seen: for the things which are seen are temporal; but the things which are not seen are eternal* (emphasis added).

In Romans 8:18, Paul declares emphatically:

> *I consider that our present sufferings are not worth comparing with the glory that will be revealed in us"* – a fact Peter alludes to, *"And the God of all grace, who called you to his eternal glory in Christ, after you have suffered a little while,* **will himself restore you and make you strong, firm and steadfast** (1 Pet. 5:10, emphasis added).

This is God's means and method of working out His eternal purposes in the lives of His children. In order to grow and develop profound faith, we must go through testing periods that allow Jesus to perfect His work in us.

Chapter 7

PRAYER MAKES TREMENDOUS POWER AVAILABLE

The power of God is at your command through prevailing prayer. Might power, beyond human comprehension, is released through prevailing prayer. Prayer is the divine generator of God's power. An inveterate missionary put the position succinctly, "Much prayer, much power, little prayer, little power; no prayer, no power."The scripture confirms this truth. A passage of the Bible that graphically and distinctly asserts this fundamental truth is Exodus 17:8-13.

"Then came Amalek, and fought with Israel in Rephidim. And Moses said unto Joshua, Choose us out men, and go out, fight with Amalek: tomorrow I will stand on the top of the hill with the rod of God in mine hand. So Joshua did as Moses had said to him, and fought with Amalek: and Moses, Aaron, and Hur went up to the top of the hill. And it came to pass, when Moses held up his hand, that Israel prevailed: and when he let down his hand, Amalek prevailed. But Moses hands were heavy; and they took a stone, and put it under him, and he sat thereon; and Aaron and Hur stayed up his hands, the one on the one side, and the other on the other side; and his hands were steady until

the going down of the sun. And Joshua discomfited Amalek and his people with the edge of the sword" (Exod. 17:8-13).

It is to be noted in the above passage that to impress upon Israel the importance of prayer, God made success and failure alternate with its continuance and discontinuance. Moses, Aaron, and Hur were struck by the fact that the fluctuations in the battle coincided with the motions of Moses' hands. This is, no doubt, a lesson of great value for the church – the fact that we only prevail in battle through the weapon of prayer.

The greatest cause of powerlessness in the contemporary Church is prayerlessness. Where there is prayerlessness, there is invariably less power than is required to accomplish and execute kingdom exploits. Lack of understanding of the significance and the principles that govern prayer have caused majority of God's people to be ineffective in prayer and kingdom service. The obvious consequence is that people caught up in this all too common trend in the Household of Faith, regress from ineffective prayer into the sin of prayerlessness, which stifles their ability to receive the continuous flow of divine power necessary to be effective in God's service.

Let us examine the following scriptures as we appreciate the astonishing power that the earnest prayer of the believer produces:

"And David built there an altar unto the LORD, and offered burnt offerings and peace offerings. So the LORD

was intreated for the land, and the plague was stayed from Israel" (2 Sam. 24:25).

"And the people cried unto Moses; and when Moses prayed unto the LORD, the fire was quenched" (Num. 11:2).

"Now when Solomon had made an end of praying, the fire came down from heaven, and consumed the burnt offering and the sacrifices; and the glory of the LORD filled the house. And the priests could not enter into the house of the LORD, because the glory of the LORD had filled the LORD's house" (2 Chr. 7:1-2)

"And the LORD appeared to Solomon by night, and said unto him, I have heard thy prayer, and have chosen this place to myself for an house of sacrifice. If I shut up heaven that there be no rain, or if I command the locusts to devour the land, or if I send pestilence among my people; If my people, which are called by my name, shall humble themselves, and pray, and seek my face, and turn from their wicked ways; then will I hear from heaven, and will forgive their sin, and will heal their land. Now mine eyes shall be open, and mine ears attent unto the prayer that is made in this place" (2 Chr. 7:12- 15).

"When my soul fainted within me I remembered the LORD: and my prayer came in unto thee, into thine holy temple" (Jonah 2:6-8).

"When my life was ebbing away, I remembered you, LORD, and my prayer rose to you, to your holy temple" (Jonah 2:6-8, NIV).

"And when they had prayed, the place was shaken where they were assembled together; and they were all filled with the Holy Ghost, and they spake the word of God with boldness" (Acts 4:31)

"Then Peter arose and went with them. When he was come, they brought him into the upper chamber: and all the widows stood by him weeping, and shewing the coats and garments which Dorcas made, while she was with them. But Peter put them all forth, and kneeled down, and prayed; and turning him to the body said, Tabitha, arise. And she opened her eyes: and when she saw Peter, she sat up. And he gave her his hand, and lifted her up, and when he had called the saints and widows, presented her alive" (Acts 9:39-41).

"And when he looked on him, he was afraid, and said, What is it, Lord? And he said unto him, Thy prayers and thine alms are come up for a memorial before God" (Acts 10:4).

It is worthy of note from the above scriptures that as the people of God prayed, power was made available from on high to deal with their specific situations. Prayer makes the difference!

I believe your testimony of answered prayer would be next to go on record!

Hear God's oath:

"Call unto me, and I will answer thee, and show thee great and mighty things, which thou knowest not" (Jer. 33:3).

This is profound! What an opportunity never to be missed!

...every human problem on earth is represented by a solution in the Word of God; the connection being prayer.

According to James 5:16, "*...the effectual fervent prayer of a righteous man availeth much.*" The Amplified version of the Bible renders it, "*...the earnest (heartfelt, continued) prayer of a righteous man makes tremendous power available [dynamic in its working]*". What a promise! Effective, fervent prayer is a generator of tremendous power that penetrates into and deals with every situation. Every time we pray, and do so in agreement with the word of God, God's mighty power is released and made available to deal with situations and brings victory and breakthrough into seemingly impossible circumstances. As I often say to my congregation, "every human problem on earth is represented by a solution in the Word of God; the connection being prayer." Notice, however, the characteristics of the prayer being examined - it must be fervent, earnest, heartfelt and continued. God's power released through prayer has been greatly instrumental in changing the destinies of nations. Prayer breaks through satanic resistance that holds nations bound and establishes God's counsel. According to Lynne Hammond, effective prayer does move mountains and change lives. In the Old

Testament, it stopped times and made the sun stand still. It won wars and brought fire from heaven. In the New Testament, it worked miracles, opened prison doors and sent angels to the rescue.

A wonderful, practical example of this is found in Daniel chapter 10; which gives us profound insight into what happens in the spirit realm when we pray.

"In those days I Daniel was mourning three full weeks. I ate no pleasant bread, neither came flesh nor wine in my mouth, neither did I anoint myself at all, till three whole weeks were fulfilled" (Daniel 10:1-2)

As Daniel continued to pray, angel Gabriel was dispatched from heaven to reveal the fierce satanic battle that withheld the answers that God had released in response to his prayer.

There are demonic hierarchical powers over regions, cities and nations.

"Then said he unto me, Fear not, Daniel: for from the first day that thou didst set thine heart to understand, and to chasten thyself before thy God, thy words were heard, and I am come for thy words. But the prince of the kingdom of Persia withstood me one and twenty days: but, lo, Michael, one of the chief princes, came to help me; and I remained there with the kings of Persia" (Daniel 10: 12-13).

We see the impact that Daniel's prayer had had on the governmental structures both in the spirit and natural realm.

According to Paul, "...*we wrestle not against flesh and blood, but against principalities, against powers, against the rulers of the darkness of this world, against spiritual wickedness in high places*" (Eph. 6:12).

Mike Bickle argues that Daniel understood the angelic and demonic powers working behind the scenes to affect the king of Persia. He saw the demonic prince (principality) over Persia warring against Israel by seeking to stir up the king of Persia against Israel (Daniel 10: 13, 20-21). The angel came because of Daniel's prayer (Daniel 10:12). If Daniel had not prayed, the two angels would not have been dispatched from heaven; a situation reminiscent of Acts 12, where there was also an angelic intervention in a very desperate and critical situation following a time of intense and protracted prayer:

"*Peter therefore was kept in prison:* **but prayer was made without ceasing of the church unto God for him**... *And, behold, the angel of the Lord came upon him, and a light shined in the prison: and he smote Peter on the side, and raised him up, saying, Arise up quickly. And his chains fell off from his hands. And the angel said unto him, Gird thyself, and bind on thy sandals. And so he did. And he saith unto him, Cast thy garment about thee, and follow me. And he went out, and followed him; and wist not that it was true which was done by the angel; but thought he saw a vision. When they were past the first and the second ward, they came unto the iron gate that leadeth unto the city; which opened to them of his own accord:*

and they went out, and passed on through one street; and forthwith the angel departed from him" (Acts 12:5, 7-10, emphasis added).

As in the previous case, tremendous power was released through the earnest prayer of the church that caused angelic intervention in this situation. Had the church not prayed, Peter would have suffered the same fate as James (Acts 12:2).

Also in 2 Chronicles 20:1-6, we find another incredible account of divine intervention through prayer:

"It came to pass after this also, that the children of Moab, and the children of Ammon, and with them other beside the Ammonites, came against Jehoshaphat to battle. Then there came some that told Jehoshaphat, saying, There cometh a great multitude against thee from beyond the sea on this side Syria; and, behold, they be in Hazazontamar, which is Engedi. And Jehoshaphat feared, and set himself to seek the Lord, and proclaimed a fast throughout all Judah. And Judah gathered themselves together, to ask help of the Lord: even out of all the cities of Judah they came to seek the Lord. And Jehoshaphat stood in the congregation of Judah and Jerusalem, in the house of the Lord, before the new court, And said, O Lord God of our fathers, art not thou God in heaven? andrulest not thou over all the kingdoms of the heathen? and in thine hand is there not power and might, so that none is able to withstand thee?"

During the reign of King Jehoshaphat, King of Judah, enemies from neighbouring nations invaded Judah.

As stated, the Bible says *"Jehoshaphat feared and set himself to seek the Lord, and proclaimed a fast throughout Judah"* (verse 3).

This incident brought the people of Judah together to seek help of the Lord through prayer and fasting. King Jehoshaphat's prayer as recorded in verse 12 is noteworthy:

"O our God, wilt thou not judge them? for we have no might against this great company that cometh against us; neither know we what to do: **but our eyes are upon thee**" (emphasis added).

This scripture made clear what drove King Jehoshaphat into prayer and fasting: *"no might against this great company that cometh against us..."* Judah was invaded by enemies too great for Jehoshaphat and his people to combat militarily; so they resolved to fight the battle using formidable spiritual weapons – prayer and fasting. The nation of Judah expressed total dependence on God in the midst of this great battle. They said to God decisively, *"...our eyes are upon you."* The people of God were in a seemingly hopeless and dire situation. A situation that was insurmountable, by man's assessment. But they chose to depend and rely unreservedly, on God. God takes this degree of trust very seriously.

What was the result?

"For the children of Ammon and Moab stood up against the inhabitants of mount Seir, utterly to slay and destroy

them: and when they had made an end of the inhabitants of Seir, every one helped to destroy another. And when Judah came toward the watch tower in the wilderness, they looked unto the multitude, and, behold, they were dead bodies fallen to the earth, and none escaped. And when Jehoshaphat and his people came to take away the spoil of them, they found among them in abundance both riches with the dead bodies, and precious jewels, which they stripped off for themselves, more than they could carry away: and they were three days in gathering of the spoil, it was so much" (vv. 23-25).

What a mighty weapon God has given to His Church to fight the cause of the enemy! We are equipped with the dynamic and formidable weapon of prayer to overturn and demolish satanic fortresses, and gain victory in every situation the enemy brings our way. To Jeremiah God said, *"See, I have this day set thee over the nations and over the kingdoms,* **to root out, and to pull down, and to destroy, and to throw down, to build, and to plant"** (Jer. 1:10, emphasis added). This assignment, charge or mandate is for every child of God today. We are called and set over the nations to utterly destroy the bands of wickedness, to undo the heavy burdens, and to let the oppressed go free, and break every yoke (Isaiah 58:6), and execute the judgement of God over wicked and evil forces of the devil. Our sphere of operation transcends our communities, regions, individual nations. We have a global mandate in this regard.

In Jeremiah 50: 20-23 God says, *"Thou art my battle axe and weapons of war: for with thee will I break in pieces the nations, and with thee will I destroy kingdoms; And with thee will I break in pieces the horse and his rider; and with thee will I break in pieces the chariot and his rider; With thee also will I break in pieces man and woman; and with thee will I break in pieces old and young; and with thee will I break in pieces the young man and the maid;I will also break in pieces with thee the shepherd and his flock; and with thee will I break in pieces the husbandman and his yoke of oxen; and with thee will I break in pieces captains and rulers."*

Prayer, therefore is not just a means of getting blessings from or enhancing intimacy with God, it is also a formidable weapon of warfare *"mighty through God to the pulling down of strongholds"* (2 Cor. 10:4).

Chapter 8

PRAYER – A SURE PLACE OF SUPERNATURAL PROTECTION AND REST

The Bible says:

> *And David stayed in strongholds in the wilderness, and remained in the mountains in the Wilderness of Ziph. Saul sought him every day, God did not deliver him into his hands* (1 Sam. 23:14).

> *Therefore he said unto Judah, Let us build these cities, and make about them walls, and towers, gates, and bars, while the land is yet before us; because we have sought the LORD our God, we have sought him, and he hath given us rest on every side. So they built and prospered.* (2 Chr. 14:7)

David's enemy – Saul – desperately sought an occasion to assassinate him, but *"God did not deliver David into his hands."* In other words, Saul could not get at him. Saul was intent on destroying David, but the difficult job he had was that because David was in the stronghold, in the very presence of God, Saul had to engage God in a battle, and defeat Him before he could get at David. What an impossible task! David knew the benefits of God's stronghold first hand! He testifies, *"The LORD is my rock, my fortress and my deliverer; my God is my rock, in whom I take refuge, my shield and the horn of my salvation, my stronghold"* (Psalm 18:2 NIV). Further, speaking of those who fear the Lord he writes, *"Thou shalt hide them in the secret of thy presence from the pride of man: thou shalt keep them secretly in a pavilion from the strife of tongues"* (Psalm 31:20). David's soul was sheltered perpetually in the fortress of God. In the presence of the Lord, the enemy cannot get at the believer.

Job tells us there is a secret place, known and available only to the believer in Christ Jesus:

"There is a path which no fowl knoweth, and which the vulture's eye hath not seen: The lion's whelps have not trodden it, nor the fierce lion passed by it" (Job 28: 7 – 8).

This is a path that is secure and protected from all demonic powers which offers maximum protection for the children of God as they seek refuge in Him.

It is a place hidden in God that no vulture's eye has seen; a place of refuge that no lion's whelps (principalities and power) pass by – not even the lion itself, Satan can operate in – the place of prayer!

The Bible says, *"God understandeth the way thereof, and he knoweth the place thereof. For he looketh to the ends of the earth, and seeth under the whole heaven"* (Job 28: 23 – 24). Indeed, "The name of the Lord is a **strong tower: the righteous runneth into it, and is safe**" (Prov. 18:10, emphasis added). Psalm 24:8 tells us of how invincible this place of refuge is: "…Who is this King of glory? **The LORD strong and mighty, the LORD mighty in battle**" (emphasis added).

In Psalm 91:1 we are told, *"He that dwells in the secret place of the Most High shall abide under the shadow of the Almighty."*

...to have God's greatest protection over your life, you need to be a dweller of His secret place

Both the words "stayed" in 1 Sam. 23:14 and "dwelleth" in Psalm 91:1 are worth noting. These words indicate that to have God's greatest protection over your life, you need to be a resident of His secret place. Visitors to the secret place seem to be excluded. In other words, prayer has got to be the lifestyle of the believer. Prayer to the believer must be a lifestyle to offer this degree of protection; never an occasional activity. Notice how frequently our first text tells us that Saul, David's arch-enemy sought him: daily! It is amazing the overwhelming protection we have in God that we often take for granted. The Bible declares, *"The eternal God is thy refuge, and underneath are the everlasting arms: and he shall thrust out the enemy from before thee; and shall say, Destroy them"* (Deut. 33:27). Underneath our every step are God's everlasting arms. Accordingly, when we go through situations and circumstances in life, we are kept by the power of Christ's in-destructible life. Jesus says, "My sheep hear my voice, and I know them, and they follow me: And I give unto them eternal life; **and they shall never perish, neither shall any man pluck them out of my hand. My Father, which gave them me, is greater than all; and no man is able to pluck them out of my Father's hand**" (John 10:27-29, emphasis added).

Undoubtedly, the enemy of our souls, the devil, his demons and agents seek occasions to destroy us at any given opportunity, but for the protection of God over our lives. 1 Peter 5:8 says *"Be sober, be vigilant; because your adversary the devil, as a roaring lion, walketh about, seeking whom he may devour."* However, the scriptures you have read above should help you appreciate the victory you have in Christ Jesus.

Between verses 2 and 13 of Psalm 91, we see the profound benefits of seeking divine protection in God. Verse 9, for instance, drives the point to an interesting conclusion:

"Because thou hast made the Lord, which is my refuge, even the most High, thy habitation." Notice the choice is yours! The above scripture says, *"because thou has made the Lord... thy habitation..."* The decision of where you seek refuge has to be made by you. Interestingly, only the Most High offers the degree of protection that the believer needs. There is no true protection anywhere else. Remember, *"The eternal God is thy refuge, and underneath are the everlasting arms..."* (Deut. 33:27).

PRAYER PREPARES YOU FOR THE RAPTURE

Jesus, dealing with end-time events said something very profound and worth noting in Luke 21:7-12, 35-36.

"And they asked him, saying, Master, but when shall these things be? and what sign will there be when these things shall come to pass? And he said, Take heed that ye be not deceived: for many shall come in my name, saying, I am Christ; and the time draweth near: go ye not therefore after them. But when ye shall hear of wars and commotions, be not terrified: for these things must first come to pass; but the end is not by and by. Then said he unto them, Nation shall rise against nation, and kingdom against kingdom: And great earthquakes shall be in divers places, and famines, and pestilences; and fearful sights and great signs shall there be from heaven. But before all these, they shall lay their hands on you, and persecute you, delivering you up to the synagogues, and into prisons, being brought before kings and rulers for my name's sake" (verses 7-12).

In verse 35, Jesus warns:

*"For as a snare shall **it come on all them that dwell on the face of the whole earth**"* (emphasis added). Undoubtedly, Jesus was referring to all the issues covered in the entire chapter until this verse. But more profoundly, He was warning the Church about the inevitability of the events as analysed. What does that mean, you may ask? It simply means there is

absolutely nothing the Church can do to stop these events unfolding. However, in verse 36, He says:

"Watch ye therefore, and pray always, that ye may be accounted worthy to escape all these things that shall come to pass, and to stand before the Son of man" (emphasis added). Here, Jesus is emphasising a very critical point: the inevitability of the end-time events (snares - verse 35) notwithstanding, watching and praying **always** will help the Church to escape *"all these things that shall come to pass"* (the snare), and be deemed worthy to stand before the "son of man." Events culminating into the second coming of Jesus will unravel suddenly and will take place on a world-scale simultaneously, as Christ has stated in Luke 17:34-35. It is fitting to reason that those who are accounted worthy to *"stand before the son of man "* are those deemed worthy to be raptured. In sum, the point being emphasised here is the role prayer plays to get the saints of God prepared for the rapture.

PRAYER IS THE FOUNTAINHEAD OF TRUE KINGDOM FRUITFULNESS

> *[It is He]* **Who has qualified us [making us to be fit and worthy and sufficient] as ministers***and dispensers of a new covenant [of salvation through Christ], not [ministers] of the letter (of legally written code) but of the Spirit; for the code [of the Law] kills, but the [Holy] Spirit makes alive* (2 Cor. 3:6, Amplified Bible, emphasis added).

> Communion with God is a salient condition of true spiritual growth. It is the soil in which all graces of the divine life root themselves ...

All kingdom exploits draw effectiveness from the anointing that comes through prayer. Every work of eternal value in the kingdom of God has been fostered and consummated by prayer. It has been rightly said that 'nothing on earth is ever established without serious and protracted prayer.' A question to Evan Roberts as to the secret of the blazing revival he was involved in received the following answer, "there is no secret, it is only ask and receive". No man can do a great and enduring work for God who is not first a man of prayer, and no man can be a man of prayer who does not devote quality time to praying, especially secret prayer.

The Bible declares, "...*but the people that do know their God, shall be strong and do exploits*" (Daniel 11:32b). Strength for divine exploits in God's kingdom comes from knowing Him through intimate relationship that results from a life-style of prayer.

In the word of David Macintyre, "Those who have turned many to righteousness have laboured early and late with the weapon called All-prayer".

Communion with God is a salient condition of true spiritual growth. It is the soil in which all graces of the divine life root themselves, leading us into richer influence and wider usefulness. We can do but little for God's kingdom by human means; it is the anointing that makes the difference.

According to Kenneth Copeland, anointing, as described in the Bible, can be defined as "God on flesh doing those things that flesh cannot do." It is God doing those things only He can do, and doing them through a flesh-and-blood, earthly vessel. To be anointed by God means to be empowered by Him for the task or position to which He has called you.

The position is well summed-up thus:

> *Then he answered and spake unto me, saying, This is the word of the LORD unto Zerubbabel, saying, Not by might, nor by power, but by my spirit, saith the LORD of hosts* (Zech. 4:6).

In a rather poetic fashion, Bill Hybels puts the succinctly:

"When we work, we work; when we pray, God works…" According to Laurence Scupoli, prayer is the means by which we obtain all the graces which rain down upon us from the divine fountain of goodness and love. David Macintyre affirms that, "Through prayer our graces are quickened, and holiness is wrought in us". "Holiness", says Hewitson, "is a habit of the mind – a setting of the Lord continually before one's eyes, a constant walking with God as one with whom we are agreed."

PRAYER CHANGES LIVES AND RE-FOCUSES DESTINY

In prayer, Hannah overcame barrenness and became a joyful mother. In prayer Jabez, a man born *in* and *with* sorrow, whose name actually meant sorrow, became profoundly successful. The amazing work of prayer was vividly demonstrated in the life of a man who had his life dramatically changed by a desperate encounter with God.

JACOB

So Jacob was left alone, and a man wrestled with him till daybreak. When the man saw that he could not overpower him, he touched the socket of Jacob's hip so that his hip was wrenched as he wrestled with the man. Then the man said, "Let me go, for it is daybreak." But Jacob replied, "I will not let you go unless you bless me." The man asked him, "What is your name?" "Jacob," he answered. Then the man said, "Your name will no longer be Jacob, but Israel, because you have struggled with God and with men and have overcome." Jacob said, "Please tell me your name." But he replied, "Why do you ask my name?" Then he blessed him there. So Jacob called the place Peniel [which means "face of God"], saying, "It is because I saw God face to face, and yet my life was spared (Gen. 32:24-29).

The life of Jacob remains a point of reference of the exceptional work of genuine encounter with God.

Esau hated Jacob because he had stolen his blessing. Quite naturally, Esau sought revenge and threatened to kill Jacob who had to flee. However, 20 years later, Jacob had to return home with his wives and children. Esau, who had waited all those years for revenge, was on the way to meet him with an army of 400 men. This was the dire and desperate situation that drove Jacob to the presence of God.

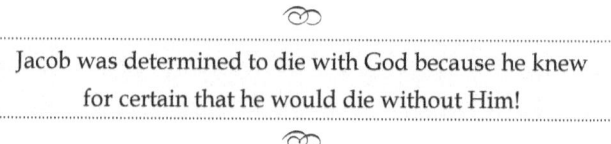

> Jacob was determined to die with God because he knew for certain that he would die without Him!

The same night, Jacob hurried his two wives, their two maids, 11 children and all of his belongings across the Jabbok River. When Jacob finally had a moment to himself, he sought solace in the presence of the Lord; in the process, a stranger suddenly appeared in the darkness and began to wrestle with him. Neither opponent prevailed until the amazing stranger sprained Jacob's thigh. But Jacob held on, realising that he had come face to face with God. This was Jacob's finest hour. It was the turning-point in his life. Jacob was determined to die with God because he knew for certain that he would die without Him! Although he was wounded and hurting, Jacob's desire for God was greater than his pain. As the dawn approached, the angel of the Lord said, "...*Let me go, for the day breaketh*". And he [Jacob] said, I will not let thee go, except thou bless me" (Gen. 32:26). The angel replied, "... *What is thy name*"? (Gen. 32:27).

"And he said, Thy name shall be called no more Jacob, but Israel: for as a prince hast thou power with God and with men, and hast prevailed" (Gen. 32:28).

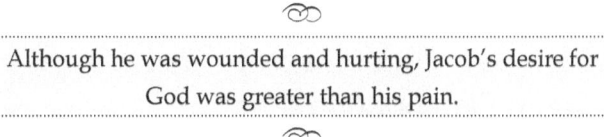

Although he was wounded and hurting, Jacob's desire for God was greater than his pain.

In essence, Jacob prevailed against the angel because of his desperate desire for a miracle from God. In a sudden and dramatic turn of events, the same night, God miraculously changed Esau's heart so that he forgave Jacob for all the wrongs he had done.

The phrase *"there wrestled a man with him until..."* (Gen. 32:24) in the scripture under consideration is note-worthy. Jacob wrestled and did not let go until he became Israel – a prince with God. A profound lesson that can easily be gleaned from this life-transforming scripture, no doubt, is the fact that any significant breakthrough in life almost always involves a wrestling, a fight, a battle and the list goes on, in prayer. The reason for this rests in the fact that life, at its best, is a battle ground, never a play ground. More often than not, life offers what you demand and never so much of what you deserve. Accordingly, the life of Jacob here offers a stunning portrait of the key of notable breakthrough in life, delineating the basic scriptural principles that underscore impressive and remarkable achievements in life. Breakthrough in life is achieved in the realm of firmness and decisiveness – where decision is translated into energy.

It is to be noted that Jacob did not become a Prince by praying fainthearted, fear-ridden and fragile prayer. He was bold, courageous, and assertive in his demand, and God honoured him.

PETER

Another example of a dramatic change of destiny resulting from an encounter with Jesus was the life of Peter. An encounter with Jesus altered Peter's destiny drastically.

"And he brought him to Jesus. And when Jesus beheld him, he said, Thou art Simon the son of Jona: thou shalt be called Cephas, which is by interpretation, A stone" (John 1:42).

A world of limitless possibilities was opened for Peter with this simple, but highly impactful encounter.

According to Gill, Christ not only calls Simon by his present name, at first sight of him, but tells him what his future name should be; and which imports, not only that he should be a lively stone in the spiritual building, the church, but should have a considerable hand in that work, and abide firm and steadfast to Christ, and his interest, notwithstanding his fall; and continue constant and immoveable until death, as he did.

Considering the vast and highly significant exploits that Peter was destined to accomplish in God's kingdom, as one pre-ordained to proclaim Christ's name to the Jews, such a profound and life-changing encounter was no doubt, expedient. Why? Because name declares identity! Sadly, many have been functioning without a true sense of identity. Peter was one of the several key people in scripture whose names God changed, because of the unique calling He had on their lives. Peter was limited and weak before his encounter with Jesus. His name (Simon) which meant "instability" was changed to "a rock" through a prophetic utterance. Before this life-transforming encounter with Jesus, Peter was misaligned with the unique and peculiar destiny God had for him. Let us reflect for a moment on some of the outstanding exploits Peter accomplished in God's Kingdom, a man of unstable personality could never have achieved so much for God. It is apt to conclude that Jesus knew this fact about Peter, hence the 'overhaul' of his personality well ahead of time.

Jabez was inappropriately named by his sorrowful mother, "because I bore him in sorrow" by reason of her **present** calamity. In the same vein, Benjamin was wrongly named, "Benoni" - "the son of my sorrow" - by his dying mother, Rachel. However, his father who saw beyond the prevailing and contemporaneous situations surrounding his birth, named him Benjamin - "the son of my right hand", or "the son of my strength." Out of that prophetic word of Jacob came the lineage of King Saul, the first king who reigned over Israel.

Peter was an ordinary man before his life-transforming encounter with Jesus. His life was banal, colourless and of little or no significance whatsoever, until he came in contact with the unchanging changer of men, the rewriter of history – Jesus Christ.

It is evident that the above scripture opens up a vast field of reflection. We shall only indicate two of the many directions in which it applies.

God focuses more on your future than your present.

The phrase *"Thou art ...thou shall be called"* bears huge significance in the above scripture. When Jesus looked at Peter, He saw what man could not perceive in him. He saw in Peter a world of unlimited possibilities. Jesus saw beyond Peter's present position, He saw his future. He saw an apostle in Peter – a divine instrument that would bear the name of Christ to the Jews, *"But contrariwise, when they saw that the gospel of the uncircumcision was committed unto me, as the gospel of the circumcision was unto Peter; For he that worked effectually in Peter to the apostleship of the circumcision, the same was mighty in me toward the Gentiles"* (Gal. 2:7-8). He saw in Peter a great healing evangelist whose shadow would heal the sick on the streets of Jerusalem (Acts 5:15-16). Jesus' knowledge of Peter undoubtedly, surpassed what he knew about himself. In Isaiah 55: 8-9, Prophet Isaiah reveals the mind of God on the matter, *"For my thoughts are not your thoughts, neither are your ways my ways, saith the* L{\small ORD}*. For as the heavens are higher than* *the earth, **so are my ways higher than your ways, and my thoughts than your** **thoughts**"* (emphasis added). By the same token, Jesus deals with you on the basis of His pre-ordained plans for your life. His dealing with man transcends man's present position or status in life. The vital lesson remains that God does not consult your past and present to determine your future. As a matter of fact, God pre-ordains a man's destiny long before he is born. Destiny is discovered, never created by man. God said to Jeremiah, *"Before I formed you in the womb I knew you, before you were born I set you apart; I appointed you as a prophet to the nations"* (Jer. 1:5, NIV).

The Lord certainly knows what you are today and what your future holds. An encounter with Jesus reveals, not only your God-given destiny, but your possibilities in life.

An encounter with Jesus marks a turning point in life.

There is no indelible or enduring breakthrough in life outside Christ. A great and enviable life does not happen by accident, it is not a product of luck either. As said, your personal success will never be achieved through man-made, self-help programs that ignore God and obedience to His laws. Success in life is a choice and it requires acute desire, determination, and faith. Those who refuse to allow life to dictate what happens to them, but instead, choose to make life happen, in the words of Philip Baker, boldly break away from the security of mediocrity and eagerly chase God's best for their lives. An enviable life, a life that is more than just average and defies the status quo needs good partnership with God. Paul declares, *"Not that we are of ourselves to think anything as of ourselves;* **but our sufficiency is of God***"* (2 Cor. 3:5, emphasis added). In Philippians 4:13, Paul says, *"I can do all things* **through Christ which strengtheneth me***"* (emphasis added).

Peter's encounter with Jesus marked a remarkable turning point in his life. That was the beginning of Peter's rise to stardom. There was a great deal of possibilities and potentials in Peter he did not realise until he met with his creator. The prophetic utterance of the all-knowing Christ *"Thou art ...thou shall be called"* (John 1:42), like a pendulum swung Peter's destiny from instability and mediocrity to fame, prominence and glory. In the same vein, it does not matter how, where, and by whom you were born; it is of no relevance what your history has been: destitute, down-trodden or a never-do-well, an encounter with Jesus will mark a fresh and astonishing beginning for you.

Chapter 9

PRAYER REVEALS THE WILL OF GOD

> *But as it is written, Eye hath not seen, nor ear heard, neither have entered into the heart of man, the things which God hath prepared for them that love him. But God hath revealed them unto us by his Spirit: for the Spirit searcheth all things, yea, the deep things of God. For what man knoweth the things of a man, save the spirit of man which is in him? Even so the things of God knoweth no man, but the Spirit of God. Now we have received, not the spirit of the world, but the spirit which is of God; that we might know the things that are freely given to us of God* (1 Cor. 2:9-12).

The will of God is revealed and known through prayer. Prayer is the access route into the heart of God. Without a life committed to persistent prayer, one is oblivious of what the perfect will and purpose, and indeed, plans of God for one's life are.

Moses declares, "*The secret things belong unto the Lord our God: but those things which are **revealed** belong unto us and to our children for ever, that we may do all the words of this law*" (Deut. 29:29, emphasis added). God reveals His present and future plans to people who are close to His heart. Prophet Amos clearly states, "*Surely the Lord GOD will do nothing, but he revealeth his secret unto his servants...*" From a personal perspective, the word *'servant'* in the above scripture means those who would obey His voice, given that the prime characteristic of a servant is obedience. (Amos 3:7). For instance, God revealed His plan to Noah about His intention to destroy mankind because of the wickedness of man long before the event took place. Consequently, Noah was given the onerous task to build an ark.

"And God said to Noah, "The end of all flesh has come before Me, for the earth is filled with violence through them; and behold, I will destroy them with the earth" (Gen. 6:13)

What an assignment! But God could only vest such vast responsibilities on His trusted *friends* – those close to His heart.

In the same vein, God did not execute His intended plan against Sodom and Gomorrah until He had revealed it to and talked it over with Abraham. Hear God ruminating over His plans and the felt duty to first reveal them to His friend – Abraham. One could literarily feel the heart of God panting over the matter:

> *And the Lord said, Shall I hide from Abraham that thing which I do; Seeing that Abraham shall surely become a great and mighty nation, and all the nations of the earth shall be blessed in him? For I know him, that he will command his children and his household after him, and they shall keep the way of the Lord, to do justice and judgment; that the Lord may bring upon Abraham that which he hath spoken of him* (Gen. 18:17).

Yet, these were plans well within the ability of God to execute without necessarily having to consult with man. He is sovereign; He can do anything without any impute whatsoever, from man.

How on earth was such a relationship ever possible? As said earlier, the simple answer is fellowship, relationship and intimacy. Regarding Moses God boasted, *"…Hear now my words: If there be a prophet among you, I the Lord will make myself known unto him in a vision, and will speak unto him in a dream. My servant Moses is not so, who is faithful in all mine house. With him will I speak mouth to mouth, even apparently, and not in dark speeches; and the similitude of the Lord shall he behold"* (Num. 12:6-8). And of Simeon it was said, *"And, behold, there was a man in Jerusalem, whose name was Simeon; and the same man was just and devout, waiting for the consolation of Israel: and the Holy Ghost was upon him. And it was revealed unto him by the Holy Ghost, that he should not see death, before he had seen the Lord's Christ. And he came by the Spirit into the temple: and when the parents brought in the child Jesus, to do for him after the custom of the law"* Luke 2:25-27).

As we wait on the Lord in prayer, God reveals His will to us; most essentially, His plans and purposes for our lives. In His Word God speaks to us, but in prayer, we speak to God. Constant communication with our heavenly father is vital if we truly want to know His plans for our lives. George Sweeling argues, "Nothing lies beyond the reach of prayer except that which lies *outside* the will of God". Knowledge of the will of God is crucial if we are to have God's best for our lives.

Let us consider the following scriptures on the subject:

"Behold, the former things are come to pass, and new things do I declare: before they spring forth I tell you of them" (Isaiah 42:9).

"Call unto me, and I will answer you, and show you great and mighty things, which you know not" (Jer. 33:3).

"At that time Jesus answered and said, I thank thee, O Father, Lord of heaven and earth, because thou hast hid these things from the wise and prudent, and hast revealed them unto babes. Even so, Father: for so it seemed good in thy sight. All things are delivered unto me of my Father: and no man knoweth the Son, but the Father; neither knoweth any man the Father, save the Son, and he to whomsoever the Son will reveal him" (Matt. 11:25-27).

"And he said unto them, Unto you it is given to know the mystery of the kingdom of God: but unto them that are without, all these things are done in parables: That seeing they may see, and not perceive; and hearing they may hear, and not understand; lest at any time they should be converted, and their sins should be forgiven them" (Mark 4: 11-12).

"Howbeit when he, the Spirit of truth, is come, he will guide you into all truth: for he shall not speak of himself;

but whatsoever he shall hear, that shall he speak: and he will shew you things to come. He shall glorify me: for he shall receive of mine, and shall shew it unto you. All things that the Father hath are mine: therefore said I, that he shall take of mine, and shall shew it unto you" (John 16:13-15).

"Now to him that is of power to stablish you according to my gospel, and the preaching of Jesus Christ, according to the revelation of the mystery, which was kept secret since the world began, But now is made manifest, and by the scriptures of the prophets, according to the commandment of the everlasting God, made known to all nations for the obedience of faith" (Rom. 16:25-26).

The will of God is revealed to the saint in the secret place. As said, there is a limit to what friends can discuss in the public. The nature of the subject-matter of a discussion determines the right avenue for it. God deals with us on a personal level and would always choose the secret place to unfold His will and purposes to us. God spoke to Abraham in the secret place when He led him out of his father's house to the land He later revealed to him (Gen. 12:1). In the same vein, God spoke to Samuel in the secret place when He commissioned him and revealed His future plans to him (1 Sam. 3:10-11). God speaks in clear terms to the praying saints. Except the believer chooses to live in isolation or detachment from his source, he can never be confused or be oblivious of the will and leading of God for his life.

Chapter 10

PRAYER HAS POWER TO CHANGE THE PLANS OF GOD

Prayer does not only change situations and circumstances, prayer does change God's plans. The Bible is replete with examples of God having to change His mind through the power of persuasive prayers, especially intercession.

Here lies one of the greatest puzzles of all time! The Bible says that God is all knowing; in fact, He knows the end from the beginning (Isaiah 46:9-11), and He does not change (Num. 23:19). He is same yesterday, today and forever (Heb. 13:8). How does this fit with God's positive response to prayers which ask for a change to His stated plans? Detailed examination of scriptures reveals that there is always a place where God's sovereignty and man's responsibility find harmony.

Two principles are identified:

Principle 1: when man repents of his sin, God repents of His judgement.

God told the young King Solomon at the very beginning of His reign, *"If my people, which are called by my name, shall humble themselves, and pray, and seek my face, and turn from their wicked ways; then will I hear from heaven, and will forgive their sin, and will heal their land* (2 Chr. 7:14). God would hear the prayer of His people and heal the land when and only when His people do the following:

- shall humble themselves
- and pray
- and seek God's face,
- and turn from their wicked ways

Note the word "then" in the above scripture. It indicates that God's responsibility starts when man has completed his. We see this trend throughout the word of God – that God is ever ready to change His mind in relation to judgment when His people repent of their sins.

Someone has said, "…as humans, we do not know the future, so God sometimes presents things to us as though they will happen, when He knows that they will not. Our responses are then based on what is presented to us. We may then pray and the situation seems to change. As far as we are concerned, God has changed His plans – although with His knowledge of the future, none of God's plans changed at all. All we have done is caught up with some of God's knowledge of the future."

Let us now examine some specific examples:

PROPHET JONAH AND THE NATION OF NINEVEH

> *So the people of Nineveh believed God, and proclaimed a fast, and put on sackcloth, from the greatest of them even to the least of them. For word came unto the king of Nineveh, and he arose from his throne, and he laid his robe from him, and covered him with sackcloth, and sat in ashes...And God saw their works, that they turned from their evil way; and God repented of the evil, that he had said that he would do unto them; and he did it not* (Jonah 3:5, 6 & 10 KJV).

The power to prevail with God was never more clearly demonstrated in the Bible than when a pronouncement of divine judgement was averted through repentance, prayer and fasting. *"Yet forty days", declared Jonah, "and Nineveh shall be overthrown"* (Jonah 3:4).

The reaction of the Ninevites was spontaneous; and God, I believe, viewed this as a sign of repentance: The King of Nineveh proclaimed a national fast, not just for humans, but also for beasts, and the people cried unto God for mercy.

And the people said, *"Who knows God may yet repent (change His mind) and turn from His fierce anger, so that we perish not."*

...whenever God finds 'a faithful few' who stand in the gap, even in the eleventh hour, and humble themselves with prayer and fasting, He is ever ready to change His mind ...

The Ninevites' repentance, expressed through fasting, moved God to repent of the judgement He had intended to bring upon them; and He did not do it. In other words, God changed His mind regarding the judgment He had earlier pronounced against them.

Jonah's message of impending judgment was therefore, averted by the repentance of the people of Nineveh. This is very much in keeping with the nature of God. God has already covenanted:

"At what instant I shall speak concerning a nation, and concerning a kingdom, to pluck up, and to pull down, and to destroy it; If that nation, against whom I have pronounced, turn from their evil, I will repent of the evil that I thought to do unto them" (Jer. 18:7, 8).

The position of God on the subject is very clear, when man repents from his sins; God repents in respect of His judgment. The repentance of man provokes God's repentance concerning judgment! The Old Testament abounds with instances of this kind. It therefore, stands to reason that whenever God finds 'a faithful few' who stand in the gap, even in the eleventh hour, and humble themselves with prayer and fasting, He is prepared to change His mind in relation to any judgment He might have intended to execute. This is distinctly demonstrated in the conversation Abraham had with God about the impending judgment on Sodom and Gomorrah.

SODOM AND GOMORRAH

God was intent on destroying Sodom and Gomorrah. But Abraham, the friend of God, would do whatever it takes to avert the judgement of God on the land. Abraham approached God and said: *"Will you destroy the righteous with the wicked? What if there are fifty righteous people in the city? Will you really sweep it away and not spare the place for the sake of the fifty righteous people in it? Far be it from you to do such a thing – to kill the righteous with the wicked, treating the righteous and the wicked alike. Far be it from you! Will not the Judge of all the earth do right?"* (Gen.18:23-24).

The Lord answered, 'if I find fifty righteous people in the city of Sodom, I will spare the whole place for their sake.'

> *Then Abraham spoke up again: Now that I have been so bold as to speak to the Lord, though I am nothing but dust and ashes, what if the number of the righteous is five less than fifty? Will you destroy the whole city for lack of five people? If I find forty-five there, he said, I will not destroy it. Once again he spoke to him, What if only forty are found there?" He said, For the sake of forty, I will not do it. Then he said, May the Lord not be angry, but let me speak. What if only thirty can be found there? He answered, I will not do it if I find thirty there. Abraham said, "Now that I have been so bold as to speak to the Lord, what if only twenty can be found there? He said, For the sake of twenty, I will not destroy it. Then he said, May the Lord not be angry, but let me speak just once more. What if only ten can be found there? He*

> *answered, For the sake of ten, I will not destroy it. When the Lord had finished speaking with Abraham, he left, and Abraham returned home* (Gen. 18:27-33).

All that God is looking for is a man, if He can find more than one, that is even better (Deut. 32:30), that would make up the hedge, and stand in the gap before God for the land that He would not destroy it (Ezek. 22:30). We can see that notion clearly demonstrated in these accounts.

A condition for not destroying the land was God finding people (intercessors) to stand in the gap, pleading for mercy from God for the land. God has already covenanted, *"If my people, which are called by my name, shall humble themselves, and pray, and seek my face, and turn from their wicked ways; then will I hear from heaven, and will forgive their sin, and will heal their land"* (2 Chr. 7:14).

This, no doubt, speaks of the nature and character of God, and it is profoundly encouraging and of immense benefit in the midst of an impending judgment!

In the word of Arthur Wallis, "This action on the part of God presents us with a theological problem. God is revealed as omniscient, as One Who sees the end from the beginning. His foreknowledge is complete and infallible. His character and counsel are immutable. 'I the Lord do not change'". However, he affirms that these are the attributes of the Almighty, and our common sense tells us that without them God would not be God.

It is certain that God foreknew, when He sent Jonah that Nineveh would repent and His judgment would be averted. This then appears to be God's purpose for sending Jonah, that He might extend mercy towards them. This nature of God is sufficiently demonstrated in 2 Peter 3:9:

"...but is longsuffering toward us, not willing that any should perish, but that all should come to repentance." The same scripture is more cleanly presented in the God's Word Translation:

"... Rather, he is patient for your sake. He does not want to destroy anyone but wants all people to have an opportunity to turn to him and change the way they think and act."

God appeared to have driven this attribute to an astonishing limit when, even the repentance of King Ahab attracted God's mercy.

GOD'S RESPONSE TO KING AHAB'S FAST

These unique attributes of God are clearly demonstrated in God responding to the fasting of even, a heathen king, Ahab, in other to avert imminent judgment. King Ahab, the husband of Jezebel, had committed abomination before God.

No previous king of Israel was as wicked as Ahab. In a swift move to unleash His judgement against Ahab, God voiced His displeasure against his evils and that of his wife – Jezebel.

This prompted Ahab to seek forgiveness with fasting. Fasting and repentance are often associated, because true fasting brings about a spirit of repentance.

God said:

"And it came to pass, when Ahab heard those words, that he rent his clothes, and put sackcloth upon his flesh, and fasted, and lay in sackcloth, and went softly. And the word of the Lord came to Elijah the Tishbite, saying, Seest thou how Ahab humbleth himself before me? because he humbleth himself before me, I will not bring the evil in his days: but in his son's days will I bring the evil upon his house" (I Kings 21:29).

So we can see that repentance lifted God's judgment from Ahab.

This powerful spiritual principle still applies today, and is consistent with God's promise to Israel:

*"Say unto them, As I live, saith the Lord **God, I have no pleasure in the death of the wicked; but that the wicked turn from his way and live: turn ye, turn ye from your evil ways; for why will ye die, O house of Israel?** Therefore, thou son of man, say unto the children of thy people, The righteousness of the righteous shall not deliver him in the day of his transgression: as for the wickedness of the wicked, he shall not fall thereby in the day that he turneth from his wickedness; neither shall the righteous be able to live for his righteousness in the day that he sinneth. When I shall say to the righteous, that he shall*

surely live; if he trust to his own righteousness, and commit iniquity, all his righteousnesses shall not be remembered; but for his iniquity that he hath committed, he shall die for it. ***Again, when I say unto the wicked, Thou shalt surely die; if he turn from his sin, and do that which is lawful and right; If the wicked restore the pledge, give again that he had robbed, walk in the statutes of life, without committing iniquity; he shall surely live, he shall not die.*** *None of his sins that he hath committed shall be mentioned unto him: he hath done that which is lawful and right; he shall surely live"* (Ezek. 33:11-16, emphasis added).

Principle 2: God's response to intercession.

The second valid explanation behind God changing His mind is based on the principle of His response to intercession.

According to R.A. Torrey, prayer moves the hand that moves the world. Richard Trench was succinct when he said, "Prayer is not overcoming God's reluctance, but laying hold of His highest willingness." Prayer averts God's judgement! He told Ezekiel, *"And I sought for a man among them, that should make up the hedge, and stand in the gap before me for the land, that I should not destroy it: but I found none"* (Ezek. 22:30). If God can find just one person who will seek His face, the tide of events can be turned.

Let us examine some examples:

ABRAHAM AND ABIMELECH

And Abraham journeyed from thence toward the south country, and dwelled between Kadesh and Shur, and sojourned in Gerar. And Abraham said of Sarah his wife, She is my sister: and Abimelech king of Gerar sent, and took Sarah. But God came to Abimelech in a dream by night, and said to him, Behold, thou art but a dead man, for the woman which thou hast taken; for she is a man's wife. But Abimelech had not come near her: and he said, Lord, wilt thou slay also a righteous nation? Said he not unto me, She is my sister? and she, even she herself said, He is my brother: in the integrity of my heart and innocency of my hands have I done this. And God said unto him in a dream, Yea, I know that thou didst this in the integrity of thy heart; for I also withheld thee from sinning against me: therefore suffered I thee not to touch her. Now therefore restore the man his wife; for he is a prophet, and he shall pray for thee, and thou shalt live: and if thou restore her not, know thou that thou shalt surely die, thou, and all that are thine (Gen. 20:1-7).

Abraham had lied about his wife – Sarah. Consequently, Abimelech took Sarah to be his. David Guzikwas is of the view that "Abraham's concern was probably not because Sarah looked like a young beauty at 90 years of age. We can surmise that she was reasonably attractive at that age, but more importantly she was connected to one of the richest and most influential men of the region." God had closed the wombs of King Abimelech's wives so that none of his wives could give birth to children. However, when Abraham prayed, God healed Abimelech and his household, *"So Abraham prayed unto God: and God healed Abimelech, and his wife, and his maidservants; and they bare children. For the LORD had fast closed up all the wombs of the house of Abimelech, because of Sarah Abraham's wife* (Gen. 20: 17-18).

MOSES

Another landmark example is found in Exodus 32: 7-10:

And the Lord said unto Moses, Go, get thee down; for thy people, which thou broughtest out of the land of Egypt, have corrupted themselves: They have turned aside quickly out of the way which I commanded them: they have made them a molten calf, and have worshipped it, and have sacrificed thereunto, and said, These be thy gods, O Israel, which have brought thee up out of the land of Egypt. And the Lord said unto Moses, I have seen this people, and, behold, it is a stiffnecked people: Now therefore let me alone, that my wrath may wax hot against them, and that I may consume them: and I will make of thee a great nation.

God, in His holy wrath wanted to destroy the nations of Israel as a result of their sins. But when Moses prayed, the Lord turned away from His anger, choosing to extend the hand of mercy rather than that of judgment towards His people. The Bible says, *"And*

Moses besought the LORD his God, and said, LORD, why does your wrath grow hot against your people, whom you have brought forth out of the land of Egypt with great power, and with a mighty hand?" (vv11-12).

Bad as the situation was, God's love for Israel made Him unwilling to destroy the nation in the first place.

However, after Moses prayed - as a result of Moses' prayer- the Bible says: *"And the Lord repented of the evil which he thought to do unto his people"* (v 14). Even Aaron that misled God's people was spared God intended judgment by the prayer of Moses.

"For I was afraid of the anger and hot displeasure, with which the LORD was angry with you to destroy you. But the LORD hearkened unto me at that time also. And the LORD was very angry with Aaron and would have destroyed him: and I prayed for Aaron also the same time" (Deut. 9:19-20).

HEZEKIAH

King Hezekiah was a good king of Judah. He introduced sweeping religious reforms and brought back the Law of Moses to the land. He destroyed the high places and idol worship from the land. He brought the nation of Israel back to the service of God. However, Hezekiah became sick to the point of death.

"In those days was Hezekiah sick unto death. And Isaiah the prophet the son of Amoz came unto him, and said unto

him, *Thus saith the* LORD, *Set thine house in order: **for thou shalt die, and not live***" (Isaiah 38:1, emphasis added).

No doubt, the news of his imminent and impending death struck his heart. However, Hezekiah's immediate reaction to this glooming report moved God to change His plans concerning him, and thus, marked a turning point in his life:

"*Then Hezekiah turned his face toward the wall, and prayed unto the* LORD, *And said, Remember now, O Lord, I beseech thee, how I have walked before thee in truth and with a perfect heart, and have done that which is good in thy sight. And Hezekiah wept sore*" (vv 2-3).

What was the outcome of his prayer?

"*Then came the word of the* LORD *to Isaiah, saying, Go, and say to Hezekiah, Thus saith the* LORD, *the God of David thy father, I have heard thy prayer, I have seen thy tears: behold, I will add unto thy days fifteen years*" (vv 4-5).

God's plan for Hezekiah's life was changed because he prayed. Perhaps, it should be stressed that if a prophet of God delivered a message, such was held with utmost gravity. It was held as, indeed, a message from the Lord. Prophet Isaiah did not go to Hezekiah on his own volition, but as the mouthpiece of God; yet, with unflinching, uncompromising and steadfast resolve, Hezekiah dared to storm the throne of grace for mercy. God's will was for Hezekiah to die. His prayer changed the mind of God. Every child of God should draw solace from this biblical account. There is absolutely nothing God cannot and will not do for those that have faith in His ability and mercy. God's unqualified invitation remains opened:

"Seeing then that we have a great high priest, that is passed into the heavens, Jesus the Son of God, let us hold fast our profession. **For we have not an high priest which cannot be touched with the feeling of our infirmities;** *but was in all points tempted like as we are, yet without sin.* **Let us therefore come boldly unto the throne of grace, that we may obtain mercy, and find grace to help in time of need"** (Heb. 4:14-16, emphasis added).

Take whatever situation you are faced with to the Lord today, solution awaits you at the throne of grace. Every situation a child of God faces, no matter the intensity or duration is subject to change. Yours is no exception!

Chapter 11

PRAYER - THE BATTLEFIELD OF THE BELIEVER

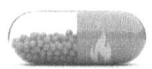

Believers in Christ are in constant battle with the devil and all his hellish hosts. The battle between light and darkness in ever raging, and is becoming fiercer by the day. Our belief and confidence in Christ Jesus is under constant bombardment. We are at such a critical time in God's kingdom that, unless we are fully persuaded of our beliefs and individual faith in the Lord, we stand the chance of being swept away by the ferocious wind that is bellowing unceasingly, causing doubts and unbelief in the minds of many. There is no better time that Paul's admonition, calling on the believers in Christ to work out their salvation with fear and trembling should resonate and be heeded than now. *"Wherefore, my beloved, as ye have always obeyed, not as in my presence only, but now much more in my absence, work out your own salvation with fear and trembling"* (Phil. 2:12).

It is certain that the battle of the age cannot be engaged in and won in any other way than through the involvement of God. Prayer puts God on the scene! The Bible affirms, *"He will keep the feet of his saints, and the wicked shall be silent in darkness; for by strength shall no man prevail"* (1 Sam. 2:9). Notice that in the midst of battles, the God of battle will be a shelter over the believer if he engages God through prayer.

Prophet Zephaniah declares, *"The Lord your God is with you, the **Mighty Warrior who saves** [a victorious warrior, NASB]. He will take great delight in you; in his love he will no longer rebuke you, but will rejoice over you with singing* (Zephaniah 3:17, NIV, emphasis added). God is the mighty warrior that saves and delivers. With God in the battle, victory is certain!

In the midst of perhaps, the great challenge of his reign as king of Judah, Jehoshaphat prayed:

*"...for we have no might against this great company that cometh against us; neither know we what to do: **but our eyes are upon thee"*** (2 Chr. 20:12, emphasis added). With this degree of faith and unflinching confidence expressed in His ability to deliver, God rose to the challenge, and gave His people landmark victory over their enemies (2 Chr. 20:22-29).

David had a personal testimony in this regard.

Emphatically, he declares:

*"For this shall every one that is godly pray unto thee in a time when thou mayest be found: surely in the floods of great waters they shall not come nigh unto him. **Thou art my hiding place; thou shalt preserve me from trouble; thou shalt compass me about with songs of***

deliverance... I will instruct thee and teach thee in the way which thou shalt go: I will guide thee with mine eye" (Psalm 32:6-8, emphasis added). The secret place of the Almighty remains the most secured place to dwell in, *"Whoever dwells in the shelter of the Most High will rest in the shadow of the Almighty"* (Psalm 91:1, NIV). It is the one place that the enemy cannot operate in. David further explains reasons why the Lord goes to this extent to protect the righteous:

"He does not delight in the strength of the horse; He does not take pleasure in the legs of a man. ***The LORD favors those who fear Him****, Those who wait for His lovingkindness"* (Psalm 147: 10-11, NASB, emphasis added). The favour of the Lord is the secret! So, there is something in common between 'favour' and 'protection'. It appears that the degree of protection that operates in the lives of those who fear the Lord, is the working of divine favour over them.

The nature of the battle between light and darkness is clearly depicted in the Bible, and the intention of the enemy spelt out in great details.

Let us consider the following scriptures:

"The enemy said, I will pursue, I will overtake, I will divide the spoil; my lust shall be satisfied upon them; I will draw my sword, my hand shall destroy them" (Exod. 15:9, KJV).

This is more clearly stated in the New Living Translation:

"The enemy boasted, 'I will chase them and catch up with them. I will plunder them and consume them. I will flash my sword; my powerful hand will destroy them" (Exod. 15:9).

"Remember thy congregation, which thou hast purchased of old; the rod of thine inheritance, which thou hast redeemed; this mount Zion, wherein thou hast dwelt... ***Thine enemies roar in the midst of thy congregations; [have created disturbances, or raised tumults] they set up their ensigns for signs... They have cast fire into thy sanctuary, they have defiled by casting down the dwelling place of thy name to the ground... They said in their hearts, Let us destroy them together****: they have burned up all the synagogues of God in the land. We see not our signs: there is no more any prophet: neither is there among us any that knoweth how long...Thine enemies roar in the midst of thy congregations; or, have roared; i.e. have created disturbances, or raised tumults"* (Psalm 74: 2,4,7-9, emphasis added).

"The thief cometh not, but for to steal, and to kill, and to destroy: I am come that they might have life, and that they might have it more abundantly" (John 10:10)

Consequently, all through the ages, we see events that, all too well give credence to our line of thought in this regard. In modern times, the threat of murder, acts of terrorism, genocide, acts of violence beyond precedence, and gruesome beheading of innocent lives as being perpetuated by such evil and satanic organisations as ISIS, only prove the trail of satanic forces at work. Wherever we look today in our world, we see individuals caught up in the web of addiction, violence, divorce, inner turmoil, immorality, witchcraft and spiritual confusion. The destruction spreads like a virus in society, leaving behind a wake of anger, fear and despair. The result is, fear, confusion, moral breakdown and spiritual anarchy.

We understand from scriptures that our *"battle is not against flesh and blood, but against the rulers, against the authorities, against the world powers of this darkness, against the spiritual forces of evil in the heavens"* (Eph. 6:12, Holman Christian Standard).

Victory against satanic forces is only possible in the place of prayer. If the Church would not pray, the devil and his hordes of demonic spirits find a clean ground to wreak havoc against God's people. If the battle against the enemy will be won by the church, we must persist in prevailing prayer to break the devil's stronghold and dislodge him completely. We have what it takes to get the job done! Paul affirms:

"For the weapons of our warfare are not carnal, but mighty through God to the pulling down of strong holds" (2 Cor. 10:4).

T.D. Jakes puts the position succinctly when he said:

"Prayer is vital to spiritual warfare because we must commune with God to put on His armor. We must communicate with him to receive His battle plan, and sometime He tells us of battles to come. Then we can allow Him to prepare us. As a result of maintaining an attitude of prayer, whenever and however the enemy strikes, we are suited up for warfare and ready to fight and win. Although we do not live in a constant state of warfare, we do live in s constant attitude of prayer because the enemy is roaming the earth, seeking whom he may devour...Prayer connects us to God, and God knows the strategies and battle plans that will defeat the enemy."

Prayer brings the power of God to bear in our battles against the power and forces of darkness. In prayer we are strengthened, invigorated and rein-enforced to face the onslaught of the devil and his cohorts.

A knee that is constantly bent in prayer belongs to a life that cannot be bent or broken by the enemy.

Remember the seven sons of Sceva's encounter with Satan.

> *Then certain of the vagabond Jews, exorcists, took upon them to call over them which had evil spirits the name of the Lord Jesus, saying, We adjure you by Jesus whom Paul preacheth. And there were seven sons of one Sceva, a Jew, and chief of the priests, which did so. And the evil spirit answered and said, Jesus I know, and Paul I know; but who are ye? And the man in whom the evil spirit was leaped on them, and overcame them, and prevailed against them, so that they fled out of that house naked and wounded* (Acts 19:11-20).

Prayer made the difference between Paul and the sons of Sceva. A praying believer, not only bears recognition before God, his position of spiritual authority is known and respected by the enemy. Never underestimate the power of prayer!

PRAYER HEALS

"The Lord will strengthen him upon the bed of languishing..." (Psalm 41:3).

"And the inhabitant shall not say, I am sick: the people that dwell therein shall be forgiven their iniquity" (Isaiah 33:24).

The power of God is generated through prayer to heal the sick.

James declares emphatically, *"Is any one among you suffering? Let him pray. Is any cheerful? Let him sing praise. Is any among you sick? Let him call for the elders of the church, and let them pray over him, anointing him with oil in the name of the Lord; and the prayer of faith will save the sick man, and the Lord will raise him up; and if he has committed sins, he will be forgiven"* (James 5: 13-15).

It is note-worthy that this scripture admonishes that we have been healed already – not going to be healed - irrespective of the sickness or disease you have in your body right now

Divine healing often takes place by activating and claiming the promises of God's word. For instance, Psalm 103:3 teaches that we have been healed of all our diseases. It is note-worthy that this scripture admonishes that we have been healed already – not just going to be healed – of whatever sicknesses or diseases you have in your body right now. This no doubt, points the believer to the finished work of Jesus on the cross of Calvary. The Bible says, *"And having spoiled principalities and powers, he made a shew of them openly, triumphing over them in it"* (Col. 2:15).

Your assignment therefore, is to constantly renew your mind in this regard and claim that which is yours through your covenant relationship with Christ.

Further, in Isaiah's profound prophecy, we are admonished: *"He is despised and rejected of men; a man of sorrows, and acquainted with grief: and we hid as it were our faces from him; he was despised, and we esteemed him not. Surely he hath borne our griefs, and carried our sorrows: yet we did esteem him stricken ,smitten of God, and afflicted. But he was wounded for our transgressions, he was bruised for our iniquities: the chastisement of our peace was upon him; and with his stripes we are healed"* (Isaiah 53:3-5).

Notice too, that the above scripture tells us that the finished work of Jesus on the cross had vicariously paid for our sicknesses and diseases. Note the phrase *"griefs and sorrows"* in the above scripture. The healing package, not only makes provision for the healing of the body but of anything that causes the believer to suffer grief and sorrow; in other words, the healing package makes provision for the healing of the total man! Your assignment, therefore, is to constantly renew your mind in this regard and claim that which is yours through your covenant relationship with Christ. You have to believe that in Christ Jesus you are already healed. Believe it in the face of all odds, and then begin to claim your healing through the power of confession – confessing the word of God on divine healing. In the words of Charles Capp, "God's principles of faith and confession unlock the supernatural to work for you." Mark 11:23-24 teaches: *"For assuredly, I **say** to you, whoever **says** to this mountain, 'Be removed and be cast into the sea,' and does not doubt in his heart, but **believes** that those things he **says** will be done, he will have whatever he **says**. Therefore I **say** to you, whatever things you ask when you pray, **believe** that you receive them, and you will have them"* (emphasis added). Notice the emphasis on the words "say" and "believe" in the above scripture. There is a divine link. What you say is shaped by what you believe. Your words are a product of your belief system. Matthew 12:34 says, *"... For out of the abundance of the heart the mouth speaketh."* Paul makes the connection in Romans 10:10 when he said:

> ∞
> ─────────────────────────────
> There are spiritual principles involved in claiming divine healing as a child of God.
> ─────────────────────────────
> ∞

"For with the heart one believes unto righteousness, and with the mouth confession is made unto salvation." Jesus, in our earlier text – Mark 11:24 says, "...whatever things you ask when you pray, believe that you receive them, and you will have them." There are spiritual principles involved in claiming divine healing as a child of God. Let us explore some of them briefly.

- *As said, you must believe in the finished work of Jesus on the Cross of Calvary. In other words, believe that He died for you and all the benefits that followed His sacrificial death belong to you as of right. Constantly renew your mind with this thought.*

- *Build your faith on the word of God. The Bible teaches, "...faith cometh by hearing, and hearing by the word of God"* (Rom. 10:17). Search and meditate on scriptures that promise you divine healing as a believer in Christ Jesus, and build your faith on them. Isaiah 55:11 highlights the nature and the integrity of the word: *"So shall my word be that goeth forth out of my mouth: it shall not return unto me void, but it shall accomplish that which I please, and it shall prosper in the thing whereto I sent it."* Every word of God has a mission which it accomplishes without fail.

Here are some of such healing scriptures in the word of God:

> *"Who forgiveth all thine iniquities; who healeth all thy diseases; Whore deemeth thy life from destruction; who crowneth thee with lovingkindness and tender mercies"* (Psalm 103:3-4).

> *"Surely he hath borne our griefs, and carried our sorrows: yet we did esteem him stricken, smitten of God, and afflicted[5] But he was wounded for our transgressions, he was bruised for our iniquities: the chastisement of our peace was upon him; and with his stripes we are healed"* (Isaiah 53:34-5).

> *"He sent his word, and healed them, and delivered them from their destructions"* (Psalm 107:20; Psalm 147:18).

In the word of Steward Perowne, "The Word by which the heavens were made, Psalms 33:6 , is seen to be not merely the expression of God's will, but his messenger mediating between himself and his creatures."

> *"Confess your faults one to another, and pray one for another, that ye may be healed. The effectual fervent prayer of a righteous man availeth much"* (James 5:16).

> *"And it shall come to pass in that day, that his burden shall be taken away from off thy shoulder, and his yoke from off thy neck, and the yoke shall be destroyed because of the anointing"* (Isaiah 10:27).

> *"Behold, I give unto you power to tread on serpents and scorpions, and over all the power of the enemy: and nothing shall by any means hurt you"* (Luke 10:19).

The process of divine healing up to this stage serves to prepare you for the next two significant stages which are:

1. **Praying and asking God to heal you**. According to our text - Mark 11:24 we are to translate our desires into prayer. Much more significantly, James 5:16 teaches that, *"...The earnest (heartfelt, continued) prayer of a righteous man **makes tremendous power***

available [dynamic in its working] (Amplified, emphasis added). What prayer does in relation to divine healing is to generate the power that is needed to bind the devil and the spirit of infirmity, and produce healing. We see the connection between prayer and divine healing further vividly stated in James 5:16. It says, *"...pray one for another, that ye may be healed..."* The connection is also made in James 5:14: *"Is any sick among you? let him call for the elders of the church; and let **them pray over him**, anointing him with oil in the name of the Lord."*

2. **After praying, believe that you have received your healing.** The Bible says, *"...when ye pray, believe that ye have them..."* (Mark 11:24). We are to believe in the power of prayer. Failure to believe in the power of prayer will rob you of receiving divine healing. It is of no use praying without believing that your prayer will work for you. We pray in the first place because we believe that our prayer will work for us.

3. **Finally, appropriate or decree your healing.** Once again, Mark 11:23 tells us that, *"...whosoever shall say unto this mountain, Be thou removed, and be thou cast into the sea; and shall not doubt in his heart, but shall believe that those things which he saith shall come to pass; he shall have whatsoever he saith."* Faith is released by speaking faith-guarded and faith-inspired words. As seen, speaking words is emphasised three times in this one verse, and the Lord commands us to believe that what we say will come to pass. The last part of this verse says, *"He shall have whatsoever he saith."* If we follow this instruction and begin to speak words in faith that line up with God's Word, then we will have the positive results that follow.

The process of divine healing or the prayer of faith must follow this pattern. It should never start from speaking to the mountain, why? Because you have not 'loaded' yourself with the requisite power which only comes through believing in the finished work of Jesus, meditating on scriptures, and praying. Remember, the structure remains: "whatsoever thing you desire, when you pray, believe that you receive them and you shall have them" (Mark 11:24).

The Bible is inundated with records of divine healing. The classic case of the Old Testament King, Hezekiah, serves as a soul-stirring and soul-inspiring example of the connection that exists between prayer and divine healing.

Hezekiah

> *In those days was Hezekiah sick unto death. And Isaiah the prophet the son of Amoz came unto him, and said unto him, Thus saith the Lord, Set thine house in order: for thou shalt die, and not live. Then Hezekiah turned his face toward the wall, and prayed unto the Lord, And said, Remember now, O Lord, I beseech thee, how I have walked before thee in truth and with a perfect heart, and have done that which is good in thy sight. And Hezekiah wept sore. Then came the word of the Lord to Isaiah, saying, Go, and say to Hezekiah, Thus saith the Lord, the God of David thy father, I have heard thy prayer, I have seen thy tears: behold, I will add unto thy days fifteen years (Isaiah 38: 1-5).*

The first line of verse one of the above scripture points to the severity of King Hezekiah's illness – quite reminiscent of the Bible's account of Elisha's sickness – *"Now Elisha was fallen sick of his sickness whereof he died"* (2 Kings 13:14). On the basis of both scriptures, the following conclusions are valid:

Prayer, indeed, prevailing prayer has profound power over sicknesses and diseases. We see this truth run like a golden thread throughout the Bible.

- Every sickness has a mission from the enemy; sickness being one of his weapons. While some are commissioned to kill as in both cases above, a whole lot are merely assigned to cause distractions. The children of God must not be oblivious of this fact. The Bible declares we must not be unaware of the enemy's devices (2 Cor. 2:11).

- Prayer, indeed, prevailing prayer has profound power over sicknesses and diseases. Prayer is a mighty weapon that breaks the yoke of sickness, its root cause, and liberates the captive completely. When the cause is removed, the effect ceases!

Hezekiah's experience provides a lasting example of what can happen when we claim God's promises of healing through prayer. The Bible declares that when Hezekiah heard the information about his imminent death, he sought God intensely and passionately: *"Then Hezekiah turned his face toward the wall,* ***and prayed unto the Lord,*** *And said, Remember now, O Lord, I beseech thee, how I have walked before thee in truth and with a perfect heart, and have done that which is good in thy sight. And Hezekiah wept sore"* (verse 2-3, emphasis added). Hezekiah, though a king, was just an ordinary man with a situation like any of us. In his hour of great trial, challenges and pain, he sought the Lord diligently, and God showed up and proved Himself mighty on his behalf. The Bible says, *"Then came the word of the Lord to Isaiah, saying, Go, and say to Hezekiah, Thus saith the Lord, the God of David thy father, I have heard thy prayer, I have seen thy tears: behold, I will add unto thy days fifteen years"* (verses 4-5).

What an astonishing outcome of prevailing prayer! Praise God, prayer works!

PART 3

BIBLICAL PERSPECTIVE TO PRAYER

Chapter 12

PRINCIPLES OF A BIBLE-CENTRED PRAYER

There are many contributing, Bible-based factors to successful prayer. If prayer must yield its desired and anticipated result, it must adhere to some salient and fundamental principles, few of which would be examined under this heading.

THE NAME OF JESUS

All things are possible through the name of Jesus. God hath highly exalted Him, and given Him the name which is above every name, that at the name of Jesus every knee should bow. There is power to overcome every circumstance in the world through the name of Jesus. The Bible declares, *"Neither is there salvation in any other: for there is none other name under heaven given among men, whereby we must be saved"* (Acts 4:12).

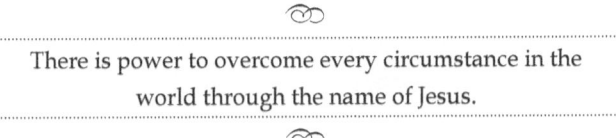

There is power to overcome every circumstance in the world through the name of Jesus.

The overall most significant requirement or condition of prevailing prayer is the powerful name of Jesus. Praying in the name of Jesus not only capsules our prayer with heaven-backed authority and power, it gives our prayer divine access to the throne of grace. It is what flings the gate of heaven open for our prayer to have its way to God. What gives the believer a legal right to the throne of grace is the name of Jesus. It is like a ticket to a stadium to watch a football match. Access would be denied if a spectator does not have a valid ticket. Even so, access to God has been denied a number of people who have not come to understand the significance of this requirement. Prayer becomes an exercise in futility if one does not understand the vital place of the name of Jesus in prayer. Not understanding the biblical principles that govern prayer has caused many of God's children to be ineffective in prayer. Consequently, many are frustrated and have regressed from being ineffective in prayer into the sin of prayerlessness.

Praying in the name of Jesus not only capsules our prayer with heaven-backed authority and power, it gives our prayer divine access to the throne of grace.

Jesus said unequivocally, "*And whatsoever ye shall ask **in my name**, that will I do, that the Father may be glorified in the Son. If ye shall ask any thing in my name, I will do it*" (John 14:13-14, emphasis added).

According to Barnes' notes on the Bible, "In my name... is equivalent to saying on my account, or for my sake. If a man who has money in a bank authorizes us to draw it, we are said to do it in his name. If a son authorises us to apply to his father for aid because we are his friends, we do it in the name of the son, and the favour will be bestowed on us from the regard which the parent has to his son. So we are permitted to apply to God in the name of his Son Jesus Christ, because God is in him well pleased Matthew 3:17, and because we are the friends of his Son he answers our requests. Though we are undeserving, yet He loves us on account of His Son... No privilege is greater than that of approaching God in the name of his Son; no blessings of salvation can be conferred on any who do not come in his name."

There are two areas of great caution to be noted in John 14:13-14.

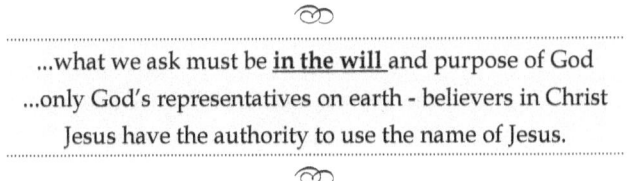

...what we ask must be **in the will** and purpose of God
...only God's representatives on earth - believers in Christ Jesus have the authority to use the name of Jesus.

First, the phrase, "*whatsoever ye ask in my name*" raises very serious issues deserving due elaboration. The extent and limit of the promise are both to be noted. It is "*whatsoever ye shall ask,*" and it is '*ask in My name.*' This means, we ask as 'My representatives on earth...

as persons doing My work, living in My spirit, seeking as I have sought to do the will of the Father...'" In other words, what we ask must be in the will and purpose of God. Second, only God's representatives on earth - believers in Christ Jesus have the authority to use the name of Jesus. Notice that *"the sacrifice of the wicked is an abomination to God"* (Pro. 21:27). Praying in the name of Jesus is a well-guarded privilege, exclusively reserved for the children of the kingdom. It is not an offer to the whole world.

The name of a person can only be used when we seek to enforce his will and further his interests. This gives the condition of a successful prayer. Accordingly, the mere use of the name of Jesus in prayer does not guarantee answer from heaven. It is the understanding we have of the person of Jesus – who He really is, and appropriating His power through faith in His name - that gives us the desired result.

It is the understanding we have of the person of Jesus – who He really is and appropriating His power through faith in His name that gives us the desired

We see this truth demonstrated in the account of the sons of Sceva, earlier referred to in the book of Acts:

> *Then certain of the vagabond Jews, exorcists, took upon them to call over them which had evil spirits the name of the Lord Jesus, saying, We adjure you by Jesus whom Paul preacheth. And there were seven sons of one Sceva,*

> *a Jew, and chief of the priests, which did so. And the evil spirit answered and said, Jesus I know, and Paul I know; but who are ye? And the man in whom the evil spirit was leaped on them, and overcame them, and prevailed against them, so that they fled out of that house naked and wounded (Acts 19:13-16).*

It is evident that this consideration opens up a vast field for reflection. We shall indicate one or two of the many directions in which it applies:

First, relationship with Jesus is what gives the believer the legal right to pray in His name. The above scripture reveals that one can pray in the name of Jesus, and yet be void of the power and authority the name carries. Second, the legal right and entitlement to pray in the name of Jesus cannot be transferred, or vested in another as in a power of attorney; you have to know Jesus for yourself. Notice the apparent error and misconception in the sons of Sceva attempting to execute mighty spiritual exploit *"in the name of Jesus whom Paul preacheth"* (v.13). It indicates that these men were not only void of the requisite understanding of the significance of the name of Jesus, they had no relationship whatsoever with Him. Our relationship with Jesus is what gives us the legal entitlement and authority to pray in His name and receive any blessings we desire of Him.

Jesus says, *"If ye abide in me, and my words abide in you, ye shall ask what ye will, and it shall be done unto you"* (John 15:7). Abiding in Him and His Word (same as

Jesus Himself) abiding in us is the comprehensive requirement that qualifies us to pray in the name of Jesus. Otherwise, a spiritual fraud is committed! The use of another person's name or property without his express or implied permission results in the commission of the crime of fraud or theft. For instance, if the police were to discover that another person fraudulently uses my full name, he has committed a crime by the sheer fact that he uses a false identification. It is, therefore, intimacy with Christ that gives us the legal right and permission to pray in the name of Jesus!

THE POWER OF THE NAME OF JESUS IN THE EARLY CHRUCH

There is, no doubt, a marked difference between the case we have just examined and the remarkable episode at the Beautiful Gate in Acts chapter 3.

> *And a certain man lame from his mother's womb was carried, whom they laid daily at the gate of the temple which is called Beautiful, to ask alms of them that entered into the temple; Who seeing Peter and John about to go into the temple asked an alms. And Peter, fastening his eyes upon him with John, said, Look on us. And he gave heed unto them, expecting to receive something of them. Then Peter said, Silver and gold have I none; but such as I have give I thee: In the name of Jesus Christ of Nazareth rise up and walk. And he took him by the right hand, and lifted him up: and immediately his feet and ankle bones received strength. And he leaping up stood, and*

> *walked, and entered with them into the temple, walking, and leaping, and praising God* (vv2-8).

Peter and John had gone up to the temple at the hour of prayer, which was approximately three o' clock in the afternoon. There was a lame man lying at the gate of the temple. He had been lame all of his life – he was born lame. He asked Peter and John for money. Peter looked at the lame man and said, "Look on us." The lame man looked at them expecting to receive something from them. The Peter said, *"Silver and gold have I none; but such as I have give I thee."* Peter knew that he had something to offer the lame man, but it was not what the lame man was expecting. Peter knew what was best for the lame man in the circumstance. He knew the usual alms collection which the lame man had resorted to, as a result of his situation, would not change his circumstances. In Peter's view, the lame man needed heaven's intervention, not the momentary and limited act of pity and benevolence he had enjoyed from men and women for so long.

Accordingly, Peter declared, *"Silver and gold have I none; but such as I have give I thee:* **In the name of Jesus Christ** *of Nazareth rise up and walk"* (Acts 3:6). In, essence, Peter gave the lame man what he had, and what he had was the name of Jesus, and a miracle followed; the lame man was healed. That which kept him in bondage for decades was broken and he was set free.

It is note-worthy that Peter attributed the miraculous healing of the lame man to faith and the great power inherent in the name of Jesus, *"And his name through faith in his name hath made this man strong, whom ye see and know: yea, the faith which is by him hath given him this perfect soundness in the presence of you all"* (verse 16). The lame man was healed with the weapon of the name of Jesus. Peter emphasised this truth to the awe-stricken crowed that witnessed the healing, affirming that the healing of the lame man was not the work or design of man but the miraculous work of God, through the name of Jesus, and by faith in His name.

IN HIS NAME, THROUGH FAITH IN HIS NAME

The name of Jesus means the authority of Jesus Christ. It is the name of Jesus that gives the believer the authority over the devil and guarantees answer to the command of faith. The believers in Christ Jesus are vested with great power and authority in the name of Jesus, or through faith in the power of Jesus to access the unlimited treasures of heaven. The name of Jesus is the access code or the secret password to the provisions of God for humanity. The Bible says:

"And the seventy returned again with joy, saying, Lord, even the devils are subject unto us through thy name... Behold, I give unto you power to tread on serpents and scorpions, and over all the power of the enemy: and nothing shall by any means hurt you" (Luke 10:17, 19).

The name of Jesus meant something very special to the early church. It was the basis of their existence; it was the core and seal of approval of their mission...

Interrogating Peter and John in Acts 4, Annas and Caiaphas, the high priest asked, *"By what power, or by what name, have ye done this?"* Notice that they did not deny the miraculous healing of the lame man. Second, they acknowledged that a supernatural power, released through the name of Jesus had brought healing to the lame man, and they wanted to know why Peter and John were praying or doing miracles in 'that name'. To the enquiry Peter replied:

*"Be it known unto you all, and to all the people of Israel, that by the name of Jesus Christ of Nazareth, whom ye crucified, whom God raised from the dead, even by him doth this man stand here before you whole. This is the stone which was set at nought of you builders, which is become the head of the corner. Neither is there salvation in any other: **for there is none other name under heaven given among men, whereby we must be saved**"* (verses 10-12, emphases added).

The name of Jesus meant something very special to the early church. It was the basis of their existence; it was the core and seal of approval of their mission, it was the message they were commissioned to preach, it was the power behind the message, and the basis of heaven validation of their calling. According to Terry Law, "the name [of Jesus] had been delegated to them, they had received a power of attorney to use the Name, and casting out of demons, they went about raising the dead by the power of the Name."

Further, the high priest called and threatened Peter and John *"not to speak at all nor teach in the name of Jesus"* (verse 18). They realised that the power and force behind the great exploits of the disciples was the authority and power the name of Jesus carries. Stopping the disciples from praying in the name of Jesus was as good as literarily, bringing the mission of Jesus on earth to a halt. The high priest knew it. The disciples knew it too. The disciples were simply not prepared to entertain anything that would either limit or hinder this great assignment the Master had delegated to them. So they replied, *"for we cannot but speak of what we have seen and heard"* (verse 20). They were ready to die for the cause of the gospel, preaching in the name of Jesus.

THE BELIEVERS' PRAYER

Being released from arrest and incarceration, Peter and John returned to the other apostles, gathered the other believers together, and began to praise God for the mighty miracle God had wrought in the lame man. In the great prayer forum they asked:

"... grant unto thy servants, that with all boldness they may speak thy word, By stretching forth thine hand to heal;

*and that signs and wonders may be done by the **name of thy holy child Jesus**"* (Acts 4:29-30, emphasis added). Notice the emphasis on *signs and wonders being done in the **name of Jesus***, indicating that signs and wonders are only possible in "His Name".

The name of Jesus was accounted for as the basis of the great revival of the early church. The Sanhedrin Council could readily identify with the reality of the time. The early Church had suddenly become a force to reckon with, and had put the streets of Jerusalem in great fear and confusion. The Sanhedrin Council had become very indignant and upset at the spread of the name of Jesus in Jerusalem and all the astonishing miracles that accompanied it. Once again, the apostles were arrested and incarcerated for further questioning. They questioned: *"...Did not we straitly command you that ye should not teach in this name? and, behold, ye have filled Jerusalem with your doctrine, and intend to bring this man's blood upon us."*

The high priests had the apostles beaten, and again warned them never to speak in the name of Jesus... They were trying to stop the force of God that was healing the sick and bringing revival.

This was the true account of what the early church was doing in the name of Jesus, and it came from the lips of the religious leaders of their day. The doctrine of the early church was the doctrine of "the Name".

They had literally filled the city of Jerusalem with this doctrine. Mighty miracles, beyond precedence, and attributed to the name of Jesus, were recorded in Jerusalem and everywhere the disciple carried the Good News of Jesus to. The great authority and power in the name of Jesus severely disturbed the religious leaders of the time. After the ascension of Jesus, preaching and performing astonishing miracles in the name of Jesus, was the proverbial "straw that broke the camel's back" for the Jewish leaders. They thought the Lord's exit meant the end of His mission on earth. Unfortunately, the present church has not come to realise the limitless power there is in the name of Jesus. As a result, it has become merely a signature to the prayers of some, rather than a powerful key that gives us legal rights to the presence of God, and all His divine treasures and provisions for mankind.

> *Blessed be the God and Father of our Lord Jesus Christ,* ***who hath blessed us with all spiritual blessings in heavenly places in Christ****: According as he hath chosen us in him before the foundation of the world, that we should be holy and without blame before him in love: Having predestinated us unto the adoption of children by Jesus Christ to himself, according to the good pleasure of his will* (Eph. 1:3-5, emphasis added).

"According as his divine power **hath given unto us all things that pertain unto life and godliness***, through the knowledge of him that hath called us to glory and virtue"* (2 Peter 1:3, emphasis added).

"For His divine power has bestowed upon us all things that [are requisite and suited] to life and godliness, through the [full, personal] knowledge of Him Who called us by and to His own glory and excellence (virtue)" (2 Peter 1:3, Amp. Bible).

The high priests had the apostles beaten, and again warned them never to speak in the name of Jesus. They made frantic effort to stop the doctrine that was filling the city - trying to stop the force that was behind the incredible healings and the astonishing exploits that gave birth to the revival inferno that had engulfed, not only Jerusalem, but *"...in all Judaea, and in Samaria, and unto the uttermost part of the earth"* (Acts 1:8). However, the Bible testifies that the apostles, *"... departed from the presence of the council, rejoicing that they were counted worthy to suffer shame for **his name**"* (Acts 5:41, emphasis added).

They were suffering for the authority of God that had been delegated to them through the power of the name of Jesus. Consequently, they were being beaten because that name placed a great power on their lips.

Notice the reason they rejoiced – *"that they were counted worthy to suffer shame for **His name.**"* How intriguing! How fascinating! How enthralling! They suffered not just for the course of the gospel, but for the cause for which the "name" had been given. They suffered for the authority of Jesus that had been delegated to them, through the power of the name of Jesus. Consequently, they were beaten because that name placed a great power on their lips.

It is certain that the progress of the early church did not occur without opposition. But rather advanced it, and therein lies the challenge and encouragement to us: to accept the truth of its message and to be faithful in following its courageous example, in the face of all odds.

The revival that started in Jerusalem invariably spread to other places. Philip the evangelist went down and preached in Samaria. And what was the outcome? The Bible says, *"But when they believed Philip preaching the things concerning the kingdom of God, and **the name of Jesus Christ**, they were baptized, both men and women"* (Acts 8:12, emphasis added).

Philip preached the kingdom of God and **the name of Jesus Christ**. Revival followed as the name of Jesus was proclaimed in Samaria. The sick were healed in that name, the lame walked in that name; the blind had their sight restored in that name.

In Acts 9 we see the fascinating story surrounding the dramatic conversion of Saul of Tarsus. Saul, notorious for persecuting Christians, had left Jerusalem after obtaining a letter from the Sanhedrin Council granting him authority to arrest Christians in Damascus. But while on the road to Damascus he had a dramatic, life-changing conversion experience, which struck him blind. Saul was lead into the city of Damascus, still in the state of blindness and had to wait for three days and nights without any food or water. In the process, the Lord appeared to a disciple in Damascus by the name of Ananias and said *"Arise and go to the street called Straight and inquire at the house of Judas for one called Saul of Tarsus, for behold, he is praying. And in a vision he has seen a man named Ananias coming in and putting his hand on him, so that he might receive his sight"* (Acts 9:11). Quite naturally, having heard of the great atrocities Saul had committed against the Christian body in Jerusalem, Ananias bluntly refused 'to do the honour.'

But to the hesitant Ananias the Lord said, *"Go, for he is a chosen vessel of mine to bear **My name** before Gentiles, kings and the children of Israel. For I will show him how many things he must suffer for My sake"* (Acts 9:15-16, emphasis added).

After his conversion, Saul (Paul) started preaching in the synagogue in Damascus, to the amazement of those that knew him and had heard of the great atrocities he had done to the church in Jerusalem. And they asked, *"Isn't he the man who raised havoc in Jerusalem among those **who call on this name**? And hasn't he come here to take them as prisoners to the chief priests?"* (verse 21 NIV, emphasis added). The people knew that Paul had eventually, not only identified with, but preaches the **name** that had caused great consternation in Jerusalem.

After a close examination of the book of Acts, only one conclusion can be drawn: that the early church was consumed with the power of the name of Jesus. The name of Jesus meant everything to them! With the astonishing and incredible miracles that were wrought in the name of Jesus, I believe the apostles would like to conclude with Julius Caesar's famous dictum: "*Vini. Vidi. Vici,*" meaning: "We came. We saw. We conquered." Indeed, they *came* into the fullness of their ministry, with the name of Jesus delegated to them as a power of attorney. They **saw** breath-taking miracles in the name of Jesus. Of course, they **conquered** and quashed all oppositions and persecutions in *that* name! The position is the same today. There is no situation, no matter the intensity or duration that is confronted with the power and authority in the name of Jesus, that remains the same. Your life may have been shattered by the storm of life, but rejoice, God knows how to rebuild your broken walls. He knows the way of the storm! The Bible declares that God has control over the storm; in fact, He sits upon the storm (Pro. 29:10).

David declares the formidable weapon we have in the name of Jesus as he spoke from a very personal experience:

> *All nations compassed me about:* ***but in the name of the*** L*ORD* ***will I destroy them****. They compassed me about; yea, they compassed me about:* ***but in the name of the*** L*ORD* ***I will destroy them****. They compassed me about like bees: they are quenched as the fire of thorns: for* ***in the name of the*** L*ORD* ***I will destroy them****. Thou hast thrust sore at me that I might fall: but the* L*ORD helped me* (Psalm 118:10-13, emphasis added).

Notice that the phrase, *"in the name of the Lord, I will destroy them"* is emphasised three times in this short passage of scripture, which gives the indication that every challenge in David's life was confronted and overcome in the all-powerful name of Jesus. What was true for David is true for you today. In verses 14-15, David boasted *"****The*** L***ORD*** ***is my strength and song, and is become my salvation.*** *The voice of rejoicing and salvation is in the tabernacles of the righteous: the right hand of the* L*ORD doeth valiantly* (emphasis added)." Here, David made a public declaration of not just his faith in the God of Israel in the midst of battle, but the fact that his entire life is dependent and reliant on Him. The right hand of the Lord is engaged in battle through the power and authority that is in His name. In one of His most motivating and highly inspirational Psalms, David highlights the connection between trust in the name of the Lord and victory in battle. He writes:

> *Some trust in chariots, and some in horses: but we will remember the name of the* L*ORD our God. They are*

> *brought down and fallen: but we are risen, and stand upright* (Psalm 20:7-8).

Where you place your trust determines the outcome of your battle. This is always the case! If that has not proved the point, I am pretty sure this next passage will:

"Why do the heathen rage, and the people imagine a vain thing? The kings of the earth set themselves, and the rulers take counsel together, against the LORD, and against his anointed, saying, Let us break their bands asunder, and cast away their cords from us. He that sitteth in the heavens shall laugh: the LORD shall have them in derision. Then shall he speak unto them in his wrath, and vex them in his sore displeasure" (Psalm 2:1-5).

The degree of the battle God takes upon Himself on your behalf is determined by the degree of the trust you have in Him.

THE PRESENT DAY CHURCH AND THE NAME OF JESUS

Undoubtedly, what applied to the early church is also applicable to the present day church. The name of Jesus has been given to us as a weapon of warfare, as the legal basis for receiving all that God has provided us with, and as the power of attorney to exercising all of God's authority and power on the earth.

The Bible teaches, *"And Jesus came and spake unto them, saying,* **All power is given unto me in heaven and in earth**. *Go ye therefore, and teach all nations, baptizing them in the name of the Father, and of the Son, and of the Holy Ghost"* (Matt. 28:18-19, emphasis added).

"All power is given unto me in heaven and in earth..."

How was Jesus empowered, and who gave Him power? The answer to these questions is found in the following three scriptures:

"And Jesus, when he was baptized, went up straightway out of the water: and, lo, the heavens were opened unto him, and he saw the Spirit of God descending like a dove, and lighting upon him: And lo a voice from heaven, saying, This is my beloved Son, in whom I am well pleased" (Matt. 3:17-18).

"And Jesus returned in the power of the Spirit into Galilee: and there went out a fame of him through all the region round about" (Luke 4:14).

"How God anointed Jesus of Nazareth with the Holy Ghost and with power: who went about doing good, and healing all that were oppressed of the devil; for God was with him" (Acts 10:38).

In the first scripture, we see that after His baptism, Jesus had the heavens opened unto Him. He as it were, had a direct and unrestricted access to heaven. In Luke 4:14, we see Jesus being more abundantly strengthened after His conflict with the devil. The 40 days and nights fast of Jesus, no doubt, prepared Him for a new phase in ministry – the ministry of miracles, signs and wonders. After His fasting experience, Jesus exploded!

Acts 10:38, however, is far more succinct in providing an answer to our question. It traces the anointing that was upon Jesus to His father. God was the anointer. So when Jesus said, *"All power is given unto me in heaven and in earth..."* (Matt. 28:18), He was speaking about the treasure the Father had bestowed upon Him which, according to Acts 10:38, enabled Him to do the astonishing exploits that have been accredited to Him in the Bible.

Notice that immediately after Jesus said all power had been given unto Him – a clear statement of omnipotence – He commanded the disciples to go in that power, *"...and teach all nations, baptizing them in the name of the Father, and of the Son, and of the Holy Ghost"*(verse 19). "In that single act", says Terry Law, "Jesus was granting the power of attorney to His disciples to go with His power, and to go "in His Name." Other than the 'Name', Jesus had invariably transferred the power He had received from the Father to the disciples for the continuation of Kingdom exploits. Jesus appeared to be saying in essence, 'this is the secret of my exploits on earth, have it, it is now yours, carry on with the job.' And what was the result? *"And they went forth, and preached everywhere, the Lord working with them, and confirming the word with signs following..."* (verse 20).

In a very profound fashion, Mark's Gospel added a dimension to Matthew's teaching on the subject. And it says:

"And he said unto them, Go ye into all the world, and preach the gospel to every creature. He that believeth and is baptized shall be saved; but he that believeth not shall be damned. And these signs shall follow them that believe; **In my name** *shall they cast out devils; they shall speak with new tongues; They shall take up serpents; and if they drink any deadly thing, it shall not hurt them; they shall lay hands on the sick, and they shall recover"* (Mark 16:15-18, emphasis added).

What Jesus is saying in very clear terms is this: the ministry of signs, wonders and, of course, subduing the devil and his hosts of demons is only possible in His name. As a matter of fact, any level of ministry exploit is only achievable in His name. Let us have a list of the things Jesus said could be done in His name.

"In my name..."

- They shall cast out devils
- they shall speak with new tongues
- they shall take up serpents;
- and if they drink any deadly thing, it shall not hurt them;
- they shall lay hands on the sick, and they shall recover

With this commission, and the accompanying power and authority, the disciples of Jesus, past and present, have been fully equipped to accomplish and fulfil the assignment the Master has left for the Church. It must be stressed that the Church would be held accountable for the assignment and the sceptre of authority – the name of Jesus – the Master has given to it.

The notable difference between this and the earlier case we considered centres on the fact that Peter and John, being Jesus' disciples were God's representatives on earth, and were therefore, privileged by virtue of their position, to pray or make demands in the name of Jesus. The position is, no doubt, different with the sons of Sceva, who in all ramifications, were fantasists who, in quest of popularity and self-gain, fraudulently laid claim to the privileges that had not been bestowed on them. They had neither relationship nor faith in the Lord Jesus.

In His letter to the Philippians Church, Paul gives us a tremendous illumination on the power in the name of Jesus.

He writes, *"Wherefore God also hath highly exalted him, and given him a name which is above every name: That at the name of Jesus every knee should bow, of things in heaven, and things in earth, and things under the earth; And that every tongue should confess that Jesus Christ is Lord, to the glory of God the Father"* (Phil. 2:9-11).

"...things *in heaven, and things in earth, and things under the earth...*" includes angels and demons. The name of Jesus is therefore superior to any name that is named in those three realms: heaven, earth, and under the earth.

Myles Monroe teaches that, "...the strength of prayers prayed in the name of Jesus is covenantal authority. We pray to the Father based on our relationship with Christ, who is the Lord over the new covenant...His name is our legal authority – whether we are dealing with "heaven" (with God), "earth" (with men") or "under the earth" (with Satan). In essence, Jesus' name is our legal authority to transact spiritual business with God. 'For there is one God, and one mediator between God and men, the man Christ Jesus; Who gave himself a ransom for all, to be testified in due time (1 Tim. 2:5,6)."

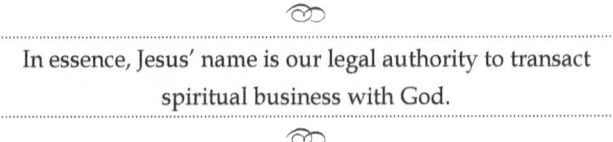

In essence, Jesus' name is our legal authority to transact spiritual business with God.

The Greek word for "ask" in the context of this scripture, according to Strong's Exhaustive Concordance, implies a demand for something due. In essence, Jesus was talking about using His name as the basis for the right or authority to demand what we need.

Acts 4:12 affirms, *"Neither is there salvation in any other: for there is none other name under heaven given among men, whereby we must be saved."* The position is further reinforced in John 14:6, *"Jesus said unto him, I am the way, the truth, and the life: no man comes unto the Father, but by me."*

For us to live the abundant life in Christ Jesus, we need to avail ourselves of the unlimited power and authority in the name of Jesus. In addition, we need to train our senses to believe, without doubt, what the Bible says about our heritage and privileges in Christ Jesus and appropriate them.

Chapter 13

PUTTING FIRST THING FIRST

Paul enjoins the believers:

> *I exhort therefore, that, **first of all, supplications, prayers, intercessions, and giving of thanks, be made for all men; For kings, and for all that are in authority**; that we may lead a quiet and peaceable life in all godliness and honesty. For this is good and acceptable in the sight of God our Saviour; Who will have all men to be saved, and to come unto the knowledge of the truth* (1 Tim. 2: 1-2, emphasis added).

Notice, Paul says, "…first of all…" that is before we pray for ourselves, our children, our churches etc. Albert Baines stressed that the phrase, "…first of all…" indicates that the subject matter of the injunction was to be regarded as "the first duty to be enjoined; the thing that is to be regarded with primary concern." It does not mean that this is to be the first thing in public worship in the order of time, but that it is to be regarded as a duty of primary importance. The duty of praying for the salvation of the whole world, however, is not to be regarded as a subordinate and secondary thing.

Kenneth E. Hagin nonetheless affirms that, "…in life we suffer many times because we don't put first things first. We let secondary things predominate and neglect thing that should be first. In our spiritual life we blame God for our failures. We wonder why certain things don't go right; when really we are not putting first thing first...many times prayers are not answered for yourself because you are putting yourself first..."

A close look at the overall theme of the verse in question, undoubtedly, elucidates the high importance God places on its subject matter - praying for the entire human race (verse1). This further explains the vital place humanity occupies in the heart of God. It is proper to suggest that the reason God asks us to give thanks for all men is because He is *"not willing that any should perish,* **but that all** *should come to repentance"* (2 Peter 3:9, emphasis added). In Christ Jesus, God has provided a way by which all of humanity could be saved. It may be observed here, that the direction to pray and give thanks for all men shows the universality or world-wide nature of Christianity and, indeed, our task in relation to the great commission, *"And he said unto them, Go you into* **all the world***, and* **preach the gospel to every creature**" (Mark 16:15, emphasis).

A command that prayer be made for all men is the centre piece of the whole chapter. That explains why its importance has to be appreciated in public worship and placed at the top of the agenda.

For what reason this has to be held with such importance was further explained in the verses that follow:

"... that we may lead a quiet and peaceable life in all godliness and honesty. For this is good and acceptable in the sight of God our Saviour; Who will have all men to be saved, and to come unto the knowledge of the truth" (vv. 2-4).

The salvation of man is uppermost in the heart of God. The whole package of salvation was geared towards giving man the opportunity to avoid eternal damnation.

PRAYER MUST BE SPECIFIC

> *Therefore I say unto you, What things soever ye desire, when ye pray, believe that ye receive them, and ye shall have them* (Mark 11: 24).

Specificity is a vital key to effective prayer. What do you want? Unfortunately, much of the prayers we pray are vague and pointless. We must realise that God is a specific God. He wants us to be specific in putting our request before Him. General prayers do not move God. Tell Him exactly what you want, and the answers you obtain would be as exact as your petition. A phrase in the Bible that never seizes to be potent stimulus or impetus to me in the place of prayer is this: *"...And God granted him that which he requested"* (1 Chr. 4:10). Let us now see who the supplicant was and what specific requests he made: *"And Jabez was more honourable than his brethren: and his mother called his name Jabez, saying, Because I bare him with sorrow. And Jabez called on the God of Israel, saying, "Oh that thou wouldest bless me indeed, and enlarge my coast, and that thine hand might be with me, and that thou wouldest keep me from evil, that it may not grieve me! And God granted him that which he requested"* (vv.9 -10).

It follows that Jabez's requests determined God's response.

Further, Abraham was very specific in his prayer – he wanted Sodom and Gomorrah spared (Gen. 18:16-33).

Hannah was specific in her prayer - she wanted a male child (1 Sam. 1:11). That was exactly what she had from the Lord (1 Sam. 1:27).

Joshua asked for the sun to stand still and it did (Joshua 10).

Hezekiah asked God for healing. God healed him (2 Kings 20).

Elijah asked God to send fire from heaven and consume the burnt sacrifice; God answered causing the people to know the reality of Gods power (1 Kings 18).

Daniel asked God for revelation. God talked with him and gave him understanding (Daniel 9)

Did you ever wonder why Jesus had to ask an obviously blind man what he wanted? In fact, the blind man cried out for mercy but Jesus still wanted to know what he wanted.

> *And Jesus answered and said unto him, What wilt thou that I should do unto thee? The blind man said unto him, Lord, that I might receive my sight* (Mark 10:51).

"What wilt thou that I should do unto thee?" He wanted to hear not only the general petition for mercy, but the distinct expression of what the man's desire was that day. Until he verbalized it, he was not healed.

The Lord wanted to get a specific request from Bartimaeus. At the point he responded, *"...Lord, that I might receive my sight"*, Jesus knew what need was uppermost in his heart which, when satisfied would bring gladness and fulfilment to him. The blind man had been crying out loud repeatedly, "Jesus, *thou Son of David, have mercy on me*" (Mark 10:47). The cry had reached the ear of the Lord. He knew what the man wanted and was ready to grant it to him. But before He did, He asked him, *"What wilt thou that I should do unto thee?"* (Mark 10:51). He wanted to hear not only the general petition for mercy, but the distinct expression of what the man's desire was. Until he verbalised it, he was not healed.

E.M. Bounds writes, "Prayer and the promises are interdependent. The promise inspires and energizes prayer, but prayer locates the promise, and gives it realization and location. The promise is like the blessed rain falling in full showers, but prayer, like the pipes, which transmit, preserve and direct the rain, localizes and precipitates these promises, until they become local and personal, and bless, refresh and fertilize. Prayer takes hold of the promise and conducts it to its marvellous ends, removes the obstacles, and makes a highway for the promise to its glorious fulfilment. While Gods promises are exceeding great and precious, they are specific, clear and personal."

In our opening Bible passage Jesus said: *"what things soever you desire when you pray, believe you receive them and you shall have them"*. The repetitive reference to the word "them" is indicative of the fact that it is the specific things we desire that we should pray for.

Andrew Murray affirms, "... Jesus desires such definite prayer for our own sakes because it teaches us to know our own needs better. Time; thought, and self-scrutiny are required to find out what our greatest need really is. Our desires are put to the test to see whether they are honest and real and are according to God's Word. We also consider whether we really believe we will receive the things we ask. Such reflective prayer helps us to wait for the special answer and to mark it when it comes." The Lord warns us against the vain repetitions of the Gentiles, who expect to be heard because they pray so much. We often hear prayers of great earnestness and fervour, in which a multitude of petitions are poured forth. The Savoir would, undoubtedly, have to respond to some of them by asking: 'What do you want?'

Prayer must be an unambiguous and distinct expression of definite need, and not a vague repetition of our desires for blessings. God moves on specific requests because they are indications of our deep desires for them in the first place.

Chapter 14

PRAYER MUST BE EFFECTUAL AND FERVENT

> ...*The earnest (heartfelt, continued) prayer of a righteous man makes tremendous power available [dynamic in its working] Elijah was a human being with a nature such as we have [with feelings, affections, and a constitution like ours]; and he prayed earnestly for it not to rain, and no rain fell on the earth for three years and six months. And [then] he prayed again and the heavens supplied rain and the land produced its crops [as usual]* (James 5:16-18, Amp. Bible).

According to the Word English Dictionary, the word **'effectual'** means "producing or capable of producing an intended effect; adequate; valid or binding, as an agreement or document. It also means that which is, "capable of or successful in producing an intended result; effective (of documents, agreements, etc) having legal force." The word **'fervent'**, according to the Word English Dictionary means, "having or showing great warmth or intensity of spirit, feeling, enthusiasm, etc, ardent: a fervent admirer; a fervent plea; hot; burning; glowing." The Bible teaches that we are always to be "...fervent in spirit..." (Rom. 12:11). W.E. Vine affirms that the word translated "fervent" in the above scripture means to be hot; to boil.

Strong's Exhaustive Concordance of the Bible shares a thrilling illumination on the subject. It confirms that figuratively, it means "to be earnest". According to Kenneth E. Hagin, the Greek word *agonizomai*, translated, "labouring fervently" indicates a striving, a wrestling. This gives a clear indication of what the Bible means when it assets that Jacob wrestled with an angel (Gen. 32:24), and that Epaphras was "labouring fervently" for the Colossians Christians in prayer (Col. 4:12). Prayer, at its best, is a 'wrestling', a 'fight', and a 'labour', never an executive compilation of needs before the Lord.

Jesus is our perfect example of both terms together. His prayer was effectual, at the same time fervent. The Bible says:

"And being in an agony [of mind], He prayed [all the] more earnestly and intently, and His sweat became like great clots of blood dropping down upon the ground" (Luke 22:44, Amp. emphasis added). Prayer avails much. According to a popular saying amongst the Jews, "He who prays surrounds his house with a wall stronger than iron."

According to Andrew Murray, prayer is the one great power which the Church can exercise in securing the working of God's omnipotence in the world. However, James tells us the salient ingredients of the kind of prayer that prevails with God. It is the prayer that is effectual and fervent!

THE PRAYER THAT AVAILS MUCH

The golden question is: "what prayer avails much", or "makes tremendous power available [dynamic in its working] according to the Amplified Bible?

In answering the question, recourse must be made to the background of this sobering teaching by the Apostle. Notice that verse 16 of the book and chapter under consideration was dealing with the crucial issue of sin and healing. And it admonishes: "*Confess your faults one to another, and pray one for another, that ye may be healed...*" Though he seems to be speaking about praying for those who are sick, the overall command is specifically to "pray for one another."

It is important to note that to be effective and fervent in prayer; our sense of righteousness must be secured by faith. Analysis of the above scripture leads us in many directions. James says that the "effectual, fervent prayer of a righteous man avails much." Let us begin with the result. The term "avails much" is a potent stimulus, and gives us the necessary impetus to pray. What does it mean? The amplified Bible says that this kind of prayer "makes tremendous power available. When I pray the prayer of faith, I make the power of God available to the situation.

However, James tells us the salient ingredients of the prayer of faith - it is effectual; it is fervent. Praying effectively demands that we pray with an unflinching, steadfast and uncompromising determination. The blind Bartimaeus sought healing with a dogged, unyielding and unrelenting faith.

"And they came to Jericho: and as he went out of Jericho with his disciples and a great number of people, blind Bartimaeus, the son of Timaeus, sat by the highway side begging. And when he heard that it was Jesus of Nazareth, he began to cry out, and say, Jesus, thou son of David, have mercy on me. And many charged him that he should hold his peace: but he cried the more a great deal, Thou son of David, have mercy on me. And Jesus stood still, and commanded him to be called. And they call the blind man, saying unto him, Be of good comfort, rise; he calleth thee. And he, casting away his garment, rose, and came to Jesus. And Jesus answered and said unto him, What wilt thou that I should do unto thee? The blind man said unto him, Lord, that I might receive my sight. And Jesus said unto him, Go thy way; thy faith hath made thee whole. And immediately he received his sight, and followed Jesus in the way" (Mark 10:46-52).

The prayer of Bartimaeus and all the actions associated with it offer a stunning portrait of an ingredient of prayer of faith – the need to be effectual or effective. Prayer, to avail much, must be effectual.

> There are many ways that fervency can be expressed. It is different for each of us. To some it may be expressing volume, to others tears. It does not really matter as long as something is coming out of your heart.

In the same vein, the amplified Bible also gives us a thrilling insight into what it means for prayer to be fervent. The word *"fervent"* is expanded as **heartfelt** and **continual**. We must really believe in the subject-matter of our prayer. We cannot pray with no actual feeling and expect our prayers to make power available. I believe in praying with other tongues, but as powerful as that can be, praying with other tongues alone it is not enough. The Bible tells us that when we pray in tongues our understanding is unfruitful. It is hard to feel anything when we have no understanding. We must also pray with understanding because that is where we will be fervent or "heartfelt" in our prayer.

There are many ways that fervency can be expressed. It is different for each of us. To some, it may be expressed through shouting, joy, to others through tears. It does not really matter as long as something is coming out of your heart. Without that, you will not be very effective.

Finally, the amplified Bible says this word also implies continual. This does mean we have to pray all the time until we see the result. The result will surely manifest, but we have to keep our faith applied. God responds to our requests within the framework of His integrity. We find a convincing elucidation of this in Hebrews 6:15-19:

> *And so, after he had patiently endured, he obtained the promise. For men verily swear by the greater: and*

> *an oath for confirmation is to them an end of all strife. Wherein God, willing more abundantly to shew unto the heirs of promise the immutability of his counsel, confirmed it by an oath: That by two immutable things, in which it was impossible for God to lie, we might have a strong consolation, who have fled for refuge to lay hold upon the hope set before us: Which hope we have as an anchor of the soul, both sure and stedfast, and which entereth into that within the veil.*

God does not just give us what we need; He gives to us in abundance. Paul prayed, "But my God shall supply all your need according to his riches in glory by Christ Jesus" (Phil. 4:19). God has everything in abundance. God has His storehouse full of blessings. We only need to know how to access His storehouse. We have to keep our heart open to hear more insight from the Lord as to what else might need to be released in prayer by faith. This is where praying in other tongues can be a powerful aid. Every time we think of the situation we can thank God for the answer and spend some time praying in tongues over the situation. We need to keep this attitude until we see the result or until God releases us from the task.

> We have to keep our heart open to hear more insight from the Lord as to what else might need to be released in prayer by faith. This is where praying in other tongues can be a powerful aid.

A RIGHTEOUS MAN

Prayer is the voice of our life. As a man lives so he prays. Not the words or thoughts with which he is occupied at set times of prayer, but the bent of his heart as seen in his desires and actions, is regarded by God as his real prayer. The life speaks louder and truer than the lips. To pray well I must live well. He who seeks to live with God, will learn so to know His mind and to please Him, that he will be able to pray according to His will. Think how Elijah, at his first message to Ahab, spoke of "the Lord God, before whom I stand." Think of his solitude at the brook Cherith, receiving his bread from God through the ravens, and then at Sarepta through the ministry of a poor widow. He walked with God, he learned to know God well; when the time came, he knew to pray to a God whom he had proved. It is only out of a life of true fellowship with God that the prayer of faith can be born. Let the link between the life and the prayer be clear and close. As we give ourselves to walk with God, we shall learn to pray – Andrew Murray.

The prayer of a righteous man availeth much. That is, a man who has the righteousness of Christ, not only as a garment covering him, but as a life-power inspiring him, as a new man "created in righteousness and true holiness" (Eph. 4:24). A man that lives as "the servant to righteousness" (Rom. 6:16,19; 1 John 3:22). When Christ gave His great prayer promises on the night He was betrayed, it was to those who keep His commandments. *"If ye love Me, ye will keep My commandments; and I will pray the Father, and He will give you another Comforter"* (John 14:15-16). It is only when the righteous man stirs up himself and rouses his whole being to take hold of God that the prayer availeth much. Just as Jacob said: "I will not let thee go" and the importunate widow gave the unjust Judge no rest, until they had what they wanted, in the same vein, effectual fervent prayer does not fail to deliver the intended outcome. And then comes the effectual fervent prayer of many righteous. When two or three agree, there is the promise of an answer; how much more when hundreds and thousands unite with one accord to cry to God to display His mighty power on behalf of His people.

Let us join those who have united themselves to call upon God for the mighty power of His Holy Spirit in His Church.

YOU MUST ASK IN FAITH

God does business with man only on the basis of faith. The Bible says "...*whatever is not of faith is sin*" (Rom 14:23). And "...*whatever you ask in prayer, you will receive, if you have faith*" (Matt. 21:22). God gets involved in the affairs of man when He sees faith. Faith, therefore, is man's express invitation to God to intervene in the issues pertaining to his life. It is his legal authority permitting God to have a say in his affairs. Jesus said to the Woman with the issue of blood, "... *Daughter, be of good comfort;* ***your faith has made you whole****. And the woman was made whole from that hour*" (Matt. 9:22, emphasis added). It is interesting that Jesus did not say to the woman 'thy much struggle, elbowing your way through the crowd, has made thee whole.' No. But "...*thy faith has made thee whole.*" In the same vein, Jesus adjudged blind Bartimaeus qualified for healing because of his uncompromising faith. Jesus said to him, "*Go thy way; thy faith hath made thee whole. And immediately he received his sight, and followed Jesus in the way*" (Mark 10: 52).

In Luke 5, the Bible gave a narrative of a man being helped by his friends, through the roof to receive healing in Jesus' healing rally. Very significantly, the Bible attributed the sick man's healing to what Jesus saw, "*And when he saw their faith...*" (v.20). So faith was what drew Jesus' attention to the man's ordeal, and he was healed.

In His landmark message on the subject of faith, Jesus affirms:

> ...*Have faith in God. For verily I say unto you, That whosoever shall say unto this mountain, Be thou removed, and be thou cast into the sea; and shall not doubt in his heart, but shall believe that those things which he saith shall come to pass; he shall have whatsoever he saith. Therefore I say unto you, What things soever ye desire, when ye pray, believe that ye receive them, and ye shall have them* (Mark 11:22-24).

Faith in God is what turns situations around. It is the mighty force that moves the mountain; without it God lacks the ability to intervene in any situation.

Chapter 15

PRAYER MUST BE CONSISTENT WITH GOD'S WORD

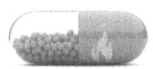

Prevailing prayer must be based on the word of God. God never does anything outside His word. He is bound by His word. His estimation of His word confirms this, *"...for thou hast magnified thy word above all thy name"* (Psalm 138:2). Faith can only begin where the will of God is known, and the word of God is the will of God. Accordingly, when we ask anything that God has promised in His word, then we are assured that we are praying in accordance with His will. Jesus said emphatically: *"If ye abide in me, and my words abide in you, ye shall ask what ye will, and it shall be done unto you"* (John 15:7). And John says, *"And this is the confidence that we have in him, that, if we ask any thing according to his will, he heareth us"* (1 John 5:14).

Prayer must be consistent with the word of God to attract answers from Him.

God cannot deny His word. When prayers are based on God's word, sufficient and credible grounds to answer those prayers are present. Why? Because the word of God is what nourishes and energises prayer.

This principle is laid bare in scripture. The Bible says, *"In the beginning was the Word, and the Word was with God, and the Word was God. The same was in the beginning with God. All things were made by him; and without him was not anything made that was made"* (John 1:1-3).

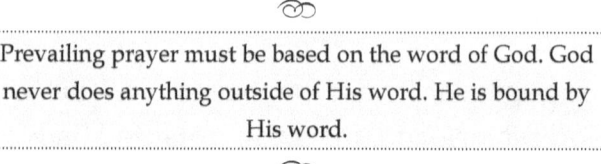

Prevailing prayer must be based on the word of God. God never does anything outside of His word. He is bound by His word.

God had entwined with His word even long before creation. Note the phrase, *"in the beginning was the Word"*, which gives the indication that the Word pre-existed everything and anything God created. In fact, the Word is the creative, executive instrument of God on earth. The Word of God accomplishes the will of God in the earth. Hebrews 11:3 goes to the core of the matter, *"Through faith we understand that the worlds were framed by the word of God, so that things which are seen were not made of things which do appear."* Of profound significance is the phrase, *"...and the Word was God"* (John 1:1). The Word was not only with God at creation; the Word was, and is indeed, God. Then He was made flesh – manifested as Jesus the Son – and dwelt among us (John 1:14). In essence, God and His Word are one.

We have an interesting connection between prayer and the word of God in Daniel 9:1-2:

> *In the first year of Darius the son of Ahasuerus, of the seed of the Medes, which was made king over the realm of the Chaldeans; In the first year of his reign I Daniel understood by books the number of the years, whereof the word of the LORD came to Jeremiah the prophet, that he would accomplish seventy years in the desolations of Jerusalem.*

While reading the word of God, it came to the realisation of Daniel that the seventy-year captivity of Jerusalem which had been prophesied by Jeremiah was soon to be completed. Daniel had been studying the book of Jeremiah, and understood as a result that God was going to leave the Jews in captivity 70 years, then punish Babylon for their iniquity. (Jer. 29:10, 14; 25:11-13). But he also understood from prophecy, that it was going to be the Medes and Persians that would destroy Babylon and avenge the destruction of the temple (Jer. 51:11), also that they would ultimately be the ones to let the Jews return to their homeland and restore their worship in the temple. (Isaiah 45:1-5, 13).

The action that followed was consequent on what Daniel had read from God's word. He set his face to seek God through prayer and fasting (Daniel 10). There was a high probability that had Daniel not studied the word, God's people could have overstayed in captivity.

YOU MUST BE MOTIVATED PROPERLY

*Call unto me, and **I will answer thee**, and show thee great and mighty things, which thou knowest not* (Jer. 33:3, emphasis added).

If you ask anything in My name, I will do it (John 14:14).

Every good gift and every perfect gift is from above, and cometh down from the Father of lights, with whom is no variableness, neither shadow of turning (James 1:17).

Generally, the above scriptures give a very clear indication of God's unwavering readiness to bless His children. It is His desire to give us all good things! However, God does not bless arbitrarily. Certain criteria are examined and thoroughly scrutinised by God before He promotes, answers the prayers or generally changes the position of a man. The issue of intent or motive is supreme in the heart of God when it comes to where He chooses to place His blessings.

Apostle James nailed down the futility of praying with a wrong motive, "*You ask, and receive not, **because you ask amiss, that you may spend it upon your lusts***" (James 4:3, emphasis added). Having the wrong motive in asking disqualifies our prayers from yielding the desired results. Further, there is a clear indication in Psalm 75: 6-7, that God would judge a man's heart before He considers him for elevation, "*For promotion cometh neither from the east, nor from the west, nor from the south. **But God is the judge**: he putteth down one, and* *setteth up another"* (emphasis added). Notice that it is well within God's prerogative to promote one and put another down. The basis of His judgment is the heart of a man. So a man's heart determines how far he can go with God, and the extent he can go in life. This is a critical matter, no doubt. You only need to look at just few cases in the word of God to understand why God places such 'heavy price-tag' on breakthrough in life.

As part of God's transitional strategy for the nation of Israel into the Promised Land, He addressed this highly significant matter:

"For the LORD thy God bringeth thee into a good land, a land of brooks of water, of fountains and depths that spring out of valleys and hills; A land of wheat, and barley, and vines, and fig trees, and pomegranates; a land of oil olive, and honey; A land wherein thou shalt eat bread without scarceness, thou shalt not lack any thing in it; a land whose stones are iron, and out of whose hills thou mayest dig brass. When thou hast eaten and art full, then thou shalt bless the LORD thy God for the good land which he hath given thee. Beware that thou forget not the LORD thy God, in not keeping his commandments, and his judgments, and his statutes, which I command thee this day: Lest when thou hast eaten and art full, and hast built goodly houses, and dwelt therein; And when thy herds and thy flocks multiply, and thy silver and thy gold is multiplied, and all that thou hast is multiplied; **Then thine heart be lifted up***, and thou forget the LORD thy God, which brought thee forth out of the land of Egypt, from the house of bondage...*

And thou say in thine heart, *My power and the might of mine hand hath gotten me this wealth. But thou shalt remember the* LORD *thy God: for it is he that giveth thee power to get wealth, that he may establish his covenant which he sware unto thy fathers, as it is this day"* (Deut. 8:7-13, 17-18, emphasis added).

Uzziah was significantly favoured and mightily blessed by God, no doubt (2 Chr. 26). Like his father and grandfather before him, according to Donnie Martin, Uzziah began his reign well. He showed much promise as a godly ruler that would lead Judah back to God and the restoration of God's blessings. But over the years, as God blessed Uzziah, a secret enemy began to invade his heart ever so subtly. So subtle was this enemy that Uzziah was not aware of what was happening to him until he had been dealt the fatal blow.

What was this subtle enemy that defeated Uzziah, you say? Simple! He allowed God's blessing to get to his head. In other words, Uzziah became proud, arrogant and haughty. Somewhere amidst all the wealth and popularity, he lost sight of the fact that God was the source of his blessing. He ended in shame and reproach, not being able to handle God's blessing for his life. Hear Uzziah's final demise or 'eulogy':

> *But when he was strong,* **his heart was lifted up to his destruction:** *for he transgressed against the LORD his God, and went into the temple of the LORD to*

burn incense upon the altar of incense (2 Chr. 26:16, emphasis added).

Jeshurun also received God's uncommon blessing and elevation, but notice the path God's blessing led him, *"But Jeshurun waxed fat, and kicked: thou art waxen fat, thou art grown thick, thou art covered with fatness; then he forsook God which made him, and lightly esteemed the Rock of his salvation"* (Deut. 32: 15), and the sad and regrettable statistics goes on. How devastating!

If God sees that my spiritual life will be furthered by giving the things for which I ask, then He will give them, but that is not the end of prayer or a life devoted and dependent on God.

I postulate that the blessings of God in our lives are to motivate us to render exceptional service to Him, as a token of appreciation. Given the sad outcome as stated, resulting from the inability of some to *handle* God's blessing appropriately, the issue of weighing a man's heart as a prerequisite for promoting him becomes critical to God. Consequently, the degree of God's blessing that flows in a man's life is not only determined and pre-judged by God, it is also an indication of the measure of blessings the condition of a man's heart has qualified him to handle. The obvious question then is: 'can you handle God's blessings without suffering the same demise as Uzziah'? 'Attitude always determines altitude'. One cannot but concede with the famous dictum of Henry

Longfellow which states in part: "The heights by great men reached and kept were not attained by sudden flight..." In context, a man's level of attainment or achievement in life is determined principally, by his attitude!

PART 4

COMMON MISCONCEPTIONS ABOUT PRAYER

Chapter 16

PRAYER: NOT AN ACTIVITY BUT A LIFESTYLE

Very often we hear of activities describing prayer, and quite erroneously, our perception of prayer is curtailed and miniaturised by these *activities* that are embedded in the act of prayer. For instance, we label some of our church events as 'prayer meetings', 'prayer forums', 'prayer conferences', 'prophetic prayer conferences', and the list goes on. It should be stressed that as appealing, captivating and enthralling these events often are, neither the events nor the captions they bear, describe the true meaning of prayer. Prayer is not an activity. Prayer is a spiritual sacrifice; it is the offering up of the soul and its best affections heavenward. According to Johnson, "Prayer is not the compilation of long words or flowery lingo. It is not the language of the "holy people". Neither is prayer some sophisticated language of regular church goers, nor an object you *use* only when you need something or when you fall into some horrendous situations." Prayer is a 'life'- a lifestyle of God's Saints.

Much of the misconceptions that surround the concept of prayer centre significantly, on the views held by many about what true Bible-centred prayer entails.

This has gone a long way to shape the general approach of many to the subject of prayer. For instance, prayer has been widely defined, at least within the Christian circle, as 'communication between God and man'. A definition manifestly flawed for lack of depth as to what true Bible-based prayer entails.

While the above definition, undoubtedly, contains some elements that describe what prayer is, it should be stressed that it leaves much to be desired. The said definition deals only on 'procedure', if you like, the 'hows' of prayer while neglecting its substance.

In-depth study of scriptures reveals that prayer is not just communication between man and his creator, but that prayer is both communication and communion (deep heart-to-heart intimacy and affection) between God and man.

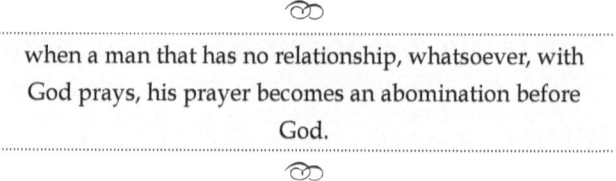

when a man that has no relationship, whatsoever, with God prays, his prayer becomes an abomination before God.

Every communication with God that meets the criteria of an authentic Bible-centred prayer must flow from the springboard of pre-existing intimate relationship between God and man; such that if there is no relationship between God and man, any attempt by man to engage in any form of communication with God becomes an exercise in futility.

Accordingly, when a man that has no relationship, whatsoever with God prays, his prayer becomes an abomination before God. Such 'prayer', no doubt, meets the communication criteria (supposed talking to God) quite alright, but lacks the vital and essential ingredient (communion) that causes such communication to receive heaven's validation.

Prayers are therefore answered, not on the basis of being communication, but on the basis of being both communion and communication! As a matter of fact, the element of communion with God qualifies prayer for answers than communication. Communication flows from communion; and communion is founded upon union. Communion is the rocket-buster that takes our prayer before the throne of grace.

Heaven is inundated with barrage of communications (seeming prayers), but very little communication flowing from the platform of communion with the father. According to E.M Bounds, "The conditions of praying are the conditions of righteousness, holiness, and salvation...Life growing in its purity and devotion will be a more prayerful life."

There are degrees or depths of communication. Whether we realise it or not, we engage in communication with different people based on different degrees of relationships or intimacy we maintain with them. In essence, the degree of intimacy we have with people determines not just what we say or communicate with them, but also the depth of such communication.

This one element (intimacy), not only shapes the nature of the conversations I hold with my wife for instance, it is what makes such conversations of a different kind from that which I hold with friends, even my best friend!

I know a great deal about my wife's interests. I know her likes and dislikes. I know her favourite food, what kind of books she likes to read. I know so much about her. This is because I have spent many years in close communion with her. I have come to know her in an intimate and loving fashion that has enhanced and fostered close relationship between us.

My top secrets are safely lodged in the custody of my wife; but only few friends of mine know any such secrets. My wife knows virtually everything about me. Within the first few months of our marriage, I gave her access to the 'vault' that holds such information, and vice versa. No friend of ours holds any such information about us, because the very nature of our relationship does not call for it.

This is the underlying principle, indeed, the basis on which prayers are answered by God. Everything, as far as our relationship with God is concerned, rises and falls on this one principle – intimacy, relationship. The closer we commune with God, the better we know Him. Prayer is the vital means of building and fostering close relationship and intimacy with God. This is the reason God deals with us more in the *secret* place. Friends have a great deal to share in the secret, but very little in the public.

Jesus says, "*If ye abide in me, and my words abide in you, ye shall ask what ye will, and it shall be done unto you*" (John 15:7).

Notice, the phrase "*and my words abide in you*" is rendered in another scripture: "*and I abide in you*" (John 15:4). What Jesus is saying in essence is that if we abide in Him, and He abides in us, we shall ask whatever we desire and it shall be granted to us. That makes an abiding relationship with the Lord the criteria for granting our requests. We are only qualified to pray, if we have an enduring and persistent relationship with the Lord. Notice that His abiding in us necessarily follows our abiding in Him. In other words, our abiding in the Lord is a sine quo nun for His abiding in us; and the abiding of His word in us is the means by which we abide in Him. It is also the proof that we do have a steadfast and eternal relationship with the Lord.

According to J.I. Packer, "I believe that prayer is the **measure of the man spiritually**, in a way that nothing else is..." (emphasis added).

God said of Abraham:

"... *Shall I hide from Abraham that thing which I do; Seeing that Abraham shall surely become a great and mighty nation, and all the nations of the earth shall be blessed in him? For I know him, that he will command his children and his household after him, and they shall keep the way of the Lord, to do justice and judgment; that the Lord may bring upon Abraham that which he hath spoken of him"* (Gen. 18:17-19).

We could trace the genesis of this relationship to Gen.12: 1-3, when God established a covenant with Abraham:

> *Now the LORD had said to Abram, Get you out of your country, and from your kindred, and from your father's house, to a land that I will show you: And I will make of you a great nation, and I will bless you, and make your name great; and you shall be a blessing: And I will bless them that bless you, and curse him that curses you: and in you shall all families of the earth be blessed…*

The dealing of God with Abraham, from this humble beginning, was on the premise of a well – established relationship. God and Abraham were in intimate relationship. The testing of Abraham by God - demanding an offering in Isaac, further authenticated this relationship. Remember, God said in the end, "… *for now I know that thou fearest God, seeing thou hast not withheld thy son, thine only [son] from me"* (Gen. 22: 12).

The principle, therefore, is that what qualifies a man to pray and have his prayers answered is not his much talking, or his eloquence in the presence of God (communication), but his **identity** with God (communion).

Very succinctly, Jesus puts the position this way:

*"I am the good shepherd, and **know my sheep**, and am known of mine"* (John 10:14, emphasis added).

To that we may add another highly significant declaration of Christ I believe that could help us build the picture that strengthens our line of thought in this regard.

> The principle, therefore, is that what qualifies a man to pray and have his prayers answered is not his much talking, or his eloquence in the presence of God (communication), but his identity with God (communion).

In Matthew 7: 20 -22, Jesus admonishes:

"...by their fruits you shall know them. Not everyone that said to me, Lord, Lord, shall enter into the kingdom of heaven; but he that does the will of my Father which is in heaven. Many will say to me in that day, Lord, Lord, have we not prophesied in your name? and in your name have cast out devils? and in your name done many wonderful works?"

Communion and oneness with the father remain, as always, the underlying factor for a healthy relationship with God. On the basis of communion, man can worship, and his worship receives God's approval, he can pray, and his prayers are heard, he can give of his substance to God, and it is accepted.

The Bible declares,

> *The sacrifice of the wicked is abomination: how much more, when he brings it with a wicked mind? (Pro. 21:27).*

> *The sacrifice of the wicked is an abomination to the LORD: but the prayer of the upright is his delight* (Pro. 15:8).

For us to have access to His blessings, God says, it must be on the basis of relationship, fellowship and intimacy.

Prayer, no doubt, plays a key role in knowing the Lord. It is a splendid tool for enhancing relationship with God. The point being emphasised is this, you must not relate with God only when you think you need His blessings or only when you need some spectacular intervention of His power. Do not pray only when you are faced with difficulties. God does not want to be used as a Cash Machine. He wants friends, people to reason and relate with like Abraham, people to spend time with like David, Moses, and Daniel.

As earlier stated, in my early days as a Christian, we were taught that God was in search of 'a man' that would fulfil His divine purposes on earth. Such teachings were often captioned "the man God uses." We were 'set on fire for God' by those powerful and impactful teachings that left us looking for every opportunity to give our utmost to God in every area of our lives. Over time, that changed. Today, instead of God using man, man now appears to be on the 'driving seat' of his life; running the course of his life in total isolation of his maker. Man has reduced God, at best, to a 'father Christmas.' God has become a puppet who has lost His will to the lust and greed of man.

Matson could not be more succinct when he said:

"Prayer is not something to be added after approaches in our search for the will of God have been tried and have failed. No, we should pray as we use the personal resources God has given us."

The above discourse does not in any way diminish the place of communication in prayer. The communication of man with his maker occupies an integral part of his relationship with the Divine. In the book of Hosea God demands:

"Return, O Israel, to the LORD your God, For you have stumbled because of your iniquity. **Take words with you and return to the LORD.** *Say to Him, "Take away all iniquity And receive us graciously, That we may present the fruit of our lips. "Assyria will not save us, We will not ride on horses; Nor will we say again, 'Our god,' To the work of our hands; For in You the orphan finds mercy"* (Hosea 12:2-3, emphasis added).

Without communication with God, man has lost contact with his source, and needless to say that such has far-reaching consequences. However, as said, what qualifies man for the rare privilege of having audience with the King of Kings is his place in God; without which his prayer becomes "the sacrifice of the wicked…" (Prov. 15:8, Prov. 21:27).

In the Sermon on the Mount, Jesus spoke greatly on the significance of communication with God:

"Ask and it will be given to you; seek and you will find; knock and the door will be opened to you. For everyone who asks receives; the one who seeks finds; and to the one who knocks, the door will be opened. "Which of you, if your son asks for bread, will give him a stone? Or if he asks for a fish, will give him a snake? If you, then, though you are evil, know how to give good gifts to your children, how much more will your Father in heaven give good gifts to those who ask him" (Matt. 7: 7-10).

On another occasion, Jesus taught, not just how to engage in communication in prayer, but the place of importunity (constant communication) with God in prayer:

> *And He said to them, Which of you who has a friend will go to him at midnight and will say to him, Friend, lend me three loaves [of bread], For a friend of mine who is on a journey has just come, and I have nothing to put before him; And he from within will answer, Do not disturb me; the door is now closed, and my children are with me in bed; I cannot get up and supply you [with anything]? I tell you, although he will not get up and supply him anything because he is his friend, yet because of his*

shameless persistence and insistence he will get up and give him as much as he needs. So I say to you, Ask and keep on asking and it shall be given you; seek and keep on seeking and you shall find; knock and keep on knocking and the door shall be opened to you. For everyone who asks and keeps on asking receives; and he who seeks and keeps on seeking finds; and to him who knocks and keeps on knocking (Luke 11: 5-10 Amplified Bible).

The Lord enjoys our constant communication with Him, no doubt! Our prayer is like a sweet-smelling aroma before the throne of grace. David prayed; *"Let my prayer be accepted as sweet-smelling incense in your presence. Let the lifting up of my hands in prayer be accepted as an evening sacrifice"* (Psalm 141:2, God's Word Translation). However, such communication must flow from a well-established relationship with the Lord.

Part 5
UNDERSTANDING THE POTENCY OF PRAYER

Chapter 17

PRAYER: A PREREQUISITE FOR BREAKTHROUGH IN LIFE

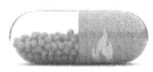

God is the architect of your life. He is the master builder with a master plan. It is important to constantly confer with Him to [ensure] that your building, or perfection, is created in conformance with the details of the original blueprint for your life. The ideal arrangement is for the architect to be on the premises during construction. Therefore, it is essential that you hold meetings with God every day. When the architect Himself is there, He can tell you, "No, no -- don't do that! Move the beam to the right. A little further. Good. The foundation isn't strong enough; put a little more cement right there." If God is with you at all times, He will offer specific counsel for everything you ask. Walk with God; let your architect dwell with you... How do you start rebuilding a damaged house? If a house is ruined by an earthquake, you may need to begin by renewing the foundation. Yet the first step is to visit the architect and check the specifications written on the original blueprints. God is the master builder of [your life] and ... He kept the prospectus tucked deep inside His heart. Naturally, we must consult with Him if we are to assist the reconstruction. He has all the answers; all He must do is research the plan and verify how He created us because He will re-create us according to that prototype. – Paul Werner.

Paul declares unequivocally, *"Not that we are sufficient of ourselves to think anything as of ourselves;* ***but our sufficiency is of God"*** (2 Cor. 3:5, emphasis added).

In the awe-inspiring and soul-stirring words of Richard Newton, we see the incredible relationship that exists between a man's commitment to prayer and his level of attainment in life.

He said:

> "The principal cause of my leanness and unfruitfulness is owing to an unaccountable backwardness to pray. I can write or read or converse or hear with a ready heart; but prayer is more spiritual and inward than any of these, and the more spiritual any duty is the more my carnal heart is apt to stare from it."

For the child of God, prayer is the ladder that transports him to his desired haven. Great achievements in life are almost always a product of a persistent, sustained and irrevocable association with God. Success outside Christ is not only impracticable or implausible, it is incomprehensible. The position could not be more succinct than James presents it:

"Every good gift and every perfect gift is from above*, and cometh down from the Father of lights, with whom is no variableness, neither shadow of turning"* (James 1:7, emphasis added). Notice that this scripture points exclusively to God being the sole source of your blessings.

There is simply no life outside of Christ. Christ is the life; any life outside of Christ is a sure way that leads to crisis.

There is simply no life outside Christ. Christ is **the** life! Any life outside Jesus is a sure way that leads to crisis! Paul alluded to this deep spiritual truth when he said, *"For to me to live is Christ, and to die is gain"* (Phi. 1:21). Also in Galatians 2:20, Paul says: *"I am crucified with Christ: nevertheless I live; yet not I, but Christ liveth in me: and the life which I now live in the flesh I live by the faith of the Son of God, who loved me, and gave himself for me."*

It is a fundamental and irrefutable fact that for man to live his dreams and have a bespoke life, he needs to partner with Jesus throughout his pilgrimage on earth. Proverb 16:3 states, *"Commit thy works unto the Lord, and thy thoughts shall be established."* Solomon's famous injunction here reminds us that any form of success proceeds from the generous hands of God. The Bible is clear that this includes material, professional, marital and spiritual successes; indeed, success in every sphere of life. In fact, no one finds success based on their own ingenuity, resourcefulness or astuteness. The "self-made" person, so revered in modern society, is a myth. No one creates themselves. The Bible is clear that everything about our lives is a gift. Therefore, even though we exert ourselves to succeed as full participants in the journey of life with God, we could not work, speak, or act without the body, mind, and spirit God has given us. Because God has given these things freely, we can be sure that success also is God-given. Man is, therefore, severely limited without a close touch with his maker through prayer.

Fraser of Brea declares, "I find myself better or worse [in life] as I decay and increase in prayer." David Macintyre affirms, "If prayer is hindered, even though it may be hindered by devotion to other duties of [life], the health of the soul is impaired." And Henry Marty laments in his diary thus, "want of private devotional reading and shortness of prayer, through incessant sermon-making, had produced much strangeness between God and my soul".

"Because of this truth", says Dr. Jerald Daffe, "success can just as easily be lost as it can be gained. In the scriptural worldview, this occurs when we choose to refrain from dedicating ourselves and our plans to God's kingdom and glory, thus splitting our souls and our motivations into parts."

Man, outside of Christ is still in a deplorable state, even at his best. Man's assignment therefore, is to connect with the source of power and blessing. Have you wondered why the Bible is replete with the phrase: "in him"? The next time you come across the golden phrase, "in him" or "in Christ" in your Bible, slow the pace of your reading, examine and identify what the Bible says you are in Christ (identity) or can accomplish in Christ.

> *According as he hath chosen us in him before the foundation of the world, that we should be holy and without blame before him in love: In whom we have redemption through his blood, the forgiveness of sins, according to the riches of his grace;In whom also we have obtained an inheritance, being predestinated according to the purpose of him who worketh all things after the counsel of his own will* (Eph. 1:4,7& 11).

The said phrase tells you what your position and inheritance are through Christ. Your identity in Christ is what qualifies you for blessings! A man whose life is an accurate description of this principle was Isaac. The Bible testifies:

> *Then Isaac sowed in that land, and received in the same year an hundredfold: and the LORD blessed him. And the man waxed great, and went forward, and grew until he became very great: For he had possession of flocks, and possession of herds, and great store of servants: and the Philistines envied him* (Gen. 26: 12-14).

Why was Isaac so great? Who was behind his greatness? What was the source of his blessing? The answer to all of the questions is succinct: God! The Bible says in verse 12 that God blessed him. So God was the source of Isaac's blessing. Isaac did not become great and successful by chance. Great destinies are not a product of luck or chance, but of choice and gruesome determination. There are always reasons attributable to man's success in life. As seen in this passage, Isaac's seed was a potent stimulus to God blessing him.

Henry Wadsworth Longfellow earlier referenced, was famous for saying:

"The heights great men reached and kept, were not obtained by sudden flight. But they, while their companions slept, were toiling upward in the night."

Remember that success is the maximum utilisation of the ability God has endowed you with. David amplified the position when he said in Psalm 75:6 - 7 " *For promotion cometh neither from the east, nor from the west, nor from the south.* ***But God is the judge****: he putteth down one, and setteth up another"* (emphasis added). God judges who to be promoted. The exclusive right and prerogative is His. Our relationship with Him in prayer, therefore, is what qualifies us for a consideration for promotion and progress in life.

In his thrilling insight into the indispensable position of prayer in his life, Borden of Yale said, *"I have only missed my morning watch once or twice this term...I can easily believe that it is next in importance to accepting Christ. For I know that when I don't wait upon God in prayer and Bible study, things go wrong."*

Psalm 127: 1-2 offers an authentic platform to expound this truth further:

"Except the Lord build the house, they labour in vain that build it: except the Lord keep the city, the watchman waketh but in vain. It is vain for you to rise up early, to sit up

late, to eat the bread of sorrows: for so he giveth his beloved sleep."

Zechariah reported the position succinctly:

"Then he answered and spake unto me, saying, This is the word of the LORD unto Zerubbabel, saying, Not by might, nor by power, but by my spirit, saith the LORD of hosts" (Zech. 4:6).

Between Psalm 120 and 127, we see a common theme that runs like a golden thread – the fact that those who achieve stardom in life do so with the help of the Almighty. Observe how in each of these songs the heart is fixed upon God only. Read the first verses of these Psalms from Psalm 120, and they run thus: "I cried unto the Lord" "I will lift up mine eyes to the hills", "Let us go unto the house of the Lord." "Unto thee will I lift up mine eyes", "If it had not been the Lord", "They that trust in the Lord", giving an indication of a life that is very dependent on the Lord.

An examination of the lives of the great saints of God in the Bible reveals a common trend: they were overly successful, fruitful, and prosperous, against all odds, achieved the seemingly impossible tasks, faced the most gruesome challenges of life, and yet, did tremendous exploits for God. One of the very secrets of their exceptional achievements in life was their dependence on God through prayer.

We shall consider some examples here:

KING UZZIAH

There was no life in which this lesson resonates with incredible insight more than that of a king whose life was marked with long, uninterrupted series of victories and fame.

Uzziah, (also called Azariah in 2 Kings 14:21-22; 15:1-6) whose name meant 'Yahweh is my strength' was a king of the ancient Kingdom of Judah, and one of Amaziah's sons, whom the people appointed to replace his father (2 Chr. 26:1). He was one of the kings mentioned in the genealogy of Jesus in the Gospel of Matthew.

Uzziah struck it rich and achieved stardom at a tender age of sixteen as he ascended the throne of the leadership of Judah amidst overwhelming legitimacy – great acceptance of the people.

> *Then all the people of Judah took Uzziah, who was sixteen years old, and made him king in the room of his father Amaziah* (2 Chr. 26: 1).

His achievements were detailed in 2 Chronicles 26:1-15.

Beginning in verse 6, the writer of 2 Chronicles details the success of Uzziah which was broadly summarised in verse 5. We have seen consistently that this is the pattern of the literature in the books of Kings and Chronicles. That is, kings are introduced, summarised, and then discussed in an extended narrative. As we move into the explanation section, we find a king on top of his leadership capacity. The reader is left to wonder, however, whether things can stay that way for young Uzziah.

"And he went forth and warred against the Philistines, and brake down the wall of Gath, and the wall of Jabneh, and the wall of Ashdod, and built cities about Ashdod, and among the Philistines. And God helped him against the Philistines, and against the Arabians that dwelt in Gurbaal, and the Mehunims. And the Ammonites gave gifts to Uzziah: and his name spread abroad even to the entering in of Egypt; for he strengthened himself exceedingly. Moreover Uzziah built towers in Jerusalem at the corner gate, and at the valley gate, and at the turning of the wall, and fortified them. Also he built towers in the desert, and digged many wells: for he had much cattle, both in the low country, and in the plains: husbandmen also, and vine dressers in the mountains, and in Carmel: for he loved husbandry" (vv 6-10).

Uzziah's legacy begins with his military exploits. The International Standard Bible Encyclopaedia comments on why this makes sense, given the history of his family:

The unpopularity of his father, owing to a great military disaster, must have remained present in the mind of Uzziah, and early in his reign, he undertook and successfully carried through an expedition against his father's enemies of twenty years before, only extending his operations over a wider area. The Edomites, Philistines and Arabians were successively subdued (these being members of a confederacy which, in an earlier reign, had raided Jerusalem and nearly extirpated the royal family); the port of Eloth, at the head of the Red Sea, was restored to Judah, and the city rebuilt; the walls of certain hostile towns, Gath, Jabneh and Ashdod, were razed to the ground, and the inhabitants of Gur-baal and Maan were reduced to subjection. Even the Ammonites, east of the Jordan, paid tribute to Uzziah.

Verses 6 and 7 focus on God's involvement in aiding Judah against the pagan Philistines. These military accomplishments brought Uzziah fame even southward into Africa, as the kings of the ancient near East grew restless, wondering if they could be the next to face Judah's mighty army.

Verses 9 and 10 show Uzziah recognized that military success required a strong defence, so he fortified Jerusalem and desert outposts with towers. Towers were built for several reasons. First, they were the spy and communication system which quickly alerted the military if borders had been breached. Lookouts were posted in towers to watch the horizons for any signs of foreign invasion, and signals were put into effect for long-distance communication between towers and cavalry. This function was likely fulfilled by the towers Uzziah built in the desert. And he made in Jerusalem engines, invented by cunning men, to be on the towers and upon the bulwarks, to shoot arrows and great stones withal. And his name spread far abroad; for he was marvellously helped, till he was strong.

In the word of another, this passage provides a behind-the-scenes look at Uzziah's military success. His success is not attributed to a claim to divine status, as was common for neighbouring kings, but rather God blessed his careful preparation. His armies were known both by their extensive training and their smart organization. Uzziah even employed a secretary to keep them properly divided. He knew that hand-to-hand combat, having the right number of soldiers in the right places on the battlefield was paramount for success. His organization was impressive, with 307,500 soldiers serving under 2,600 family leaders, amounting to nearly 120 soldiers per division/leader. Uzziah completely funded the soldiers' equipment from the royal court. In the past, the men had often been responsible to furnish their own battle gear. Uzziah understood mathematics and engineering. His impressive military mind invented primitive catapults and trained warriors to operate them. In hand-to-hand combat, such machines must have been especially lethal. As a result, Uzziah's fame spread, yet the text is clear that the king did not stand alone. Through God's help, Uzziah achieved military and technological excellence.

WHAT WAS THE SECRET OF UZZIAH'S SUCCESS?

Do you know the secret behind Uzziah's ability to succeed in everything he endeavoured to do – administratively, militarily, agriculturally, in inventions, in engineering etc? Verse 7 of our text contains the very simple reason:

"God helped him". In a more emphatic manner, the word of God declares that "for he [Uzziah] was marvellously helped, till he was strong." (v.15).

Dear Saint, the Bible says, *"John answered and said, A man can receive nothing, except it be given him from heaven"* (John 3:27). Our world today is full of short-sighted, gullible men and women who, like King Herod, would not give God the glory due to Him. They are ever prepared to ascribe any level of achievements and successes in their lives, either to their unique personalities or unparalleled and uncommon abilities. God is totally out of their record of achievement. As a result, our society is replete with *self-made* millionaires, *self-made* billionaires, etc. A very glaring lesson we have learnt so far in this book, especially under the heading being considered, is that God is the source of all abilities, potentials, achievements, wealth etc. In the words of Socrates (c. 470 BC – 399 BC), a classical Greek (Athenian) philosopher: "As for me, all I know is that I know nothing…" Albert Einstein concurs, "Whoever undertakes to set himself up as a judge of Truth and Knowledge is shipwrecked…" "My religion", he adds, "consists of a humble admiration of the illimitable superior spirit who reveals himself in the slight details we are able to perceive with our frail and feeble mind" (emphasis added).

The word translated "help" in verse 15 comes from a Hebrew word that means "surrounds." So God was fully involved in the affairs of King Uzziah. In all his battles, political, military, business enterprises God "surrounded" him, such that whoever wanted to contend with Uzziah, invariably had to take God on first! His affairs were conducted under the full glare of God. Heaven had in place *divine surveillance* over the life of King Uzziah. God's blessing was the secret behind King Uzziah's success.

> Through habitual seeking of the face of God, it wasn't difficult for Uzziah to please God with his life

In-depth study of Scriptures reveals the very reason why God lavished His favour on this young ruler. According to Jim Cymbala, "…events leading to Uzziah's success were not accidents of providence – such things do not exist in the spiritual realm. Rather they were the result of something that Uzziah was habitually doing. Scripture reveals that "he [Uzziah] continued to seek God in the days of Zechariah, who had understanding through the vision of God; and *as long as he* [Uzziah] *sought the Lord*, God prospered him" (2 Chr. 26:5 NASB).

Through habitual seeking of the face of God, it was not difficult for Uzziah to please God with his life: "*And he did that which was right in the sight of the Lord…*" (verse 4).

It was not when Uzziah sought success that he found it, but when he sought God.

Notice there was a direct connection between seeking and success in the reign of King Uzziah. It was not when Uzziah sought success that he found it, but when he sought God!

E.M. Bounds was succinct when he said, "Jacob wrestled, not so much with a promise, as with the Promiser. We must take hold of the Promiser, lest the promise prove nugatory. Prayer may well be defined as that force which vitalizes and energizes the Word of God, by taking hold of God, Himself. By taking hold of the Promiser, prayer reissues, and makes personal the promise. "There is none that stirreth up himself to take hold of Me," is God's sad lament. "Let him take hold of My strength, that he may make peace with Me," is God's recipe for prayer."

The word "sought" emphasises continued inquiry and devotion. It comes from a word which meant "to tread a place or path." It depicted someone regularly going to a place, seeking or searching, and, as a result, treading a path. As long as Uzziah regularly sought the Lord, God made him to prosper.

This formula for success was not just true for Uzziah, and his day, it is for every child of God, who dares to do what Uzziah did – passionately seek God. Psalm

14:2 tells us the high premium God places on the very act of seeking His face.

> *The Lord looked down from heaven upon the children of men, to see if there were any that did understand, and seek God (KJV).*
>
> *The Lord looked down from heaven upon the children of men to see if there were any who understood, dealt wisely, and sought after God, inquiring for and of Him and requiring Him* [of vital necessity] (Amp. Bible).

The value of seeking God is clearly illustrated in the following prophecy given to Israel by a prophet of God:

"The Spirit of God came on Azariah son of Oded. He went out to meet Asa and said to him, "Listen to me, Asa and all Judah and Benjamin. The LORD is with you when you are with him. If you seek him, he will be found by you, but if you forsake him, he will forsake you" (2 Chr. 15:1-2).

It is worth noting the time period during which Uzziah was seeking the Lord and enjoying divine favour, as a result. The Bible says it was "*...in the days of Zechariah, who had understanding in the visions of God...*" (verse 4). Both the period of time that Uzziah sought God and the personality of the individual he sought God under are vitally important to our discussion. First, it was in the days of Zechariah that God lavished His love and favour on Uzziah. Now in an attempt to address the second issue raised above, we must seek to know the profile of the man - Zechariah that produced such a brilliant protégée in Uzziah. While it is clear from biblical history that the Zechariah here referred to was not the prophet whose book is included among the books of the Minor Prophets in the Bible, he was nonetheless, a person of repute, who had a fervent and passionate relationship with God. He was a man with a touch of heaven upon his life, a man with an unrestricted access to the invisible things of the Spirit. His life shaped and influenced the young ruler – Uzziah to be a seeker of God. It is very important and soul-stirring that Uzziah was said to have associated with a man that *"had understanding in the visions of God..."* (verse 4, emphasis added). Lack of these qualities in Zechariah would have rendered nugatory every move by Uzziah to seek God through him.

What a lesson for today 'Zechariahs'! You cannot be a mentor over the upcoming generations of 'Uzziahs' while you have little or no understanding whatsoever, of the ways of God. A Latin phrase: *Nemodat quod non habet*, sums the position quite appropriately: "You cannot give what you do not have."

A. W. Tozer's view on the subject illustrates the point perfectly:

"Every believer has had or will sometime have the experience of leaning hard on the example of someone wiser and more spiritual than himself and looking to him for counsel and guidance in the Christian Life... Happy is the newborn babe in Christ who can find a pure and holy soul whom he can take as a model and from whom he can learn the ways of the Kingdom. Such a one can act as a mentor to save the young Christian from many mistakes and pitfalls into which he otherwise might fall. Much is said about this in the Scriptures and many examples are found there. Joshua had his Moses; Elisha had his Elijah and Timothy his Paul. It speaks well of the humility of the younger men that were willing to learn and of the patience of the older ones that were willing to teach. Had Moses, for instance, withdrawn his company and refused to be bothered with young Joshua the history of Israel would have been different, as it would have been also if Joshua had been too proud and self-assured to sit at the feet of Moses."

It is a fact of life that leaders cannot *show* the way until they *know* the way! The account we have of Zechariah here is, in a way (albeit with marked difference in some respects), reminiscent of what the Bible presents us with about Eli who, more or less, lost fellowship with God. But for God's direct intervention, Eli would not have been able to produce a successful protégée in Samuel, because he had lost the *vision* of God himself.

"For I have told him that I will judge his house for ever for the iniquity which he knoweth; because his sons made themselves vile, and he restrained them not. And therefore I have sworn unto the house of Eli, that the iniquity of Eli's house shall not be purged with sacrifice nor offering for ever" (1 Sam. 3:13,14). We urgently need 'heaven-

recognised' 'Zechariahs' in the present day Church – people who will motivate and encourage the upcoming generation of believers to conform to God's image, and maintain a healthy relationship with Him.

Chapter 18

HANNAH - A WOMAN IN NEED

The life of Hannah epitomises, in so many ways, the lives of ordinary people in the Church today, irrespective of their needs. Hannah had a need, and it was crucial! A need so intensive, challenging, it encapsulates acute moral degradation; and it caused her pain. The Bible says she was childless. Hannah's inability to produce children had huge implications under the Mosaic covenant which promised to reward obedience to God's law with fruitfulness.

The summary of the benefits and curses of the Law as given to Moses by God shows that if the nation were to be obedient there would not be any childless couples, or even animals, among the people. It also shows that God Himself is capable of either shutting up the wombs of women or opening it as he wishes (Exod. 23:26, Deut. 7:14).

Without children, Hannah looked like a failure. Many people would assume she was "not right with God." The problem probably goes back to the misinterpretation of Psalm 127:3 *"Lo, children are heritage of the LORD: and the fruit of the womb is his reward"*. This verse was written in light of Deuteronomy 7:12-14 (quoted above) and was under the Mosaic covenant.

Hannah's situation was further exasperated by the abhorrent attitude of her mate – Peninnah who took advantage of the latter's situation to torment her. Peninnah provoked Hannah because she was childless. The world, the flesh and devil will provoke us over things that the Lord withholds from us. They will try to make us fret on purpose! They may even throw it in our faces that it is the Lord who did this to us. The temptation will then be to turn against the Lord and blame Him.

Notice that the time that should have been the most spiritual blessing to Hannah was apparently when her adversary attacked the most viciously. Peninnah was determined to destroy her joy in the Lord and her appreciation for the kindness of her husband. There are many ugly motivations that could have been behind this, but the point is the results - it destroyed Hannah's joy. The devil will use your kids, family, spouse, and much more to destroy your joy and increase your depression, or to cause it just when you should be rejoicing or receiving a blessing. In it all, Paul enjoins us to, "*...endure hardness, as a good soldier of Jesus Christ*" (2Tim. 2:3).

Now let us explore some important highlights of this biblical account:

"*Now there was a certain man of Ramathaimzophim, of mount Ephraim, and his name was Elkanah, the son of Jeroham, the son of Elihu, the son of Tohu, the son of*

Zuph, an Ephrathite: And he had two wives; the name of the one was Hannah, and the name of the other Peninnah: and Peninnah had children, but Hannah had no children. And when the time was that Elkanah offered, he gave to Peninnah his wife, and to all her sons and her daughters, portions: But unto Hannah he gave a worthy portion; for he loved Hannah: but the Lord had shut up her womb. And her adversary also provoked her sore, for to make her fret, because the Lord had shut up her womb" (1 Sam. 1:1-2,4-5,6).

Notice the three "symptoms" that come up here. Hannah fretted, she wept and she would not eat. These are all things that go with depression, anxiety, eating disorders, and other such like. Physical symptoms are very much a part of life when one is afflicted with depression or anxiety. At such times, we must allow the word of God to speak expressly to our situation. The Bible teaches that *"we have not an high priest which **cannot be touched with the feeling of our infirmities**; but was in all points tempted like as we are, yet without sin"* (Heb. 5:4, emphasis added). He understands the situation far more than we do. The High Priest of our soul, Jesus Christ, has been through similar, even worse situations. He, therefore, has a word for your situation. Search the scripture today, and get that word, *"Search the scriptures; for in them ye think ye have eternal life: and they are they which testify of me"* (John 5:39). One word from the Lord can alter the course of your life!

Hannah's situation could be summarised thus:

- Barrenness – inability to have children.

- The perennial problem of a "crowded marriage".

- The generic problem inherent in polygamy - it genders strife.

- A long wait; unfulfilled aspiration.

- Depression or anxiety arising from her situation. Hannah's first problem was that her husband had married another woman. (It seems most likely that Hannah was the first wife, since she is mentioned before Penninah).

Hannah probably felt like a failure given that she could not produce children. The Bible says, *"And she was in bitterness of soul, and prayed unto the LORD, and wept sore"* (1 Sam. 1:10). Guilt played a major role in these problems. Too often, there is a real or imagined guilt or insufficiency that causes the afflicted to condemn or torment themselves. Where there has been sin, God is able to forgive. However, very often it is an artificial, man-made guilt that has nothing to do with reality as God sees it. Hannah decided to do something drastic about her problem; something she had not done this before. She entreated the Lord and made a vow to Him. Notice in verse 10 that she was in bitterness of soul. But, what did she do? She prayed unto the Lord and wept sore to Him. These are sacrifices God will not despise.

"The sacrifices of God are a broken spirit: a broken and a contrite heart, O God, thou wilt not despise" (Psalm 51:17).

Lord may not answer us right away; He does hear and will answer in His time and way. Remember that Hannah had been suffering under this burden for years, though we are not told exactly how long.

In the verses that followed 1Samuel 1:12-14 we see the events that marked a turning point in the life of Hannah, *"And it came to pass, as she continued praying before the LORD, that Eli marked her mouth. Now Hannah, she spake in her heart; only her lips moved, but her voice was not heard: therefore Eli thought she had been drunken. And Eli said unto her, How long wilt thou be drunken? put away thy wine from thee."*

The secret key to Hannah's breakthrough was her perseverance. This was clearly spelt out in the following phrase, *"as she continued praying before the LORD."* Hannah did not only pray, she prayed with zest, utter determination and indefatigability. She would not let go until she had what she desired. In essence, Hannah was determined to translate desire into miracle.

However, to further exasperate the situation, Eli, the high priest, totally misjudged her. His immediate supposition was that she was wicked and needed to repent. Without seeking further knowledge of the situation he rebuked her rather forcefully.

Someone is going to misunderstand each one of us at some point too. More often than not, it will probably be the "spiritual" people in our lives - the pastor or his wife, parents, siblings or spouses, a leader in the Church or someone who thinks they are very "spiritual" and wise. It may be that the very ones who should be ministering to us will misjudge and make false accusations. They will assume we are "not right with God."

Hannah did not accept the accusation neither was she rude, but she explained the condition of her sorrowful spirit, though she didn't go into detail or tell exactly why (1 Sam. 1:15-16). There is a time to reject accusations, even the accusations of our own hearts, *"For if our heart condemn us, God is greater than our heart, and knoweth all things. Beloved, if our heart condemn us not, then have we confidence toward God And whatsoever we ask, we receive of him, because we keep his commandments, and do those things that are pleasing in his sight"* (1 John 3:20-22). This is because sometimes our own treacherous hearts will condemn us even when we are striving to do those things that are pleasing to God.

Hannah had poured out her soul before the Lord and spoken to Him out of the abundance of her complaint and grief. This is a description of a soul in deep distress. Those of us who have suffered these things will easily recognise that feeling. There is a time to pour out your complaint before the Lord. The title of Psalm 102 says, A Prayer of the afflicted, when he is overwhelmed, and poureth out his complaint before the LORD. And David cries out in Psalm 142,

> *I cried unto the LORD with my voice; with my voice unto the LORD did I make my supplication. I poured out my complaint before him; I shewed before him my trouble. When my spirit was overwhelmed within me, then thou knewest my path...*

...we are safer laying them (our problems) there (in His presence) than anywhere else, for He understands the true depth or our suffering and is full of compassion and mercy!

Even though the act of complaining is not a desirable habit of life, the Bible, however, says that the Lord accepts the complaint of the overwhelmed and miserable spirit. And, after all, perhaps we are safer laying them there than anywhere else, for He understands the true depth or our suffering and is full of compassion and mercy! Psalm 86:15 says *"But thou, O Lord, art a God full of compassion, and gracious, longsuffering, and plenteous in mercy and truth. And remember, He is greater than our heart."*

> *Then Eli answered and said, Go in peace: and the God of Israel grant thee thy petition that thou hast asked of him. And she said, Let thine handmaid find grace in thy sight. So the woman went her way, and did eat, and her countenance was no more sad*(1Sam 1:17-18).

Eli may not have even known that he was speaking a prophecy here, but he was nevertheless. As the high priest, God reserved the right to use him thus (John 11:51). Hannah believed him and acted upon it, she showed her confidence that God would answer according as she was told. She ate again and her countenance was no more sad. What a sweet testimony to her faith in the Lord. She knew she had her answer, and she took it by faith (Heb. 11:1).

God answered her prayer - probably one of many prayers. However, she waited long and sorrowed much before she got her original desire. For a barren woman even a few years is a long wait, partly because she is reminded every month of her inability to conceive. The Lord blessed her not only with Samuel, but also by giving her other children as well (1Sam. 2:21), thus doing exceeding abundantly above what she asked of thought, (Eph. 3:20).

In her thrilling testimony to the goodness of God, she said, *"For this child I prayed; and the LORD hath given me my petition which I asked of him: Therefore also I have lent him to the LORD; as long as he liveth he shall be lent to the LORD. And he worshipped the LORD there"* (1 Sam. 1:27-28).

Hannah attributed her miracle to the Lord. In the next chapter she glorified the Lord and gave him the glory due unto His name. She also kept her vow. She gave Samuel to the Lord.

However, we must not lose sight of the fact that the Bible traces Hannah's ordeal to a highly significant and insightful point, "*And her adversary also provoked her sore, for to make her fret,* **because the LORD had shut up her womb**" (1 Sam.1:6, emphasis added). For what reason the Lord "closed" Hannah's womb, we are not told. However, what is hugely important to our discussion is that, even though the Lord placed barrenness on Hannah for whatever reason, Hannah was able to change the course of her life through hell-shattering; yoke-destroying and life-transforming prayer! What a lesson?

Chapter 19

KING HEZEKIAH

The life of Hezekiah presents us with another breathtaking and soul-inspiring experience in so many respects, given the weight it lends to our discussion.

"In those days was Hezekiah sick unto death. And Isaiah the prophet the son of Amoz came unto him, and said unto him, Thus saith the Lord, Set thine house in order: for thou shalt die, and not live" (Isaiah 38:1).

The above scripture details the darkest moments of the life of Hezekiah who was the twelfth king of Judea, a man of exceptional qualities who ushered in a sweeping and radical reforms that reinstated the worship of God to Judah at a time when Judea had sunk to the bottom of political and spiritual depravity.

We are not told how Hezekiah became sick. All we are told was that Hezekiah was sick. To us, under this heading, that is all that is important, because it is not what happens to a man that really matters but his *reaction* to what happens to him, his ability to navigate through the situation life throws at him without being overcome by it, is what is important. In essence, it is a man's reaction to the challenges of life that determines the outcome, no matter the experience!

It must be stressed that Hezekiah was not only said to be sick, *"he was sick unto death"* (2 Kings 20:2, Isaiah 38:1). In other words, death was hanging over him.

One can all too well imagine how perplexed Hezekiah must have been at the news of his imminent or impending death from not just a friend, but a Prophet of high repute like Isaiah.

Second, it must be noted that Hezekiah was not just a King; he was a man who feared God greatly, and maintained such a fervent relationship with Him like king Uzziah. Notice the impeccable record he had before the Lord:

"And he did that which was right in the sight of the Lord, according to all that David his father did…He trusted in the Lord God of Israel; so that after him was none like him among all the kings of Judah, nor any that were before him. ***For he clave to the Lord, and departed not from following him, but kept his commandments, which the Lord commanded Moses. And the Lord was with him; and he prospered whithersoever he went forth****: and he rebelled against the king of Assyria, and served him not"* (2 Kings 18:3,5-7, emphasis added).

Can you imagine a man of such exceptional testimony, and close association with God being afflicted by Satan. At the time of Prophet Isaiah's visit to Hezekiah, it was fitting for Hezekiah to have assumed a lot of things, not least, the possibility of such visit being intended as a forum of praying in *agreement* to avert or overcome the sickness he was suffering from. After-all, they had shared burdens in prayer together before. It could have also been a casual visit from Isaiah who was, but a personal friend of his. The fact that Hezekiah himself was a man of prayer meant that he might have expected God to have had a personal and direct dealing with him on such a crucial matter, as conveyed by Prophet Isaiah. So, nothing could have prepared Hezekiah for the *grim* report he had received from God through such a distinguished and high-profile Prophet like Isaiah. In all, Hezekiah expected to recover from his ailment. If anything, he expected a message of hope in this dire moment of his life. Instead, it was *"Thus saith the Lord, Set thine house in order: for thou shalt die, and not live"* (Isaiah 38:1).Let us try and put this message in context: from a personal perspective, this message reads like: 'Hezekiah, I am here on a pretty serious business. I am sorry to inform you that God has decided not to heal you of your sickness. He has, therefore sent me to inform you to put the business of your home in order: if you have not written a Will, please do so. Appoint the next leader of your family because, this sickness is going to kill you.' What a message!

Remember, our focus is not so much on the message Prophet Isaiah delivered but on Hezekiah's reaction to the message. Well, again, many options were undoubtedly, opened to Hezekiah upon receiving this message of doom:

First, he could have "lost his cool with" Isaiah, accusing him of harbouring evil desires against him. Reason? A man who is intimate with God is not intimidated by man or by any situation.

Second, as a Prophet of great repute, known nationally as a man that *heard* from God, Hezekiah could have quickly engaged Prophet Isaiah in some sort of *urgent* prayers intent on averting the imminent evil. His reaction upon receiving the news of his impending demise was that of unwavering and uncompromising faith in the God he had known and maintained close relationship with all along. Instead of relying on *man* (Prophet Isaiah) to help plead his case with God or stand in the gap for him, he took matters with God himself, in an attitude that suggests: 'I also have access to the God from whom this message came.' I have served Him to the best of my ability; I have walked righteously before him. I was the one that opened and cleansed the Temple of the Lord, and reinstated the true worship of Jehovah to Judah. My credentials are straight before Him. I have had a very close and fervent relationship with Him. I have the experience of approaching and supplicating before Him. I do not need a *middle-man* between God and me. I know Him; He is my God. He has heard me on matters of grim and ghastly nature before, He will hear me again!' After all, the Bible enjoins us "...*forget not all His benefits*" (Psalm 103: 2).

The fact that he allowed Prophet Isaiah to leave the palace before he approached God on the matter, buttresses how private he regarded his relationship with God. He must have reasoned, 'issues of this importance are better thrashed out in the *closet*; these are not issues to be put in the public domain. David Macintyre was succinct when he said, "communication with God discovers the excellence of His character." Neither did Hezekiah's regard Prophet Isaiah's pronouncement as the final verdict on the matter. No! He took his destiny into his own hands and supplicated before God.

He said, "... *Remember now, O LORD, I beseech thee, how I have walked before thee in truth and with a perfect heart, and have done that which is good in thy sight. And Hezekiah wept sore*" (Isaiah 38:2-3). This prayer touched the heart of God and marked a significant turnaround in this situation! Even though God orchestrated this whole process, He did not mind putting His integrity on the line in changing His mind about its outcome, after Hezekiah had prayed.

The conclusion of this awful situation was astounding:

"*Then came the word of the LORD to Isaiah, saying, Go, and say to Hezekiah, Thus saith the LORD, the God of David thy father,* **I have heard thy prayer, I have seen thy tears: behold, I will add unto thy days fifteen years**" (Isaiah 38:4-5, emphasis added).

What a mighty weapon we have in prayer!

GOD'S POWER AND WILLINGNESS TO ANSWER PRAYER

> "...there is another truth that has come to me with wonderful clarity as I studied the teaching of Jesus on prayer. The Father waits to hear every prayer of faith. He wants to give us whatever we ask for in Jesus' Name. We have become so accustomed to limiting the wonderful love and the great promises of our God, that we cannot read the simplest and clearest statements of our Lord without qualifying them. If there is one thing I think the Church needs to learn, it is that God intends prayer to have an answer, and that man has not yet fully conceived of what God will do for the child who believes that his prayer will be heard. God hears prayer." – **Andrew Murray.**

God derives special pleasure in answering the prayers of His people. The Bible portrays God as a father that is habitually in fervent love with His children. This is seen, not just in His ability, but in His willingness to respond to the prayers of His children. Often, the reward of prayer is so conspicuous that it is scarcely possible to ignore the connection between the petition and the answer. God has not only called men to seek Him but has covenanted to allow the petition of the saints to weigh heavily on His heart.

"I have not spoken in secret, in a dark place of the earth: I said not unto the seed of Jacob, Seek ye me in vain: I the L<small>ORD</small> *speak righteousness, I declare things that are right"* (Isaiah 45:19).

"I have not spoken in secret, in a corner of the land of darkness; I did not call the descendants of Jacob [to a fruitless service], saying, Seek Me for nothing [but I promised them a just reward]. I, the Lord, speak righteousness (the truth – trustworthy, straightforward correspondence between deeds and words); I declare things that are right" (Isaiah 45:19, Amp.).

In the words of Zacharias Fomum, "God has ordained prayer as the mechanism through which redeemed people will share His sovereignty with Him. The praying saints can move God who can move the universe in any direction. This means that the praying saint can determine all that happens in the universe."

As said, God has committed Himself to answer the prayer of His saints, in most cases, in ways out of the ordinary. He has put His integrity on the line in this matter.

We are told that God is love! By implication, it means that God does not just have a "property" or "nature" called love, He is love Himself, *"He that loveth not knoweth not God; for God is love"* (1 John 4:8). An electricity plant, for instance, generates electricity not by nature but by design. It is manufactured with the sole ability to generate electricity. God is an embodiment of love. Everything He does is from 'the love' perspective. God operates constantly with the objectivity of love in mind. When the believers pray, God responds in love to meet their needs. This explains why even when mankind was in acute rebellion against God, God still considered it appropriate to redeem him by sending His only begotten son – Jesus to die vicariously in order to change man's eternal destiny. We see this vividly demonstrated in the following scriptures: *"**For God so loved the world** that he gave his only begotten Son, that whosoever believeth in him should not perish, but have everlasting life"* (John 3:16, emphasis added).

"But God commendeth his love toward us, in that, while we were yet sinners, Christ died for us" (Rom. 5:8).

In Christ Jesus, God no doubt, gave His best to the undeserving world - an unmerited gesture. The Bible says, *"Behold, what manner of love the Father hath bestowed upon us, that we should be called the sons of God …"* (1 John 3:1). It is incomprehensible! But as said, God's willingness to answer prayers is directly in consonance with His 'make-up', which is love. To E.M. Bounds, "Nothing is clearer than that prayer has its only worth and significance in the great fact that God hears and answers prayer."

God could boast of His unflinching determination to answer the prayer of the believer. We can draw inspiration from the following scriptures:

"And call upon me in the day of trouble: I will deliver thee, and thou shalt glorify me" (Ps 50:15).

"Ask, and it shall be given you; seek, and ye shall find; knock, and it shall be opened unto you" (Matt. 7:7).

"**For every one that asketh receiveth**; and he that seeketh findeth; and to him that knocketh it shall be opened" (Luke 11:10, emphasis added)

"And whatsoever ye shall ask in my name, that will I do, that the Father may be glorified in the Son. If ye shall ask any thing in my name, I will do it" (John 14:13-14).

"Hitherto have ye asked nothing in my name: ask, and ye shall receive, that your joy may be full" (John 16:24).

Finally, in Jeremiah 33:2-3, God expresses an unequivocal commitment to answer the prayer of the saint. *"Thus saith the Lord the maker thereof, the Lord that formed it, to establish it; the Lord is his name; Call unto me, **and I will answer thee**, and show thee great and mighty things, which thou knowest not"* (Jer. 33:2-3, emphasis added). This is far more than a promise. This is a promise backed by guarantee! There is a huge difference between an *ordinary* cheque, and a cheque backed by guarantee!

> *After this I looked, and, behold, a door was opened in heaven: and the first voice which I heard was as it were of a trumpet talking with me; which said, Come up hither, and I will shew thee things which must be hereafter* (Rev. 4:1).

The most intriguing scripture on the subject of prayer, God's delight and, in fact, His commitment in answering prayer to me is Hebrew 6: 13-19:

> *For when God made promise to Abraham, because he could swear by no greater, he sware by himself, Saying, Surely blessing I will bless thee, and multiplying I will*

> *multiply thee. And so, after he had patiently endured, he obtained the promise. For men verily swear by the greater: and an oath for confirmation is to them an end of all strife. Wherein God, willing more abundantly to shew unto the heirs of promise the immutability of his counsel, confirmed it by an oath: That by two immutable things, in which it was impossible for God to lie, we might have a strong consolation, who have fled for refuge to lay hold upon the hope set before us: Which hope we have as an anchor of the soul, both sure and stedfast, and which entereth into that within the veil...*

Notice that, "*By two immutable things*" (God's counsel and God's oath), we have been given such hope that is "*an anchor of our soul, both sure and stedfast, and which entereth into that within the veil*" (v. 19).

Bob Tornado affirms that if God had sworn by anything finite, that thing might fail, and then the obligation would be at an end, but he has sworn by what is infinite, and cannot fail; therefore his oath is of eternal obligation.

By this, God determines to give a second "immutable" thing, an oath validated by a swearing by His own self, placing His own reputation upon this immutable contract.

Notice, that the counsel of God came first and then the oath. It takes both to assure the fearful and distrustful nature of man to trust in the immutable word of the

Lord. The word, "immutable", in the Greek dictionary means to be "unchangeable, unalterable", that which cannot be perverted from its original intent and purpose. Such is the nature of the counsel of God, which is etched in the granite of His own substance and character, a God who CANNOT lie! That calls the compassion and mercy of God into play. He who knows the heart of man better than man himself, in a divine act of quelling the distress and agony of man's own mind concerning what His counsel provides, lowers Himself to an act of making an oath, a solemn covenantal promise, which necessitates a "swearing unto", or a binding statement of such contract. By this, God determines to give a second "immutable" thing, an oath validated by a swearing by His own self, placing His own reputation upon this immutable contract. Since He could swear by nothing less than Himself, given that everything else besides Him is subject to change and alteration, He swore by Himself. He is unchangeable and unalterable, and by that single act of swearing, we have been given an unfailing promise, that He who has begun this good work will indeed, finish it. The immutability of His counsel and oath, *"in blessing I will bless thee and in multiplying I will multiply thee"*, is such that heaven and earth could pass away, but this solemn word of affirmation and confirmation will never pass from existence. Time will not stop His counsel and oath from having their fulfilment in the hearts of mankind.

Part 6

PRAYER ENFORCERS

(THINGS THAT MUST ACCOMPANY PRAYER)

Chapter 20

THE WORD OF GOD – KEY PRAYER ENFORCER

In the words of D. L. Moody, *"Prayer is hardly ever mentioned in the Bible alone, it is prayer and earnestness; prayer and watchfulness, prayer and thanksgiving. It is an instructive fact that throughout scripture prayer is always linked with something else…"*

> For any prayer to achieve its objective, it must be in company of some fundamental, yet highly significant building blocks of the Christian faith. This is of supreme importance! Otherwise prayer becomes a futile exercise.

For any prayer to achieve its objective, it must be in company of some fundamental, yet highly significant building blocks of the Christian faith. This is of supreme importance! Otherwise, prayer becomes a futile exercise. God holds the key to all knowledge. He has the key to heaven where all of our mercies, blessings, favours, revelations, insights, wisdom, etc are locked up. But it is our responsibility to *"knock"* at the door of heaven, well informed of vital biblical principles, until God opens the door and gives us what we need. Under this heading, we shall examine just few of those things that must accompany prayer to yield the desired result.

PRAYER AND THE WORD OF GOD

"The Word of God is the fulcrum upon which the lever of prayer is placed, and by which things are mightily moved. God has committed Himself, His purpose and His promise to prayer. His Word becomes the basis, the inspiration of our praying, and there are circumstances under which, by importunate prayer, we may obtain an addition, or an enlargement of His promises. It is said of the old saints that they, "through faith obtained promises." There would seem to be in prayer the capacity for going even beyond the Word, of getting even beyond His promise, into the very presence of God, Himself." – EM Bounds.

> In many of its aspects, prayer is dependent upon the Word of God. Without the Bible our prayers have no foundation.

In many of its aspects, prayer is dependent upon the Word of God. Without the Bible our prayers have no foundation. True faith always finds its validity or authenticity in the Word. Because it has pleased Him to commit Himself to us in the Word of Promise, we feel encouraged to approach Him on its merits and integrity. The Word of God is vital in prayer because the Bible reveals much about prayer. Besides,

God uses His word to facilitate the supernatural. A reverence for God's holy Name is closely related to a high regard for His Word.

The viral connection between prayer and the word is clearly delineated in the following words of our Lord Jesus Christ:

"If ye abide in Me, and My words abide in you, ye shall ask what ye will, and it shall be done unto you" (John 15:7).

The Word of God is the food, by which prayer is nourished and made strong. Prayer, like man, cannot live by bread alone, "but by every word which proceedeth out of the mouth of the Lord...

The verb, "abide" means "continue", "remain", "stay", "dwell" or "steadfast" in Greek and is used no less than 12 times in John 15:4-16. The same word is used in John 8:31 when Jesus said that those who continue in His word are His disciples indeed. Accordingly, abiding in the Lord requires an obligation of adhering strictly to the words of God, regarding them as true and authoritative in every respect. Abiding in the Lord requires certain attributes which affirm its existence in the life of the believer. For instance, 1John 2:6 says, *"He that saith he abideth in him ought himself also so to walk, even as he walked."* To abide in Him, according to Frangipane, is to live in ceaseless fusion with His passions. "The Word of God", affirms EM Bounds, "is a great help in prayer. If it be lodged and written in our hearts, it will form an out flowing current of prayer, full and irresistible. Promises, stored in the heart, are to be the fuel from which prayer receives life and warmth, just as the coal, stored in the earth, ministers to our comfort on stormy days and wintry nights. The Word of God is the food, by which prayer is nourished and made strong." Prayer, like man, cannot live by bread alone, "but by every word which proceedeth out of the mouth of the Lord...Unless the vital forces of prayer are supplied by God's Word, prayer, though earnest, even vociferous, in its urgency, is, in reality, flabby, and vapid, and void. The absence of vital force in praying can be traced to the absence of a constant supply of God's Word, to repair the waste, and renew the life. He who would learn to pray well, must first study God's Word, and store it in his memory and thought.

Prayer, being a dialogue with our heavenly father, its most essential element must be ability to hear the voice of God in response to ours. This is contrary to the view widely held in some Christian circles which see prayer as an opportunity to go before God with "an unending shopping list", regarded as prayer requests. This accounts for the lack of emphasis we see today on such teaching as 'how to hear the voice of God through an intense study of His word'. It must be stressed, too, that the misguided emphasis on the use of the gift of prophecy in the contemporary church has also done more harm than good in this regard. Apart from the fact that majority of ministers of God today regard themselves prophets, and must prophecy, as it were, to validate their calling and demonstrate their ability to *hear from God,* the misguided use of prophecy in the modern church has denied the word of God its rightful place. *'Human-baked'* prophecies have been erroneously substituted for the word of God in some Christian organisations.

This has resulted in the average believer having a very narrow conception of the word. The absence of proper understanding and application of the word of God has reduced the quality of our lives and our services to God. This is so because kingdom exploit is a product of divine revelation gained from the word of God. So persuaded in his convictions about the nature and integrity of the word of God, Emmanuel Kant warns: "The existence of the Bible, as a book for the people, is the greatest benefits which the human race has ever experienced. Every attempt to belittle it is a crime against humanity." The Bible testifies in Daniel 11:32, **"... but the people that do know their God shall be strong, and do exploits"** (emphasis added).

In his very insightful word to the young men, John writes, *"I have written unto you, fathers, because ye have known him that is from the beginning. I have written unto you, young men, because ye are strong, and the word of God abideth in you, and ye have overcome the wicked one"* (1 John 2:14). Notice what gave the young men in John's era strength. Abiding in the word of God! Through it they overcame the evil one. Any wonder then why many believers are easily defeated by the devil? Lack of abiding in the word of God is a weapon we have inadvertently given to the devil to fight us with. Do not forget the word of God is a formidable weapon of warfare – the Sword of the Spirit (Eph. 6:17); consequently, when we do not abide in the word of God, the devil gains and we lose. Further, Jesus says, *"My sheep hear my voice, and I know them, and they follow me: And I give unto them eternal life; and they shall never perish, neither shall any man pluck them out of my hand. My Father, which gave them me, is greater than all; and no man is able to pluck them out of my Father's hand"* (John 10:27-29). It is in the place of abiding that we are equipped with divine strategies both for warfare and, of course, the next level of our lives. It is my conviction that no child of God is able to live above his perception or impression of the word of God. The understanding of the word of God we run the course of our lives with determines greatly, the quality of the life we live.

The gift of prophecy is a valid, authentic, and Bible-based gift of the Holy Spirit! It must however, be utilised under the guidance of the word of God. Quite sternly Peter warns, *"We have also a more sure word of prophecy; whereunto ye do well that ye take heed, as unto a light that shineth in a dark place, until the day dawn, and the day star arise in your hearts: Knowing this first, that no prophecy of the scripture is of any private interpretation. For the prophecy came not in old time by the will of man: but holy men of God spake as they were moved by the Holy Ghost"* (11 Pet. 1: 19-21, emphasis added); to which Paul adds, *"All scripture is given by inspiration of God, and is profitable for doctrine, for reproof, for correction, for instruction in righteousness: That the man of God may be perfect, thoroughly furnished unto all good works"* (2 Tim. 3: 16 - 17).

In the strict application of the word of God, the believer is to be taught the Bible- precept upon precept - (*For precept must be upon precept, precept upon precept; line upon line, line upon line; here a little, and there a little Isa 28:10*), and encouraged to study the word as an essential tool for enhancing spiritual growth and intimacy with God. He must not be taken out of this obligation which he owes to God and himself through a barrage of prophecies often 'coded' *"the Lord said I should tell you…"* which has resulted in many believers today not having the right attitude towards the word of God. Many contemporary Christians do not see any reason whatsoever, to spend time studying the word of God, let alone building their destinies on it. Henry H. Halley said quite blatantly: "EVERYBODY ought to Love the Bible, Everybody ought to be a Regular Reader of the Bible. Everybody ought to strive to Live by the Bible's teachings. The Bible ought to have central place in the life and working of every Church; and in every pulpit. THE PULPIT'S ONE BUSINESS

IS THE SIMPLE EXPOSITORY TEACHING OF GOD'S WORD." Constant attention must be drawn to the indispensable place of the word of God in the believer's life. Paul was succinct when he admonished his young *protégé* - Timothy, "*Till I come, give attendance to reading, to exhortation, to doctrine*" (1 Tim. 4:13).

As Timothy advanced as a Minister of the word, Paul saw the need to inculcate in him the disciplineof earnest and resolute study of the word of God. He said to him:

"*Study to shew thyself approved unto God, a workman that needeth not to be ashamed, rightly dividing the word of truth*" (2 Tim. 2:15).

Another version of the Bible puts it this way:

"*Carefully study to present thyself approved unto God, a workman that needeth not to be ashamed, rightly handling the word of truth*" (The Douay-Rheims Bible).

Paul knew that with ability comes responsibility, and that if Timothy would ever make his "calling and election sure" (2 Pet. 1:10), and make full proof of his ministry (2 Tim. 4:5), he needed to have an intense and firmer grip on the word of God than just *reading* it. Only a constant and in-depth study of the word of God would suffice; because, in the words of another, "when you read, you skim the surface, [but] when you study, you discover the treasure."

The commitment of the contemporary believer to the word of God must not be any less. We are admonished to *"Search the scriptures."* **Why? Because,** *"for in them ...ye have eternal life: **and they are they which testify of me**"* (John 5:39, emphasis added). We are to teach, instruct and guide the believer to fully appreciate the unique place of the word of God in his life, giving him the necessary aid to engage in meaningful study of the word. Jude admonishes the Church: *"But ye, beloved, building up yourselves on your most holy faith..."* (verse 20).

The Psalmist estimation of the word illustrates the point perfectly. The word of God was everything to the Psalmist. In Psalm 19: 7-10 for instance, the Psalmist says

> *The law of the Lord is perfect, converting the soul: the testimony of the Lord is sure, making wise the simple. The statutes of the Lord are right, rejoicing the heart: the commandment of the Lord is pure, enlightening the eyes. The fear of the Lord is clean, enduring for ever: the judgments of the Lord are true and righteous altogether. More to be desired are they than gold, yea, than much fine gold: sweeter also than honey and the honeycomb.*

Further, in Psalm 119:1-8, the Psalmist affirms:

> *Blessed are the undefiled in the way, who walk in the law of the Lord. Blessed are they that keep his testimonies, and that seek him with the whole heart. They also do no iniquity: they walk in his ways. Thou hast commanded us to keep thy precepts diligently. O that my ways were*

> *directed to keep thy statutes! Then shall I not be ashamed, when I have respect unto all thy commandments. I will praise thee with uprightness of heart, when I shall have learned thy righteous judgments. I will keep thy statutes: O forsake me not utterly.*

Writing from a very personal experience, Smith Wigglesworth said emphatically, *"There is one thing God has given me from my youth up, a taste and relish for my Bible…It seems better to me to get the Book of books for your soul, for the strengthening of your faith and the building up of your character in God, so that all the time you are being changed and made meet to walk with God."*

It is to be noted that God Himself esteems His word above His names, *"…for thou hast magnified [exalted NIV] thy word above **all** thy name"* (Psalm 138:2b, emphasis added). The "name" of God refers to His authority and reputation. A proper understanding of this translation is that God exalted His Word above all other things that are under His authority. The Lord says, *"Heaven and earth shall pass away, but my words shall not pass away"* (Matt. 24:35).

The point was well driven home in the words of Andrew Murray:

"Before prayer, God's word strengthens me by giving my faith its justification and its petition. And after prayer, God's word prepares me by revealing what the Father wants me to ask. In prayer God's word brings me the answer, for in it the Spirit allows me to hear the Father's voice... Listening to God's voice is the secret of the assurance that He will listen to mine...My willingness to accept His words will determine the power my words have with Him. What God's words are to me is the test of what He Himself is to me. It shows the uprightness of my desire to meet Him in prayer."

George Muller's unparalleled success in evangelistic labours had been attributed to two causes to which he was habitually committed: his unusual prayerfulness, and his habit of reading the Bible on his knees.

It is this connection between His word and our prayer that Jesus points to when He said, *"If ye abide in Me, and My words abide in you, ye shall ask what ye will, and it shall be done unto you"* (John 15:7).

The incredible weight of the message Jesus conveys in this passage is better understood by reference to another passage of Scriptures where Jesus made his intent clearer. For instance, in John 15:4, Jesus says, "Abide in me, and I in you..." As a condition to having His abiding presence in us, Jesus says we must abide first in Him. However, instead of *"ye in me and My words in you"* as in John 15:7, we have, "ye in me and *I* in you". Both scriptures find consensus in the fact that the abiding of His word is the equivalent of God Himself abiding in us. The Word is the 'gateway' of God into the life of the believer. 'A man's words are as good as the man'! In His promises Jesus gives Himself away, making Himself accountable to whoever would receive His promises.

The Bible says Jesus is the living word of God. "*In the beginning was the Word, and the Word was with God, and the Word was God. The same was in the beginning with God. All things were made by him; and without him was not any thing made that was made... And the Word was made flesh, and dwelt among us...*" (John 1:1-3,14).

The *written* word therefore, was given to reveal the *living* Word – the Lord Jesus Christ - to us.

The words of Smith Wigglesworth drive the point home:

"I cannot understand God by feelings. I cannot understand the Lord Jesus Christ by feelings. I understand God, and I understand Jesus through the Word of God. God is everything the Word says He is. Get acquainted with God through the Word. Get acquainted with the Lord Jesus Christ through the Word." Abraham Lincoln, on the other hand, believes that "the Bible is the best gift God has ever given to man. All the good from the Saviour of the world," he affirms, "is communicated to us through this book." What an estimation and endorsement of the word of God!

In Proverbs 4:20-22, God highlights the inestimable value of feeding constantly on His word, "*My son, attend to my words; incline thine ear unto my sayings. Let them not depart from thine eyes; keep them in the midst of thine heart for they are life unto those that find them, and health to all their flesh."*

The above scripture, no doubt, opens up a vast field for reflection.

1. In the first place, we need to attend or listen or pay close attention to or have high regard for the word of God, "*My son, attend to my words...*" (verse 20)

2. Second, we are called to incline our ears unto the teaching of God's word, accepting it as authoritative in every respect. We are to open our ears to God's word, and God's word alone, "*incline thine ear unto my sayings*" (verse 20).

3. We are to have a firm grip on the word of God, "*Let them [my words] not depart from thine eyes...*" We are to look as well as listen to God's word. "*Therefore we ought to give the more earnest heed to the things which we have heard, lest at any time **we should let them slip**"* (Heb. 2:1, emphasis added). Guess who could let the word of God we have heard slip? The Bible says: *we*! The only antidote for this being to "Let the word of Christ dwell in you richly..." (Col. 3:16).

4. Finally, we are to keep or store up the word of God in our hearts, "*keep them in the midst of thine heart...*" (verse 21). The Psalmist says, "*Thy word has I hid in mine heart...*" (Psalms 119:11).

While the Gospels are instrumental at bringing us abreast with Jesus' *mission* and *activities* on earth, the epistles bring to the lime light the implications, consequences, and impact of such activities in the life and destiny of the believer.

In sum, if the *written* word, as discussed, is given to reveal the *living* word – Jesus Christ, there is no greater disservice we can do to ourselves than to handle the God's word with levity and degree of nonchalance. God's word in any context means the entire Bible not just the Gospels. No one studies and lives only the Gospels and lives a victorious Christian life. "The four Gospels", affirms Kenneth E. Hagin, "are a history of the life of Jesus: His works, His saying, and His deeds. In the Gospels we see Jesus dying, but if we don't go further than the Gospels, we won't know why he died…it is only in the epistles where we learnt what this living Word, Jesus Christ, wrought for us in His death, burial and resurrection." This is a valid argument, and I endorse it. While the gospels are instrumental at bringing us abreast with Jesus *'mission* and *activities* on earth, the epistles bring to the lime light the implications, consequences, and impact of such activities in the life and destiny of the believer. For instance, it was in the epistles that we read that, consequent upon Jesus' death and resurrection:

"… he hath made him to be sin for us, who knew no sin; that we might be made the righteousness of God in him" (2 Cor. 5:21).

"Christ hath redeemed us from the curse of the law, being made a curse for us: for it is written, Cursed is every one that hangeth on a tree: That the blessing of Abraham might come on the Gentiles through Jesus Christ; that we might receive the promise of the Spirit through faith" (Gal. 3:13,14).

In his soul-stirring letter, Apostle Paul writes:

"Wherefore remember, that ye being in time past gentiles in the flesh, who are called uncircumcision by that which is called the Circumcision in the flesh made by hands; That at that time ye were without Christ, being aliens from the commonwealth of Israel, and strangers from the covenants of promise, having no hope, and without God in the world: ***But now in Christ Jesus ye who sometimes were far off are made nigh by the blood of Christ.*** *For he is our peace, who hath made both one, and hath broken down the middle wall of partition between us; Having abolished in his flesh the enmity, even the law of commandments contained in ordinances; for to make in himself of twain one new man, so making peace; And that he might reconcile both unto God in one body by the cross, having slain the enmity thereby: And came and preached peace to you which were afar off, and to them that were nigh"* (Eph. 2: 11-17, emphasis added).

In his book, *Life Overflowing*, Bishop T.D. Jakes gave an exposé of the deep mystery behind the incredible revelation Paul had of the church that has enriched the Gospels in such an astonishing fashion. He believes that, Paul had a revelation from God about the Gentiles and the Church, and without that revelation, he would never have been able to fulfil his calling. God had revealed to him the mystery of the church, and he was consumed with it. He became the greatest expositor of God's blueprint for the church that has ever lived. If you pulled all of his epistles out of the New Testament, the church would be lost, because Paul defines and articulates the functioning of the New Testament church. Without Apostle Paul, we never would have understood how we were to function as the literal body of Christ. In his epistles, Paul unveils before our eyes God's glorious church. Pulling away the curtain of ignorance and darkness, he reveals to believers what the church really is and how the body of Christ is ordained by God to operate in this earth.

It is therefore, fitting to perceive the epistles as the practicality of the spirit and teachings of the gospels. The believer is to study them as he does the teachings of Jesus and the Old Testament, in order to be well informed and adequately equipped.

Chapter 21

REASONS WHY THE WORD OF GOD IS VITAL IN PRAYER

Both the word of God and prayer have a divine link, the knowledge of which is of immeasurable benefit in prevailing prayer. Every provision of God for man is revealed and known through the word of God. The legitimacy of our request in prayer is determined and tested to the extent to which the word of God makes provision for it, and is in conformity with the word. We cannot therefore, pray outside the word of God. If we do, we are out of His will. Any prayer that is prayed out of the will of God cannot receive heaven's validation, and is therefore, an exercise in futility. Consequently, God's word determines the ambit or confines of our prayer. Further, the effectiveness of our prayer depends a great deal on the strength it draws from the word of God. In the words of R.A. Torrey, "Triumphant prayer is almost impossible where there is neglect of the study of the Word of God...Prayer that is born of meditation upon the Word of God is the prayer that soars upward most easily to God's listening ears...all that God is, and all that God has, is at the disposal of prayer. Prayer can do anything that God can do, and as God can do everything, prayer is omnipotent."

Let us now examine the immeasurable significance of the word of God in prayer.

> There is no better way to make God an integral part of our prayer than using His Word in prayer. This process guarantees praying in agreement with His will.

1. God's word is of great significance in prayer because God and His word are one (John 1:1). This is clearly illustrated in God's estimation of His word. God does not only submit to the authority of His word, He is incapable of doing anything outside of His word, "*…for thou hast magnified thy word above all thy name*" (Psalm 138:2). However, Henry Morris' caution is of tremendous importance: "It is impossible to place the inspired, inerrant Word of God on too high a pedestal, for God Himself honours it above His name! The Word is not greater than God, for He wrote it by His Spirit, but it is greater than His "Name," which represents Him, and all that He is and does. His Word, however, represents Him more fully than His name alone can do; in His Word, in fact, His name is revealed."

   There is no better way to make God an integral part of our prayer than using His Word in prayer. This process guarantees praying in agreement with His will.

2. God's Word is of importance in prayer because it is the means of achieving God's purpose in the earth. Indeed, God's Word is the executor of God's purposes on earth. Gbile Akanni affirms that "God, all through the ages, has done every one of His works by his Word. God does not at anytime need to run up and down, gathering materials here and there before getting His work done. All He does is to speak His word…" "The scripture", he adds, "is God's comprehensive equipment for resetting the direction

of your life. Apart from the Word, God has no other equipment, so comprehensive, complete, and adequate for training you..." In essence God relies on His Word to perform His purposes on earth. We have compelling clarification of this fact in the following Scriptures:

"Through faith we understand that the worlds were framed by the word of God, so that things which are seen were not made of things which do appear" (Heb. 11:3).

"In the beginning God created the heaven and the earth. And the earth was without form, and void; and darkness was upon the face of the deep. And the Spirit of God moved upon the face of the waters. **And God said, Let there be light: and there was light"** (Gen. 1:1-3). In his book, *'The Power of The Prophetic Blessing'*, John Hagee shares an astonishing insight on the above scripture, "The statement "God said..." occurs ten times in the first chapter of Genesis, establishing the power of words. With one statement, God removed the force of darkness over the earth. He said, "Let there be light," and the marvellous and mysterious power of light was born...God continued to create the universe with the supernatural power of prophetic speech."

The nature and integrity of God's word is firmly established in Isaiah 55: 10-11:

"For as the rain cometh down, and the snow from heaven, and returneth not thither, but watereth the earth, and maketh it bring forth and bud, that it may give seed to the sower, and bread to the eater: So shall my word be that goeth forth out of my mouth: it shall not return unto me void, but it shall accomplish that which I please, and it shall prosper in the thing whereto I sent it."

"He sent his word, and healed them, and delivered them from their destructions." (Ps. 107:20).

3. The Word has authority. When God the Father created the universe, He did it through His Son, the Word. The Word spoke a word and there was light, life, people and heavenly bodies. When we proclaim the Word, it becomes a declaration in the spiritual kingdom – the Word still has the same power. When we call on the living Word, it has the power to give life and to re-create. The very nature and integrity of the word of God makes praying based on the word of God a tremendous treasure. On the authority of Isaiah 55:11, the following conclusions about the Word of God are valid:

   a. God sends His Word for definite purposes

   b. Every Word God sends out returns to Him

   c. No word of God returns to Him empty

   d. Every word of God accomplishes its purpose

   e. Every Word of God prospers in its mission.

   The Bible declares, "*God is not a man, that he should lie; neither the son of man, that he should repent: hath he said, and shall he not do it? or hath he spoken, and shall he not make it good?*" (Num. 23:19). IF God is His Word and God and His Word are one, as earlier established, the "Word" could safely be substituted for "God" in the above Scripture. And in Hebrews 4:12, we read that "*…the word of God is quick, and powerful, and sharper than any two edged sword, piercing even to the dividing asunder of soul and spirit, and of the joints and marrow, and is a discerner of the thoughts and intents of the heart.*"

4. "*But we will give ourselves continually to prayer, and to the ministry of the word*" (Acts 6:4). In this statement, the Apostles recognised that to be effective in prayer they must devote themselves to the ministry of the word, attesting to the fact that the word of God forms the basis of true Kingdom prayer. The Word of God offers the believer the spiritual authority to base his prayer. It gives the believer the divine guidelines that must govern his prayer. Jesus,

during His temptation alluded to this guideline in His constant reference to the phrase, "*It is written...*" (Luke. 4:4, 8, and "*It is said...*" (Luke. 4:14).

"And the devil said unto him, If thou be the Son of God, command this stone that it be made bread. And Jesus answered him, saying, **It is written***, That man shall not live by bread alone, but by every word of God. And the devil, taking him up into an high mountain, shewed unto him all the kingdoms of the world in a moment of time. And the devil said unto him, All this power will I give thee, and the glory of them: for that is delivered unto me; and to whomsoever I will I give it. If thou therefore wilt worship me, all shall be thine. And Jesus answered and said unto him, Get thee behind me, Satan:* **for it is written***, Thou shalt worship the Lord thy God, and him only shalt thou serve. And he brought him to Jerusalem, and set him on a pinnacle of the temple, and said unto him, If thou be the Son of God, cast thyself down from hence: For it is written, He shall give his angels charge over thee, to keep thee...And Jesus answering said unto him,* **It is said***, Thou shalt not tempt the Lord thy God"* (Luke 4: 1-10,14).

5. Jesus makes the indwelling of His word in the believer as a condition for answering the believer's prayer. In John 15:7 Jesus says, "*If ye abide in me, and my words abide in you,* **ye shall ask what ye will***, and it shall be done unto you*" (emphasis added). As noted above, it is not enough for the believer to know just how to pray, neither is the numbers of hours he spends in prayer or the kind of prayer he prays what is important to Jesus here. It is the conviction the believer has of the word of God that determines the final outcome of his prayer. Paul admonishes, "*Let the word of Christ dwell in you richly in all wisdom; teaching and admonishing one another in psalms and hymns and spiritual songs, singing with grace in your hearts to the Lord*" (Col. 3:16).

While man looks on his prayer, Jesus looks on man's relationship with Him and the place His eternal Word occupies in man's life. In this the admonition of Paul, *"Let the word of Christ dwell in you richly in all wisdom; teaching and admonishing one another in psalms and hymns and spiritual songs, singing with grace in your hearts to the Lord "* (Col. 3:16) resonates with incredible wisdom. God only answers petitions that his Son has had a hand in formulating. *"If we ask anything according to his will he hears us"* (1 John 5:14).

6. Praying Scripture-centred prayer enhances spiritual growth. You actually learn what God says about certain situations, and by praying His Word you will see His results. Many people have testified that just by praying the healing scriptures they have been healed, physically and mentally.

7. The Word reveals God's will and priorities. God introduces His will in the Word. If our prayer lives are to be revitalised so that prayer becomes both fruitful and fulfilling, we must make it a discipline to pray in accordance with the word of God, following its instruction and guidance in prayer. We must endeavour to make the revelation of God's will as revealed in His word both the foundation and basis of our prayers. When we pray the Word we pray the will of God, and when we pray according to the will of God, the Word says our prayers will be answered (1 John 5:14-15). Scriptural praying is allowing the revelation of God's will as revealed through His Word to form the very basis of our prayers.

8. God's word is *"living and powerful"* (Heb. 4:12); God's word is *Spirit and life"* (John 6:63). Consequently, when our prayer is based on the word of God, we have the confidence that our prayers are *living, powerful, spiritual* (not in the flesh, John 6:63), and administering *life*.

Consequently, when our prayer is based on the word of God, we have the confidence that our prayers are living, powerful, spiritual (not in the flesh, John 6:63), and administering life.

9. Further, faith which is an indispensable ingredient of any Bible-based prayer is a product of the word of God: "So then faith cometh by hearing, and hearing by the word of God" (Rom. 10:17). The deep importance of this truth reverberates with greater clarity when we consider the concept of faith in light of Romans 14:23, "...for whatsoever is not of faith is sin" (emphasis added). "... the just shall *live by his faith*" (Habk.2:4, Rom. 1:17, Gal. 3:11) remains God's indisputable *standard of living* for the believer. So faith then becomes the *Sine qua non* (essential and indispensable requirement) of **any** relationship with God. Essentially, what that means is that the whole spectrum of the believer's life, not just his prayer, is governed by faith. And the source of faith, as seen, is the word of God (Rom. 10:17). What you need is to know the mind of God through His word and you are smooth sailing. The following experience of D. L Moody on the subject is stupendous and illustrates the point, "One day I read in the tenth chapter of Romans, 'Now faith cometh by hearing, and hearing by the word of God.' I had closed my Bible, and prayed for Faith. I now opened my Bible, and began to study, and Faith has been growing ever since."

10. Finally, we must also trace the importance of scripture-based praying to the fact that both the word of God and prayer are weapons of warfare, a combination of which undoubtedly, yields greater results. The Bible says, "*For the weapons of our warfare are not carnal but mighty in God for pulling down strongholds, casting down arguments and every high thing that exalts itself against*

the knowledge of God, bringing every thought into captivity to the obedience of Christ, and being ready to punish all disobedience when you obedience is fulfilled" (2 Cofinthians10:4-6). It is important that you study these verses properly and understand them. Pray that the Holy Spirit opens your eyes to see the deep meaning of each word.

Kenneth E. Hagin acknowledges that believing according to the word requires a conscious decision to live beyond your five senses. Faith is a *sixth* sense, so to speak. Faith is believing God's word in your heart or spirit…you see, your head will fight you if it hasn't been renewed sufficiently with the word of God. Your own mental thinking will try to keep you in the natural realm. But if you'll just persist in believing God's word in your heart, you'll grow strong in faith. And no matter what your head tells you, you'll get results The Bible says so. I know from experience. I've proven the Word to be so time after time in the midst of tremendous opposition."

In sum, it must be stressed that you only receive answers to your prayers when such prayers are in agreement with the word of God. When you have a need you want to pray about, first search the Scripture that promises what you need, meditate on it, and let it be the basis of your prayer. It gives a foundation for your faith. That leads us to the next topic of great importance:

PRAYING THE WORD: THE BELIEVER'S DESTRUCTIVE WEAPON

Hudson Taylor said: "We (Christians) are supernatural people: born again through a supernatural birth, driven by a supernatural power and nourished by supernatural food, taught by a supernatural Teacher from a supernatural Book." From E.W. Kenyon's perspective, fasting and long hours of prayer do not build faith.....reading books about faith and men of faith and their exploits stirs in the heart a deep passion for faith, but does not build faith. The Word alone is the source of faith. Andrew Murray contends that little of the Word with little prayer is death to the spiritual life. Much of the Word with little prayer gives us sickly life. Much of prayer with little of the Word gives more life, but without steadfastness. A full measure of the Word and prayer each day gives a healthy and powerful life. Faith comes from hearing the message, and the message is heard through the Word (Rom.10:17). Without faith we cannot pray because prayer without faith does not please God (Heb.11:6). God affirms His Word and His promises with an oath (Heb.6:16-17). He cannot be unfaithful to His Word. God reveals Himself in His Word. He shows His character to us through His Word. The promises in the Word are in line with His being and His character, to which He can never be unfaithful.

The Bible says, *"For the word of God is living and powerful, and sharper than any two-edged sword, piercing even to the division of soul and spirit, and of joints and marrow, and is a discerner of the thoughts and intents of the heart"* (Heb. 4:12).

Word praying means taking the words of the scripture, under the illumination of the Holy Spirit and turning them into prayer, applying them to specific situations.

One excellent way of praying powerful prayer, therefore, is praying the scriptures. It is an incredible experience to turn the Bible, especially the Psalms into a prayer manual. Praying the word is a tremendous way of making sure that you are praying within the will of God. The Bible is the will of God. That way one is certain not to be praying amiss, according to James 4:3, *"You ask, and receive not, because you ask amiss, that you may spend it upon your lusts."*

Word praying means taking the words of the scripture, under the illumination of the Holy Spirit and turning them into prayer, applying them to specific situations. A key element of scripture praying is personalising the words of the Bible to suit your specific needs. For instance, when you come across phrases like, "thou shall be blessed...", you could either say, "I shall be blessed" or, better still, "I am blessed", as we see in Deuteronomy 28 below.

When we speak and pray the Scriptures, we are coming into agreement with God, and His power is released to answer our prayers. It is a *breed* of prayer of faith or declaratory prayer, and it is *"mighty through God to the pulling down of strongholds"* (2 Cor. 10:4).

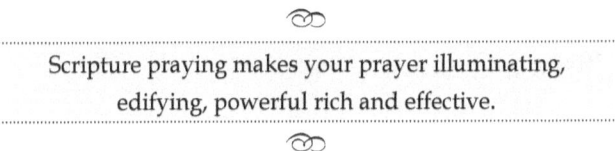

Scripture praying makes your prayer illuminating, edifying, powerful rich and effective.

This is a powerful way of engaging in warfare, especially in the area of overcoming satanic strongholds. Just recall the temptation of Jesus by Satan for a brief moment. Jesus employed no other weapon than the one He deemed most powerful and formidable for the occasion – The word. Praying the word of God is the believer's weapon of mass destruction, Satan finds scripture praying most frustrating and uncomfortable.

Scripture praying makes your prayer illuminating, edifying, powerful, rich and effective. It so anchors your prayer on the word of God that you know you are praying according to the perfect will of God!

God is always moved by His word, he cannot deny His word. The main method by which God speaks to man is through His word – the Bible, and the main way through which man speaks to God is through prayer. When a man reads God's word and hears God speaking to Him through it and he responds to what he has heard through prayer and obedience, fellowship with God is established.

It is interesting to note that the early disciples of Jesus practised word praying when they faced severe persecution from the Jewish authorities. They were arrested, beaten warned not to preach in the name of Jesus Christ any more.

Instead of being discouraged, they went on to do spiritual warfare in prayer in the mighty name of Jesus. The manner in which they prayed is a clear example of scripture praying. Quoting Psalm 2, the disciples prayed:

"And being let go, they went to their own company, and reported all that the chief priests and elders had said unto them. And when they heard that, they lifted up their voice to God with one accord, and said, Lord, thou art God, which hast made heaven, and earth, and the sea, and all that in them is: Who by the mouth of thy servant David hast said, Why did the heathen rage, and the people imagine vain things? The kings of the earth stood up, and the rulers were gathered together against the Lord, and against his Christ. For of a truth against thy holy child Jesus, whom thou hast anointed, both Herod, and Pontius Pilate, with the Gentiles, and the people of Israel, were gathered together, For to do whatsoever thy hand and thy counsel determined before to be done. And now, Lord, behold their threatenings: and grant unto thy servants, that with all boldness they may speak thy word, By stretching forth thine hand to heal; and

that signs and wonders may be done by the name of thy holy child Jesus" (Acts 4:23-30).

Also Old Testament prayers like Ezra's prayer in Nehemiah 9:6-37 are rehearsals of biblical history and biblical texts.

Later on the Bible says, *"With great power the apostles continued to testify to the resurrection of the Lord Jesus, and much grace was upon them all"* (Acts 4:33). What an incentive to get into the practice of scripture praying! It is powerful, it is result-oriented!

Do not forget, everything God created He brought under the authority of His word. So the word of God has both authoritative and persuasive influence over every creature of God. For instance, the Bible teaches *"Through faith we understand that the **worlds were framed by the word of God**, so that things which are seen were not made of things which do appear"* (Heb.11:3, emphasis added). By the same token, the word of God not only pre-exists all of God's creatures (John 1:1), it maintains dominance and superiority over everything that exists in the universe, including mankind.

We find this truth fully substantiated in the following scriptures:

"O earth, earth, earth, hear the word of the LORD" (Jer. 22:29)

"Give ear, O ye heavens, and I will speak; and hear, O earth, the words of my mouth" (Deut. 32:1).

"*Hear, you peoples, all of you, listen, earth and all who live in it, that the Sovereign LORD may bear witness against you, the Lord from his holy temple*" (Micah 1:2).

Scripture praying can further be illustrated as follows:

"*Because I hearken diligently unto the voice of the LORD my God, to observe and to do all His commandments, the LORD has set me on high above all nations of the earth, as a result...I am blessed in the city, I am blessed in the field. The fruit of my body is blessed, and the fruit of my ground is blessed, and the fruit of my cattle is blessed, the increase of thy kine is blessed, and the flocks of thy sheep are blessed. I am blessed when I come in, and I am blessed when I go out. The LORD shall cause my enemies that rise up against me to be smitten before my face: they shall come out against me one way, and flee before me seven ways. The LORD shall command the blessing upon me in my storehouses, and in all that I set my hand unto; and He shall bless me in the land which the LORD my God gives me...And all people of the earth shall see that I am called by the name of the LORD; and they shall be afraid of me. And the LORD shall make me plenteous in goods, in the fruit of my body, and in the fruit of my cattle, and in the fruit of my ground, in the land which the LORDS wore unto my fathers to give me. The LORD shall open unto me His good treasure, the heaven to give the rain unto my land in his season, and to bless all the work of my hand: and I shall lend unto many nations, and I shall not borrow. And the LORD shall make me the head, and not the tail; and I shall be above only, and I shall not be beneath; as I hearken unto the commandments of the*

LORD my God, which He commands me, to observe and to do them" (Deut.28:1, 3-8, 10-13).

"Though my beginning was small, yet my latter end should greatly increase" (Job 8:7).

"Because I obey and serve the Lord, I shall spend my days in prosperity, and my years in pleasures" (Job 36:11).

"Lord your anger lasts but for a moment, in your favour is life: my weeping endures only for a night but my joy comes in the morning" (Psalm 30:5).

"I shall not die, but live, and declare the works of the LORD" (Psalm 118:17).

"You, eternal God are my refuge, and underneath are your everlasting arms. You will drive out my enemies before me, saying, "Destroy him!" (Deut. 33:27).

"My sun shall no more go down; neither shall my moon withdraw itself: for the LORD shall be my everlasting light, and the days of my mourning shall are ended" (Isaiah 60:20).

Chapter 22

PRAYER - THANKSGIVING, PRAISE AND WORSHIP

True biblical prayer is often inextricably linked with thanksgiving, praise and worship. In fact, thanksgiving, praise and worship are themselves different expressions of our desires (prayer) to God. As God's redeemed people, we are called to offer these as acts of reverence to God.

> *But you are a chosen generation, a royal priesthood, a holy nation, His own special people, that you may proclaim the praises of Him who called you out of darkness into His marvelous light* (1 Pet. 2:9).

We were chosen to declare praise, worship and thanksgiving. We are called into the ministry of Royal Priesthood with the concomitant privileges and responsibility of offering God praise, worship and thanksgiving.

In his insightful work, Derek Prince observes that "three things are closely associated: thanksgiving, praise and worship; yet they are distinct. The trio can be likened to the colours of the rainbow that are distinct but blend into one another. Very simply, I would say that we thank God for what He does, particularly for what He does for us. We praise God for His greatness. But worship relates us to God in His holiness".

Psalm 100:4 tells us to, "*Enter his gates with thanksgiving and his courts with praise*" Those are the two steps of approach to God. You come into the gates with thanksgiving, and then you move further into the courts with praise. Even at that, there is a point of variance between the two concepts: While thanksgiving is the expression of our gratitude to God for the blessings and benefits we have received and experienced from Him, praise expresses our admiration of God's greatness, perfection, exceptional intervention in crises situation or His work at creation. Let me point out an incredible out-working of thanksgiving in the ministry of Jesus. In John 6, we find the account of Jesus feeding the five thousand:

> *And Jesus took the loaves; and when he had given thanks, he distributed to the disciples, and the disciples to them that were set down; and likewise of the fishes as much as they would.*

It is interesting to note, reading this scripture that Jesus did not pray. All He did was to give thanks. It was the giving of thanks over five loaves and two fishes that made this small amount of food to be sufficient to feed five thousand people. Amazing!

Note what the Scriptures say a little further on:

> *(Howbeit there came other boats from Tiberias nigh unto the place where they did eat bread, after that the Lord had given thanks:).* What a confirmation.

Indeed, what released the miracle was an attitude of thanksgiving; thanksgiving then becomes a "multiplying agent" of God's resources in the believer's life.

Praise and worship are powerful weapons God has given to His Church. Next to the word of God, two of our most powerful offensive weapons against the enemy are praise and worship. Battles were fought and won by God's people in the Old Testament by simply singing praises to God. Paul and Silas understood the secret of the divine explosives that are inherent in praise and worship (Acts 16:25-34).

This is briefly laid out in the following scripture:

> *Let the high praises of God be in their mouth, and a two-edged sword in their hand; To execute vengeance upon the heathen, and punishments upon the people; To bind their kings with chains, and their nobles with fetters of iron; To execute upon them the judgment written: this honour have all his saints. Praise ye the* LORD *(Psalm 149:6-9).*

Interestingly, the Bible says in Psalm 8:2:

> *Out of the mouth of babes and sucklings hast thou ordained strength because of thine enemies, that thou mightest still the enemy and the avenger.*

Satan is "the enemy and avenger". He needs to be silenced because he is constantly accusing the believers in Christ Jesus before God (Rev. 12:10). The responsibility to silence the devil is ours, not God's, because He has given us the power and authority to do so (Psalm 91: 13, Luke 10:19).

Every word in the Bible, Old Testament and New that means "worship" or is translated "worship" is always descriptive of an attitude. It is inherent in man's nature to worship. We tend to worship what we love, adore, admire and seek after. Mankind is invariably dedicated to what he worships. It is not difficult therefore, to identify who our God is in reality. Whatever occupies a man's heart becomes his "god" (Ezek. 14:3). Whoever man adores and worships becomes his "god". This heart requirement is so vital because the power of worship is based on our right relationship with God. Our worship is indicative of the integrity of our hearts towards God.

There are also certain specific postures associated with worship all through the Scripture — bowing the head, bowing down the upper part of the body and, in particular, extending the arms with hands reaching upwards. All of these are important and carries eternal significance only if the heart is right towards God. In the soul-inspiring words of Campbell Morgan, "The supreme thing is worship. The attitude of worship is the attitude of a subject bent before the King... The fundamental thought is that of prostration, of bowing down."

The Connection

Psalm 100:4 offers a clear approach into God's presence, *"Enter into his gates with thanksgiving, and into his courts with praise: be thankful unto him, and bless his name."* In context, thanksgiving serves as a key that unlocks the gate into God's presence, while praise takes one further into God's court where requests are made.

Just as one visiting a friend cannot begin to speak to him two or three houses from where he lives, but would, of necessity, gain access to him at the intended address before he begins to speak and share intimacy with his friend, it is absolutely impossible to gain audience with God without first, accessing His presence through thanksgiving and praise. For prayer to mount up to God's presence, thanksgiving and praise must unlock both the gate and the court where He is. This unveils the significance of Psalm 91: 1-2: *"O come, let us sing unto the LORD: let us make a joyful noise to the rock of our salvation.* **Let us come before his presence with thanksgiving***, and make a joyful noise unto him with psalms"* (emphasis added).

God's presence cannot be approached arbitrarily. It is not a play ground or an open field. Neither is it readily opened to everyone. For one to seek and find

God, the prescribed pattern must be followed. This is what makes God's presence a much secured place to be. In Psalm 91: 1-7, David went to the heart of the matter:

*"He that dwelleth in the secret place of the most High shall abide under the shadow of the Almighty. I will say of the LORD, He is my refuge and my fortress: my God; in him will I trust. Surely he shall deliver thee from the snare of the fowler, and from the noisome pestilence. He shall cover thee with his feathers, and under his wings shalt thou trust: his truth shall be thy shield and buckler. Thou shalt not be afraid for the terror by night; nor for the arrow that flieth by day; Nor for the pestilence that walketh in darkness; nor for the destruction that wasteth at noonday. A thousand shall fall at thy side, and ten thousand at thy right hand; **but it shall not come nigh thee**"* (emphasis added).

Notice the phrase, *"it shall not come nigh thee"* in verse 7. It points to what the psalmist says in verse 2 – the secret place being a refuge and fortress. The Bible says, *"The name of the LORD is a fortified tower; the righteous run to it and are safe"* (Pro. 18:10, NIV). The practicality of the security that is available in the presence of God was enjoyed by David (1 Sam. 23:14).

The way into God's presence, therefore, is thanksgiving, praise, worship and prayer, and these also serve as building blocks to prevailing prayer.

PRAYER AND FAITH

> *But without faith it is impossible to please him:for he that cometh to God must believe that he is, and that he is a rewarder of them that diligently seek him"*(Heb. 11:6). Paul drove the point home, thus: *"He that spared not his own Son, but delivered him up for us all, how shall he not with him also freely give us all things?* (Rom. 8:32).

However, what makes God consider the prayer of the Saints is faith. Faith is a vital principle of prayer, because prayer is the supreme expression of our faith in God. God does business with us on the basis of our faith. Communication with God ceases to be prayer if it is void of the essential ingredient of faith.

Smith Wigglesworth puts the position quite succinctly when he said:

"I believe that there is only one way to all the treasures of God, and that is the way of faith. By faith and faith alone do we enter into knowledge of the attributes, become partakers of the beatitudes, and participate in the glories of our ascended Lord. All His promises are yea and Amen to them who believe."

It is apt to reason that you pray in the first place because you have faith. If you do not have faith, you will not pray because prayer would not serve any purpose. Faith therefore, is the rail upon which the train of prayer moves. Faith, in relation to prayer is a mind-set that fosters on the integrity of the word of God and trust in the Lord Jesus.

> *For the invisible things of him from the creation of the world are clearly seen, being understood by the things that are made, even his eternal power and Godhead; so that they are without excuse…* (Rom. 1:20).

Jesus makes the connection between faith and prayer. Consider these scriptures:

"And Jesus answering saith unto them, Have faith in God. For verily I say unto you, That whosoever shall say unto this mountain, Be thou removed, and be thou cast into the sea; and shall not doubt in his heart, but shall believe that those things which he saith shall come to pass; he shall have whatsoever he saith. Therefore I say unto you, What things soever ye desire, when ye pray, believe that ye receive them, and ye shall have them" (Mark 11:22-24).

"Jesus answered and said unto them, Verily I say unto you, If ye have faith, and doubt not, ye shall not only do this which is done to the fig tree, but also if ye shall say unto this mountain, Be thou removed, and be thou cast into the sea; it shall be done. And all things, whatsoever ye shall ask in prayer, believing, ye shall receive" (Matt. 21:21-22).

"And whatsoever ye shall ask in my name, that will I do, that the Father may be glorified in the Son" (John 14:13).

In the Jewish way of thinking, a person's name is directly linked to the person's character and prerogatives. "Prerogatives" refers to any exclusive right or privilege a person may hold. In Jesus' case, His prerogative is the right to rule, to be the Master in relation to our being the servant. This means that prayer in Jesus name is prayer that fits within the boundaries of Christ's character, seeks the will of Jesus, and is submissive to the authority of Jesus. In essence, prayer in Jesus' name is prayer offered in faith that Jesus is trustworthy, and therefore, worthy of the positions and authority He holds over us.

Faith is demonstrated in prayer in many ways. We exhibit faith in prayer through "believing". The emphasis throughout Hebrews 11 on "faith" simply means "believe."

> *For verily I say unto you, That whosoever shall say unto this mountain, Be thou removed, and be thou cast into the sea; and shall not doubt in his heart, but shall believe that those things which he saith shall come to pass; he shall have whatsoever he saith. Therefore I say unto you, What things soever ye desire, when ye pray, believe that ye receive them, and ye shall have them* (mark 11:23-24).

The prayer of faith depends on our firm and unwavering belief to work. This implies that we fail to receive what we ask in prayer when we are in doubt or are overwhelmed with our senses. The Bible says that Abraham "*...against hope believed in hope ... according to that which was spoken...And being not weak in faith, he considered not his own body...*" (Rom. 4:18,19). Abraham was undoubtedly, not operating by the five senses but by the sense of faith. He did not consider the natural circumstances. He believed what God had promised him. And that is what faith is. Faith believes that God will do what He promised. So, for Abraham, the promise of having a son in his old age was fulfilled long before Isaac was born.

Sometimes the fulfilment of a divine promise may seem to us to be delayed, but it will manifest in *"due season if we faint not"* (Gal.6:9).

A brief journey to the 'gallery of faith' (Heb. 11) would, no doubt, give you a great understanding of what an asset faith is to the believer: The exceptional and incredible record the Bible holds of some legends of faith never cease to amaze me. I find the following record most inspiring and insightful:

> *And what shall I more say? for the time would fail me to tell of Gedeon, and of Barak, and of Samson, and of Jephthae; of David also, and Samuel, and of the prophets: Who through faith* **subdued kingdoms, wrought righteousness, obtained promises, stopped the mouths of lions. Quenched the violence of fire, escaped the edge of the sword, out of weakness were made strong, waxed valiant in fight, turned to flight the armies of the aliens. Women received their dead raised to life again:** *and others were tortured, not accepting deliverance; that they might obtain a better resurrection* (Heb. 11:32-35, emphasis included).

Another way we often demonstrate faith in prayer is through expectation. In context, "expectation" means "relating" with the end product of one's prayer as if it had already manifested. It is you being engrossed in or infused with the end result of your prayer. Romans 4:17 affirms that it is the nature of God to call *"those things which be not as though they were."*

> Another way we often demonstrate faith in prayer is through expectation. In context, "expectation" means "relating" with the end product of one's prayer as if it has already manifested.

However, we see a sharp contrast from the propositions put forward under this heading in the next chapter.

Chapter 23

A CHURCH IN CONSTANT PRAYER WITHOUT FAITH

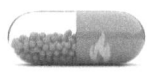

A great number of believers, sadly, perpetuate the grave error this body of believers committed in this scripture. It is shocking to know the staggering number of faith-filled believers that spend quality time in prayer, with little or no expectation, whatsoever, of the final outcome of their prayer. They pray quite alright, they have the right confessions, no doubt, but there is little or no expectation of the object of their prayer. They are not in expectation! We see this apparent deficiency in the prayer forum of one of the most powerful and influential churches of its time. In Acts 12: 1-5 we read:

> Now about that time Herod the king stretched forth his hands to vex certain of the church. And he killed James the brother of John with the sword. And because he saw it pleased the Jews, he proceeded further to take Peter also. (Then were the days of unleavened bread.) And when he had apprehended him, he put him in prison, and delivered him to four quaternions of soldiers to keep him; intending after Easter to bring him forth to the people. Peter therefore was kept in prison: but prayer was made without ceasing of the church unto God for him.

As the record indicates, this local assembly of believers were under persecution of great proportion. James, one of the leading figures of the Church, had been assassinated under the direct instruction of King Herod, *"And he killed James the brother of John with the sword"*– an event, from all indications that held the Church in utter bewilderment. If the Church ever thought that this was but an isolated event, they were profoundly mistaken. The true scale of what the Church was up against was well illustrated in the following words:

> *...he proceeded further to take Peter also. (Then were the days of unleavened bread.) And when he had apprehended him, he put him in prison, and delivered him to four quaternions of soldiers to keep him; intending after Easter to bring him forth to the people* (Acts 12 3-4).

For the first time the Church realised that it was faced with a sustained, systematic attack from the political powers of the time. The Church had to do something about it; it could not be seen to be passive in the face of an attack of this magnitude; after-all, the church is empowered to face up to challenges of this amplitude:

> *For though we walk in the flesh, we do not war after the flesh: (For the weapons of our warfare are not carnal, but mighty through God to the pulling down of strong holds;) Casting down imaginations, and every high thing that exalteth itself against the knowledge of God, and bringing into captivity every thought to the obedience of Christ* (2 Cor. 10:3-5).

The Church understood that the present battle, though orchestrated by the political powers of the day, was fuelled by strong accolades of spiritual powers.

Therefore, it was not a battle to be fought with physical weapons: *"For we wrestle not against flesh and blood, but against principalities, against powers, against the rulers of the darkness of this world, against spiritual wickedness in high places"* (Eph. 6:12). A vast array of more *powerful* and *sophisticated* weapons (truly weapons of mass destruction, fit for the battle) must be deployed. With their choice of spiritual weapon – prayer – the church no doubt, understood its position of authority in the spirit realm, and faced up to the challenge! The present day church must recognise its sphere of power and authority. If the church leaves the sphere which God has given it, it no longer has God-ordained authority.

Let us consider the following scriptures on the subject:

"Behold, I give unto you power to tread on serpents and scorpions, and over all the power of the enemy: and nothing shall by any means hurt you" (Luke 10:19).

"So shall they fear the name of the Lord from the west, and His glory from the rising of the sun. When the enemy shall come in like a flood, the Spirit of the Lord shall lift up a standard against him" (Isaiah 59:19).

"And it shall come to pass in that day, that his burden shall be taken away from off thy shoulder, and his yoke from off

thy neck, and the yoke shall be destroyed because of the anointing" (Isaiah 10:27).

"Verily I say unto you, Whatsoever ye shall bind on earth shall be bound in heaven: and whatsoever ye shall loose on earth shall be loosed in heaven. Again I say unto you, That if two of you shall agree on earth as touching an thing that they shall ask, it shall be done for them of my Father which is in heaven" (Matt. 18:18, 19).

These saints had an incredible burden in intercession - battering the gates of heaven with storms of prayer. They took the kingdom of heaven by violence. They understood that a degree of violence was needed to get certain spiritual work established. They were focused, determined and resolute! Their souls ascended to God in thick intercession; petitioning God as the flame of their prayer mounted heaven-ward. They were not going to settle for anything less than Peter being released from prison.

God has covenanted in His word:

> *If my people, which are called by my name, shall humble themselves, and pray, and seek my face, and turn from their wicked ways; then will I hear from heaven, and will forgive their sin, and will heal their land* (2 Chr. 7:14).

Catharine of Sienna was right when she said, "Perfect prayer is not attained by the use of many words, but through deep desire. This particular faith in prayer undoubtedly engages itself in *apprehending* the answer to prayers."Coleridge illustrates the point very enthusiastically, "Believe me, to pray with all your heart and strength, with the reason and the will, to believe vividly that God will listen to your voice through Christ, and, verily, to do the thing he pleaseth thereupon – this is…the greatest achievement of the Christian's warfare upon earth…"

But as we will sadly come to realise, though these brethren had a prayer burden, fiery zeal, flowed gracefully in the power of the Holy Spirit, had resilience and a mission spirit, they lacked the spirit of expectancy - they were not prepared for the final outcome of their labour in prayer! The following lesson from the experience of this church may serve to point a caution which has sometimes been too lightly heeded – praying with the final outcome of your request in view. They were, however, to be commended for their courageous, uncompromising and unyielding zeal for labouring fervently in prayer. However, the greatest ingredient of prevailing prayer was missing; faith!

For emphasis, the account of Peter's imprisonment reads:

"Peter therefore was kept in prison: but prayer was made without ceasing of the church unto God for him. And when Herod would have brought him forth, the same night Peter was sleeping between two soldiers, bound with two chains: and the keepers before the door kept the prison" (Acts 12:5-6).

However, verse 7 marked an incredible turning point in this episode:

> "And, behold, the angel of the Lord came upon him, and a light shined in the prison: and he smote Peter on the side, and raised him up, saying, Arise up quickly. And his chains fell off from his hands.

From this point, we no longer heard of what the Church was doing *in prayer*, but what heaven was doing in consequence – unleashing astonishing miracles. The reason is not far-fetched: prayer is the 'mother' of the supernatural. The supernatural is the product of intense prayer. Where prayer abounds, the supernatural abounds even more. As a result, the following miracles were recorded:

> Prayer is the 'mother' of the supernatural. The supernatural is the product of intense prayer. Where prayer abounds, the supernatural abounds even more.

- Heaven's intervention
- Angelic visitation – verse 7
- Breaking the chains of the enemy from Peter's life – verse 7
- Great deliverance – leading Peter out of prison: verse 8
- The gates of the prison, especially the iron gate, supernaturally opening – verse 10.

Hear Peter's account of the astonishing experience: "… *Now I know of a surety, that the Lord hath sent his angel, and hath delivered me out of the hand of Herod, and from all the expectation of the people of the Jews"* (verse 11).

For Peter, this experience was only reminiscent of a similar angelic intervention, leading to dramatic release from prison (Acts 5:19).

In verses 12-17 we are told

> And when he [Peter] had considered the thing, he came to the house of Mary the mother of John, whose surname was Mark; where many were gathered together praying. And as Peter knocked at the door of the gate, a damsel came to hearken, named Rhoda. And when she knew Peter's voice, she opened not the gate for gladness, but ran in, and told how Peter stood before the gate. And they said unto her, Thou art mad. But she constantly affirmed that it was even so. Then said they, It is his angel. But Peter continued knocking: and when they had opened the door, and saw him, they were astonished. But he, beckoning unto them with the hand to hold their peace, declared unto them how the Lord had brought him out of the prison. And he said, Go shew these things unto James, and to the brethren. And he departed, and went into another place.

They had been praying, without ceasing for Peter's release (12:5), yet they found it difficult to believe that God had answered their prayer. The problem was that they simply were not expecting Peter's release. They had zeal but no faith. Much could, however, be said about Rhoda's faith! A young woman who prayed with her ears at the door, expecting the miracle being prayed for to manifest. Rhoda was in all ramifications, sensitive in the spirit to know the next move which is an accurate description of a true spirit – inspired prayer. Notice when she heard the knock on the door, she acted spontaneously – she knew something had shifted in the spirit realm. Second, Rhoda *identified* Peter's voice. She knew in essence, 'this is what we have been labouring in prayer for.' She was so certain in her mind that nothing could convince her otherwise, she could not be dissuaded from her findings! Even when the praying brethren, men and women of various spiritual rankings erroneously accused her of being 'mad' due to her revelation, the Bible says, "... **she constantly affirmed that it was even so"** (verse 15, emphasis added). This is because she expected Peter's release to be the final outcome of their prayer, and it was! Answers to prayer often stare us in the face, but we cannot discern it.

ZECHARIAH AND ELISABETH: THE DOUBTING COUPLE.

> *There was in the days of Herod, the king of Judaea, a certain priest named Zacharias, of the course of Abia: and his wife was of the daughters of Aaron, and her name was Elisabeth. And they were both righteous before God, walking in all the commandments and ordinances of the Lord blameless. And they had no child, because that Elisabeth was barren, and they both were now well stricken in years* (Luke 1:5-7).

We find a similar experience being recorded about a wonderful, God fearing couple the Bible describes as being *"righteous before God"* (Luke 1:6). However, Elisabeth was said to have problem having children – a situation that no doubt needed heaven intervention, more so as we are told that they had become *"well stricken in age"* (Luke 1:7). Like many typical families, Zechariah and the wife had prayed and believed God for a child – a male child. But time had gone by and there was no sign that God was going to answer their prayer. Even with the passage of time, this godly couple kept this dire need of their lives before them. But this was not to be forever. Their hope of ever becoming parents began to fade with time, amidst great and excruciating pains. Solomon succinctly declares that *"Hope deferred makes the heart sick…"* (Pro. 13:12). This is no less true for ministers of God! Elizabeth's difficulty in having children could only be explained one way: she was barren! Bible precedence has shown that God does strategically close the womb of a woman, as does the "womb of a Church" so as to drive a couple to prayer.

Abraham and Sarah had turned to God in prayer when Sarah was barren, as had Isaac and Rebecca, and had Hannah. Fervent as they were in prayer for a son, nothing was coming forth as an answer from heaven! Their faith, no doubt, began to wane, accepting childlessness as fate in life. Henry Morris, however, sheds incredible illumination on the subject as he observes that there were four key people in the Bible who were said to be "well stricken in years" or "well stricken in age." The first were Abraham and Sarah (Gen. 18:11), the parents of Isaac, "who would be the forerunner, so to speak, of Israel and the dispensation of Law – just as Elizabeth and Zachariah (1:7,18) were to be parents of John the Baptist, the forerunner of Christ and the dispensation of grace." And all four, according to Henry Morris, "…were past child-bearing age when God sent both promised sons into their respective homes."

Zechariah, we are told was a Priest in Israel. And he had been appointed on this special day to burn incense in the Temple – he had been chosen by lot for this special duty. Unknown to Zechariah, this was a set-up by God. His moment had finally arrived, but he was totally oblivious of what God was about to do. The hour he had waited years, perhaps, decades for had come! The burning of incense in the Temple was but a share ritual. But God, in His sovereignty, had chosen such day that the lot fell on Zechariah to burn incense in the Temple to give him an experience of a life-time; but he was not prepared! While Zechariah, perhaps, anxiously and enthusiastically looked forward to the opportunity of one day being chosen to perform the ritual of burning incense in the Temple, he did not exercise such anticipation towards the weightier matter of having his prayer answered in a way out of the ordinary; a way that defiles precedence. Unknown to Zechariah, his life was about to change forever! Not only was he going to soon become a parent, Zechariah was to be a sovereign vessel, the father of a man who, "in the spirit of and power of Elijah" would turn the hearts of the fathers to their children..." (Malachi 4:6). This was to be a blessing out of the ordinary; a male child with a heaven mandate and eternal mission to earth. The Bible testifies of him, "There was a man sent from God, whose name was John The same came for a witness, to bear witness of the Light that all men through him might believe. He was not that Light, but was sent to bear witness of that Light" (John 1:6-8, emphasis added). Zechariah's story was about to change. The long wait was drawing to a fascinating close. The status he had long waited for was about to become a reality. Indeed, "...*Weeping may endure for a night, but joy comes in the morning*" (Psalm 30:5). I strongly believe that God has placed this book in your hand and led you to this chapter because the "re-writer" of history wants to change your story. Cheer up, child of God; you may have waited for so long for the miracle of your life, I declare to you, delay is no bar to the fulfilment of God's promise. Your hour has come!

But, as to be seen later in the scripture under consideration, Zechariah, like our earlier example in Acts 12, had prayed with selfless zeal, but without faith for the final outcome.

> Cheer up, child of God; you may have waited for so long for the miracle of your life, I declare to you, delay is no bar to the fulfilment of God's promise.

"And there appeared unto him an angel of the Lord standing on the right side of the altar of incense. And when Zacharias saw him, he was troubled, and fear fell upon him. But the angel said unto him, Fear not, Zacharias: for thy prayer is heard; and thy wife Elisabeth shall bear thee a son, and thou shalt call his name John. And thou shalt have joy and gladness; and many shall rejoice at his birth. For he shall be great in the sight of the Lord, and shall drink neither wine nor strong drink; and he shall be filled with the Holy Ghost, even from his mother's womb. And many of the children of Israel shall he turn to the Lord their God. And he shall go before him in the spirit and power of Elias, to turn the hearts of the fathers to the children, and the disobedient to the wisdom of the just; to make ready a people prepared for the Lord. **And Zacharias said unto the angel, whereby shall I know this? for I am an old man, and my wife well stricken in years***. And the angel answering said unto him, I am Gabriel, that stand in the presence of God; and am sent to speak unto thee, and to shew thee these glad tidings. And, behold, thou shalt be dumb, and not able to speak, until the day that these things shall be performed,* **because thou believest not my words,** *which shall be fulfilled in their season"* (Luke 1:11-20, emphasis added).

What attitude should have been expected of Zechariah – one that had spent years and decades believing God for a miracle?

Let us consider a similar situation in the word of God as we attempt to answer this highly significant question. First, it is fitting to emphasise on the basis of the above scripture, the reason Zechariah was struck dumb. The answer is found in the following words: *"...because thou **believest not** my words, which shall be fulfilled in their season"* (verse 20, emphasis added). The word "believe" and "faith" share a great deal in common.

> Zechariah doubted the ability of God to wrought the miracle as promised by the angel, but Mary's reception and reaction was that of absolute dependence and reliance on God's sovereign and unlimited power.

The word translated as faith is a Greek word "pistis", meaning "God's divine persuasion", in a sense distinct from human belief (confidence), yet involving it. But truly from the word origin is the word "peitho". Peitho means to persuade, to induce one with words to *believe*. Although the words are different in English, the New Testament only has one family of words - from the root peitho (Strong's #3982 in Greek) that are translated as both 'faith' and 'belief'. Part of the reason why the Greek (in the New Testament and Hebrew in the Old Testament) words are translated as 'faith' or 'belief', according to Luke Baker, is because English doesn't have a word 'faithed' or 'faithing', so it has to use 'believed' and 'believing'. For instance, the Bible says, "Abraham believed God, and it was counted unto him for righteousness" (Heb. 4:3).

Putting the Angels word in context, it would instead of *"because thou believest not my words…"* read, 'because you have no faith in my words…'

Zechariah's case was undoubtedly, similar to that of Mary, the mother of our Lord Jesus Christ, in that they both had the same angelic visitation. As a matter of fact, the same angel – Gabriel – did the errands! And the object of the visits was to relay God's news of child birth on both occasions. However, a point of sharp contrast exists in the way the parties received the message delivered by the angel. Whilst, as seen, Zechariah doubted the ability of God to perform the miracle as promised by the angel, Mary's reception of the message as given by the angel and her reaction as a result, was that of absolute dependence and reliance on God's sovereign and unlimited power. The Bible says, *"And Mary said, Behold the handmaid of the Lord; be it unto me according to thy word. And the angel departed from her"* (Luke 1:38). In essence, Mary said "amen" to the message of the angel, and God moved supernaturally as a result, to perform His word. You see, to know God is to be in the place of victory, the place of triumph, and the place of rest. *"Now thanks be unto God, which always causeth us to triumph in Christ…"* (2 Cor.2:14).

PRAYER AND FASTING

Fasting is aimed at withdrawing from food in order to concentrate or focus on God, His holiness, His will and purposes.

Throughout Scriptures, fasting refers to abstaining from food for spiritual purposes. It stands in distinction to hunger strike, the purpose of which is to gain political power or attract attention to a good cause. It is also different from health dieting which stresses abstinence from food for physical, not spiritual, purposes. That is not to say that these forms of 'fasting' are wrong, but their objective is different from the fasting discussed in this book, which centres on the 'God's-chosen fast' as detailed in the word of God.

Fasting is aimed at withdrawing from food in order to concentrate or focus on God, His holiness, His will and purposes. Biblical fasting always centres on God and His purposes, not on man or the person observing the fast.

In Scripture, the normal means of fasting involves abstaining from all food, but not always from fluid. There were, however, occasions in the Bible where people fasted without food and water for different period of time. For example, Queen Esther fasted without food and water for three days:

> *Go, gather together all the Jews that are present in Shushan, and fast for me, and neither eat nor drink three days, night or day: I also and my maidens will fast likewise; and so will I go in unto the king, which is not according to the law: and if I perish, I perish* (Esther 4:16).

Some could argue, given the broad title of this chapter – *"Things that must accompany prayer"*, that the believer is nowhere mandated in scripture to fast. As valid as such argument could be, it must nonetheless, be argued that Jesus, in His teaching on the subject did not leave the observance of fasting at the believer's discretion either!

> The inference is clear. In particular the parallel between prayer and fasting is without doubt. If Jesus expected His disciples to pray regularly, by the same token He expected them also to fast often.

In Matthew 6:16, Jesus in reference to fasting says, *"Moreover **when** ye fast, be not, as the hypocrites, of a sad countenance: for they disfigure their faces, that they may appear unto men to fast. Verily I say unto you, They have their reward."* With His choice of words, *"...when ye fast..."* instead of the opposite, 'if ye fast,' a valid argument could be advanced that Jesus, indeed, intended for His *followers* to fast.

It is to be noted that the same phrase is used by Jesus in relation alms giving, (*...when* thou doeth *thine* give arms, verse 2), prayer, (*...when* thou prayest, verse

5), which leaves the believer in no doubt, as to his obligations in connection with the three related duties.

With this qualification, Jesus assumed that all His disciples would practice all three of these duties. The inference is clear. In particular the parallel between prayer and fasting is without doubt. If Jesus expected His disciples to pray regularly, by the same token, He expected them also to fast often. Perhaps the strongest connection between prayer and fasting was made by Jesus in Matthew 17:21, *"Howbeit this kind goeth not out but by prayer and fasting."*

The background to the above scripture had to do with a seemingly impossible task the disciples of Jesus were faced with just after the transfiguration experience of Jesus. By Jesus' assessment of the situation, fasting was required to deal with the particular case. However, it should not be assumed that every time we pray it is to be with fasting.

The subject of fasting is covered in detail in the last chapter of this book, and my earlier book: "The Wonders of Fasting".

Chapter 24

PRAYER AND BOLDNESS (CONFIDENCE)

For prayer to be effective it must be accompanied with 'boldness'. The degree of boldness in a believer's life is a reflection of a number of antecedents, especially the level of faith he has in God, and the degree of assurance he possesses in God's ability to intervene and deal with a given situation.

Confidence, according to New Explorer Encyclopaedic Dictionary means, "The act of confiding, trusting, or putting faith in, reliance, belief, that in which faith is put or reliance had, freedom from doubt, belief in yourself and your abilities..."

Confidence - another word for boldness - is the force that launches our faith. According to Clefflo Dollar, it propels faith forward like the rocket boosters that send the Space Shuttle into orbit. Trying to operate your faith without the force of confidence is like trying to take off in an air-plane that has no engine.

The Bible says, *"Let us therefore come boldly unto the throne of grace, that we may obtain mercy, and find grace to help in time of need"* (Heb. 4:16). What an invitation! Notice, we have not only been invited to the throne of grace, we are told how to come – boldly. Boldness, in the context of this scripture, can be regarded as 'Heaven dress code' to the throne of grace. If you must heed the royal invitation, it is required that you adhere strictly to the dress code! It is to be said therefore, that heaven has no business with timid and unsure folks. Without boldness or confidence, your prayer lacks the requisite faith that will make it work; Hence in Hebrews 10:22-23, we are asked to draw near, *"... with a true heart in **full assurance of faith**... Let us hold fast the profession of our faith without wavering; for he is faithful that promised"* (emphasis added). Further, in 1 John 5:14, 15, the Bible says, *"And this is the confidence that we have in him, that, if we ask any thing according to his will, he heareth us."* In Hebrews 10:35-36, we are admonished, *"Cast not away therefore your confidence, which hath great recompence of reward And if we know that he hear us, whatsoever we ask, we know that we have the petitions that we desired of him."*

The mystery of approaching the throne of grace with boldness or confidence cannot be fully unravelled and accurately understood, and of course its almost infinite benefits fully appropriated if left only at the definitional threshold.

> We not only leave the presence of God with our prayer answered, something in addition takes place – we are impacted with greater confidence, trust, faith, boldness, and the power of God.

We see astonishing examples of the benefits of praying with confidence in some biblical accounts to be examined in greater details later. Paramount of these are the cases of the unwilling friend (Luke 11:5-8), the unjust Judge (Luke 18:6), the Canaanite woman (Matt. 15:21-28), to mention but a few. Without a doubt, unflinching confidence was the driving force that gave each supplicant the final victory - confidence in the approach, confidence in the sustained petitions, confidence believing in the final outcome before it materialised, and confidence in believing that the obstacles would be overcome at some point. That said, it is appropriate at this stage to point out that confidence or boldness, whilst it is a required ingredient that any supplicant must possess as he approaches God, it is also one of the many benefits or rewards he leaves the throne of grace with. In context, the believer goes to God in prayer in full assurance of faith; he leaves God's presence with a much greater level of assurance, trust, faith, confidence, and boldness.

Let us examine the following scriptures as we look at this issue further:

"For we have not an high priest which cannot be touched with the feeling of our infirmities…**Let us therefore come boldly** [confidence, NIV] **unto the throne of grace**, that we may obtain mercy, and find grace to help in time of need" (Heb. 4:15,16, emphasis added).

"Therefore I say unto you, **What things soever ye desire, when ye pray**, believe that ye receive them, and ye shall have them" (Mark 11:24, emphasis added).

"**Now when they saw the boldness** [confidence, AMSB] of Peter and John, and perceived that they were unlearned and ignorant men, they marvelled; and they took knowledge of them, that they had been with Jesus" (Acts 4:13, emphasis added).

In the first two scriptures, it is clear that we are asked to make confident approach to the throne of grace; confidence or boldness being made salient requirement to the presence of God. However, the last scripture gives an insight into the inestimable benefits of being in the presence of God. We not only leave the presence of God with our prayer answered, something in addition takes place – we are imparted with greater confidence, trust, faith, boldness, and the power of God. The more we pray the more confidence we have in God, the recipient of our prayer through the degree of intimacy that develops as a result.

PRAYER, LOVE AND FORGIVENESS

"Though I speak with the tongues of men and of angels, and have not charity, I am become as sounding brass, or a tinkling cymbal. And though I have the gift of prophecy, and understand all mysteries, and all knowledge; and though I have all faith, so that I could remove mountains,

and have not charity, I am nothing. And though I bestow all my goods to feed the poor, and though I give my body to be burned, and have not charity, it profiteth me nothing. Charity suffereth long, and is kind; charity envieth not; charity vaunteth not itself, is not puffed up, Doth not behave itself unseemly, seeketh not her own, is not easily provoked, thinketh no evil; Rejoiceth not in iniquity, but rejoiceth in the truth; Beareth all things, believeth all things, hopeth all things, endureth all things. Charity never faileth: but whether there be prophecies, they shall fail; whether there be tongues, they shall cease; whether there be knowledge, it shall vanish away. For we know in part, and we prophesy in part. And now abideth faith, hope, charity, these three; but the greatest of these is charity" (1 Cor. 13: 1-9, 13).

Love holds a cardinal position in our relationship with God and with one another. Love is to regulate and govern our conduct in God's kingdom.

It is well known that the word "charity" (Greek agape) is often translated "love" in the King James Version; and it means an unconditional, generous and unselfish concern for others.

The Bibles teaches that "God is love" (1 John 4:8). Love is the sum total of His character. According to Charles Finney, all God's other moral attributes, such as justice, mercy, and so on, are only expressions of His love. All true Christianity consists in is being like God – acting on His principles and grounds and having His feelings towards different [people]"

One notable peculiarity of this love is, undoubtedly, the fact that "it does not seek its own" (1 Cor. 13:5). This principle of this teaching runs through the Bible like a golden thread. Matthew 16:25 affirms that, *"Whoever desires to save his life will lose it."* "An established principle of God's government", he insists, "is that if a person aims supremely at his own interests, he will lose his own interests." The same principle is taught later in the epistles: "Let no one seek his own, but each one his neighbor's good" (Matt. 10:24, World English Bible). Also from a very personal experience, Paul writes:

"Even as I please all men in all things, not seeking mine own profit, but the profit of many that they may be saved" (v. 33). Finally, *"Let every one of us please his neighbour for his good to edification"*, Paul admonishes (Rom. 15:2). Therefore making the interests of others our supreme objective is more consistent with the principles of the law, the gospels and the epistles.

Matthew Henry reminds us that "Charity is much to be preferred to the gifts on which the Corinthians prided themselves…To sum up the excellences of charity, it is preferred not only to gifts, but to other graces, to faith and hope. Faith fixes on the Divine revelation and assents thereto, relying on the Divine Redeemer. Hope fastens on future happiness, and waits for that; but in heaven, faith will be swallowed up in actual sight, and hope in enjoyment. There is no room to believe and hope, when we see and enjoy.

But there, love will be made perfect. There we shall perfectly love God. And there we shall perfectly love one another. Blessed state! How much surpassing the best below! God is love, 1 John 4:8,16. Where God is to be seen as he is, and face to face, there charity is in its greatest height; there only will it be perfected."

It should be stressed that a proper study of the word of God reveals that love for God and love for man are inextricably tied. For instance, our relationship with God must be right if we expect God to answer our prayer. In Mark 12:30 we read, *"And thou shalt love the Lord thy God with all thy heart, and with all thy soul, and with all thy mind, and with all thy strength: this is the first commandment."* God expects us to love Him exceptionally – holding nothing back. Notice, God called this the first commandment! He rightly placed it where it belongs – first, which gives the sense of being the greatest commandment. However, in the following verse, we are told, *"And the second is like, namely this, Thou shalt love thy neighbour as thyself. There is none other commandment greater than these"* (v 31). Notice God's estimation of these commandments. He says *"There is none other commandment greater than these."* Now, in His supreme order of priority, God places Himself first in the heart of man. Who comes next? *"Thy neighbour as thyself"* – the same degree of love you have for yourself is what God requires of you for your neighbours; and it should be said that the emphasis in verse 31 is more on your neighbour than on yourself. The spotlight is nearly always on your relationship with, or better still, on how you treat people, unbelievers alike. The visible proof of what we profess to be – Christians - is the right attitude; that being what makes us "the salt of the earth" (Matt. 5:13) and "the light of the world" (Matt. 5:14). Hear God's verdict, *"By this shall all men know that ye are my disciples, if ye have love one to another"* (John 13:35). That remains His Supreme standard; love for one another! It is a well-known fact that many people do good deeds (charitable deeds) but do not have faith in Jesus Christ; others profess faith in Jesus but rarely produce good works. A deficit in either faith or good deeds will mean a bad representation of God's image and glory on the earth.

Andrew Murray affirms, "My relationship with God is part of my relationship with men. Failure in one will cause failure in the other. It isn't necessary that it be a distant consciousness of something wrong between my neighbour and myself. An ordinary current of thinking and judging – the unloving thoughts and words I allow to pass unnoticed- can hinder my prayer. The effective prayer of faith comes from a life given up to the will and the love of God. Not as a result of what I try to be when praying, but because of what I am when I'm not praying is my prayer answered by God...neither faith nor work will profit if we don't have love. Love unites us with God; it proves the reality of faith. "Have faith in God" and "Have love to men" are both essential commandments. The right relationships with the living God above me and the living men around me", affirms the erudite writer, "are the conditions for effective prayer."

FORGIVENESS

Love sums up everything about relationships. If we always love, we will have no problem being forgiving. Our relationship with God will not suffer because our relationships with people will always be in love.

> If we always love, we will have no problem being forgiving. Our relationship with God will not suffer because our relationships with people will always be in love.

So significant was this matter in the mind of our Lord Jesus that He put the need others above our Christian sacrifice. In the Sermon on the Mount, Jesus commands us to be reconciled to a brother before even bringing an offering to Him; by so doing placing our relationships with others over worship. He says, *"But I say unto you, That whosoever is angry with his brother without a cause shall be in danger of the judgment: and whosoever shall say to his brother, Raca, shall be in danger of the council: but whosoever shall say, Thou fool, shall be in danger of hell fire. Therefore if thou bring thy gift to the altar, and there rememberest that thy brother hath ought against thee; Leave there thy gift before the altar, and go thy*

way; first be reconciled to thy brother, and then come and offer thy gift"(Matt. 5:22-24).

Jesus teaches that acceptable worship is impossible if our relationship with our brother is deficient.

Christ's teaching on forgiveness constitutes an integral component of the gospels.

In His response to the disciples request centred on knowing how to pray, Jesus gave a startling warning about unforgiveness, *"For if ye forgive men their trespasses, your heavenly Father will also forgive you But if ye forgive not men their trespasses, neither will your Father forgive your trespasses"* (Matt. 6:14-15). It is made clear from the above scripture that if we refuse to forgive others, God will deny us forgiveness. Why? Because when we refuse to forgive others, we invariably deny ourselves the grounds to merit God's forgiveness. Also in His parable of the unmerciful servant, Jesus concluded, *"So likewise shall my heavenly Father do also unto you, if ye from your hearts forgive not everyone his brother their trespasses"* (Matt. 18:35). Finally, in Mark 11:25, Jesus says, *"And whenever you stand praying, if you have anything against anyone, forgive him and let it drop (leave it, let it go), in order that your Father Who is in heaven may also forgive you your [own] failings and shortcomings and let them drop"* (Amp.).

In his thrilling and insightful thought on the subject, Henry Morris submits that, this conditional promise of forgiveness significantly occurs right after the unlimited promise of answered prayer in Mark 11:23, which indicates that even mountains could be moved by prayer. The implication is that an unforgiving attitude will hinder the faith that could otherwise move mountains.

The overall lesson here is that God sees and rewards the way you treat others, either good or bad.

The scripture is replete with teachings that caution that God places high premium on, and is immensely concerned with the way we treat others. Here are a few of them:

> *When the Son of man shall come in his glory, and all the holy angels with him, then shall he sit upon the throne of his glory: And before him shall be gathered all nations: and he shall separate them one from another, as a shepherd divideth his sheep from the goats: And he shall set the sheep on his right hand, but the goats on the left. Then shall the King say unto them on his right hand, Come, ye blessed of my Father, inherit the kingdom prepared for you from the foundation of the world: For I was an hungred, and ye gave me meat: I was thirsty, and ye gave me drink: I was a stranger, and ye took me in: Naked, and ye clothed me: I was sick, and ye visited me: I was in prison, and ye came unto me* (Matt. 25:31-36).

It would, undoubtedly appear absurd, even paradoxical to think that the King of glory, the creator of the heavens and the earth would suffer hunger, thirst, nakedness, and imprisonment. It was inconceivable! It was to be a mystery- a mystery unimaginable to think that the God that owns the cattle on a thousand hills (Psalm 50:10), would suffer these things .Of course the recipients of this rather dismal and disheartening message did not spear any moment to voice their frustration.

> Then shall the righteous answer him, saying, Lord, when saw we thee an hungred, and fed thee? or thirsty, and gave thee drink? When saw we thee a stranger, and took thee in? or naked, and clothed thee? Or when saw we thee sick, or in prison, and came unto thee? (vv 37-39).

What was the Lord's interpretation of the puzzle?

"Then shall he answer them, saying, Verily I say unto you, Inasmuch as ye did it not to one of the least of these, ye did it not to me. And these shall go away into everlasting punishment: but the righteous into life eternal" (vv 45, 46).

What a verdict! At this trial appeared both the 'sheep' (the righteous) and the 'goats' (the unrighteous) and the criterion on which they were judged was their treatment of their 'brethren'.

THE BENEFITS OF HELPING THE POOR

God rewards our acts of benevolence to the poor and needy. This is clearly established in all the scriptures we have considered so far. God wants our generosity to reflect His free giving. Remember, *"By this shall all men know"* that we are 'His' if we love one to another" (John 13:35).

In Psalm 41: 1-3, we read:

"Blessed is he that considereth the poor: the LORD will deliver him in time of trouble. The LORD will preserve him, and keep him alive; and he shall be blessed upon the earth: and thou wilt not deliver him unto the will of his enemies. The LORD will strengthen him upon the bed of languishing: thou wilt make all his bed in his sickness."

It is to be noted that this scripture opens with a promise of blessing for acts of benevolence to the poor. In other words, giving to the poor entitles the giver to the following blessings:

- The Lord delivers him in time of trouble
- The Lord preserves him
- He is kept alive (longevity)
- He is blessed upon the earth
- The Lord will not deliver him into the will of the enemy
- The Lord will strengthen him when he is sick
- The Lord will heal him in sickness (the word 'sickness' in this scripture is the same word translated 'grief' in Isaiah 53).

We see eight wonderful rewards tied to acts of benevolence to the poor and needy.

However, what is meant by "considering the poor" in the above scripture can be better understood by examining yet, the following scriptures:

"Do not withhold good from those who deserve it [to whom it is due KJV] when it's in your power to help them. If you can help your neighbor now, don't say, 'Come back tomorrow, and then I'll help you." (Pro. 3:27-28 NLT).

Notice in verse 27 it says to help those who "deserve it". I have preference for the King James Version of the Bible, it says: *"to whom it is due"*. In my opinion, no one is more deserving of our help and continuous assistance than those that are in need.

The word "withhold" in verse 27 is particularly insightful. It indicates a condition of the heart – far more than the letter of the instruction given. It no doubt, suggests a plausible situation where one is in a position to render assistance and chooses not to do so. The spiritual law of sowing and reaping is spoken of here, but the main theme of these verses is your heart - the condition of your heart to bless others. When the Lord gives us an assignment to be generous towards others and we ignore it, it displeases Him because it is His nature to meet needs. We are the instruments He uses to meet the needs of others.

In Proverb 19:17, the Bible says, *"He that hath pity [cares, Moffatt Bible], upon the poor lendethunto the Lord; and that which he hathgiven will he pay him again."*

Also consider the following scriptures:

"For the poor shall never cease out of the land: therefore I command thee, saying, Thou shalt open thine hand wide unto thy brother, to thy poor, and to thy needy, in thy land" (Deut. 15:11).

"Whoso stoppeth his ears at the cry of the poor, he also shall cry himself, but shall not be heard" (Pro. 21:13).

"He that giveth unto the poor shall not lack: but he that hideth his eyes shall have many a curse." (Pro. 28:27).

"The righteous considereth the cause of the poor: but the wicked regardeth not to know it" (Pro. 29:7).

"And let us not be weary in well doing: for in due season we shall reap, if we faint not" (Gal. 6:9).

"For God is not unrighteous to forget your work and labour of love, which ye have shewed toward his name, in that ye have ministered to the saints, and do minister" (Heb. 6:10).

"My little children, let us not love in word, neither in tongue; but in deed and in truth" (1 John 3:18).

Chapter 25

THE POWER OF IMPORTUNITY IN PRAYER

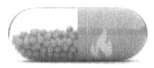

"Success is certain when the Lord has promised it. Although you may have pleaded months without evidence of answer, it is not possible that the Lord should be deaf when his people are earnest in a matter which concerns his glory. The Prophet on the top of Carmel continued to wrestle with God, and never for a moment gave way to a fear that he should be non-suited in Jehovah's courts. Six times the servant returned, but on each occasion no word was spoken but "Go again."Delayed answers often set the heart searching itself, and so lead to contrition and spiritual reformation... Elijah was a man of like passions with us: his power with God did not lie in his own merits. If his believing prayer availed so much, why not yours?.." – **Spurgeon**

Webster's New Explorer Encyclopaedic Dictionary defines importunity as: *"Overly persistent in request or demand, to press or urge with troublesome persistence."* According to the American Heritage Dictionary, importunity means *"an insistent or pressing demand."* In relation to prayer, importunity is the act of persistence and insistence in prayer, until God answers the request. It is the act of relentless, selfless and shamelessly *asking, and demanding* until you have the desired answer. We have established earlier that life does not give you what you deserve but what you consistently and insistently demand. So importunity holds a vital place in prayer as the basis on which, very often, our prayers are answered. Importunity is one of the ways in which a believer demonstrates a firm faith in God's ability and readiness to answer his prayer.

In the inspiring words of Randy Pausch, *"The brick walls are there for a reason. The brick walls are not there to keep us out. The brick walls are there to give us a chance to show how badly we want something. Because the brick walls are there to stop the people who don't want it badly enough They're there to stop the other people."*

An earlier case we looked at in Acts 12:5, the Bible records that, *"Peter ... was kept in prison:* **but prayer was made without ceasing** *of the church unto God for him"* (emphasis added). Of Hannah, it was recorded, "...as she *continued praying before the Lord..."* (1 Sam. 1:12), she had her breakthrough. And this principle appears to be built on one premise: *"He is a rewarder of them that diligently seek him"* (Heb. 11:6).

Importunity in prayer always requires a degree of resilience, tenacity, intensity, perseverance and persistence. It is prayer that pleads with God and asks Him *repeatedly* for the things we need. Importunity is undeniably, an indispensable mark of a kingdom warrior. Without it he stands the chance of being stripped of his privileges. True importune prayer then, is prayer that is drawn on and follows after God. Importunity is God's way of assessing the value you have placed on what you are asking Him to do and how desperately you need it. It is prayer that is aroused and energised by the Holy Spirit and moves our soul toward God and presses our desires upon Him repeatedly, with urgency and perseverance, while waiting until our prayers are answered. The seeming delay in answering prayer is the ground on which importunity is required.

> It appears to me that the people that have had profound personal encounters with God were those that God had to enlist in the school of protracted waiting.

In the words of E. M. Bounds, "importunate prayer is a mighty movement of the soul toward God. It is a stirring of the deepest forces of the soul, toward the throne of heavenly grace. It is the ability to hold on, press on, and wait. Restless desire, restful patience, and strength of grasp are all embraced in it. It is not an incident, or a performance, but a passion of soul. It is not a want, half-needed, but a sheer necessity… When the answer is not immediately given, the praying Christian must gather courage at each delay, and advance in urgency till the answer comes…a persistent spirit brings a man to the place where faith takes hold, claims and appropriates the blessing…

laxity, faint-heartedness, impatience timidity will be fatal to our prayer..."

The Bible presents importunity in prayer as the secret of obtaining our desire from heaven in the face of all odds. It must, however, be borne in mind that though, the waiting time that warrants importunity in prayer is always seemingly difficult to deal with in prospect; and somewhat intimidating, God never leaves us alone in the process. What is more? God not only gives us the specific desire we waited so long for, He recompenses us for the waiting time. Needless to say that in the process of time, we grow in faith, and we conform the more to the image of Jesus. The principle is explicit: as we seek God with profound desperation, according to Paul, a divine transformation takes place in our lives – we are changed into the image of the one we seek, from glory to glory (2 Cor. 3:18).

It appears to me that the people that have had profound personal encounters with God were those that God had had to enlist in the school of protracted waiting. No doubt the waiting period invariably included the fiery ordeal of great trials, the painful postponement of divine promises. At such crucial time, we must allow the period of waiting to stir our soul in fervent prayer towards the throne of grace. Undoubtedly, the enemy uses the waiting time to wage his fiercest battle against our minds, pulling its deadliest weapons against our ability to see any credit in waiting for a just and loving father. The enemy's singular mission at such times is to challenge the integrity, validity and authenticity of the word of God. Once this is achieved, the very essence of our belief, indeed, faith in God is dealt a devastating blow!

...the waiting time should be a testament to our ability to hold on, press on, and wait, a restless desire, restful patience, and strength of grasp in the face of all odds.

The waiting time should be a testament to our ability to hold on, press on, and wait; a restless desire, restful patience, and strength of grasp in the face of all odds.

For Abraham, it appeared the longer God's promise for a child was delayed, the more his faith in God grew. For the 25 years period that Abraham waited for the fulfilment of God's promise, the Bible declares:

> *And being not weak in faith, he considered not his own body now dead, when he was about an hundred years old, neither yet the deadness of Sarah's womb:*

He staggered not at the promise of God through unbelief; but was strong in faith, giving glory to God (Rom. 4:19-20).

This scripture describes the waiting period of Abraham; the period he bore the pains and agony of importunity. The 25 years of bearing the shame and reproach of childlessness, by human standard. The Bible testifies that Abraham's faith was more fervent and stronger at the end than the beginning. In other words, the longer God's promise was delayed, the more Abraham's faith grew. What a lesson for the would-be saints in the college of importunity. In the words of Bob Sorge, "our human tendency is to believe that the longer a promise remains unfulfilled, the chances of the promise coming to pass are diminished with every passing moment. But the Abraham-kind-of faith grows during the season of waiting because it is daily strengthening itself in God's word."

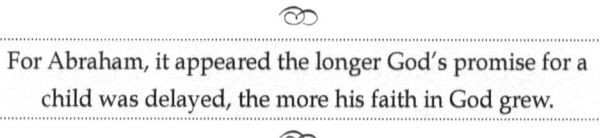

For Abraham, it appeared the longer God's promise for a child was delayed, the more his faith in God grew.

Very persuasively, John Gill asserts that there is no reason to stagger at, or hesitate about any of the promises of God, since they are made by him that cannot lie; his faithfulness is engaged to perform them; with him all things are possible; every promise is in Christ, yea and amen, and never did any fail; and yet so it is, that some of God's children, through unbelief do stagger at the promises of God; thinking either that they are too great for them, or demur upon them through difficulties which attend them: Abraham never doubted the faithfulness of God, he *was strong in faith*; nothing moved him, no difficulties discouraged him, he made no demur or remonstrate upon the promise, nor had the least hesitation in his mind about the accomplishment of it; but was fully assured that so it would be, as God had said; and thus, he was giving glory to God, ascribing to Him the glory of His veracity, faithfulness, power, grace, and goodness, as all such who are strong in faith do; such persons bring the most glory to God, and are the most comfortable in their own souls.

The seemingly absurd or contradictory proposition of a loving father putting those closest to His heart on the 'waiting line' has been an issue of much thinking and rumination for me for quite some time. On the surface, it seems to create *all sorts of paradoxes. From a human perspective, it seems no explanation would suffice. However, being a principle that is affirmed so frequently in the word of God, one cannot but arrive at the conclusion that God uses the 'golden period' of waiting to produce a greater maturity and fruitfulness in His special vessels. It appears the greater the exploits God purposes and destines to use one to accomplish in the earth, the more readily He enlists one in the school of waiting and importunity, as a means of training and equipping the vessel for the tasks ahead.*

We see this clearly in the life of one of God's greatest prophets and the forerunner of Jesus – John the Baptist:

"And the child grew, and waxed strong in spirit, **and was in the deserts till the day of his shewing unto Israel***"* (Luke 1:80, emphasis added).

John Gill affirms that John the Baptist "was not brought up in the schools of the prophets, nor in the academies of the Jews, or at the feet of any of their Rabbis and doctors; that it might appear he was not taught and sent of men, but of God: nor did he dwell in any of the cities, or larger towns, but in deserts; partly that he might be fitted for that gravity and austerity of life, he was to appear in..."

The significance and vastness of John's God-ordained assignment could very well explain the necessity of the waiting.

> *And his father Zacharias was filled with the Holy Ghost, and prophesied, saying, And thou, child, shalt be called the prophet of the Highest: for thou shalt go before the face of the Lord to prepare his ways; To give knowledge of salvation unto his people by the remission of their sins, Through the tender mercy of our God; whereby the dayspring from on high hath visited us, To give light to them that sit in darkness and in the shadow of death, to guide our feet into the way of peace* (Luke 1: 67, 76-79).

It then makes sense to expect the all-knowing and compassionate God to use the waiting time to groom His chosen vessels before they are deployed to their lines of duty.

One can then see the credit in Paul taking refuge in Arabia shortly after his dramatic conversion. He said of himself, *"Neither went I up to Jerusalem to them which were apostles before me; but I went into Arabia, and returned again unto Damascus"* (Gal. 1:17). Many of the authorities on Paul allude to the fact that he spent the first two or three years after his conversion in Arabia. This must have come within the three years that intervened between his conversion and his first visit to Jerusalem. There is no question as to the rationale behind God's leading and direction that led him to Arabia. Every vision of God has a birthing place. I believe Arabia was to Paul a place where the dust of his most startling conversion finally settled down. After such a sudden change of direction and focus, Paul undoubtedly, needed a place of seclusion for much reflection based on the vision he had near Damascus. This move was highly required for intellectual and theological readjustment before God would equip and release him for his God's ordained assignment.

It should be made abundantly clear that God's waiting time is not forever, it is for a season. Further, the waiting time is always greatly rewarded by God: Isaiah dealt profoundly with this matter in, at least, two portions of his book: In Isaiah 40: 31 the Bible says, *"But they that wait upon the* LORD *shall renew their strength; they shall mount up with wings as eagles; they shall run, and not be weary; and they shall walk, and not faint."* Then, Isaiah 64:4, says, *"For since the beginning of the world men have not heard, nor perceived by the ear, neither hath the eye seen, O God, beside thee, what he hath prepared for him that waiteth for him. The waiting process attracts high premium from God; it is never a wasted time."*

JACOB'S ENCOUNTER WITH AN ANGEL – A PORTRAIT OF IMPORTUNITY IN PRAYER

The case of Jacob is remarkable in many respects, significantly because of the valuable lesson it gives us in respect of importunity in prayer.

> *And Jacob was left alone; and there wrestled a man with him until the breaking of the day. And when he saw that he prevailed not against him, he touched the hollow of his thigh; and the hollow of Jacob's thigh was out of joint, as he wrestled with him. And he said, Let me go, for the day breaketh. And he said, I will not let thee go, except thou bless me. And he said unto him, What is thy name? And he said, Jacob. And he said, Thy name shall be called no more Jacob, but Israel: for as a prince hast thou power with God and with men, and hast prevailed* (Gen. 32:24-28).

The account of Jacob wrestling with the angel is a story found in the Book of Genesis 32, and referenced elsewhere, such as Genesis 35:1-7 and Hosea chapter 12. The account includes the renaming of Jacob as "Israel", literally "He who struggles with God."

Jacob wanted God to bless him and protect him from his brother's anger; but it was not to be without a price! It involved a fight, struggle, pain, frustration and near defeat.

In life you may encounter many "falls", but you must not be defeated! Proverbs 24:16 says, *"For a righteous man falls seven times and rises again"* Micah declares, *"Rejoice not against me, O my enemy: when I fall, I shall arise; when I sit in darkness, the LORD shall be a light unto me"* (Micah 7:8).

The life of Jacob here offers a stunning portrait of the true spirit of importunity.

He wrestled all night with the angel holding tight, determined to persevere. When day broke, the angel gave in and blessed Jacob by changing his name from Jacob to Israel, which means "a Prince with God." Jacob left limping as a reminder of this (Gen. 32:24-32).

The being with which Jacob wrestled is variously described as an angel, a man, or God. Jacob asks the being his name, and while he did not receive an answer, Jacob named the place where they wrestled Peniel saying, *"because I saw God face to face, and yet my life was spared"* (Gen. 32:29-30).

Importunity is therefore, an intense and persistent wrestling with God, a fight for triumph until victory is achieved. Prayer is a fiercely contested conflict. The enemy is never drawn to the negotiating table where cease-fire is on the agenda. In the word of S. D. Gordon, "prayer is a contest of wills. If Satan's will, persistence, and determination outlasts that of the petitioner, the petitioner is defeated. But the petitioner has the advantage because of Christ's victory and never needs to suffer defeat. Importunity combined with perfect faith is unconquerable."

The story of Jacob above paints a picture of intense battle between two individuals with opposing objectives. The angel was intent on leaving; Jacob on the other hand, needed a blessing at all costs. He was unprepared to substitute anything for his desire. The angel wrestled with Jacob and Jacob wrestled in return. Jacob knew that this encounter could just be a one in a life time experience; so he threw everything into it to get the blessing he so desperately needed out of the angel. "...*I will not let you go until you bless me*" (Gen. 32:26) was his resolve. And he paid the ultimate price to have his desire met. According to Josh Billings, the usefulness of the postage stamp consists in its ability to stick to one thing until its purpose is achieved - gets the letter to its final destination. Jacob was driven with unparalleled determination and tenacity; the end result, undoubtedly, justified his agony.

The dislocation of his joint could not deter him either. He wrestled even more ferociously. He had his goal firmly ahead of him – to be blessed! He would not take 'no' for an answer.

Andrew Murray could not be more correct when he said, "... a perseverance which strengthens the faith of the believer against all which may seem opposed to the answer is a real miracle; it is one of the impenetrable mysteries of the life of faith... It might seem strange that after having prayed with the certainty of being heard, and having seen therein the will of God, we should still need to continue in prayer. Nevertheless it is so. In Gethsemane, Jesus prayed three times in succession. On Carmel Elijah prayed seven times; and we, if we believe the promise of God without doubting, shall pray until we receive the answer. Both the importunate friend at midnight and the widow who besieged the unjust judge are examples of perseverance in seeking the end in view."

In Newt Gingrich's view, "Perseverance is the hard work you do after you get tired of doing the hard work you already did." Importunate praying is the earnest inward movement of the heart toward God.

Why was Jacob so desperate for a continuous encounter with the angel, you may ask? God had been with Jacob, no doubt, but his was a life bedevilled with crisis emanating from within his family. Esau, his brother, had vowed to kill him as a result of their turbulent history not least because Jacob, along with his mother had tricked their father into giving Jacob a blessing that was meant for Esau. And up to this point, Esau had never forgiven Jacob for what he had done. Jacob was on a journey back to Canaan, and knew that Esau was bent on revenge. Jacob saw heaven's intervention as the only way out of his predicament.

> *And he said, Thy name shall be called no more Jacob, but Israel: for as a prince hast thou power with God and with men, and hast prevailed* (Gen. 32:28).

As stated, the biblical account of Jacob under consideration leaves us with lessons of great proportion. It is almost always the fact that to do anything of significance in life or in the kingdom of God, one must know what he wants and pursue it with selfless and unhindered determination. One of the passages of scripture that has been of tremendous blessing to me as a Shepherd of God's people for a good number of years now has been this:

> *Thus Solomon finished the house of the LORD, and the king's house: and all that came into Solomon's heart to make in the house of the LORD, and in his own house,* **he prosperously effected** [successfully accomplished, ESV] (2 Chr. 7:11, emphasis added).

This could not have been without rugged determination and a resolve to be a 'finisher'.

It appears to me that only few things in life can be accomplished without having to go again and again. The fact of life is that we do not always get what we ask for all at once. Hear the words of a veteran on the subject, *"Perseverance is a great element of success. If you only knock long enough and loud enough at the gate, you are sure to wake up somebody"* - Henry Wadsworth Longfellow. The only way in which we can enjoy God is through faith. God loves importunate prayer so much that He will not give us much blessing without it.

The believer must learn the secret of "wrestling" with God in order to get what he wants.

Jacob desperately wanted to receive what God had destined for him, by all means. So he fought gallantly for it. We see from this account that even though the angel was reluctant blessing Jacob, but because of the latter's unyielding and unbending attitude the angel blessed him anyway, making him a Prince with

God. Jacob did not become a Prince of God by being complacent or praying faithless and faint-hearted prayer. With God, virtually nothing is impossible. In the word of another, "someone doing it [repeatedly] interrupts the person saying it cannot be done."

Andrew Murray affirms that of all the mysteries of the prayer world, the need for persevering prayer is one of the greatest. We cannot easily understand why the Lord, who is so loving and longing to bless us, should have to be petitioned time after time, sometimes year after year before the answer comes the power of believing prayer is considerable; real faith can never be disappointed. It knows that to exercise its power, it must be gathered up, just like water, until the stream can come down in full force. Prayer must often be "heaped up" until God sees that its measure is full. Then the answer comes. Every single believing prayer has its influence. It is stored up towards an answer which comes in due time to whomever perseveres to the end. However, insight into this truth should lead the believer to cultivate the corresponding attitudes of patience, faith, waiting and praise, which are the secret of his perseverance.

Concerning Abraham, the Bible says, *"Who against hope believed in hope, that he might become the father of many nations, according to that which was spoken..."* (Rom. 4:18, emphasis added). What was the result? *"...after he had patiently endured, he obtained the promise"* (Heb. 6:15, emphasis added).

Jesus not only taught the need to persevere in prayer theoretically (Luke 11, 18), His life was a practical demonstration of what it meant to develop resilience in prayer. In an act of determined persistence in prayer, it was said of Jesus, *"And being in an agony he **prayed more earnestly**: and his sweat was as it were great drops of blood falling down to the ground"* (Luke 22:44, emphasis added). What a portrait of importunate in prayer! It must be earnest, firm and unrelenting. The Amplified version of the Bible in James 5:16 highlight the salient components of importunate prayer and its outcome, in a very significant way:

*"The **earnest (heartfelt, continued)** prayer of a righteous man makes tremendous power available* **[dynamic in its working]** *(emphasis added)"*.

Faith holds the answer as a promissory note based on the promise. It sees it from afar, rejoices in it and praises God for it. It was said of the legends of faith:

"… but having seen them afar off, and were persuaded of them, and embraced them, and confessed that they were strangers and pilgrims on the earth" (Hebrew 11:13).

It is in persevering in prayer and praise that the heart is put in its best position, not just in anticipation of the promise, but of regarding those things that be not as though they were. This is the faith that possesses the blessing of the blessed Lord. Do not let delay shake your faith; each prevailing prayer is a step closer to your victory.

In the words of an unknown author, "When the world says, "Give up," Hope whispers, "Try it one more time."

And the same chapter of the Bible references Elijah as a man who engaged in importunate prayer with astonishing results.

Jesus taught importunity in prayer not only by engaging in the act Himself, He emphatically recommended importunate prayer as a secret of obtaining our greatest miracles from God...

"Elias was a man subject to like passions as we are, and he prayed **earnestly** that it might not rain: and it rained not on the earth by the space of three years and six months. And he prayed again, and the heaven gave rain, and the earth brought forth her fruit" (James 5:17-18). Elijah's prayer was earnest, and no doubt, fervent and persistent hence it received heaven's backing. No matter the degree of delay we experience in having our desires fulfilled or materialised, God wants us to unashamedly come to Him again and again.

Jesus emphatically recommended importunate prayer as a secret of obtaining our greatest miracles from God – miracles that could have been denied the supplicant but for persistence in prayer. In the process, Jesus gave two landmark parables to illustrate the inestimable value of persistence in prayer (the parables of the persistent friend – Luke 11, and the persistent widow – Luke 18), details of which are discussed in chapters 26 and 27 of this book.

The hour of waiting is indeed, challenging and frustrating – *"Hope deferred maketh the heart sick..."* (Prov. 13:12); but Paul offers the believer a convincing approach that makes the whole process less daunting:

> *And so, after he [Abraham - NIV] had patiently endured, he obtained the promise. For men verily swear by the greater: and an oath for confirmation is to them an end of all strife. Wherein God, willing more abundantly to shew unto the heirs of promise the immutability of his counsel, confirmed it by an oath: That by two immutable things, in which it was impossible for God to lie,* **we might have a strong consolation**, *who have fled for refuge to lay hold upon the hope set before us: Which hope we have as an anchor of the soul, both sure and stedfast, and which entereth into that within the veil* (Heb.6:15-19, emphasis added).

The Oxford Dictionary defines the word 'consolation' as *"The comfort received by a person."* Note what the writer of Hebrews asserts would provide the believer strong consolation (comfort) in the short and difficult time of waiting:-

- The immutability of His counsel (v17) – the fact that His counsel is unchangeable, durable, dependable, stable, reliable.

- His counsel being confirmed by an oath (v17) –The fact that God's promises are ratified and strengthen by an oath. Paul teaches, *"For all the promises of God in him are yea, and in him Amen, unto the glory of God by us"* (2 Cor. 1:20).

- The two immutable things... (v18) -The phrase, *"by two immutable things"* means: 'The promise and the oath of God'. The promise pledged His faithfulness and justice; the oath affirms all the infinite perfections of the Godhead.

- The fact that it is impossible for God to lie, (v18). It is not in God's nature to lie. The Bible says, *"God is not a man, that he should lie; neither the son of man, that he should repent: hath he said, and shall he not do it? or hath he spoken, and shall he not make it good?"* (Num. 23:19).

We are told by the scripture under consideration that these will give the believer the much needed, "consolation...*to lay hold upon the **hope set before us: Which hope we have as an anchor of the soul, both sure and stedfast, and which entereth into that within the veil**"* (v19, emphasis added).

The New International Version of the Bible offers a more transparent explanation on the subject:

> *And so after waiting patiently, Abraham received what was promised. Men swear by someone greater than themselves, and the oath confirms what is said and puts an end to all argument. Because God wanted to make the unchanging nature of his purpose very clear to the heirs of what was promised, he confirmed it with an oath. God did this so that, by two unchangeable things in which it is impossible for God to lie, we who have fled to take hold of the hope offered to us may be greatly encouraged. We have this hope as an anchor for the soul, firm and secure. It enters the inner sanctuary behind the curtain* (Heb. 6:15-19).

I will like to end this chapter with the thought provoking words of two veterans:

"I have walked that long road to freedom. I have tried not to falter; I have made missteps along the way. But I have discovered the secret that after climbing a great hill, one only finds that there are many more hills to climb. I have taken a moment here to rest, to steal a view of the glorious vista that surrounds me, to look back on the distance I have come. But I can only rest for a moment, for with freedom come responsibilities, and I dare not linger, for my long walk is not ended" – Nelson Mandela.

"Never give in. Never give in. Never, never, never, never – in nothing, great or small, large or petty – never give in, except to convictions of honour and good sense. Never yield to force. Never yield to the apparently overwhelming might of the enemy" – Winston Churchill.

Chapter 26

THE PARABLE OF THE IMPORTUNATE FRIEND

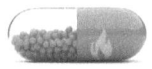

*And he said unto them, Which of you shall have a friend, and shall go unto him at midnight, and say unto him, Friend, lend me three loaves; For a friend of mine in his journey is come to me, and I have nothing to set before him? And he from within shall answer and say, Trouble me not: the door is now shut, and my children are with me in bed; I cannot rise and give thee. I say unto you, Though he will not rise and give him, because he is his friend, yet because of his **importunity** he will rise and give him as many as he needeth. And I say unto you, Ask, and it shall be given you; seek, and ye shall find; knock, and it shall be opened unto you. For every one that asketh receiveth; and he that seeketh findeth; and to him that knocketh it shall be opened* (Luke 11:5-10, emphasis added).

It is interesting to note that the basis for this parable was a request made by one of Jesus' disciples, yearning to be taught how to pray: *"And it came to pass, that, as he was praying in a certain place, when he ceased, one of his disciples said unto him, Lord, teach us to pray, as John also taught his disciples"* (verse1). Of no less importance is the fact that, of the myriads of miracles the disciples of Jesus had seen Him perform, which obviously were done under the full glare of the disciples, their primary and utmost interest was not on how to 'do miracles' or 'how to cast out demons' but on "*how to pray.*" How striking! Here is an incredible lesson for today's disciples of Jesus Christ. Prayer, undoubtedly, remains the key that accesses all that heaven holds for mankind.

In this parable a man was in dire need. He was obviously grappling with an emergency situation – a visitor at an inconvenient hour. In the process he remembered a friend whom he considered could help him out of the situation, and headed for his house. However, at no time was this man oblivious of the difficulties the late hour posed, but because of the severity of the prevailing situation – a friend at home with no food to set for him – he would confront all odds to overcome the seemingly insurmountable situation.

This parable opens up very thrilling insights and a vast field for our reflection.

It is evident that the friend had 'full stock' of bread and would have given him as much as he needed but for the following obstacles:

1. It was too late – mid night
2. The door was already shut
3. He was already in bed
4. The children were also in bed.

Now, the supplicant would either have to overcome these obstacles or allow them to deter him; the choice was his! He could hear these excuses of his friend and decide to leave in despair or confront them head-on.

It is to be noted that whatever way his decision went, it had far-reaching consequences. If he chose to insist and persist, and of course, persevere against all odds, he could persuade his friend to open the door and meet his needs. But if he gave-up in frustration, then he could grapple with his situation much longer. As noted above, the choice was his.

But thank God, the lesson the parable conveys is 'perseverance that takes no refusal or makes provision for an alternative.' Now, the final outcome of his perseverance as recorded in verse 8 leaves us with exceptional grounds for reflection:

*"I say unto you, Though he will not rise and give him, because he is his friend, yet because of his **importunity** he will rise and give him as many as he needeth"*

(emphasis added). The word 'importunity' is rendered in the Amplified version of the Bible as *'shameless persistence and insistence,'* which brings out the meaning more clearly:

"I tell you, although he will not get up and supply him anything because he is his friend, yet because of his shameless persistence and insistence he will get up and give him as much as he needs" (Amplified Bible).

Using the word of Vince Lombardi, "The difference between a successful person and others is not a lack of strength, not a lack of knowledge, but rather a lack in will."

Finally, his perseverance paid off. He succeeded in persuading his friend to get out of bed to meet his need. Amazing! But notice what did the job! The Bible says it was not the fact that they were friends. All along, the unwilling friend knew who the *supplicant* was; his identity was never in doubt. The unwilling friend's refusal to get out of bed and respond to his friend's need was not based on lack of knowledge of who the 'supplicant' was. He knew who was at the door knocking all along. Once again, verse 5 stated quite clearly the reasons why the friend was kept outside knocking. But, as said, verse 8 attributed the turn of event to the supplicant's refusal to give up.

It is to be noted, however, that in this parable Jesus was illustrating the potency of importunity in prayer using, as a case study, the unwilling friend who did not want to be disturbed at night; the centre message being if reluctant and hard-hearted men could yield to the influence of importunity, how much more will a loving, compassionate heavenly father, who do not sleep, and greatly delights in bestowing benefits upon the needy, grant the requests of those who call upon Him!

Bob Sorge's thrilling insight adds incredible weight to the subject: He writes, "When I study the lives of those who had profound personal encounters with God's Glory, almost all of them had a common denominator in their history: a protracted season of waiting on God before the visitation of Glory."

Importunity overcomes demonic obstacles that seek to hinder our prayer. Daniel's experience went to the heart of the matter. In Daniel 10:12 we read the account of an angelic intervention that eventually broke the siege of a demonic power that held answer back from Daniel:

"Then said he unto me, Fear not, Daniel: for from the first day that thou didst set thine heart to understand and to chasten thyself before thy God, thy words were heard, and I am come for thy words."

When Daniel prayed, God answered immediately, but demonic forces over the region of Persia prevented the immediate manifestation of the answer God had dispatched. In the word of the angel we see an acute explanation for the delay:

"But the prince of the kingdom of Persia withstood me one and twenty days: but, lo, Michael, one of the chief princes, came to help me; and I remained there with the kings of Persia" (verse 13).

It is important to stress that the main theme of the book of Daniel under this heading is the dynamic power of persistence in prayer in the face of all odds. As the battle from the demonic power intensified,

Daniel prayed even the more. Even though Daniel did not see any manifestation of the answer to his prayer, there was no drop in his tenacity and momentum in prayer. After a period of persistent and protracted prayer, Daniel, like all the other cases we have considered so far, gained victory over the enemy. Through Daniel's persistence, the enemy's resistance was broken and the answer that had been sent in response to Daniel's prayer came through. Satanic forces are always at work prohibiting the answer to your prayer from manifesting. However, the power of importunity always serves as a formidable antidote to such experience.

Stephen Nielsen shares a brilliant insight on the significance of this parable and I endorse it. According to him:

1. Importunity is an appeal to the friendship of God for our friends. As we see in this story, a man goes to his friend at midnight to ask for bread for another friend in need. Here God represents the friend that the man goes to for bread. Therefore, when we go to prayer on behalf of a friend, we must always appeal to God as a friend. And we go to Him and have hope in our importune prayers not only because we believe He is our friend but also because we are confident that He is a friend of our friend — the one we care about and are asking Him to help. He in fact is a better and more faithful friend to the needy then we are. As Andrew Murray has said, "When we go to God as a friend of the poor and the perishing, we can count on His friendliness." This knowledge of the friendship of God is the hope and endurance of our importunity. It is what keeps us asking.

2. Importune prayer goes beyond friendship. We can certainly place our hope in God as a friend; we can rely on Him to answer our prayers because He is our friend and because we have befriended the poor. But importune prayer does not have its primary basis on friendship. Its real basis comes from the urgency of the need and the persistence of our asking on behalf of that need. Hence, in the story the friend did not get up and give to the man on the basis of his friendship but because of his persistence based on his great need. Therefore, I believe that the teaching here is that we ought not to place our hope in answers to prayers solely on the basis that God is our friend, but rather on the basis of our importunity.

3. Importune prayer keeps asking with a shameless boldness. In the parable, the man went to his friend at midnight and kept asking him for bread until, finely, he got up and gave him as much as he needed. I think we can see clearly here that when the man came asking for bread he did not come with any reluctance, that is, with any guilt, embarrassment, or unworthiness because of the lateness of the night. No, he did not think of himself at all. He thought only of his poor friend in need of food. So he came boldly, without shame, expecting food from a good friend. This I believe is the heart of importunity — to have no regard for ourselves, but to be so caught up with the needs of another that we think only of that need and how our friend God can fill it.

4. Importune prayer keeps increasing in intensity. Immediately after Jesus told the parable He explained the meaning of persistence in prayer — to keep asking, seeking, and knocking (vv. 9 and 10). Hence, He explained that this was how the man asked for bread, with this kind of intense persistence. Therefore this is what true importunity is: to first ask; then with more persistence, to seek; then with even more persistence and intensity, to knock. Asking is where prayer begins. Seeking intensifies our prayer and keeps

it going. Knocking keeps it going even stronger until we receive what we ask for.

The subject of importunity was so great in the mind of Jesus that He was prepared to teach on it again. A point to note is that each time Jesus taught on the subject of prayer, the element of importunity was frequently used as a tool to illustrate, not just the need to persevere in prayer, but as an integral part of a heaven-backed prayer. For instance, in His Sermon on the Mount, Jesus emphatically highlighted the need to employ progression in prayer, from *asking to seeking,* and finally to *knocking*, all denoting different levels of intensity in our requests.

"Ask, and it will be given to you; seek, and you will find; knock, and it will be opened to you. For everyone who asks receives, and he who seeks finds, and to him who knocks it will be opened ... If you then, being evil, know how to give good gifts to your children, how much more will your Father who is in heaven give good things to those who ask Him" (Matt. 7:7-11).

Chapter 27

THE PERSISTENT WIDOW AND THE CANAANITE WOMAN

In another parable Jesus highlighted the significance of importunity in prayer:

"And he spake a parable unto them to this end, that men ought always to pray, and not to faint; Saying, There was in a city a judge, which feared not God, neither regarded man: And there was a widow in that city; and she came unto him, saying, Avenge me of mine adversary. And he would not for a while: but afterward he said within himself, Though I fear not God, nor regard man; Yet because this widow troubleth me, I will avenge her, lest by her continual coming she weary me. And the Lord said, Hear what the unjust judge saith. And shall not God avenge his own elect, which cry day and night unto him, though he bear long with them? I tell you that he will avenge them speedily. Nevertheless when the Son of man cometh, shall he find faith on the earth?" (Luke 18:1-8).

The central lesson in both parables is the same – the inestimable value of perseverance in prayer. Notice as we all do, this woman described as a widow, had an adversary who tormented her repeatedly. This undoubtedly, symbolises the adversarial relationship that exists between the believer and the enemy of his soul – the devil. Simply put, the Bible says:

*"Be sober, be vigilant; because **your adversary** the devil, as a roaring lion, walketh about, seeking whom he may devour:"* (1 Pet. 5:8, emphasis added).

The devil is every believer's adversary. And by implication, *every* child of God must regard the devil as an adversary, and must constantly launch a ferocious attack against him, his demons and his kingdom. We are not to be ignorant of his devices (2 Cor. 2:11).

The woman in this parable was in a critical situation, and needed help at all cost. She could not help herself, and there was only one source help could come from for her, – the Judge. Unfortunately, the Judge who knew her situation perfectly well would not avenge her of her adversary for no particular reason. Notice that refusal by the Judge to intervene and get justice for the supplicant did not necessarily lessen the burden of her adversary on her. It is fitting to reason that repeated refusal by the Judge, with time had escalated the pressure of the situation on her. The Bible says, *"Hope deferred makes the heart sick: but when the desire is fulfilled, it is a tree of life"* (Pro. 13:12).

But she did not relent; she persevered. She had no one-else to turn to but the Judge, and she was persuaded that it was within the prerogative of the Judge to rescue her from her deadly adversary. The situation was tense, it was critical. It might have been life-threatening! 'A desperate situation; a situation of this magnitude', she must have reasoned within herself, 'requires extra-ordinary measures.' So the less than humane manner the Judge might have threatened her on previous visits did not matter at all! What was of importance, huge importance at that, was gaining the attention of the Judge, persuading him to look into her matter.

After repeated visits, the woman's perseverance finally paid off! The Judge finally gave in to her pressure. Says the unjust Judge, "...*Though I fear not God, nor regard man; Yet because this widow troubleth me, I will avenge her, lest by her continual coming she weary me*" (vv 4-5).

Jesus likened God to the unjust Judge only in the sense of being so compassionate He could be moved by persistence. The Lord most assuredly promises to answer prayer. The Bible says, "You are the one who hears prayers. Everyone will come to you" (Psalm 65:2, *God's Word Translation*).

Note and ruminate on the following scriptures:

"Ask, and it shall be given you; seek, and ye shall find; knock, and it shall be opened unto you" (Matt. 7:7).

"Again I say unto you, That if two of you shall agree on earth as touching any thing that they shall ask, it shall be done for them of my Father which is in heaven." (Matt. 18:19).

"And all things, whatsoever ye shall ask in prayer, believing, ye shall receive" (Matt. 21:22).

"Therefore I say unto you, What things soever ye desire, when ye pray, believe that ye receive them, and ye shall have them" (Mark 11:24).

"If ye then, being evil, know how to give good gifts unto your children: how much more shall your heavenly Father give the Holy Spirit to them that ask him?" (Luke 11:13).

"And whatsoever ye shall ask in my name, that will I do, that the Father may be glorified in the Son. If ye shall ask any thing in my name, I will do it" (John 14:13-14).

"And in that day ye shall ask me nothing. Verily, verily, I say unto you, Whatsoever ye shall ask the Father in my name, he will give it you" (John 16:23).

"Let us therefore come boldly unto the throne of grace that we may obtain mercy, and find grace to help in time of need" (Heb. 4:16)

"And this is the confidence that we have in him, that, if we ask any thing according to his will, he heareth us: And if we know that he hear us, whatsoever we ask, we know that we have the petitions that we desired of him" (1 John 5:14-15).

And finally, in Jeremiah 33:3, God urges the believer: "Call unto me, and I will answer thee, and show thee great and mighty things, which thou knowest not".

These passages of scripture tell us there can be no question about God's ability and intention to hear the prayer of the righteous. This should be an authentic ground for the believer to build a solid, unwavering faith to persist and persevere in his request, knowing that God is not a man that should lie (Num. 23:19).

Other than Jesus' teaching on the subject, we see the act of importunity engaged in throughout the Bible.

THE CANAANITE WOMAN

The parable of the persistent widow bears reminiscence to the encounter the Canaanite woman had with Jesus, whose initial request for healing for her daughter was resisted by Jesus; but prevailed after insisting that she could, indeed, have her need met in spite of Jesus' unwillingness.

"And, behold, a woman of Canaan came out of the same coasts, and cried unto him, saying, Have mercy on me, O Lord, thou son of David; my daughter is grievously vexed with a devil. But he answered her not a word. And his disciples came and besought him, saying, Send her away; for she crieth after us. But he answered and said, I am not sent but unto the lost sheep of the house of Israel." "Then came she and worshipped him, saying, Lord, help me. But he answered and said, It is not meet to take the children's

bread, and to cast it to dogs. And she said, Truth, Lord: yet the dogs eat of the crumbs which fall from their masters' table. Then Jesus answered and said unto her, O woman, great is thy faith: be it unto thee even as thou wilt. And her daughter was made whole from that very hour" (Matt. 15:22-28).

> This woman persisted, insisting that she could, in fact, benefit from the ministry of Jesus, ... This was another very desperate supplicant who was faced with a fiery and life-threatening situation.

The woman persisted, insisting that she could, in fact, benefit from the ministry of Jesus, notwithstanding the Lord's initial refusal to heed her request. This was another very desperate supplicant who was faced with a fiery and life-threatening situation. Not even when she was by inference referred to as a dog did she give up. Rather, she engaged in a holy argument with Jesus! What does that tell us about the glorious act of importunity? Importunity is giving credit to your case before the Lord, insisting that your case is, indeed, worth the audience of the King of glory. Importunity takes place when the supplicant, not only refuse to take 'no' for an answer, but engages in intense and legitimate argument giving reasons why he must have his needs met. She pointed out that even the dogs get to eat the crumbs that fall from the master's table.

"And she said, Truth, Lord: yet the dogs eat of the crumbs which fall from their masters' table" (Matt. 15:27).

On hearing this, Jesus declared the greatness of her faith and delivered her daughter.

In this story, Jesus is showing us that His main calling during His lifetime was to the Jewish people and not to other peoples of the world. When He sent out the twelve disciples in Matthew 10, He told them, *"Go not into the way of the Gentiles, and into any city of the Samaritans enter ye not: But go rather to the lost sheep of the house of Israel"* (v.5-6). Even Paul testified that, *"Jesus Christ was a minister of the circumcision"* (Rom. 15:8). When the Bible refers to the "circumcision," it is referring to the Jewish people.

You see, Jesus was born as the Jewish Messiah–as their promised Holy One. He came to them to fulfil all the Old Testament prophecies concerning Him. It was only after He was rejected by them, that the message was offered to all people.

So, the children referred to in Matthew 15:26 are the Jewish people. The dogs are a picture of the Gentiles–that is, everyone who is not a Jew. Jesus came to His own people (John 1:11). Just as it would not be right to allow our children to go hungry while we feed our pet dogs, Jesus would not spend His ministry reaching the Gentiles when He was called to go to the Jews.

> Not even when she was by inference referred to as dog did she give up. Rather, she engaged in a holy argument with Jesus!

The good news is that Jesus was willing to give to the Canaanite Woman that which was exclusively reserved for the Jews because of her persistent faith, as shown in her importunate plea. Thank God, after the rejection of Jesus by the Jewish people, "salvation is come unto the Gentiles" (Rom. 11:11). According to the apostle Paul, we Gentiles were *"without Christ, being aliens from the commonwealth of Israel, and strangers from the covenants of promise, having no hope, and without God in the world"* (Eph. 2:12).

Yet through Jesus Christ we *"who sometimes were far off are made nigh by the blood of Christ"* (Eph. 2:13). We have been given the full blessings of being the children of God. And, though Jesus will again reach out to the Jewish people, we know that He will never turn from us because we are Gentiles.

Abraham also set a striking example for us in this regard. This is the prayer that calls upon the greatness of God and requires an answer out of that greatness. In this, Abraham discovered some secrets that will serve us well.

> Elijah repeated and urged his prayer seven times ere the raincloud appeared above the horizon, heralding the success of his prayer and the victory of his faith

The repeated intercessions of Abraham for the salvation of Sodom and Gomorrah present an early example of the necessity for, and benefit deriving from importunate praying. Jacob, wrestling all night with the angel, gives significant emphasis to the power of a dogged perseverance in praying, and shows how, in spiritual things, importunity succeeds, just as effectively as it does in matters relating to time and sense.

> Daniel had answers to his prayer put on hold for twenty-one day. But he persisted and eventually prevailed against the demonic powers laid hold on the answer God had dispatched from heaven in response to his prayer.

Finally, Moses prayed forty days and forty nights, seeking to stay the wrath of God against Israel, and his example and success are a stimulus to present-day faith in its darkest hour. Elijah repeated and urged his prayer seven times before the raincloud appeared above the horizon, heralding the success of his prayer and the victory of his faith. Daniel had answers to his prayer put on hold for twenty-one day. But he persisted and eventually prevailed against the demonic powers laid hold on the answer God had dispatched from heaven in response to his prayer.

From the foregoing discussion on the significance of importunity, the following conclusions as discussed in the next chapter are valid.

Chapter 28

VITAL LESSONS IN THE SCHOOL OF IMPORTUNITY

Life is a compilation or record of experiences. Some are of good, motivating and uplifting nature, others are quite the opposite by human standards. What however, we must remember, irrespective of the situations we are faced with in life, is that very often God wills differently.

In Isaiah 55:8-13, Prophet Isaiah went to the heart of the matter. In it, we see a pungent elucidation of this truth:

> *For my thoughts are not your thoughts, neither are your ways my ways, saith the* L<small>ORD</small>*. For as the heavens are higher than the earth, so are my ways higher than your ways, and my thoughts than your thoughts. For as the rain cometh down, and the snow from heaven, and returneth not thither, but watereth the earth, and maketh it bring forth and bud, that it may give seed to the sower, and bread to the eater: So shall my word be that goeth forth out of my mouth: it shall not return unto me void, but it shall accomplish that which I please, and it shall prosper in the thing whereto I sent it. For ye shall go out with joy, and be led forth with peace: the mountains and the hills shall break forth before you into singing, and all the trees of the field shall clap their hands. Instead*

> *of the thorn shall come up the fir tree, and instead of the brier shall come up the myrtle tree: and it shall be to the* LORD *for a name, for an everlasting sign that shall not be cut off.*

The above scripture highlights the existence of two different planes: the superior heavenly plane and the subordinate earthly plane. On the heavenly plane exists the whole counsel of God: His will, purposes, ways and thoughts. On the earthly plane are man's ways and thoughts, far inferior and, most times, at variance with God's ways.

DAVID – A Man Subjected to God's Supreme Will

In 1 Chronicles 17, after David ascended the throne of Israel, he embarked on a very ambitious reform, which included an unflinching determination to build a befitting temple for God. Prophet Nathan originally conceded with the idea. But at night, God spoke to Nathan and sent him to Kind David with a massage that was totally different from what David had in mind:

> *Go and tell David my servant, Thus saith the* LORD, **Thou shalt not build me an house to dwell in**: *For I have not dwelt in an house since the day that I brought up Israel unto this day; but have gone from tent to tent, and from one tabernacle to another. Wheresoever I have walked with all Israel, spake I a word to any of the judges of Israel, whom I commanded to feed my people, saying, Why have ye not built me an house of cedars? Now therefore thus shalt thou*

say unto my servant David, Thus saith the LORD *of hosts, I took thee from the sheepcote, even from following the sheep, that thou shouldest be ruler over my people Israel: And I have been with thee whithersoever thou hast walked, and have cut off all thine enemies from before thee, and have made thee a name like the name of the great men that are in the earth. Also I will ordain a place for my people Israel, and will plant them, and they shall dwell in their place, and shall be moved no more; neither shall the children of wickedness waste them any more, as at the beginning, And since the time that I commanded judges to be over my people Israel. Moreover I will subdue all thine enemies. Furthermore I tell thee that the* LORD *will build thee an house* (verses 4-10, emphasis added).

Here is an example of how God's ways and plans override man's greatest agenda. While it is absolutely impossible for man to rise from his level to God's plane, it is highly possible for God's ways and thoughts to be brought down to man. God says that His word that goes forth from His mouth is like the rain and the snow that bring heaven's life-giving moisture to earth.

In Galatians 6:9 we are admonished, "*And let us not be weary in well doing:* ***for in due season we shall reap, if we faint not***" (emphasis added).

The very reality of life has thought us that God's due season is very often at variance with man's. Knowing God's timing is very crucial for proper understanding of God's leading and direction for our lives. A man's life must run or operate in accordance with God's plans, timing and direction, lest he misses God's vital guidance and provisions for his life.

Jesus understood the valuable lesson of divine timing. The Bible records that when he heard of Lazarus' illness, "... *he abode two days still in the same place where he was*" (John 11:6). God hardly ever does things to suit our timeframe. Very often, we easily get discouraged because of this. In this passage of scripture, Jesus was obviously not operating on earthly timing, as in our daily understanding of time.

Kairos, on the other hand, refers to something more significant and has high implications on God's dealings with man as in the unfolding of events that pertain to his life and destiny. Kairos measures moments and seasons, not seconds, minutes or hours.

The ancient Greeks had two words for time: *chronos* and *kairos*. The former – *chronos* – still being in use today has the same background meaning as words like chronological and anachronism. It refers to clock time – time that can be measured – seconds, minutes, hours, years. *Kairos*, on the other hand, refers to something more significant and has high implications on God's dealings with man as in the unfolding of events that pertain to his life and destiny. Kairos measures moments and seasons, not seconds, minutes or hours. Further, it refers to the *right* moment, the perfect timing and season. Where *chronos* is quantitative, *kairos* is qualitative. While man very often judges events at the threshold of chronos time, God operates events by divine timing – *kairos*. Daniel alluded to this fact when he said, "*And he changeth the times and the seasons...*" Only the creator of times and seasons has the sole prerogative to put such changes in place. God deals with us on the basis of His unique and distinct program and destiny for our lives. Accordingly, we experience various seasons in life based God's specific and explicit program that is uniquely designed for us individually. A man's season of certain blessings is inextricably tied to the destiny God has designed for him. For instance, my season of some specific blessings is different from yours - that is if such blessings are part of God's package for your life, in the first place. There is a common ground between seasons of specific blessings and importunity in prayer. Understanding of divine timing is crucial in the school of importunity in almost all cases. Very often, we importunate in prayer when we think that certain blessings we are due for are being delayed or, worse off, have eluded us completely. The cardinal lesson in this regard, therefore, is the huge need for the believer to search the mind of God in specific cases, to ascertain His divine timing for most of the things we ask for in prayer. This does not, in the least, indicate that all cases that require importunity in prayer have something to do with man operating outside of God's timing for his life. As in the case of Daniel, in some, if not majority of cases, we are denied certain breakthroughs for a period of time because of demonic interference in place which only persistence in prayer can help to deal with.

> God deals with us on the basis of His unique and distinct program and destiny for our lives. Accordingly, we experience various seasons in life based God's specific and explicit program that is uniquely designed for us individually.

> There is a common ground between seasons of specific blessings and importunity in prayer.

Let us briefly examine some of the significant lessons in the school of importunity:

1. Importunity enhances greater relationship between the believer and God. As earlier observed, when God holds blessings back from the believer, it is for the believer to engage in prayer at a higher dimension, this, in process, increases his knowledge of God and His ways, which in turn strengthens his relationship with God.

2. Importunity in prayer helps the believer develop the virtue of patience. Waiting which results in importunity must be seen as part of life and a tool God uses to build patience in us. Patience is undoubtedly, a fundamental virtue a believer is expected to develop and nourish in his life. We need to be reminded that patience is a fruit, and not a gift of the Spirit! One of the

significant differences between the fruit and gifts of the Holy Spirit is the fact that though, they are *"the work of one and the same Spirit..."* (1 Cor. 12:11), the fruit of the Spirit which, in a sense speaks of the believer's level of maturity in Christ, is the adorning ornament the believer presents to God. It is the special beautification or divine glamorisation of our lives before God. In essence, fruit is what we offer God. Gifts of the Spirit, on the other hand, are God's gifts to the believer. Patience, being fruit of the Spirit, therefore, is essential for the proper development and functionality of the believer, and the route to its attainment must be esteemed highly.

3. Importunity in prayer teaches one never to allow unfavourable circumstances to keep one from prevailing in prayer and having our needs met in God. All the cases we have explored under this broad heading, summarily, leave us with the invaluable lesson that without perseverance in prayer, the believer will never experience some levels of breakthrough in life. The case of the importunate friend (Luke 11), for instance, is condensed in one vital lesson:

"So I say to you, Ask and keep on asking and it shall be given you; seek and keep on seeking and you shall find; knock and keep on knocking and the door shall be opened to you. For everyone who asks and keeps on asking receives; and he who seeks and keeps on seeking finds; and to him who knocks and keeps on knocking, the door shall be opened." (Luke 9-11).

Significant breakthrough in life is almost always a product of much battle. Fight with this understanding in mind that, *"To turn aside the right of a man before the face of the most High, To subvert a man in his cause, **the L*ord* approveth not"** (Lam. 3: 35-36, emphasis added). The rights and privileges of the saints of God are well safeguarded and guaranteed in Christ.

4. Importunity in prayer teaches that there is no obstacle that waiting on the Lord in prayer cannot overcome. For the man that went to his friend at middle of the night, the four obstacles his unwilling friend advanced as being reasons he could not meet his friend's need were overcome with resolve, determination and perseverance (Luke 11). The widow did not get discouraged when the judge denied her repeatedly. No, she kept going back with renewed energy, resolve and flaming intensity in her request; the judge was rather the one that got weary (Luke 18:1-8). Importune prayer then is prayer that has strength of heart; it never faints, never grows weary, and never gets discouraged until it achieves its objectives. I have had a firsthand experience in this regard. In 1991, shortly after I completed my Legal Training as a lawyer, the enemy attacked me severely with a life-threatening disease. Something unique about this disease was that it had no name. Of the numerous hospitals I visited, none could find accurate diagnosis for my ailment, yet I was in grave pain, and my life was ebbing away like a piece of heated ice block. My health so deteriorated with the passage of time that all hope of ever recovering faded away. I sought every help I knew, but to no avail. Needless to say that I was confused and fearful for my life. However, as often the case with man, after all personal efforts had failed; I took my case to the greatest physician – Jesus. Perhaps, you expect me to say I had an instant breakthrough as a result. No! It took a fight. I laboured in prayer. I engaged in gruesome fasting. I stormed the throne of grace with unflinching resolve. Having exhausted all the solutions man could offer in the beginning, I knew it would either be God or never. My perseverance, after a painful period of three years, finally paid off. My breakthrough came after I had prayed and persevered in prayer, taking 'no' for an answer. To God be the glory!

5. Importunity teaches that God purposely designs waiting periods for His chosen vessel. The overarching reason, according to Bob

Sorge is because [God] is preparing them for a visitation of Glory. As said, waiting is part of life and one of God's formidable tools for developing his battle axes.

6. Importunity enables the believer to be stronger in prayer. We are strengthened through prayer, and our ability to pray increases as we tarry in prayer. A divine exchange takes place in prayer. The praying believer relinquishes his weakness and takes on the strength of God. Isaiah 40: 28-31 declares, *"Hast thou not known? hast thou not heard, that the everlasting God, the Lord, the Creator of the ends of the earth, fainteth not, neither is weary? there is no searching of his understanding. He giveth power to the faint; and to them that have no might he increaseth strength. Even the youths shall faint and be weary, and the young men shall utterly fall: But they that* **wait upon the Lord shall renew their strength**; *they shall mount up with wings as eagles; they shall run, and not be weary; and they shall walk, and not faint"* (emphasis added).

In the place of fervent prayer, the believer is refreshed and invigorated. What a blessing!

7. Importunity increases the anointing of the Holy Spirit over your life. God is the source of all Kingdom power. The Holy Ghost is the enabling power for kingdom services. Our frequency at His throne invariably increases His power in your life, which in turn, increases your effectiveness in Kingdom service. Paul declares: *" Not that we are sufficient of ourselves to think anything as of ourselves; but our sufficiency is of God; Who also hath made us able ministers of the new testament; not of the letter, but of the spirit: for the letter killeth, but the spirit giveth life"* (2 Cor. 3:5-6). Also in Daniel 11:32, we are told, *"And such as do wickedly against the covenant shall he corrupt by flatteries: but the people that do know their God shall be strong, and do exploits."* Persistent prayer is the life-blood of the believer. Great men and women of God down through the ages have alluded to the effectiveness this in their lives.

8. Through incessant prayer, the believer takes on the nature, character and personality of God. The Bible says, *"But we all, with open face beholding as in a glass the glory of the Lord, are changed into the same image from glory to glory, even as by the Spirit of the Lord"* (2 Cor. 3:18). As we constantly behold His face, we are changed into the image of the One we gaze at.

9. Prayer of importunity enables us to grow in faith. As we stand on God's word in persistent prayer, faith grows along because, *"... faith comes by hearing, and hearing by the word of God"* (Rom.10.17). Importunity increases our dependence on God. It helps us appreciate our vulnerability and frailty which calls for childlike dependence on God. The life of David was an accurate portrait of this. In 1 Samuel 17, we see a little shepherd boy's faith overcome the nation's fear.

10. Importunity increases God's protection over your life. God's presence is undoubtedly, the most secured place to be. The greater the time you spend in the presence of God, the more secured you are. The enemy knows it:

"And David abode in the wilderness in strong holds, and remained in a mountain in the wilderness of Ziph. And Saul sought him every day, but God delivered him not into his hand" (1 Sam. 23:14). Psalm 91: 1 also says, "He that dwelleth in the secret place of the most High shall abide under the shadow of the Almighty." Please note the words "abode" in our first scripture and "dwelleth" in the second, both give the impression of habitation, permanence and repetition. The Bible declares that, "The eternal God is your refuge, and underneath are the everlasting arms: and he shall thrust out the enemy from before you; and shall say, Destroy them" (Deut. 32:27).

There is a significant caveat to the thoughts shared above. It is found in the soul-stirring and thought-provoking words of

Gloria Copeland, "God is a shield [but] He can't be a shield to you when you live your life in opposition to Him. You have to walk in His ways." I whole-heartedly endorse her opinion. It is the person that dwells IN the secret place of the Most High that shall abide under the shadow of the Almighty (Psalm 91:1). The protection the Almighty offers does not extend to those who 'dwell' outside the secret place. Remember, "... *whoso breaketh an hedge, a serpent shall bite him.*" (Eccl. 10:8).

11. Importunity increases your authority over satanic powers.

"Because thou hast made the Lord, which is my refuge, even the most High, thy habitation; There shall no evil befall thee, neither shall any plague come nigh thy dwelling. For he shall give his angels charge over thee, to keep thee in all thy ways. They shall bear thee up in their hands, lest thou dash thy foot against a stone. Thou shalt tread upon the lion and adder: the young lion and the dragon shalt thou trample under feet" (Psalm 91: 9-13, emphasis added). Luke 10:19 says, "Behold, I give unto you power to tread on serpents and scorpions, and over all the power of the enemy: and nothing shall by any means hurt you."

12. The School of importunity is God's training ground for His 'generals.'

When God wants to place a man in a rare and special service in His Kingdom, He sends him to the School of importunity – the Training Camp. Zacharias Fomum could not be more correct when he said, "God is calling a band of overcomers to co-operate with Him to a degree that He is not calling all others who believe in His Son and love Him. He is calling a few to whom he wants to reveal, in a special way, His final plan for the battle against Satan and his hosts. When He finds such people and reveals His purpose to them, they will make importunate "knocking" their one business and so co-operate with God to bring His Kingdom. Such people will pay a very high price – loneliness, intensity in prayer, ever increasing wrestling, and increased attacks from hell – but they are people who will neither rest night nor day nor give God a second's rest, but pray until the Lord appears in the clouds to establish the Kingdom…"

13. Importunate people are rewarded. Importunity is rewarding. No doubt, it takes time and causes agitation for a time; but the reward outlasts the waiting. David affirms,"…*weeping may endure for a night, but joy cometh in the morning*" (Psalm 30:5). "*A woman when she is in travail hath sorrow, because her hour is come: but as soon as she is delivered of the child, she remembereth no more the anguish, for joy that a man is born into the world*" (John 16:21).

    Jesus guarantees the importunate saint's reward in the parable of the Importunate Widow in the following words, "*And shall not God avenge his own elect, which cry day and night unto him, though he bear long with them? I tell you that he will avenge them speedily. Nevertheless when the Son of man cometh, shall he find faith on the earth?*" (Luke 18:7-8). Notice our Lord promises to avenge the importunate believer 'speedily.' This might appear odd with the spirit of importunity – which means 'a long wait, perhaps in agony!' It is submitted that there is no contradiction whatsoever either in relation to the word in question or anywhere in the Bible. It appears to me that Jesus seems to be promising even greater reward to the importunate saint by opting to reward Him *speedily*. In essence, He appears to be promising to make up for the seemingly wasted time – the waiting time. Put in context, a Christian couple that waited for five years in prevailing prayer before being able to conceive, could unarguably, be said to have had their waiting time rewarded when they were blessed with a set of triplets. The Bible says, God "…*is a rewarder of them that diligently seek him*" (Heb. 11:6).

14. Importunity increases boldness. It is an irrefutable fact that boldness is a product of fervent, prevailing prayer:

*"Now when they saw the **boldness** and unfettered eloquence of Peter and John and perceived that they were unlearned and untrained in the schools [common men with no educational advantages], **they marvelled; and they recognized that they had been with Jesus"** (Acts 4:13, Amplified Bible, emphasis added). The disciples were ordinary men by every human standard; but standing before the greatest religious thinkers of the day – The Sanhedrin Council - and defending their faith before them, their personalities, perspectives and purposes completely changed because of their contact with Jesus. So apparent was the sudden change that even members of the Sanhedrin Council took note of it. The Bible says they marvelled, however, they recognised that they had been with Jesus.*

15. Importunity is the business of the matured saints. While only mature believers would exercise the degree of resilience and perseverance required to importunate in prayer, it is fitting to conclude that importunity itself produces greater maturity in us.

16. Importunity achieves its objectives.

    "For ye have need of patience, that, after ye have done the will of God, ye might receive the promise. Cast not away therefore your confidence, which hath great recompense of reward" (Heb. 10:35-36). God holds the key to the heavens where all our blessings, favour, revelations, directives and insights are locked up (James 1:7). It is our responsibility, therefore, to "knock" at the door of heaven until He opens it and gives us what we want.

Consequently, be rest assured that whatever the situation you are faced with today, your mountain is not immutable. Knock and knock harder, and the door will be opened.

INTENSIFICATION OF PERSISTENCE

> *Our Lord Jesus thought it of such importance that we should know the need of perseverance and importunity in prayer, that He spake two parables to teach us this. This is proof sufficient that in this aspect of prayer we have at once its greatest difficulty and its highest power. He would have us know that in prayer all will not be easy and smooth; we must expect difficulties, which can only be conquered by persistent, determined perseverance –*
> Andrew Murray

THE THREE STAGES OF PRAYER

In His teaching on the subject of prayer, Jesus opened for us the three levels or stages of prayer – the stages of asking, seeking and knocking. The stages grow in intensification as they progress, and each stage lends strength to the other.

"Ask, and it shall be given you; seek, and ye shall find; knock, and it shall be opened unto you: For every one that asketh receiveth; and he that seeketh findeth; and to him that knocketh it shall be opened" (Matt. 7:7-9).

"So I say to you, Ask and keep on asking and it shall be given you; seek and keep on seeking and you shall find; knock and keep on knocking and the door shall be opened to you. For everyone who asks and keeps on asking receives; and he who seeks and keeps on seeking finds; and to him who knocks and keeps on knocking, the door shall be opened" (Luke 11:9-10).

What does the Lord mean by the phrase: *"Ask and keep on asking, and you will receive?"* He is saying, 'intensify the process of prayer, drive prayer to its limit. Go beyond just asking, seek as you ask. Seek and keep on seeking and you will find. And go even deeper in seeking. Let seeking give way to knocking – fierce deliberate asking and seeking. What will not give way to asking will give way to seeking, and if need be, knocking has to be done.'

The Lord then takes it further and said, *"For everyone who asks receives, and he who seeks finds, and to him who knocks it will be opened"* (Luke 11:10). There is, therefore, no reason why anyone should ask and not receive. If a person were to ask and not receive, it would most likely be because he did not ask persistently. If he sought and did not find, it could be because he sought superficially, for too short a time, and gave up. If he knocked and it was not opened to him, it could be that he walked away just as the Lord was just about to open to him.

There are believers whose prayer lives are at the level of asking. They receive what is available at the asking plane. They will receive all that is available at the asking plane, only if they fulfil the conditions for having prayer answered.

The Asking Stage

Asking is where the journey begins. It is the elementary stage. It is a product of our abiding in Christ. According to Benny Hinn, "Asking begins in the outer court. This is where we make our request known...This is where we ask and receive. This where we come to the Lord and make our desires and needs known to Him...This is where we are cleansed by the blood as we confessed our sins. This is where we find Him faithful and just to forgive us...It is in the world that we must prevail in prayer as we wait upon the Lord." Every journey starts with a step! This applies too to spiritual things. God expects us to commence the salvation journey at an elementary level, and make our way up. Here is Peter's view on the matter, *"As newborn babes, desire the sincere milk of the word, that ye may grow thereby: If so be ye have tasted that the Lord is gracious"* (1 Pet. 2:2-3). The writer of Hebrews alluded to this fact when he said, ***"Therefore leaving the principles of the doctrine of Christ, let us go on unto perfection****; not laying again the foundation of repentance from dead works, and of faith toward God, Of the doctrine of baptisms, and of laying on of hands, and of resurrection of the dead, and of eternal judgment"* (Heb. 6:1-2, emphasis added).

Why is asking so important in prayer?

In Mathew 7:7-11 Jesus taught more about asking. *"Ask, and it shall be given you seek, and ye shall find knock, and it shall be opened unto you: For every one that askethrecieveth; and he that seekethfindeth; and to him that knocketh it shall be opened. Or what man is there of you, whom if his son ask bread, will he give him a stone? Or if he ask a fish, will he give him a serpent? If ye then, being evil know how to give good gifts unto your children, how much more shall your father which is in heaven give good things to them that ask him?"*

In those three verses alone, Jesus refers to asking five times. Clearly, asking is a vital part of receiving from God. Yet in Matthew 6:8, Jesus says, "Your Father knoweth what things ye have need of, before ye ask Him".

If God already knows what we need, why do we have to ask Him for it? Why would He not just give it to us?

The answer is simple. Our faith is what connects us to God. It opens the door for us to receive His provision, asking is an expression of faith.

James 4:2 says unequivocally, *"...ye have not, because ye ask not"*. In essence, even though the Omniscience God knows what we need before we ask Him, He still wants us to express our faith in asking. More significantly, God will withhold certain blessings from us until we ask for them in prayer.

In Mark 10: 46-52, we have a fascinating episode that buttresses this principle:

"And they came to Jericho: and as he went out of Jericho with his disciples and a great number of people, blind Bartimaeus, the son of Timaeus, sat by the highway side begging. And when he heard that it was Jesus of Nazareth, he began to cry out, and say, Jesus, thou son of David, have mercy on me. And many charged him that he should

hold his peace: but he cried the more a great deal, Thou son of David, have mercy on me. And Jesus stood still, and commanded him to be called. And they call the blind man, saying unto him, Be of good comfort, rise; he calleth thee. And he, casting away his garment, rose, and came to Jesus. And Jesus answered and said unto him, **What wilt thou that I should do unto thee?** *The blind man said unto him, Lord, that I might receive my sight. And Jesus said unto him, Go thy way; thy faith hath made thee whole. And immediately he received his sight, and followed Jesus in the way"* (emphasis added).

Jesus asked Bartimaeus what seems like a strange question to ask a blind man. He was however, giving Bartimaeus an opportunity to express his personal faith in Christ Jesus. Note the first word the blind man said to Jesus, *"Rabboni"*, which means Lord. He acknowledged that Jesus was Lord over his life, hence he asked Him for healing. Jesus saw his faith and healed him.

So, asking is vital. Ask today and give God opportunity to move in your situation.

The Seeking Stage

> *You will seek me and find me when you seek me with all your heart. I will be found by you," declares the Lord, "and will bring you back from captivity.[a] I will gather you from all the nations and places where I have banished you," declares the Lord, "and will bring you back to the place from which I carried you into exile* (Jer. 29:13-14).

Next is the seeking stage. Seeking is a far more intense action. The seeking stage is the plane of greater intensity. It takes far more effort and determination to pray at the seeking level than at the asking plane. In his unique categorisation, Benny Hinn regards this stage as the "Holy place... [where] stood the candlestick on one side and the table of showbread on the other..." It is a far more matured stage of knowing God, His will and purpose. That of course, does not come cheap. The anointing of the Holy Spirit comes along to give the power needed to meet the degree of intensification that is required at the seeking level. No one can seek God and find Him even at his best effort: "*...not by might, nor by power, but by my spirit, saith the LORD of hosts*" (Zech. 4:6).

The seeking stage is the 'gateway' into warfare in prayer. No one can seek passively. Many things that cannot be received asking and continuing in asking will be obtained by the seeker. A person can ask and not receive and then go away calmly. However, if he were to seek in prayer and not find, he would be totally frustrated. Few believers pray on this plane. It is costly; one must know something about laying hold on God to make progress here. The believer's anchors his hope on the word of God, and batters the gate of heaven on the basis of God's word. The need for importunity starts at this level, and grows in intensity into the knocking level.

The Knocking Stage

This is a place of utter desperation, where one has come to the end of oneself. A place where you know that unless God shows- up utter devastation is imminent.

It is also a place of divine partnership with God. Intercession forms an integral part of this stage of prayer. It is not a place for weak and faint-hearted prayer.

The prayer of Jesus at the garden of Gethsemane was a portrait of this. It was intense. It was violent. It produced sweat like drops of blood!

> *And being in an agony he prayed more earnestly: and his sweat was as it were great drops of blood falling down to the ground* (Luke 22:44).

In the words of Zacharias Fomum, "This is the prayer of violence in the spiritual world. Praying at this plane means that the total man-spirit, soul and body, is engaged in prayer. Were God to fail to answer at that plane, the praying person would be finished permanently." Therefore, the warning of Jesus to His disciples must be heeded at this critical stage of prayer: *"Howbeit this kind goeth not out but by prayer and fasting"* (Matt. 17:21). This is so because very often, it takes a demonic siege to cause blockade in the spirit realm, not allowing God's blessing to come through to the believer, as in the case of Daniel (Daniel 10). So, fasting is required in such cases to break through the siege, and release the blessing. Victory is guaranteed to those who would go through persistence in asking, seeking, enduring the fierceness of the battle of knocking night and day, with tears and groans for a season, as seen in all the cases we have examined under this heading. Note there is no failure except in no longer trying!

PART 7
COMMON BLOCKADES TO PRAYER

Chapter 29

HINDRANCES TO PRAYER

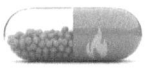

We have so far established the absolute, unconditional and infinite love of God for man. The Bible is replete with this great teaching that has formed the core of God's relationship with man. Jeremiah 31:3 says, *"The Lord hath appeared of old unto me, saying, Yea, I have loved thee with an everlasting love: therefore with lovingkindness have I drawn thee."* Note the word 'everlasting,' which indicate that God's love is infinite. In John 3:16 which is the climax of God's expression of love for humanity, we are told, *"For God so loved the world, that he gave his only begotten Son, that whosoever believeth in him should not perish, but have everlasting life."* Romans 5:8 affirms, *"But God commendeth his love toward us, in that, while we were yet sinners, Christ died for us."* It is apparent that the gift of salvation is undoubtedly, an absolute work of grace. Truly, it is **"not by works of righteousness which we have done, but according to his mercy he saved us**, by the washing of regeneration, and renewing of the Holy Ghost; Which he shed on us abundantly through Jesus Christ our Saviour; That being justified by his grace, we should be made heirs according to the hope of eternal life" (Titus 3:5-7, emphasis added).

It is fitting to reason that if God so loved us as to extend the gift of grace to us at our fallen Adamic state, He would very much be prepared to answer our prayers now as heirs of the kingdom.

It is apt to reason that if God so loved us as to extend the gift of grace to us at our fallen Adamic state, He would very much be prepared to answer our prayers now as heirs of the kingdom. The Bible says, *"For the eyes of the Lord run to and fro throughout the whole earth, to shew himself strong in the behalf of them whose heart is perfect toward him"* (2 Chr. 16:9). *The NIV Bible capsules it thus: "For the eyes of the LORD range throughout the earth to strengthen those whose hearts are fully committed to him."* In fact, the beautiful psalm of David describes God as, *"… our refuge and strength,* **a very present help in trouble"** (emphasis added). Notice if you will, the wording which the Bible takes time to highlight: *"a very present help"* (Psalm 46:1). When it comes to prayer, God has transcended the threshold of His love for man as the basis to answer man's prayer. He has covenanted to answer the prayer of the saints. Jesus proclaims in Matthew 21:22, *"And all things, whatsoever ye shall ask in prayer, believing, ye shall receive."* That is a covenantal promise! The believer's life must be a life of answered prayer. In His teaching on prayer, Jesus taught His disciples to pray daily for bread, ask daily for forgiveness, for deliverance from the evil one, and for our daily needs and to have answer prayers daily.

According to John Rice, "it is perfectly normal for an obedient child to ask for food every meal time and get it, get all he wants, and eats until he is perfectly satisfied."

It is the Lord's delight to give us what we ask of Him in prayer. Like David, we should all pray, *"O God, hear my prayer; give ear to the words of my mouth"* (Psalm 54:2). If Christians do not believe in the efficacy of prayer, there would be no reason for us to ask anything of God. He is the one who tells us that we can have confidence that our prayers ascend to Him. *"And this is the confidence that we have toward him, that if we ask anything according to his will he hears us. And if we know that he hears us in whatever we ask, we know that we have the requests that we have asked of him"* (1 John 5:14-15). While as Christians we pay lip-service to the superlatives in that sentence ("whatever" and "anything"), how often do we really believe it?

However, the reality of life has taught us that many of our prayers do not receive answers from God. It should be stressed that unanswered prayer is not the result of God's unwillingness to respond to our requests, but because of the hindrances that get on our way. Charles Finney was once so burdened with the critical situation of asking and not receiving that he decided to examine the principal causes of such phenomenon. Amongst other things, he affirms that *"...Everyone that asketh receiveth, but there certainly is a "great gulf" between the asking and receiving that is a great stumbling block to many."*

> It is important to know from the outset that I am the only one who can hinder my prayers. You are the only one who can hinder your prayers...

There are times when it feels like our prayers are reaching the ceiling and going no further; times when we are lying face-down on the floor and feel that our prayers are rising no higher than the fibres of the carpet. While we can be sure that God does hear our prayers, there are times when He chooses not to heed or answer them.

It is important to know from the outset that the believer is the only one who can hinder his prayers. Indeed, you are the only one who can hinder your prayers. I cannot hinder your prayers anymore than you can hinder mine. While we may have done much to hinder our prayers, we are not necessarily even aware of this. Let us now examine some of the very crucial reasons why prayer may go unanswered.

A CLOSED HEAVEN

> *And your heavens which are over your head shall be bronze, and the earth which is under you shall be iron. The Lord will change the rain of your land to powder and dust; from the heaven it shall come down on you until you are destroyed* (Deut. 28: 23-24).

> *If I shut up heaven that there be no rain, or if I command the locusts to devour the land, or if I send pestilence among my people…* (11 Chr.7:13).

> *And also I have withholden the rain from you, when there were yet three months to the harvest: and I caused it to rain upon one city, and caused it not to rain upon another city: one piece was rained upon, and the piece whereupon it rained not withered. So two or three cities wandered unto one city, to drink water; but they were not satisfied: yet have ye not returned unto me, saith the Lord. I have smitten you with blasting and mildew: when your gardens and your vineyards and your fig trees and your olive trees increased, the palmerworm devoured them: yet have ye not returned unto me, saith the Lord* (Amos 4:7-9).

> *As soon as Jesus was baptized, he went up out of the water. At that moment heaven was opened, and he saw the Spirit of God descending like a dove and alighting on him* (Matt. 3:16).

A consideration of the condition of the heaven that is over a believer's life is of great significance and has huge implications. This ought to be given considerable attention by everyone that truly desires a momentous and symbolic breakthrough in life.

When the heavens are closed, plans, no matter how articulated, are in disarray, and destiny ruined. The repercussions of closed heavens are far more than can be can exhaustively examined in any work of literature. However, attempt would be made to consider this vital subject to a depth that would, at least, give a concise understanding of what closed heavens means, and what its effect could be in the life of the saint of God.

A closed heaven situation could be understood from the perspective of a drought phenomenon. When heavens hold back rains in the physical sense, then, draught is in place. The situation is exactly the same when examining the subject of closed heavens from a spiritual perspective; given that rain in scriptures often represents the outpouring of the Holy Spirit upon men. It represents the pouring forth of blessings on men. In Deuteronomy 11:16-17, it says – *"Take heed to yourselves, that your heart be not deceived, and ye turn aside, and serve other gods, and worship them; And then the LORD's wrath be kindled against you, and He shut up the heaven, that there be no rain..."* Although this is mainly referring to a physical condition, it can also apply to the spiritual realm. As we can see from this verse, sin causes a "closed heaven." It holds back the "rain" or the blessings of God. It shuts down any revelation or insight into the future. It blocks the wisdom, knowledge, and understanding of God from getting through to His people. It blinds them from seeing Jesus as He really is. James 1:7 gives a clear indication of the significant position heaven occupies in the life of the believer in this respect. It says, *"Every good gift and every perfect gift is from above, and cometh down from the Father of lights, with whom is no variableness, neither shadow of turning."* Consequently, when the heavens are closed, blessings, divine rain and answers to prayer are held back. This, undoubtedly, causes suffering, frustration and despair.

It is to be noted, as made abundantly clear from scriptures that everyone – man, woman, locality, church or nation appears to have 'its own heaven'. Accordingly, the heaven could be opened over a man and yet closed over his wife, or opened over a wife and closed over a husband. We have striking illustration of this in the following two scriptures:

"And thy heaven that is over thy head" (Deut. 28:23).

*"And Jesus, when He was baptized, went up straightway out of the water: and, lo, the heavens were **opened unto Him**…"* (Matt 3:16, emphasis added).

Gbile Akanni's insightful thought will invariably enhance our understanding of the subject. He affirms, "… Each man operates vertically under a "heaven space". It is marked out for each person. If the heavens over a man, over a family or over a church should be closed, it may not be applicable to all men around him. This further shows that each of us is responsible for the condition of the heavens over our heads. It is possible for you to seek for your heavens to be opened just as Jesus; our LORD deliberately did as he came to Jordan. When it opened, it opened unto him. Several men were standing there, but theirs remained closed. This is an individual response to this message. Each man should check what the condition of the heavens is over his head. Do not assume that it is well. Do not just be carried along with men around you."

When the heavens are closed, prayers are prayed but there are no answers from heaven.

IS YOUR HEAVEN OPEN?

We desperately need an open heaven over us. We need wisdom, inspiration, divine insight, grace, mercy in our time of crucial need. We need answers to our prayers; we need heaven intervention in the affairs of our lives.

In Ezekiel 1:1, we read, *"Now it came to pass in the thirtieth year, in the fourth month, in the fifth day of the month, as I was among the captives by the river of Chebar, that the heavens were opened, and I saw visions of God."* Ezekiel 1:3 goes on to say, *"The word of the LORD came expressly unto Ezekiel the priest, the son of Buzi, in the land of the Chaldeans by the river Chebar; and the hand of the LORD was there upon him."* Here we see that the "heavens" had to be opened before Ezekiel could see, hear, or be touched by God. All the darkness and distance between him and God was conquered. He was uplifted into the glories of the upper world. Heaven was opened to him. Resultantly, he saw great and excellent things - displays of Divine Glory. Immediately, his ears were opened to hear a word from the Lord. It came expressly and accurately to him. It came in the fullness of light and power - so much so that it took possession of him and dwelt richly in him. He then felt the constraining power of God reviving and supporting him. Actually, at this time, he was filled with His power and the influence of a prophetic spirit - giving him the gift and word of prophecy.

In John 1:51, the Lord Jesus said something very intriguing to Nathanael at his first meeting him – *"And He saith unto him, Verily, verily, I say unto you, Hereafter ye shall see heaven open, and the angels of God ascending and descending upon the Son of man."* What He was relating to Nathanael was that there would be a perpetual intercourse opened between heaven and earth for him. And it would all come about through the medium of Him - the Messiah. Clear and abundant revelations of God's will would be made unto him. All mysteries shut up and hidden would be revealed. He would enjoy angelic protection and assistance. This would all prove that Jesus is indeed Who He claimed to be - the Messiah.

This verse in particular draws us back to Genesis 28:12, which gives the account of Jacob experiencing an "open heaven". The Bible says, *"And he dreamed, and behold a ladder set up on the earth, and the top of it reached to heaven: and behold the angels of God ascending and descending on it."* Here, "ladder" is depicted as the medium of communication between heaven and earth. As we had seen in John 1:51, Jesus Christ is that medium. He is the way to heaven. All God's favours come through Him.

Daniel on the subject said, "*And whiles I was speaking, and praying, and confessing my sin and the sin of my people Israel, and presenting my supplication before the LORD my God for the holy mountain of my God; Yes, whiles I was speaking in prayer, even the man Gabriel, whom I had seen in the vision at the beginning, being caused to fly swiftly, touched me about the time of the evening oblation. And he informed me, and talked with me, and said, O Daniel, I am now come forth to give you skill and understanding. At the beginning of your supplications the commandment came forth, and I am come to show you; for you are greatly beloved: therefore understand the matter, and consider the vision*" (Daniel 9:20-23).

Whilst Daniel was praying Gabriel, whom he had seen in the vision at the beginning (Daniel 8:16-17) came and touched him at the time of the evening oblation, about 3pm. Notice in verse 23 that Gabriel's commission was given at the start of Daniel's prayer. So his prayer had been answered before he had even finished. Friends, the effectual fervent prayer of a righteous man availeth much! (James 5:16). But notice the speed at which Gabriel covers the distance from heaven to earth, no more than a couple of minutes. Gabriel goes on to give Daniel some encouragement and comfort by telling him that he was greatly beloved. What a privilege and honour. We too can have the privilege and honour of having the love of

God bestowed upon us and be called the sons of God and adopted into the family of God (1 John 3:1, Rom. 8:14-17).

In the Book of Acts, we find Stephen, the first martyr, encountering an "open heaven" as well as the Apostle Peter – *"But he(Stephen) being full of the Holy Ghost, looked up steadfastly into heaven, and saw the glory of God, and Jesus standing on the right hand of God. And said, Behold, I see the heavens opened, and the Son of man standing on the right hand of God"* (Acts 7:55-56). *"On the morrow...Peter went up upon the housetop to pray about the sixth hour: And he became very hungry, and would have eaten: but while they made ready, he fell into a trance, And saw heaven opened, and a certain vessel descending unto him, as it had been a great sheet knit at the four corners; and let down to the earth"* (Acts 10:9-11). Stephen saw "the heavens opened." This is a figurative expression denoting that he was permitted to see into the eternal world. Heaven came down to him - giving him a view of the happiness he was going to. Peter also saw "heaven opened." This was also a common mode of speaking found in the Hebrew Scriptures. It depicted the sky above as a vast expanse opened to present an opportunity for anything to descend. It was an emblem of the opening and revealing of some sort of mystery. Notice that Peter had this experience after he prayed. His heart ascended to God in prayer - preparing him to receive the discoveries of divine grace and favour.

Lastly, in the book of Revelation, Apostle John, experiencing an "open heaven" said,

> *After this I looked, and, behold, a door was opened in heaven: and the first voice which I heard was as it were of a trumpet talking with me; which said, Come up hither, and I will show thee things which must be hereafter* (Rev. 4:1).

> *And I saw heaven opened, and behold a white horse; and He that sat upon him was called Faithful and True...* (Rev. 19:11).

In both cases, John was permitted to look into the world above. In the first instance, heaven was pictured as a door that remained shut to those on the earth. However, as soon as it was opened for him, he heard the voice of the Lord calling him higher in order to get a better view of future happenings. In the second incident, he was given the opportunity to see into the heavens and behold the Lord Jesus Himself as the Triumphant, Conquering, and soon coming King.

The significance of open heavens therefore, can be summarised thus:

When the heavens were opened for the Prophet Ezekiel, he saw the "visions of God"...accurately heard and understood the word of the Lord...and was mightily strengthened by the "hand of the LORD" for the task ahead of him. When baptizing Jesus, John the Baptist saw the heavens open and the Holy Ghost descend like a dove upon the Son of God. This all happened as a result of Jesus' prayer. Nathanael was told by the Lord that he would experience Jacob's ladder - an "open heaven" where the angels of God would ascend and descend with the blessings from above. It would all happen through Christ and for His glory and name's sake. While Peter was praying, he received an "open heaven" whereby he was enabled to tap into the mysteries concerning the calling of the Gentiles. And John the Revelator experienced an "open heaven" whereby he was given "visions from God" concerning end-time events and the Second Coming of Jesus.

Chapter 30

SELFISH MOTIVES

The strongest indication we have in the Word of God on the subject of hindrances to prayer is James 4:3, *"You ask and do not receive, because you ask wrongly, to spend it on your passions."* Our Master did not say it was wrong to pray in the corners of the street, but He did say it was wrong to have the motive to be seen of men. If our prayer must amount to anything before God, it is imperative that our motives be scrutinised under the full glare of the Holy Spirit.

Edwin Robinson was succinct when he said, "The world is …a kind of kindergarten where millions of bewildered infants are trying to spell God with the wrong blocks." It is certain that unless we attain to a certain level of spiritual maturity, we would very likely ask God for things for the wrong reasons. The Bible asserts, *"…the natural man receiveth not the things of the Spirit of God: for they are foolishness unto him: neither can he know them, because they are spiritually discerned"* (1 Cor. 2:1).

Humans are selfish by nature. It is part of our human nature that we naturally regard our own interests ahead of the interests of others. Sadly, we even often regard our own interests ahead of God's. In 1 John 5:14 -15, the Apostle John declares,

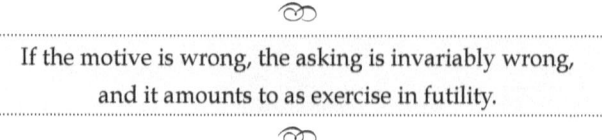

If the motive is wrong, the asking is invariably wrong, and it amounts to as exercise in futility.

"And this is the confidence that we have in him, that, if we ask any thing according to his will, he heareth us: And if we know that he hear us, whatsoever we ask, we know that we have the petitions that we desired of him" (1 John 5:14-15). Our confidence comes from asking "according to His [God's] will." We could have a scenario; however, where we could be asking God for the right thing with the wrong motive. It stands to reason, therefore, that if we do not ask according to God's will, no matter how justified in our judgment we may think we are, our prayer will still be sincerely misdirected. In essence, you may be asking God for the wrong thing for the right purpose or the right thing for the wrong purpose. Motive for wanting the subject matter of our prayer is the issue here. If the motive is wrong, the asking is invariably wrong, and it amounts to an exercise in futility. We must ask in accordance with God's will as revealed in His word. We must ask only for things that are consistent with the character and nature of God. We must ask for things that are for the spiritual benefit of ourselves or for the person on whose behalf we pray. God will not answer our self-centred and self-serving prayers. The major antidote to this problem, it appears, is to constantly examine the sincerity of our hearts, in relation our prayer objectives. Further, since the word of God is the revealer of the will of God, it is expedient for the supplicant to be convinced that his request is consistent with the word of God. Jesus has guaranteed mankind, *"If ye abide in me, and my words abide in you, ye shall ask what ye will, and it shall be done unto you"* (John 15:7).

God will not answer our self-centred, self-serving prayers. The major antidote to this problem, it appears, is to constantly examine the sincerity of our hearts, in relation to our prayer objectives.

THE SIN FACTOR

> *Behold, the LORD's hand is not shortened, that it cannot save; neither His ear heavy, that it cannot hear. But your iniquities have separated you and your God, and your sins have hid His face from you, that He will not hear* (Isaiah 59:1-2).

God has a deep abhorrence for sin. As a matter of fact, sin provokes God, and moves Him to unleash judgment if warnings are not heeded. We find an interesting example in God's reaction to the sin of Sodom and Gomorrah. And God said, *"... Because the cry of Sodom and Gomorrah is great,* **and because their sin is very grievous**; *I will go down now, and see whether* *they have done altogether according to the cry of it, which is come unto me; and if not, I will know"* (Gen. 18:20,21, emphasis added).

In this passage, God said that cry had gone out of Sodom and Gomorrah, a situation reminiscent of the biblical account of Genesis chapter 4, when Cain killed his brother Abel. God came down and said that Abel's blood had cried to Him. Both incidents cried for God's judgment.

God's nature cannot put up with sin! We see that heaven is spiritually closed because of sin. Man - whether sinner or saint - shuts heaven to himself through disobedience. Matthew Henry observes that, *"sin hinders God's mercies from coming down upon us; **it is a partition wall** that separates between us and God"* (emphasis added).

Paul warns emphatically, *"Nevertheless the foundation of God standeth sure, having this seal, The Lord knoweth them that are his. And, Let every one that nameth the name of Christ **depart from iniquity**"* (2 Tim 2: 19, emphasis added). God's standard cannot change; and He is no respecter of persons (Acts 10:34).

Draped with God's awesome glory, Prophet Habakkuk wrote, *"Thou art of purer eyes than to behold evil, and canst not look on iniquity: wherefore lookest thou upon them that deal treacherously, and holdest thy tongue when the wicked devoureth the man that is more righteous than he?"* (Hab. 1:13).

Sin has a devastating impact on the believer and his relationship with God. The believer caught in the web of sin is stripped of all his spiritual defences and is open to the enemy's attacks. The devil acknowledges that the believer in his best form of relationship and fellowship with God is protected and immune to his attacks.

"Then Satan answered the LORD, "Does Job fear God for nothing? "Have You not made a hedge about him and his house and all that he has, on every side?" (Job 1:10).

> Sin has a devastating impact on the believer and his relationship with God. The believer caught in the web of sin is stripped of all his spiritual defences and is open to the enemy's attacks.

1 Samuel 23:14 proclaims "... David abode in the wilderness in strong holds, and remained in a mountain in the wilderness of Ziph. And Saul sought him every day, but God delivered him not into his hand." Notice where David chose as his hiding place, when the enemy of his soul was intent on destroying him. He was in the very presence of God.

Israel suffered the full effect of sin in their defeat in Ai.

When the Israelites crossed the Jordan River, God gave them a mighty victory over the large city Jericho (Joshua 6). Yet when they came to the little town of Ai, they suffered a humiliating defeat. In response,

Joshua ran to God in prayer: *"And Joshua said, Alas, O Lord GOD, wherefore hast thou at all brought this people over Jordan, to deliver us into the hand of the Amorites, to destroy us? would to God we had been content, and dwelt on the other side Jordan!"* (Joshua 7:7). Rather than answering Joshua's plea for help, God told him to stop praying and deal with the sin that was in the camp.

With the conquest of Jericho, Israel was a 'victor'. But with the victory came a costly and deadly evil that instantly changed Israel's position from victory to defeat. The difference between Israel's encounter in Jericho and Ai was the presence of sin in the camp. Consequently Israel felt unable to withstand the adversary. In Joshua 7:10-11, we have a full picture of the situation:

"And the LORD said unto Joshua, Get thee up; wherefore liest thou thus upon thy face? Israel hath sinned, and they have also transgressed my covenant which I commanded them: for they have even taken of the accursed thing, and have also stolen, and dissembled also, and they have put it even among their own stuff."

The solution to the problem was not a lengthy prayer meeting but rather dealing with the hidden sin.

Though God had commanded that everything in Jericho was to be reserved as holy to Him, rather than taken as the spoils of war, Achan had seen things that he wanted in the ruins of Jericho, took them and hid them in his tent. As a result of his sin, the army of Israel was robbed of God's power and protection. The solution to the problem was not far-fetched. It was not to be found in lengthy prayer meeting, nor fasting, but in dealing with the hidden sin.

When we allow sin to hinder our prayers, we are cut off from a vital source of spiritual renewal. The effect of sin on our prayer could not be more clearly stated than is affirmed in Psalm 66:18, *"If I regard iniquity in my heart, the Lord will not hear me."*

The same principle applies to individuals as well as nations or churches. Sin blocks effective prayer. If we want God's power to be active in our daily lives through prayer, then we must confess and forsake our sin.

THE PRAYER OF THE RIGHTEOUS

God is committed to answering the prayers of the righteous. A great deal has been said to that effect. However, the following scriptures further buttress the point:

"...The effectual fervent prayer of a righteous man avails much" (James 5:16)

"But know that the Lord has set apart for Himself [and given distinction to] him who is godly [the man of loving-kindness]. The Lord listens and heeds when I call to Him" (Psalm 4:3, Amp.)

"The eyes of the LORD are upon the righteous, and his ears are open unto their cry" (Psalm 34:15)

"If thou wert pure and upright; surely now he would awake for thee, and make the habitation of thy righteousness prosperous. Though thy beginning was small, yet thy latter end should greatly increase. For enquire, I pray thee, of the former age, and prepare thyself to the search of their fathers" (Job. 8:6-8).

"For the eyes of the Lord are over the righteous, and his ears are open unto their prayers: but the face of the Lord is against them that do evil" (1Pet. 3:12).

This should act as impetus to live a life that is pleasing to God.

THE CONDITION OF THE HEART

Closely linked to the issue of sin is that of the condition of a man's heart. This is of vital importance to God. No man receives anything from God without God first examining his heart. The condition of the heart determines whether God can do business with man, and to what extent God can relate with him. We gain great illumination in the following passage of scripture on the matter:

No man receives anything from God without God having to first judge his heart.

And Samuel did that which the Lord spake, and came to Bethlehem. And the elders of the town trembled at his coming, and said, Comest thou peaceably? And he said, Peaceably: I am come to sacrifice unto the Lord: sanctify yourselves, and come with me to the sacrifice. And he sanctified Jesse and his sons, and called them to the sacrifice. And it came to pass, when they were come, that he looked on Eliab, and said, Surely the Lord's anointed is before him (1 Sam. 16:4-6).

The condition of the heart determines whether God can do business with man and to what extent God can relate with him.

Here, Samuel was commissioned to visit the house of Jesse after the demise of King Saul, to anoint one of Jesse's sons as Saul's replacement. It is certain that God had already appointed Saul's successor among Jesse's sons. Samuel was to merely authenticate that appointment. However, the sight of Eliab (Jesse's eldest son) almost caused Samuel to commit an irrevocable error. Immediately Samuel saw Eliab, his instinct moved him to want to place the anointing on him, against God's pre-ordained will and purpose.

The Bible says, *"And it came to pass, when they were come, that he looked on Eliab, and said, Surely the Lord's anointed is before him"* (v.6). God's intervention could not have been sooner. In it Samuel learnt the lesson of his life: *"But the Lord said unto Samuel, **Look not on his countenance**, or on the height of his stature; because I have refused him: for the Lord seeth not as man seeth; for man looketh on the outward appearance, but the Lord looketh on the heart"* (v.7, emphasis added).

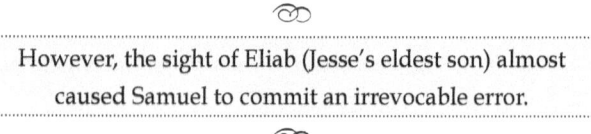

However, the sight of Eliab (Jesse's eldest son) almost caused Samuel to commit an irrevocable error.

God knew the sort of short-sighted, narrow-minded, fear – ridden and insecure leader Eliab would be, were he to become the leader of His people. The event that unfolded shortly after this incident, more than anything else, was to justify God's preference for David over Eliab.

Israel was on a battle field with the Philistines. From all indications, Goliath's appearance and rhetoric had put Israel in grave fear, even before the battle began. The Bible records:

> *A champion named Goliath, who was from Gath, came out of the Philistine camp. His height was six cubits and a span.[a] He had a bronze helmet on his head and wore a coat of scale armor of bronze weighing five thousand shekels[b]; on his legs he wore bronze greaves, and a*

> *bronze javelin was slung on his back. His spear shaft was like a weaver's rod, and its iron point weighed six hundred shekels.[c] His shield bearer went ahead of him.Goliath stood and shouted to the ranks of Israel, "Why do you come out and line up for battle? Am I not a Philistine, and are you not the servants of Saul? Choose a man and have him come down to me. If he is able to fight and kill me, we will become your subjects; but if I overcome him and kill him, you will become our subjects and serve us." Then the Philistine said, "This day I defy the armies of Israel! Give me a man and let us fight each other." On hearing the Philistine's words, Saul and all the Israelites were dismayed and terrified* (1 Sam. 17:4-11 NIV).

Right in the midst of this rather ugly situation, David appeared in the battle field and began to make enquiries as to the reward that would go to whoever could defeat goliath.

> *David asked the men standing near him, "What will be done for the man who kills this Philistine and removes this disgrace from Israel? Who is this uncircumcised Philistine that he should defy the armies of the living God?" They repeated to him what they had been saying and told him, "This is what will be done for the man who kills him. When Eliab, David's oldest brother, heard him speaking with the men, he burned with anger at him and asked, "Why have you come down here? And with whom did you leave those few sheep in the wilderness? I know how conceited you are and how wicked your heart is; you came down only to watch the battle. "Now what have I done?" said David. "Can't I even speak?" He then turned away to someone else and brought up the same matter, and the men answered him as before* (vv. 26-30).

> What made God reject Eliab made David turn away from him!

Notice David's frustration at Eliab's attitude. The Bible, very significantly, records that David "turned away [from Eliab] to someone else" (v.30). At his best, this was the true portrait of Eliab. Had Eliab been chosen the King of Israel, faced with a similar situation of this magnitude, he would have deserted God's people on the battle field. What made God reject Eliab made David turn away from him! Eliab had a grave attitude problem. This was a major deficit in his life. Making him king would not have solved his problem, it would have exasperated it. Some succeed because they are destined to but far more succeed because they are determined to. There was no such determination in Eliab to be Saul's successor.

> The sum total of a man's life is revealed by his heart. A man cannot be different from his heart. If you want to know what a man is made of, look at the product of his heart...

The Bible says, "*For promotion cometh neither from the east, nor from the west, nor from the south. But God is the judge:* **he putteth down one, and setteth up another**" (Psalm 75: 6-7, emphasis added). In context, God had to "put" Eliab down, to set up David. You see, experience is not what happens to a man, it is what a man does with what happens to him.

The sum total of a man's life is revealed by his heart. A man cannot be different from his heart. If you want to know what a man is made up of, look at the product of his heart: *"A good man out of the good treasure of his heart bringeth forth that which is good; and an evil man out of the evil treasure of his heart bringeth forth that which is evil: for of the abundance of the heart his mouth speaketh"* (Luke 6:45).

The Bible tells us that a man's heart, at its best, is "… deceitful above all things, and desperately wicked: who can know it?" (Jer. 17:9). Spiritual maturity aids us in overcoming this Adamic nature, making our hearts more pliable to the ways of God.

Chapter 31

IDOLS IN THE HEART

> Son of man, these men have set up their idols in their heart, and put the stumblingblock of their iniquity before their face: should I be enquired of at all by them? The word of the Lord came to me...Son of man, if a country sins against me by being unfaithful and I stretch out my hand against it to cut off its food supply and send famine upon it and kill its people and their animals, even if these three men – Noah, Daniel[a] and Job – were in it, they could save only themselves by their righteousness, declares the Sovereign Lord (Ezek. 14:3, 12-14).

Be careful, or you will be enticed to turn away and worship other gods and bow down to them. Then the Lord's anger will burn against you, and he will shut up the heavens so that it will not rain and the ground will yield no produce, and you will soon perish from the good land the Lord is giving you (Deut. 11:16,17).

Anything that can make the heaven over a man to become brass hinders his prayer from being heard. In these sobering passages of scripture, we find something intriguing – the presence of idols in the heart! In David's words to Solomon, we read,

> And thou, Solomon my son, know thou the God of thy father, and serve him with a perfect heart and with a willing mind: for the LORD searcheth all hearts, and

> *understandeth all the imaginations of the thoughts:* ***if thou seek him, he will be found of thee; but if thou forsake him, he will cast thee off forever*** (1 Chr. 28:9, emphasis added).

When a man has chosen another god to serve, and shifts his allegiance to that other god as an object of worship, God is provoked to anger and judgment. Here, God is not talking about statutes, or stones or any object of worship in particular. He was referring to idols of the heart. The displacement of God from His rightful place in the life of a man can be an idol. Idols in the heart can be an ambition, career, money, one's spouse, parents or desire for fame.

King Saul regarded the idol of the praises of men more than the approval of God. When confronted by the Prophet of God, he cherished his reputation more than the truth and blamed his people for something he had done. Even after he realised that David had been chosen by God Himself to assume the throne of Israel, Saul tried on several occasions, to kill God's appointed King. He was possessed and driven by the idol of self-image.

God cannot put up with a man whose heart is filled with idols; he therefore, withdraws communication from him. The operation of idols in the heart can be very subtle. It can happen without realising it. We need to constantly search our heart to know 'who' is there.

Hear God's assessment of the situation:

> *This people draweth nigh unto me with their mouth, and honoureth me with their lips; but their heart is far from me. But in vain they do worship me, teaching for doctrines the commandments of men... But those things which proceed out of the mouth come forth from the heart; and they defile the man. For out of the heart proceed evil thoughts, murders, adulteries, fornications, thefts, false witness, blasphemies: These are the things which defile a man: but to eat with unwashen hands defileth not a man (Matt. 15: 8, 9, 18-20).*

God wants all of our hearts, not some of it! The cry of His heart remains: *"My son, give me thine heart, and let thine eyes observe my ways"* (Pro. 23:26). May we heed the Master's clarion call with the urgency it deserves, and render our hearts as a living sacrifice, holy and acceptable unto the Author and Finisher of our faith.

MARITAL DISHARMONY

> *Likewise, ye husbands, dwell with them according to knowledge, giving honour unto the wife, as unto the weaker vessel, and as being heirs together of the grace of life; that your prayers be not hindered* (1 Pet. 3:7, emphasis added).

For clarity, let us examine the same scripture in another version of the Bible:

> *In the same way, you husbands must give honor to your wives. Treat your wife with understanding as you live together. She may be weaker than you are, but she is*

> *your equal partner in God's gift of new life. Treat her as you should so your prayers will not be hindered* (New Living Translation).

It is clear from the above Bible passage that broken relationship in the home, between a husband and wife will hinder prayers. Peter was saying in essence, to the husband, 'dwell with your wife with understanding, ensuring that nothing interferes with the godly, harmonious relationship the Bible prescribes.' It is to be noted that, though Peter was speaking specifically to husbands in this scripture, the principle nonetheless, applies to wives. We are admonished by Paul to, *"Recompense to no man evil for evil. Provide things honest in the sight of all men. If it be possible, as much as lieth in you, live peaceably with all men"* (Rom.12:17-18).

God takes the issue of marital harmony seriously; it is close to His heart, as we can see from the following scriptures, *"This is another thing you do. You drown the Lord's altar with tears, weeping and wailing because he no longer accepts the offerings you bring him. You ask why he no longer accepts them. It is because he knows you have broken your promise to the wife you married when you were young. She was your partner, and you have broken your promise to her, although you promised before God that you would be faithful to her. 15 Didn't God make you one body and spirit with her? What was his purpose in this? It was that you should have children who are truly God's people. So make sure that none of you breaks his promise to his wife. "I hate divorce," says the Lord God of Israel. "I hate it when one of you does such a cruel thing to his wife. Make sure that you do not break your promise to be faithful to your wife"* (Mal. 2:13-16 GNT).

Sadly, most Christians read the first part of Malachi 2:16, which says that God hates divorce, and stop there. But the verse goes on to say emphatically:

> *For the LORD, the God of Israel, saith that he hateth putting away:* **for one covereth violence with his garment, saith the LORD of hosts:** *therefore take heed to your spirit, that ye deal not treacherously* (emphasis added).

The phrase *"for one covereth violence with his garment"* is far from being an accurate translation of the true meaning of the verse. The word "garment" refers to the wife. One of the best translations of this verse is found in the Amplified Bible.

> *For the Lord, the God of Israel, says: I hate divorce and marital separation and him who covers his garment* **[his wife]** *with violence. Therefore keep a watch upon your spirit [that it may be controlled by My Spirit], that you deal not treacherously and faithlessly [with your marriage mate]* (emphasis added).

God not only hates divorce, He hates a man or woman who covers his or her mate in violence and then tries to cover it. Unfortunately, domestic violence (spouse beating) has become an epidemic in the world, and it is, most regrettably, almost as prevalent in the Church. God hates it!

God demands that we seek and maintain close harmony in our family relationships.

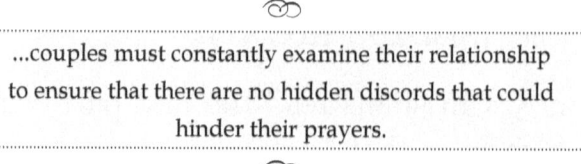

> ...couples must constantly examine their relationship to ensure that there are no hidden discords that could hinder their prayers.

The relationship between husband and wife is to reflect that which exists between Christ and His church. It is to be a relationship of absolute love, adoration and sacrifice. If Christ gave His life for the church, how can a husband do any less for his wife? This is, of course, impossible when the relationship is strained or broken. Thus couples must constantly examine their relationship to ensure that there are no hidden discords that could hinder their prayers. Many marriages are destroyed and many prayers hindered. Too often, marriages are torn apart by wrong judgments and assumptions that breed contempt. Beware lest Satan, using his most compelling lies against you, implants in your mind thoughts that fuel hatred and discord. Once the enemy succeeds in planting seeds of suspicion, hatred, bitterness and unforgiveness in your marriage, you begin to follow a dangerous path that separates you from your spouse, even while living under the same roof. This path which most assuredly breeds discord, invariably results in tragic pain which may eventually, lead to separation and divorce. Build your marriage on the solid word of God; adhering to God's blue-prints for a successful and lasting marriage.

UNFAITHFUL GIVING

An ungenerous heart is another hindrance to prayer. Let us examine the following scriptures on the subject.

"Whoso stoppeth his ears at the cry of the poor, he also shall cry himself, but shall not be heard" (Pro. 21:13).

"There are those who [generously]scatter abroad, and yet increase more; there are those who withhold more than is fitting or what is justly due, but it results only in want. The liberal person shall be enriched, and he who waters shall himself be watered" (Pro. 11:24-25).

"One person gives freely, yet gains even more; another withholds unduly, but comes to poverty. A generous person will prosper; whoever refreshes others will be refreshed. People curse the one who hoards grain, but they pray God's blessing on the one who is willing to sell. Whoever seeks good finds favor, but evil comes to one who searches for it" (Prov. 11:24-27 NIV).

"Will a man rob God? Yet ye have robbed me. But ye say, Wherein have we robbed thee? In tithes and offerings. Ye are cursed with a curse: for ye have robbed me, even this whole nation. Bring ye all the tithes into the storehouse, that there may be meat in mine house, and prove me now herewith, saith the Lord of hosts, if I will not open you the windows of heaven, and pour you out a blessing, that there

shall not be room enough to receive it. And I will rebuke the devourer for your sakes, and he shall not destroy the fruits of your ground; neither shall your vine cast her fruit before the time in the field, saith the Lord of hosts. And all nations shall call you blessed: for ye shall be a delightsome land, saith the Lord of hosts" (Mal. 3:8-12).

The wilful disobedience in not giving your tithe and offerings to the Lord can be a major blockade to prayer, especially while believing God for financial breakthrough. The position could not be clearer, **"Give, and it shall be given unto you;** *good measure, pressed down, and shaken together, and running over, shall men give into your bosom. For with the same measure that ye mete withal it shall be measured to you again"* (Luke 6:38, emphasis added).

Majority of believers have not come to terms with the fundamental principles that govern financial prosperity. The key to our receiving is our giving. When the heaven holds back the 'rain' of prosperity from us, the only solution the Bible offers is strategic sowing. The principle of seedtime and harvest is one of the Bible mysteries that defile human reasoning and comprehension. It is a principle, so fundamental, impregnable and irrevocable; it transcends the limits of time. It has God's seal of approval on it; it has been proven and tested!

The Bible says, *"And the Lord smelled a sweet savour; and the Lord said in his heart, I will not again curse the ground any more for man's sake; for the imagination of man's heart is evil from his youth; neither will I again smite any more everything living, as I have done. While the earth remaineth, seedtime and harvest...shall not cease"* (Gen. 8:21, 22).

Further, we are asked to, *"Honour the LORD with thy substance and with the firstfruits of all thine increase"*, and the result? *"So shall thy barns be filled with plenty, and thy presses shall burst out with new wine"* (Pro. 3:9-10).

When we give God back the tithe that is His to begin with, He blesses us abundantly spiritually and physically. Notice that God says He commands tithes so *"that there may be food in My house"* (Malachi 3:10). Tithe is primarily used to feed God's people spiritually! If we support the work God is doing through His faithful ministers, He promises to bless us far above anything we could imagine (Eph. 3:20-21)!

The combined effect of Malachi 3:8-12, Luke 6:38, Proverbs 11:24-27 and Proverb 3:9 leaves us with the following conclusions:

- A person that withholds from God is cursed. The only thing that breaks that curse is not the 'super-anointing' upon the Bishop or the Apostle; it is the sheer obedience of the believer that removes the curse.

- He promises not only blessings in return for obedience, but He says He will personally rebuke the devourer on our behalf.

- The measure of harvest we have in return is determined by the giver *–"For with the same measure that ye mete withal it shall be measured to you again"* – (Luke 6:38).

Paul teaches that "*...He which soweth sparingly shall reap also sparingly; and he which soweth bountifully shall reap also bountifully. Every man according as he purposeth in his heart, so let him give; not grudgingly, or of necessity: for God loveth a cheerful giver. And God is able to make all grace abound toward you; that ye, always having all sufficiency in all things, may abound to every good work*" (2 Cor. 9:5-8).

UNFORGIVENESS AND STRIFE

> *Therefore if thou bring thy gift to the altar, and there rememberest that thy brother hath ought against thee; Leave there thy gift before the altar, and go thy way; first be reconciled to thy brother, and then come and offer thy gift* (Matt. 5:23,24).

Unforgiveness and strife strike directly at our ability to pray. They are one of the most serious blockades to prayer.

Unforgiveness and strife will hinder your prayers by making your relationship with God and man unfruitful. Without forgiving others, we are left unforgiven by God. For prayer to be effective in yielding the desired outcome, unforgiveness must be dealt with! Prayer will simply not work with unforgiveness. The message could not be clearer than as taught by Jesus, "*And whenever you stand praying, if you have anything against anyone, forgive him, that your Father in heaven may also forgive you your trespasses. But if you do not forgive, neither will your Father in heaven forgive your trespasses"* (Mark 11:25-26). Jesus prayed, *"And he said unto them, When ye pray, say, Our Father which art in heaven, Hallowed be thy name. Thy kingdom come. Thy will be done, as in heaven, so in earth. Give us day by day our daily bread. And forgive us our sins; for we also forgive every one that is indebted to us. And lead us not into temptation; but deliver us from evil"* (Luke 11:2-4).

Unforgiveness does not reflect the character of Christ, and it demonstrates ingratitude for the vast forgiveness God has extended to you.

Jesus sums up the need for forgiveness in the above scriptures. Unforgiveness does not reflect the character of Christ, and it demonstrates ingratitude for the vast forgiveness God has extended to you. It cuts us from receiving God's forgiveness and short-circuits the power generated by our prayer. Releasing the people that have caused us pains will release us to make progress in every area of life. The Christian has been forgiven for the greatest of offenses. He has been forgiven for knowingly, purposely and unrepentantly transgressing the law of God. And yet, we are often slow to forgive our fellow man for the smallest of transgressions. Even the biggest of the sins committed against us is nothing compared to our transgressions against God. On reflection, Mark 11:25 earlier considered highlights the reciprocal nature of forgiveness. Jesus admonishes *"And whenever you stand praying, forgive, if you have anything against anyone, so that your Father also who is in heaven may forgive you your trespasses."* The phrase, *"so that your Father also who is in heaven may forgive you your trespasses"* is insightful. It indicates that our forgiving others is the basis for our sins being forgiven by God. It appears to me that God would answer prayer only to the degree to which man's willingness to forgive the wrongs of others allows Him. You need to resolve issues of unforgiveness in your life if you want God to hear your prayers. God will not share His temple with uncleanness, pride and sinful rebellion. Strife is acting upon unforgiveness. The need for forgiveness was modelled by Jesus, not only through His frequent teachings on the subject but by, in fact, living it out in His relationship with others. For instance, Jesus forgave the paralytic that was lowered on a mat through the roof (Mark 2:3-5), He forgave the woman caught in adultery (John 8:3-11), He forgave Peter for denying Him (John 18:15-18), He forgave the criminal on the cross (Luke 23:39-43), He forgave the people who crucified Him (Luke 23:34), finally and most significantly, He forgave you (Rom. 5:8, Ps. 103:3).

> It appears to me that God would answer prayer only to the degree to which man's willingness to forgive the wrongs of others allows Him..

It has been proven that unforgiveness is hazardous to our health. Our relationships and ability to forgive each other is viewed by God very critically. This is reflected in the Ten Commandments – six of which deal with people to people (horizontal relationships) and four with people to God (vertical relationships). God, no doubt, foreknew that we will have issues with one another hence He gave more commandments regulating our horizontal relationships than our relationship with Him.

The strongest warning against the devastating effect of strife, in my view is James 3:16 says, *"For where envying and strife is, there is confusion and every evil work."* Also in 2 Timothy 2: 24-26, Paul warns that because of strife Satan can dominate and have control over the believer, *"And the servant of the Lord must not strive; but be gentle unto all men, apt to teach, patient, In meekness instructing those that oppose themselves; if God peradventure will give them repentance to the acknowledging of the truth; And that they may recover themselves out of the snare of the devil, who are taken captive by him at his will."*

"Harmony", says Kenneth Copeland "makes the prayer system work." And he affirms, "The absence of strife is the key to getting rid of confusion and evil. It is the predominant, primary prerequisite for answered prayer...the first thing to do is begin to forgive. Get strife out of your life...Give God the opportunity to create a system of harmony around you and your prayer life will begin to work."

Before we conclude that God has simply not heard or prayers or that it is not His will to give us what we ask, we need to examine our hearts to see if unforgiveness and strife stands as a barrier between ourselves and God.

David says, *"If I regard iniquity in my heart, the Lord will not hear me"* (Psalm 66:18). Before we conclude that God has simply not heard our prayers or that it is not His will to give us what we ask, we need to examine our hearts to see i unforgiveness and strife stand as barriers between ourselves and God.

Apostle Paul warned of the consequences of unforgiveness when he told the believers at Corinth:

"To whom ye forgive anything, I forgive also: for if I forgave anything, to whom I forgave it, for your sakes forgave I it in the person of Christ; **lest Satan shouldget an advantage of us***: for we are not ignorant of his devices"* (2 Cor. 2:10,11, emphasis added).

Chapter 32

DOUBT AND UNBELIEF

> *For verily I say unto you, That whosoever shall say unto this mountain, Be thou removed, and be thou cast into the sea; and shall not doubt in his heart, but shall believe that those things which he saith shall come to pass; he shall have whatsoever he saith. Therefore I say unto you, What things soever ye desire, when ye pray, believe that ye receive them, and ye shall have them* (Mark 11: 23, 24).

> *If any of you lack wisdom, let him ask of God, that giveth to all men liberally, and upbraideth not; and it shall be given him. But let him ask in faith, nothing wavering. For he that wavereth is like a wave of the sea driven with the wind and tossed. For let not that man think that he shall receive any thing of the Lord. A double minded man is unstable in all his ways* (James 1:5-8).

Doubt and unbelief are two of the greatest hindrances to prayer. Doubt puts a believer in a state of mind where he rationalises and filters the Word of God and chooses to accept what his senses and prevailing circumstances persuade Him to believe. Doubt is similar to unbelief; it comes from a mind that is divided on what the word of God says on a given subject. Take the issue of divine healing for instance. A doubtful person would believe that God does heal, but doubts if God is able and willing to heal him. It is common to hear such believers make statements like:

"I know God heals, but…" The interjection of the word "but" in a statement or declaration of faith introduces or brings doubt into such statements, because what you say after "but" is very likely to express doubt and fear. Put in context, you are saying something like, "I know God heals, but I don't know if He will heal me."

James declares:

> …let him ask in faith, nothing wavering. For he that wavereth is like a wave of the sea driven with the wind and tossed. For let not that man think that he shall receive any thing of the Lord (James 1:6-7).

Unbelief is a condition of disbelief or obstinate rejection of the word of God.

James Burck defines unbelief as "a foundation of a false belief system that chooses to believe error instead of the word of God…" We must see unbelief for what it is: the arch-enemy of the cross of Jesus! This self-reliant core of humanity has the power to enslave people in the hopeless bond of perfectionism, chronic fear of failure, rejection, and existential despair. Faith is the victory that, day by day, overcomes the chronic world of unbelief.

Our prayers cannot be separated from our faith. If we are to ask God, we must ask with expectancy, believing in our heart of hearts that God can and will give what we desire …

Our prayers cannot be separated from our faith. In the words of another, "Faith is the power-source, but prayer switches it on." If we are to ask God, we must ask with expectancy, believing in our heart of hearts that God can and will give what we desire, provided that what we desire is really what we need and what will bring glory to Him! We are to ask with confidence and expectancy, praying out of the faith He has given us.

According to Paul Spencer, unbelief is believing something contrary to God's Word – which is the highest truth. We don't have to try so hard to do this because the world conditions us with unbelief from an early age. C.H. Spurgeon said that right believing produces right living. In her books on the unredeemed nature, the Bible teacher and author, Liberty Savard, talks about layers that the soul creates in order to protect itself. This is the soul's bottom line defence system and includes self-control, self-reliance, self-protection, self-centredness, self-defence. When we view the negative behaviour of the soul in connection with the term layers of protection then we can begin to understand the "whys" of our wrong thinking and wrong behaviour. It is obvious that it is this accumulation of wrong beliefs, or unbelief that gives rise to a sinful disposition. Sin is the inevitable response to unbelief: sin being the nature of man without intimate relationship with God. This intimate relationship demands unconditional surrender to God.

The greatest antidote to doubt and unbelief is the word of God – the final authority in every matter.

FEAR AND WORRY

"An anxious heart weighs a man down, but a kind word cheers him up" (Pro. 12:25, NIV).

"I sought the LORD, and he heard me, and delivered me from all my fears" (Psalm 34:4).

"Do not be anxious about anything, but in everything, by prayer and petition, with thanksgiving, present your requests to God. And the peace of God, which transcends all understanding, will guard your hearts and your minds in Christ Jesus" (Phil. 4:6-7).

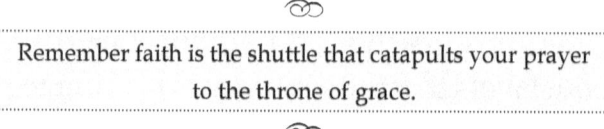

Remember faith is the shuttle that catapults your prayer to the throne of grace.

Fear and worry are also major enemies of the believer. Fear will rob the believer in Christ Jesus of the best God has for him. Anything that hinders our faith is an enemy of effective fervent prayer; fear and worry are two very destructive ones. They both have the capability to overcome faith and render the believer spiritually numb. Remember faith is the shuttle that catapults your prayer to the throne of grace. Anything that reduces or inhibits faith in the heart of the believer, therefore, is an enemy and must be avoided. We are commanded to come to the throne of grace with boldness, not with fear, anxiety, worry and uncertainty (Heb. 4:16).

Fear is faith in the wrong thing. It is believing the verdict of the devil instead of the word of God. The irony of it is that, it is far easier to have faith than to operate under the weight of fear and worry. The Bible asserts, *"An anxious heart weighs a man down, but a kind word cheers him up"* (Pro. 12:25, NIV).

The possible causes of anxiety and fear are many: conflict, health problems, dangerous situations, death, unmet needs, spiritual problems, false beliefs, etc.

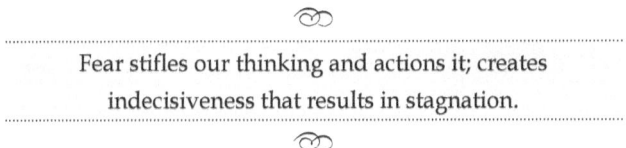

Fear stifles our thinking and actions it; creates indecisiveness that results in stagnation.

Fear stifles our thinking and actions; it creates indecisiveness that results in stagnation. I have known talented people who procrastinate indefinitely rather than risk failure. Lost opportunities cause erosion of confidence, and the downward spiral begins. It hinders us from becoming the people God wants us to be. When we are dominated by negative emotions, we cannot achieve the goals He has in mind for us. A lack of self-confidence stymies our belief in what the Lord can do with our lives.

Remember, *"...God hath not given us the spirit of fear; but of power, and of love, and of a sound mind"* (2 Tim. 1:7).

TURNING AWAY FROM THE SCRIPTURE

> *This book of the law shall not depart out of thy mouth; but thou shalt meditate therein day and night, that thou mayest observe to do according to all that is written therein: for then thou shalt make thy way prosperous, and then thou shalt have good success* (Joshua 1:8).

The word of God is the believer's manual for successful living. However, it just does not end there! Our defiance in ignoring the word of God is a sin that God does not take lightly. The reasoning is quite clear. A life outside the Bible is a life geared towards sin and unrighteousness. It breeds self-righteousness and its concomitant effects, chiefly pride. All these cause God to hide his face from us. The Bible says, *"There they cry, but none giveth answer, because of the pride of evil men. Surely God will not hear vanity, neither will the Almighty regard it"* (Job 35:12-13). Solomon asserts that prayers made from such a hardened heart are an abomination to God. *"If one turns away his ear from hearing the law, even his prayer is an abomination"* (Pro. 28:9). This finds consensus in Proverbs 21:27, where Solomon affirms that the *"The sacrifice of the wicked is abomination..."*

> To the sin-ridden Israel, God says: *"When ye come to appear before me, who hath required this at your hand, to tread my courts? Bring no more vain oblations; incense is an abomination unto me; the new moons and sabbaths, the calling of assemblies, I cannot away with; it is iniquity, even the solemn meeting. Your new moons and your appointed feasts my soul hateth : they are a trouble*

unto me; I am weary to bear them. And when ye spread forth your hands, I will hide mine eyes from you: yea, when ye make many prayers, I will not hear : your hands are full of blood" (Isaiah 1:12-15). But thank God, there was a remedy. God says, *"Wash you, make you clean; put away the evil of your doings from before mine eyes; cease to do evil; Learn to do well; seek judgment, relieve the oppressed, judge the fatherless, plead for the widow* (Isaiah 1:16-17).

When we read the words of Scripture, we position ourselves for God to speak to us. He provides the understanding we need to live lives that bring glory to Him—lives that are increasingly consistent with His standards of grace and holiness. If we ignore God's word, we are tempted to disobey what He teaches; and He will not answer our prayers. Without submitting ourselves to Scripture, we may not even know what and how to pray. We pray best and most effectively when we are saturated with the Word of God.

HOW TO OVERCOME HINDRANCES TO PRAYER

Hindrances to prayer can be overcome. Undoubtedly, overcoming hindrances to prayer requires a thorough act of reflection, self-examination and evaluation, in order to discover matters that could be preventing your prayers from yielding the desired results. Close partnership with the Holy Spirit will reveal invariably, the hidden issues that have been deflating your prayers of the necessary power to generate the desired outcome.

> Undoubtedly, overcoming hindrances to prayer requires a thorough act of reflection, evaluation and self-examination in order to discover matters that could be preventing your prayers from yielding the desired results.

The Bible teaches, *"...for the Spirit searcheth all things, yea, the deep things of God"* (1 Cor. 2:1).

As stated, God does not arbitrarily refuse to answer the prayers of the believer. When the believer's prayers are hindered, issues of sin or disobedience of a kind is almost always involved, apart from matters of demonic interference. Therefore, the key to regaining access to the throne of grace and restoring fervent fellowship with God is genuine repentance.

"But thou, O Lord, art a God full of compassion, and gracious, longsuffering, and plenteous in mercy and truth" (Psalm 86:15).

The phrase, "ready to forgive" make the message clearer in the more modern version of the Bible:

"But you, O Lord, are a compassionate and merciful God. You are patient, always faithful and ready to forgive" (God Word Translation).

And John 1:9 promises that,

"If we confess our sins, he is faithful and just to forgive us our sins, and to cleanse us from all unrighteousness."

Confession is always a remedy for sin.

This is well demonstrated by Israel in the following scripture:

> *O Israel, return unto the Lord thy God; for thou hast fallen by thine iniquity. Take with you words, and turn to the Lord: say unto him, Take away all iniquity, and receive us graciously: so will we render the calves of our lips. Asshur shall not save us; we will not ride upon horses: neither will we say any more to the work of our hands, Ye are our gods: for in thee the fatherless findeth mercy* (Hosea 14:1-3).

Israel had sinned and time of exile had begun. Israel needed to find the right words (confession) to say (verse 2). In the past, Israel had had to regain God's forgiveness through a process called atonement – offering sacrifices to God for sin, and God was no longer interested in the nation's ritualistic sacrifices that were void of penitence or repentance. Such sacrifices had no value if not backed with repentance. The writer of Hebrews says something enthralling and insightful about the dilemma Israel found itself, *"But in those sacrifices there is a remembrance again made of sins every year.* **For it is not possible that the blood of bulls and of goats should take away sins.** *Wherefore when he cometh into the world, he saith, Sacrifice and offering thou wouldest not, but a body hast thou prepared me"* (Heb. 10:3-5, emphasis added).

As a result, the nation must now come with words - words of repentance; and do the right thing, and then God would forgive their sins.

What would suffice as genuine repentance in this sense would, no doubt, require the following matters:

1. Honest realisation of one's failure and sin. In other words, the believer must honestly judge his sin in the light of God's word and the revelation of the Holy Spirit.

2. Honest confession would involve a penitent heart and sincere repentance. I think there can be no honest confession of sin, if there were not grief over it (2 Cor. 7:10). This grief of heart over sin will involve a revulsion, a turning away, a change of mind and attitude toward sin, which we call repentance. In Ezekiel 20:43, the Bible says, "*And there you shall remember your ways and all your deeds with which you have defiled yourselves, and you shall loathe yourselves for all the evils that you have committed*"(ESV).

3. A confession, in the sense that is meant in I John 1:9 would involve a *simple faith* that God is willing to forgive and cleanse us as He has promised.

In response to Israel's repentance, God said:

> *I will heal their backsliding, I will love them freely: for mine anger is turned away from him. I will be as the dew unto Israel: he shall grow as the lily, and cast forth his roots as Lebanon. His branches shall spread, and his beauty shall be as the olive tree, and his smell as Lebanon. They that dwell under his shadow shall return; they shall revive as the corn, and grow as the vine: the scent thereof shall be as the wine of Lebanon. Ephraim shall say, What have I to do any more with idols? I have heard him, and*

observed him: I am like a green fir tree. From me is thy fruit found. Who is wise, and he shall understand these things? prudent, and he shall know them? for the ways of the Lord are right, and the just shall walk in them: but the transgressors shall fall therein (Hosea 14:4-9).

Is there anything between your soul and the Saviour? Have you humbly searched your heart anew in the light of God's Word, and found nothing to hinder your prayers?

Chapter 33

THE MINISTRY OF THE HOLY SPIRIT IN PRAYER

> *Likewise the Spirit also helpeth our infirmities: for we know not what we should pray for as we ought: but the Spirit itself maketh intercession for us with groanings which cannot be uttered. And he that searcheth the hearts knoweth what is the mind of the Spirit, because he maketh intercession for the saints according to the will of God* (Rom. 8:26-28).

If we are to prevail in prayer, it is highly imperative that we be led by the Holy Spirit.

> *And I will pray the Father, and he shall give you another Comforter, that he may abide with you forever; Even the Spirit of truth; whom the world cannot receive, because it seeth him not, neither knoweth him: but ye know him; for he dwelleth with you, and shall be in you. I will not leave you comfortless: I will come to you* (John 14:16-18).

The Amplified Bible translation of the above scriptures give us the sevenfold meaning of the Greek word translated "Comforter"- Comforter, Counsellor, Helper, Advocate, Intercessor, Strengthener, or Standby.

> *And I will ask the Father, and He will give you another Comforter (Counselor, Helper, Intercessor, Advocate, Strengthener, and Standby), that He may remain with*

> *you forever— The Spirit of Truth, Whom the world cannot receive (welcome, take to its heart), because it does not see Him or know and recognize Him. But you know and recognize Him, for He lives with you [constantly] and will be in you. I will not leave you as orphans [comfortless, desolate, bereaved, forlorn, helpless]; I will come [back] to you* (John 14:16-18, Amp.)

"However, I am telling you nothing but the truth when I say it is profitable (good, expedient, advantageous) for you that I go away. Because if I do not go away, the Comforter (Counselor, Helper, Advocate, Intercessor, Strengthener, Standby) will not come to you [into close fellowship with you]; but if I go away, I will send Him to you [to be in close fellowship with you]" (John 16:7, Amp.)

As a divine person, the Holy Spirit has functions as stated in the above scriptures. He is heaven's divine administrator on earth. He carries out God's intents on earth.

Let us briefly examine each of the functions.

THE HOLY SPIRIT AS OUR HELPER

The original Greek word translated as helper - *paraclete* - means that the Holy Spirit has come to "take hold together with us." A *paraclete* is someone who can do something for you that you cannot do for yourself. The same Greek word is used in 1 John 2:1 *"My little children, these things write I unto you, that ye sin not. And if any man sin, we have an advocate with the Father, Jesus Christ the righteous."*

> As I seek the help of the Holy Spirit in prayer, He takes hold with me and renders the degree of assistance needed to see the problem through.

The Holy Spirit is a present help in all circumstances and at all times. He comes along to take hold together with me against any situation I am faced with. However, He cannot take hold unless I take hold first because He is a helper. As I seek the help of the Holy Spirit in prayer, He takes hold with me and renders the degree of assistance needed to see the problem through.

> People are generally limited in the degree of help or assistance they can render. But for the saints of God, the Holy Spirit is always available...

One weakness of humans is in our limited knowledge. We do not even know what is happening on the other side of a wall, let alone the other side of the country. We also do not know what people are planning to do, but the Holy Spirit knows everything. And He will help us to pray accurately and effectively.

One way the Holy Spirit helps us in prayer is by giving us utterance in a language for prayer which we have never learned. Thus, we can bypass our minds with their doubt and lack of understanding of what is best, and pray according to the perfect will of God. The Bible says, *"For he who speaks in a tongue does not speak to men but to God, for no one understands him; however, in the spirit he speaks mysteries"* (1 Cor. 14:2). Further, Jude 1:20 says, *"But you, beloved, building yourselves up on your most holy faith, praying in the Holy Spirit."*

People are generally limited in the degree of help or assistance they can render. But for the saints of God, the Holy Spirit is always available to you as the Comforter, to render the necessary help in any given situation.

THE HOLY SPIRIT AS OUR COUNSELLOR

The Lord Jesus referred to Him on a number of occasions as 'the Comforter' (John 14. 16, 26; 15. 26) and told the disciples that it was expedient that He should go away, otherwise, the Comforter would not come unto them (John 16. 7). Also in Jesus' farewell speech, recorded in John's Gospel (chapters 13-17), Jesus promised another Counsellor, He being the first. In essence, Jesus was informing the disciples that another person was coming to their help, who would perform all the assignments heaven had vested on Jesus when He was on earth, which further buttresses the point that this Counsellor has specific roles to accomplish. By analysing these roles, it is possible to come to an understanding of the relationship between Jesus and the Counsellor, the Spirit. Thus, the one whom John calls "another Counsellor" is to act as administrator of God's divine purpose on earth. Since the Counsellor would come only after the departure of Jesus, the Counsellor may be seen as the presence of Jesus when Jesus is absent.

Jesus' promises to dwell within His disciples are fulfilled in the Counsellor. It is no accident that the first passage containing Jesus' promise of the Counsellor (John14:16) is followed by the verse which says, *"I will not leave you as comfortless; I will come to you"* (John 14:18).

He is the inner witness or voice that speaks to the believer. He brings counsel to the believer in every area of life. The Bible says, *"For as many as are led by the Spirit of God, these are sons of God"* (Rom. 8:14 NKJ). Oh, how we need to be led by the One who knows the mind of God – the Holy Spirit.

Jesus admonishes,

> *These things have I spoken unto you, being yet present with you. But the Comforter, which is the Holy Ghost, whom the Father will send in my name, he shall teach you all things, and bring all things to your remembrance, whatsoever I have said unto you* (John 14:25-26).

THE HOLY SPIRIT AS OUR ADVOCATE

> *My little children, these things write I unto you, that ye sin not. And if any man sin, we have an advocate with the Father, Jesus Christ the righteous* (1 John 2:1).

This word 'Comforter' does help us to understand the vast functions of the Holy Spirit. It is the same word in the Greek (paraclete) as appears in 1 John 2. 1, where it is also translated 'Advocate'. Therefore, it is very well possible to substitute the word 'Advocate' for the word 'Comforter' with regard to the functions of Holy Spirit. This means there are two Advocates referred to in these passages; the one is the Lord Jesus Christ and the other is the Holy Spirit.

An advocate, Solicitor or Barrister is one who takes upon himself the case of another and argues it before the Judge in the Court of Law. He stands in the position of the accused and represents his interest before the Judge. This gives us a clear picture of the work of the Lord Jesus for us. He is our Advocate in heaven, and as such, He delights to look after the repentant sinner's interests in those awesome courts. He does not attempt to produce evidence to show our innocence. He knows that every accusation of the holy law of God against us is true, but He pleads on our behalf the value of His atoning Blood. When we sin, our Advocate presents Himself to the Father as the propitiation for our sins. As the hymn says, 'He shows His wounds and spreads His hands'. But for the heavenly intercession of His Advocate, every child of God would have lost his relationship with the Father long before now. However, he does lose his sense of peace with God when he sins. But as he confesses his sin, he has a renewal of that peace with God through the Blood of Jesus, which he knew when he first came to Him. How wonderful to have a Friend at court like this.

THE HOLY SPIRIT AS OUR INTERCESSOR

> *Likewise the Spirit also helps in our weaknesses. For we do not know what we should pray for as we ought, but the Spirit Himself makes intercession for us with groanings which cannot be uttered. Now He who searches the hearts knows what the mind of the Spirit is, because He makes intercession for the saints according to the will of God. And we know that all things work together for good to those who love God, to those who are the called according to His purpose* (Rom. 8:26-28).

In verse 26 of the above scripture, we are told that we have infirmities in the place of prayer, and more significantly that the Holy Spirit comes along to supply the needed strength. The word infirmities, according to *W.E Vine Expository Dictionary of New Testament* means: want of strength, weakness, indicating inability to produce result. No doubt, our infirmities would have kept us from producing prayer results but for the help of the Holy Spirit. What a blessing!

It is interesting that the indwelling of the Holy Spirit makes "intercession for us here on earth, as the Lord Jesus "ever liveth to make intercession for [us] in Heaven (Heb. 7:25).

THE HOLY SPIRIT AS OUR STRENGTHENER

In times of trials, we are strengthened from within, by the Holy Spirit. The Bible says, *"He that believeth on me, as the scripture hath said, out of his belly shall flow rivers of living water"* (John 7:38).

According to Spurgeon, "The Holy Spirit also divinely operates in the strengthening of the faith of believers. That faith is at first of his creating, and afterwards it is of his sustaining and increasing: and oh, brothers and sisters, have you not often felt your faith rise in proportion to your trials? Have you not, like Noah's ark, mounted towards heaven as the flood deepened around you? You have felt as sure about the promise as you felt about the trial. The affliction was, as it were, in your very bones, but the promise was also in your very heart. You could not doubt the affliction, for you smarted under it, but you might almost as soon have doubted the divine help, for your confidence was firm and unmoved. The greatest faith is only what God has a right to expect from us, yet do we never exhibit it except as the Holy Ghost strengthens our confidence, and opens up before us the covenant with all its seals and securities."

Paul brings thrilling insight to the role of the Holy Spirit as a Strengthener in His letter to the Ephesians, when he writes, *"For this cause I bow my knees unto the Father of our Lord Jesus Christ, Of whom the whole family in heaven and earth is named, That he would grant you, according to the riches of his glory, to be strengthened with might by his Spirit in the inner man"* (Eph. 3:14-16).

In Acts 2:1-13 we see the disciples filled with boldness to be witnesses. We see Peter who denied Christ three times now boldly witnessing.

This is the power to overcome sin in our life; this is the power to be a witness in our world of today by living out the gospel values in our families, work places and colleges. This is the power to overcome fear in our lives, this is the power to evangelise as the church teaches, and the power which will give us strength to do the right thing in the most trying situation of our live.

There are many more ways in which the Spirit helps us, the above mentioned are only a few of the ways. In moments of loneliness and sadness, in moments where we face huge mountains but do not know what to do or where to turn to, let us turn to the Holy Spirit. Jesus makes it clear that the Spirit is a gift for the asking (John 7:37-39).

THE HOLY SPIRIT AS OUR STANDBY

Finally, the Holy Spirit is our standby. This gives an indication of one waiting to be relied on – especially in times of emergencies. The Holy Spirit knows what you need, but He will not impose Himself on you. He is right there to help you if you ask Him. The reason you have not had the help you need is because you have not asked Him. It is too tempting to seek the help of man in our moment of trial, when as a matter of fact we should be asking the Holy Spirit to help us. We need the help of the Holy Spirit so much in prayer, not just because of all His functions to the believer as analysed, but much more because the Holy Spirit helps the believer to know the mind of God. In his insightful and compelling teaching, Paul asserts:

> *But as it is written, Eye hath not seen, nor ear heard, neither have entered into the heart of man, the things which God hath prepared for them that love him.***But God hath revealed them unto us by his Spirit: for the Spirit searcheth all things, yea, the deep things of God. For what man knoweth the things of a man, save the spirit of man which is in him? even so the things of God knoweth no man, but the Spirit of God.** *Now we have received, not the spirit of the world, but the spirit which is of God; that we might know the things that are freely given to us of God. Which things also we speak, not in the words which man's wisdom teacheth,* **but which the Holy Ghost teacheth**; *comparing spiritual things with spiritual. But the natural man receiveth not the things of the Spirit of God: for they are foolishness unto him: neither can he know them, because they are spiritually discerned. But he that is spiritual judgeth all things, yet he himself is judged of no man* (1 Cor. 2:9-14, emphasis added).

The believer, according to Paul, is oblivious of the vast provisions of God for Him, safe for the help of the Holy Spirit. Verses 9 and 10 are explicit on the point: *"But as it is written, Eye hath not seen, nor ear heard, neither have entered into the heart of man, the things which God hath prepared for them that love him"* (verse 9). Now, notice the unique function of the Holy Spirit in the next verse, as a reveller of the divine will and purposes of God to the believer:

> *But God hath revealed them unto us by his Spirit: for the Spirit searcheth all things, yea, the deep things of God* (verse 10).

THE HOLY SPIRIT AND OUR PRAYER LANGUAGE

> *And when the day of Pentecost was fully come, they were all with one accord in one place. And suddenly there came a sound from heaven as of a rushing mighty wind, and it filled all the house where they were sitting. And there appeared unto them cloven tongues like as of fire, and it sat upon each of them. And they were all filled with the Holy Ghost, and began to speak with other tongues, as the Spirit gave them utterance* (Acts 2:1-4).

"Speaking in tongues" is one of the supernatural gifts of the Holy Spirit referred to in 1 Corinthians 12:4-10.

"Glossolalia" is the most commonly accepted term for "speaking in tongues." It comes from the Greek words meaning "tongues" or "languages," and "to speak." Although not exclusively, "speaking in tongues" is primarily practiced by Pentecostal Christians. Glossolalia is the "prayer language" of Pentecostal churches. Some Christians who speak in tongues believe they are speaking in an existing language.

The first place that speaking in tongues occurred in the New Testament was in Acts 2:1-4: "*When the day of Pentecost came, they were all together in one place. Suddenly a sound like the blowing of a violent wind came from heaven and filled the whole house where they were sitting. They saw what seemed to be tongues of fire that separated and came to rest on each of them. All of them were filled with the Holy Spirit and began to speak in other tongues as the Spirit enabled them."*

This means that the tongues that were being spoken were those of a known language. The tongues were words with specific meaning and not just babbling. This is clarified in Acts 2:7-11: *"Aren't all these who are speaking Galileans? Then how is it that each of us hears them in our native language? Parthians, Medes and Elamites; residents of Mesopotamia, Judea and Cappadocia, Pontus and Asia, Phrygia and Pamphylia, Egypt and the parts of Libya near Cyrene; visitors from Rome, (both Jews and converts to Judaism); Cretans and Arabs — we hear them declaring the wonders of God in our own tongues!"*

WHAT IS THE PURPOSE OF SPEAKING IN TONGUES?

Praying always with all prayer and supplication in the Spirit, and watching thereunto with all perseverance and supplication for all saints... (Eph. 6:18).

Now to each one the manifestation of the Spirit is given for the common good. To one there is given through the Spirit the message of wisdom, to another the message of knowledge by means of the same Spirit, to another faith by the same Spirit, to another gifts of healing by that one Spirit, to another miraculous powers, to another prophecy, to another distinguishing between spirits, to another speaking in different kinds of tongues, and to still another the interpretation of tongues. All these are the work of one and the same Spirit, and he gives them to each one, just as he determines (1 Cor. 12:11)

In regard to speaking in tongues, the book of Joel (referenced in Acts 2) declares:

In the last days, God says, I will pour out my Spirit on all people. Your sons and daughters will prophesy, your young men will see visions, your old men will dream dreams. Even on my servants, both men and women, I will pour out my Spirit in those days, and they will prophesy. I will show wonders in the heaven above and signs on the earth below, blood and fire and billows of smoke. The sun will be turned to darkness and the moon to blood before the coming of the great and glorious day of the Lord. And everyone who calls on the name of the Lord will be saved (Acts 2:17-21).

Speaking in tongues is a divine experience that assists us enormously in prayer and worship. It is a flowing stream that never dries up. Jesus affirms, *"In the last day, that great day of the feast, Jesus stood and cried, saying, If any man thirst, let him come unto me, and drink.* **He that believeth on me, as the scripture hath said, out of his belly shall flow rivers of living water. (But this spake he of the Spirit, which they that believe on him should receive:** *for the Holy Ghost was not yet given; because that Jesus was not yet glorified.)"* (7:37-39, emphasis added). Speaking in tongues enriches not just your prayer life, but your spiritual life as a whole.

Let us examine some of the benefits of speaking in tongues briefly.

Speaking in tongues is a prayer language

Speaking in tongues is a supernatural prayer language. According to 1 Corinthians 14:2, when a believer speaks in tongues he is speaking supernaturally to God. Paul calls it *'mysteries'*.

> *For he that speaketh in an unknown tongue speaketh not unto men, but unto God: for no man understandeth him; howbeit in the spirit he speaketh mysteries* (1 Cor. 14:2).

Your spirit (the inner man or the real you) prays, but your mind does not understand. So in tongues, it is the real you that is talking to God. With tongues a believer is able to pray for a lengthy period of time, with the help of the Holy Spirit.

Praying in tongues is evidence of the infilling of the Holy Spirit

On three occasions in the Acts of Apostle, the Bible attributes the ability to speak in tongues to the indwelling of the Holy Spirit in man: in Acts chapter 2 – on the day of Pentecost; Acts chapter 10 – when Peter ministered to the Gentiles and Acts chapter 19 – when Paul prayed for the believers in Ephesus.

Tongues with interpretation strengthens the church

"He that speaketh in an unknown tongue edifieth himself; but he that **prophesieth edifieth the church**" (1 Cor. 14:4, emphasis added). Speaking in tongues is a main outlet of most gifts of the spirit.

Praying in Tongues is a means of personal edification:

> *He that speaketh in an unknown tongue **edifieth himself**; but he that prophesieth edifieth the church* (1 Cor. 14:4, emphasis added).

It is purely a means of personal spiritual edification. It aids us spiritually. It charges us up. It is like a blazing fire – an inferno - that engulfs the praying believer. In fact, praying in tongues is like a *spontaneous combustion* – a process of catching fire and burning as a result of heat generated by an internal chemical reaction. That is exactly what happens when we pray in tongues? We are 'set ablaze' as a result of the divine heat that comes from the Holy Ghost!

We all need this kind of praying. We cannot help others; we cannot edify others unless we ourselves have been edified.

Take time to build yourself up, by praying much in the Holy Spirit, with other tongues. According to Kenneth Hagin, "Spiritual things are similar to natural things. Jesus used natural things to explain spiritual things. In the natural, no one will be expert and keen in any area without working at it... Likewise, things of the spirit don't fall on us like ripe cherries off a tree. We will not to be expert in spiritual things unless we take time. Praying in tongues will help you to be keen to spiritual things." This is very consistent with the admonition of Jude,

Praying in tongues is a wonderful way of building ourselves up spiritually.

Praying in tongues strengthens us in the place of prayer

> Likewise the Spirit also helpeth our infirmities: for we know not what we should pray for as we ought: but the Spirit itself maketh intercession for us with groanings which cannot be uttered. And he that searcheth the hearts knoweth what is the mind of the Spirit, because he maketh intercession for the saints according to the will of God (Rom. 8:26-27).

There are times when we do not know what to pray. It would be impossible in these situations for mental praying alone to get the job done. Spiritual praying is required. Spiritual praying is praying out of your spirit in spirit-given utterances. They can be utterances in your known language, or in a tongue that is unknown to you, or sometimes in groaning. We may not always understand the entire situation surrounding a matter about which we are praying. This type of prayer is very instrumental in intercession, which is one of the greatest spiritual undertakings.

Praying in tongues is a means of magnifying God

"For they heard them speak with tongues, and magnify God. Then answered Peter" (Acts 10:46). To magnify God is to dignify Him; it is to make Him great.

Tongues brings spiritual refreshing

"For with stammering lips and another tongue will he speak to this people. To whom he said, This is the rest wherewith ye may cause the weary to rest; and this is the refreshing: yet they would not hear" (Isaiah 28:11-12). Tongues provides a 'staying power' or fortitude in the place of prayer.

In 1 Corinthians 14:15 Paul asserts: *"So what shall I do? I will pray with my spirit, but I will also pray with my understanding; I will sing with my spirit, but I will also sing with my understanding."*

Finally, Paul admonishes that the *"manifestation of the Spirit is given to every man to profit withal"* (1 Corinthians 12:7). In the words of Lester Sumrall, "Through tongues, God can bring into your life an enrichment and a spiritual blessing you have never known before as you realize and experience a new nearness to God."

PART 8
CATEGORIES OF PRAYER

(Types of Prayer)

Chapter 34

PERSONAL PRAYER

Personal prayer is the prayer of an individual speaking to God, privately. This is the main difference between this type of prayer and public or corporate prayer, which is prayer with a group or congregation of other believers. This is a very intimate and crucial time between the individual and God, where the individual talks over and deals with issues that affects him with God. It is the life - blood of Christianity. Secret prayer is what gauges your spiritual health and effectiveness as a child of God. God delights in having such fellowship with His saints. We see a typical example of this with God having to constantly and habitually share fellowship with Adam and Eve in the Garden of Eden (Gen. 3:9). Jesus Christ knew the value. He enjoyed such robust fellowship with His heavenly father. He did not take the Fatherhood of God for granted. The Bible declares, *"And in the morning, rising up a great while before day, he went out, and departed into a solitary place, and there prayed"* (Mark 1:35).

No doubt, the mighty exploits of Jesus are attributable to the power He gained from secret prayer. This was where Jesus gained power with God over men, situations and circumstances. The Bible proclaims,

"How God anointed Jesus of Nazareth with the Holy Ghost and with power: who went about doing good, and healing all that were oppressed of the devil; for God was with him" (Acts 10:38). Time alone with God is the powerhouse of the believer! It is not only where he deals with issues with God, it is where the believer comes into contact with the anointing of the Holy Spirit. The secret of power with God is the secret place! We cannot be entrusted with His precious anointing in the public place, but in the secret place. A believer or minister of the Gospel that wants to be much for God must learn to first be much with Him in the place of personal prayer. You cannot have one without the other! This is vividly demonstrated by Jesus. By His example, Jesus has shown that we are to have 'time alone with God' and that our duty in prayer is not discharged without it: we are to pray with all prayer and supplication.

Jesus' commitment to private audience with His father raises a significant ground for reflection:

1. Jesus, though perfectly holy, regarded the duty of secret prayer as of great importance.

2. The fact that He sought a solitary place for concerted fellowship - far away from the world and even from His disciples.

3. It was early in the morning - always the best time, and a time when it should not be omitted.

4. If Jesus – one that was equal with God prayed, how much more important is it for us!

In the words of Baines, "If Jesus did it in the morning, how much more important is it for us, before the world gets possession of our thoughts; before Satan fills us with unholy feelings; when we rise fresh from beds of repose, and while the world around us is still!... If that is omitted, all will go wrong, our piety will wither. The world will fill our thoughts. Temptations will be strong. Through the day, we shall find it impossible to raise our feelings to a state of proper devotion. It will be found to be true universally, that the religious enjoyment through the day will be according to the state of the heart in the morning, and can therefore be measured by our faithfulness in early secret prayer."

How different, too, was the conduct of the Saviour from those who spend the precious hours of the morning in sleep! He knew the value of the morning hours; he rose while the world was still; He saw the light as it spread abroad in the east with fresh tokens of his Father's presence, and joined with the universal creation in offering praise to the everywhere present God.

It must be stressed that a man's spiritual height is not determined by the 'volume' of the prayer he does in the public arena, but by the richness of his prayer closet.

It must be stressed that a man's spiritual height is not determined by the 'volume' of prayers he does in the public arena, but by the richness of his prayer closet. It has been said, time and again, in this book that one of the significant functions of effective prayer is to establish, foster and facilitate intimacy and affectionate personal relationship between the believer and God. This is more easily achieved through personal prayer. God deals with us as individuals, and He loves to relate with us on that basis. There are things lovers can discuss in the public, but there are many things they reserve for a private and more secured place for discussion. Public prayer is highly important but friendship with God can only be fostered through private time with Him. This is how the knowledge of God is obtained, His power activate and drawn into our lives and His divine nature gained.

> *According as his divine power hath given unto us all things that pertain unto life and godliness, through the knowledge of him that hath called us to glory and virtue: Whereby are given unto us exceeding great and precious promises: that by these ye might be partakers of the divine nature...* (2 Pet. 1:3-4).

Knowledge is imperative in our relationship with God. The above scripture tells us that the provisions of God for the believer are appropriated through knowledge: *"According as his divine power hath given unto us all things that pertain unto life and godliness, **through the knowledge of him**"* (emphasis added). The degree of God's blessing that manifests in your life, in the vast provisions of God for mankind, is dependent on, and is in direct proportion to the knowledge of God you have. This is only possible through proximity to and intimate relationship with Him.

The practice of private, personal time with God was rife amongst the saints of old, right from the patriarchs in Genesis down to the prophets and the disciple of Jesus. The great men and women of God down through the ages have testified to the effectiveness of habitually spending quality time with God. David knew the benefits of a fresh encounter with God every day. In Psalm 5:3 he prays, *"My voice shalt thou hear in the morning, O LORD; in the morning will I direct my prayer unto thee, and will look up."* In Psalm 119:147, he affirms, *"I rise before the dawning of the morning, And cry for help; I hope in Your word."*

David knew how important it was to give God the first fruits of the day, to worship before Him, and to seek help for what lay head. He understood the value of knowing His faithfulness, and His blessing early in the morning. The Bible says in Psalm 92:1-2 (NIV), *"It is good to praise the Lord and make music to Your name, O Most High, to proclaim Your love in the morning and Your faithfulness at night."* In Luke 21:38 (NIV) *"And all the people came early in the morning to hear him at the temple."* They came early in the morning to hear the words of Jesus. How fascinating and insightful! It is better to start the day with Jesus, to spend time in His presence to prepare you for the day ahead, to lay your prayers and daily itinerary, your daily schedule, your daily work pattern, and your daily routine before Him, to ask His blessing and His help, than to rush off and think we can do it all on our own without Him.

The blessings derivable from a lifestyle of persistent and undisruptive time with God are enormous. Apart from it fostering and enhancing intimacy with God, it is the place where defeat is turned into triumph. In Psalm 3:1-4 David said,

> *Lord, how are they increased that trouble me! many are they that rise up against me.Many there be which say of my soul, There is no help for him in God. Selah.But thou, O Lord, art a shield for me; my glory, and the lifter up of mine head.I cried unto the Lord with my voice, and he heard me out of his holy hill.*

David was overwhelmed by the presence of enemies and troubles. They mocked his faith in God and said, *"…There is no help for him in God."* But David knew that the secret for deliverance from trouble was in the 'secret place', *"He that dwelleth in the secret place of the most High shall abide under the shadow of the Almighty"* (Psalm 91:1).

He knew that the troubles of life are best dealt with in the secret place. It is in the secret place that divine exchange takes place: God takes over our troubles and gives us His peace. No man in his best effort is able to overcome the battles of his life. It is the anointing that the prayer of the righteous generates that makes tremendous power available to deal with the battles of life (James 5:16). David cried out to God in the midst of his troubles:

"*I cried unto the Lord with my voice, and he heard me out of his holy hill...*" (v.4), and what a difference that made! Watch what happened after David had prayed and turned his troubles and distresses over to God:

> *I laid me down and slept; I awaked; for the Lord sustained me.* ***I will not be afraid of ten thousands of people****, that have set themselves against me round about. Arise, O Lord; save me, O my God: for thou hast smitten all mine enemies upon the cheek bone; thou hast broken the teeth of the ungodly. Salvation belongeth unto the Lord: thy blessing is upon thy people* (Psalm 3:5-8, emphasis added).

In the midst of anxiety, stress, pain and fear, David did what we all should do, he cried out to the Lord in prayer. He addresses his complaint to God about not only his son Absalom, but many others who trouble him.

Regardless of what was against David, he maintained a positive and loyal heart towards God. He knew who God was. David had seen God at work on his behalf when he killed a bear, a lion and the giant goliath as a young shepherd boy. Over and over again, David had seen God work one miracle after another on his behalf!

When your way seems so hard, the burden seems too heavy to bear, when the fires of life never cease to burn, when all else seems hopeless, God will give you an escape route. In 1 Corinthians 10:13, the Bibles proclaims, *"There hath no temptation taken you but such as is common to man: but God is faithful, who will not suffer you to be tempted above that ye are able; but will with the temptation also make a way to escape, that ye may be able to bear it."*

Remember Daniel in the Lion's den? God did not take him out! Remember the 3 Hebrew boys in the fiery furnace? God did not take them out the fire, He stepped in it.

Concerning the thorn in his flesh, Paul petitioned God; and what was God's response to him, *"My grace is sufficient for thee: for my strength is made perfect in weakness. Most gladly therefore will I rather glory in my infirmities, that the power of Christ may rest upon me"* (2 Cor. 12:9).

God may not always rescue us out of our storms early, but He will be right there with us in them. God has not promised us a life free from hardship; His ultimate purpose is to reveal Himself, His love, His compassion, His power through our season of hardship.

Remember Daniel in the Lion's den? God did not take him out! Remember the three Hebrew boys in the fiery furnace? God did not take them out the fire, He stepped in. Why? Because, very often, God redeems not from, but **in** trouble.

In Isaiah 43:1-3, the Lord explains His unique position concerning the difficulties and tribulations that we often face in life:

> *But now thus saith the* LORD *that created thee, O Jacob, and he that formed thee, O Israel, Fear not: for I have redeemed thee, I have called thee by thy name; thou art mine. When thou passest through the waters, I will be with thee; and through the rivers, they shall not overflow thee: when thou walkest through the fire, thou shalt not be burned; neither shall the flame kindle upon thee. For I am the* LORD *thy God, the Holy One of Israel, thy Saviour: I gave Egypt for thy ransom, Ethiopia and Seba for thee.*

It is to be noted that as encouraging and uplifting the above promise is, the Lord did not pledge to keep us from the fire and flood of life. What He does, however, promise is to be with us in those challenging moments. The reason for this is not farfetched. It is here that character is formed. More significantly, God utilises such dire moments of our lives to train us in Christ-likeness.

Chapter 35

CORPORATE OR UNITED PRAYER

"So when they had further threatened them, they let them go, finding nothing how they might punish them, because of the people: for all men glorified God for that which was done. For the man was above forty years old, on whom this miracle of healing was shown. And being let go, they went to their own company, and reported all that the chief priests and elders had said unto them. And when they heard that, they lifted up their voice to God with one accord, and said, Lord, thou art God, which hast made heaven, and earth, and the sea, and all that in them is: who by the mouth of thy servant David hast said, Why did the heathen rage, and the people imagine vain things? The kings of the earth stood up, and the rulers were gathered together against the Lord, and against his Christ. For of a truth against thy holy child Jesus, whom thou hast anointed, both Herod, and Pontius Pilate, with the Gentiles, and the people of Israel, were gathered together, for to do whatsoever thy hand and thy counsel determined before to be done. And now, Lord, behold their threatenings: and grant unto thy servants, that with all boldness they may speak thy word, by stretching forth thine hand to heal; and that signs and wonders may be done by the name of thy holy child Jesus. And when they had prayed, the place was shaken where

they were assembled together; and they were all filled with the Holy Ghost, and they spake the word of God with boldness" (Acts 4:21-31).

Incredible power, guaranteeing astonishing outcome are released when brethren pray under corporate anointing. In the words of Yonggi Cho, "when I pray alone, I can only exercise my own individual faith. Yet, when I pray in a group, with my brothers and sisters in Christ, the power of our faith increased geometrically."

As the scripture above indicates, this was the practice of the early disciples, confronting every adverse situation that befell them jointly in an atmosphere of corporate prayers. God never fails to respond to the united request of His people. In the scripture under examination, Peter and John had been arrested and brought before the religious council. Their lives were threatened and warned never to preach in the Name of Jesus again. They went back to their company and told everyone what had happened. When they heard, they all prayed.

Tremendous power is released in united prayer. God did not only cause the miraculous release of the disciples from their captors (vv. 23-24), but the Bible says *"…by the hands of the apostles were many signs and wonders wrought among the people…."* (Acts 5:12). This was undoubtedly, caused by the power that was generated through the united prayer of the Church.

The political system of the day tried but could not stop the power of God in operation.

Moses was emphatic when he told Israel, *"How should one chase a thousand, and two put ten thousand to flight..."* (Deut. 32:30). Incredible mysteries are unfolded when the saints of God are united in prayer. According to Moses, our strength increases in geometric and not arithmetic proportion when we join forces in prayer. How is that possible? Moses says it is the presence of "the Rock" in their midst. When we gather unto Him and not unto ourselves, then our strength is multiplied because there is automatic manifestation of the power of the Holy Spirit, as Charles Spurgeon asserts, "Prayer is that slender nerve that moves the muscles of omnipotence." Jesus alludes to the same fact, and said *"Again I say unto you, that if two of you shall agree on earth as touching anything that they shall ask, it shall be done for them of My Father which is in heaven. For where two or three are gathered together in My name, there am I in the midst of them"* (Matt. 18:19-20). According to Derek Prince, the above passage is our great powerhouse as we encounter the world. In these verses are contained all the elements of power that we need to do anything we ever want to accomplish. No president, no dictator, no army commander, and no ordinary person outside the Church has the smallest fraction of power that is described and offered to all Christians in these verses. What a privilege! And what is the result? *"Whatsoever you bind on earth shall be ..."*

(Matt. 18:18). Another translation puts it thus: *"Truly I say to you, Whatever things are **fixed by you on** earth will be **fixed in heaven**: and whatever you make free on earth will be made free in heaven"* (Bible in Basic English, emphasis added).

Andrew Murray's analogy could not be further from the truth:

"God gives us a very special promise for the united prayer of two or three who agree in what they ask. As a tree has its root hidden in the ground and its stem growing up into the sunlight, so prayer needs equally for its full development, the hidden secrecy in which the soul meets God alone, and the public fellowship with those who find in the Name of Jesus their common meeting place... The bond that unites a man to his fellow men is no less real and close than that which unites him to God."

Believers are not only members of one family, but even of one body. Just as each member of the body depends on the other, and the full action of the spirit dwelling in the body depends on the union and cooperation of all, so Christians cannot reach the full blessing God is ready to bestow through His Spirit, except as they seek and receive it in fellowship with each other. It is in the union and fellowship of believers that the Spirit can manifest His full power. It was to the hundred and twenty continuing in one place together, and praying with one accord, that the Spirit came from the throne of the glorified Lord.

A classic Old Testament example will help our insight into this crucial topic.

JUDAH GAINED VICTORY OVER ITS ENEMIES

Jehoshaphat, King of Judah was faced with a monumental situation – a large powerful army from the neighbouring territories of Moab, Ammon, and Mount Seir were invading his kingdom from the east. Total annihilation was imminent without the Lord's intervention! Realising that he had no military might to meet this challenge, Jehoshaphat turned to God for help. Scripture records that, *"Jehoshaphat feared, and set himself to seek the lord and proclaimed a fast throughout all Judah"* 2 Chronicles 20:3. God's people were called to unite in public, collective fasting and prayer for God's divine intervention.

The people of Judah fasted - men, women, and children. Desperate situations require desperate measures; they desperately needed to know God's battle plan to defeat this great enemy's army.

From the initial call to prayer and fasting,

> ...*all Judah gathered themselves together, to ask help of the LORD: even out of all the cities of Judah they came to seek the LORD* (2Chr. 20:4).

This describes warfare prayer, in all its ramifications: It is asking help of the Lord.

With the people of God thus assembled, Jehoshaphat led them in prayer, reminding God of His covenant with Abraham. Jehoshaphat's prayer received an immediate, response from heaven; because, as observed by Mahesh Chavda:

"…When the corporate prayers of many joined in the name of [Jesus] are mounted on the booster rocket of our corporate fasting, our prayers suddenly take on a supernatural power that few on earth have ever seen! You can be sure that Satan fears this holy combination as no other. Every time God's people have dared to lay aside their differences or personal concerns long enough to seek God in prayer and fasting together in one mind and one accord, terrible things have happened to his dark kingdom, while wonderful and miraculous things have happened to mankind!"

Pius Quensnel asserts, "God is found in union and agreement. Nothing is more efficacious that this in prayer." The bond that binds believers corporately is inextricably linked with the force that binds us to Christ. The Church cannot fully and adequately appropriate God's provisions for it until it understands the unique and colossal power that is present when we seek God in the atmosphere of unity. David's exquisite revelation in Psalm 133: 1-3, drives the point home:

> *Behold, how good and how pleasant it is for brethren to **dwell together in unity**! It is like the precious ointment upon the head, that ran down upon the beard, even Aaron's beard: that went down to the skirts of his garments; As the dew of Hermon, and as the dew that descended upon the mountains of Zion: for there the LORD commanded the blessing, even life for evermore (emphasis added).*

The significance of unity in the Church is further elucidated in 2 Chronicles 5:13, *"It came even to pass, as the trumpeters and singers were as one, to make one sound to be heard in praising and thanking the LORD; and when they lifted up their voice with the trumpets and cymbals and instruments of music, and praised the LORD, saying, For he is good; for his mercy endures forever: that then the house was filled with a cloud, even the house of the LORD."*

In the midst of the assembly of fasting people, God spoke through one of the prophets present - Jahaziel a powerful prophetic utterance, combining encouragement, assurance and direction. God said to His people:

> *Do not be afraid nor dismayed because of this great multitude, for the battle is not yours, but God's. You will not need to fight in this battle. Position yourselves, stand still and see the salvation of the LORD, who is with you, O Judah and Jerusalem!' Do not fear or be dismayed; tomorrow to out against them, for the LORD is with you* (2 Chr. 20: 15-17).

God had already put in place a master-plan for the defeat of the enemies of His people. Unknown to Judah, God was already making things happen behind the scene. God works the same way today; it takes faith to realise that our God is moving miraculously in our lives, even when we do not even know it. What a comforting word in the midst of disaster of such magnitude.

But never forget, God only spoke after the entire nation had spent time praying and fasting. God moves only in response to the cries of His people!

In verse 16, God gave His people a most significant instruction, *"Position Yourselves…"* right in the middle of the prophetic word. This unravels the mind of God, not just for Judah, but for the present day church. There is a place beyond victory called triumph that God is taking His saints. Indeed, we are told in scriptures that we are not just conquerors, but more than conquerors.

"Nay, in all these things we are more than conquerors through him that loved us" (Rom. 8:37). God is, undoubtedly, taking us beyond the sphere of victory to the glorious place of triumph.

Victory is being able to defeat your enemies. But triumph goes far beyond mere victory. When you triumph, you come out of the battle with more than you had before! God wants to give you more. The banner of prayer we have lifted in the Church has so far brought us to the plane of victory. The Church is transiting gloriously to the brink of spectacular and unparalleled triumph, that will mark the proverbial "straw that breaks the Carmel's back" for the devil and his hordes of demons. We must press on with unflinching resolve for the final outcome of our battle against Satan and his kingdom.

It is recorded that after the battle with the enemies, Judah spent the next three days gathering the spoils – the enemies' possessions in battle - and found abundance of cattle and personal property, garments and precious vessels. They took so much that they were unable to carry it all; indeed, there was so much of it (2 Chr. 20: 25).

By no means would such astonishing miracles end with the people of old; they are still available for us - the Church today! However, as said, it would require a price. It would require a divine positioning of the church to scale beyond the limits of victory to that of triumph. The Church has got to prepare herself for this level of breakthrough; it will not come on a platter of gold. The Bible says, *"So Jotham became mighty, because he prepared his ways before the LORD his God"* (2 Chronicles 27:6). Second, it would demand a greater level of unity in the Body of Christ than there is right now. Notice, in crisis, Judah pulled together! Hence they attracted God's astonishing response. What a mighty God we serve!

Events in the Household of Faith seem to point to the contrary; people in crisis situations seem to find more sympathy out in the world than in the church. The Church seems to be more prepared to attack and devour the wounded soldiers than to offer the needed assistance. We must stick together if we are ever going to transcend our level of victory into triumph. It is in the place of unity that God commands His blessings (Psalm 133).

In response, the Bible says:

> ...Jehoshaphat bowed his head with his face to the ground: and all Judah and the inhabitants of Jerusalem fell before the Lord, worshipping the Lord. And the Levites, of the children of the Kohathites, and of the children of the Korhites, stood up to praise the Lord God of Israel with a loud voice on high. And when he had consulted with the people, he appointed singers unto the Lord, and that should praise the beauty of holiness, as they went out before the army, and to say, Praise the Lord; for his mercy endureth forever (2 Chr. 20:18-19, 21 KJV).

Jahaziel's prophetic utterance gave Judah not only the assurance that God was with them in the crisis situation, but a sense of victory ahead of the battle. This was what gave Jehoshaphat the impetus to lead Judah to the battlefield with High Praise on their lips. They believed that God spoke to them without reservation, whatsoever. In verses 22 – 30 we read the most fascinating outcome of this battle: the entire enemies' army destroyed themselves, without Jehoshaphat or his people having to resort to any military combat with them. God did not only give His people victory over their enemies, He turned the wealth of the enemies over to them (Prov. 13:22). Judah spent the next three days gathering the spoils and returning to Jerusalem amidst thunderous praise and thanksgiving. And the fame of Jehoshaphat spread to all the neighbouring nations.

This demonstrates the supremacy of spiritual power over carnal powers. While his enemies relied on carnal weapons (the arm of flesh), Jehoshaphat and his people utilised spiritual weapons. This was vividly demonstrated in yet, another battle the children of Israel were involved in. Just reminiscent of the account we are considering, God again assured His people victory over their enemies ahead of the battle. God told His people:

> *Be strong and courageous, be not afraid nor dismayed for the king of Assyria, nor for all the multitude that is with him: for there be more with us than with him: With him is an arm of flesh; but with us is the Lord our God to help us, and to fight our battles. And the people rested themselves upon the words of Hezekiah king of Judah* (2 Chr. 32:7-8).
>
> *David says, "Some nations boast of their armies and weapons, but we boast in the LORD our God"* (Psalm 20:7, New Living Translation).

The two passages quoted above highlight the outright superiority of spiritual weapons over carnal (physical weapons), and the outcome of the battle Judah was in vividly demonstrates this. In 2 Corinthians 10:4, Paul says, "… the weapons of our warfare are not carnal, but mighty through God to the pulling down of strongholds". Notice, according to Paul, spiritual weapons are formidable because God is involved in their usage. They are applied through God.

It would, no doubt, be beneficial to identify and highlight the spiritual weapons that Jehoshaphat used in this battle, as they are both relevant and applicable to present day believers.

They may be summarised as follows:

1. United prayer – Matthew 18:19-20
2. Collective public fasting – Esther 4:16
3. The Gift of prophecy – 1 Cor. 14:3
4. Biblical Praise and Worship – Psalm 149:6-9:

The Bible says, *"On the fourth day they held an assembly in the Valley of Berakah — for there they blessed the Lord; that is why the place is called the Valley of Berakah to this day. Then all the men of Judah and Jerusalem, with Jehoshaphat at their head, returned to Jerusalem with joy; for the Lord had given them joy over their enemies. They came to Jerusalem, with harps, lyres, and trumpets, to the house of the Lord."* (2 Chr. 20: 26-28).

As said, these weapons are still as potent as they were when Jehoshaphat used them in the battle against the enemies of Judah.

Mighty Miracles in His Name

God says, *"If my people which are called by **my name**, shall humble themselves and pray, and seek my face, and turn from their wicked ways; then will I hear from heaven and will forgive their sin and heal their land"*(II Chr. 7:14, emphasis added).

In the last two scriptures, the issue of "name" resonates as a salient condition for the fulfilment of God's promises that attention cannot but be given to it.

More than one Christian gathering 'in His name' is the basis of the rest of the promises. That is the force, the pillar, and indeed, the foundation of all that we have said under this heading. Matthew 18:18-20 gives the indication that once that condition is met then, *"... Whatsoever ye shall bind on earth shall be bound in heaven: and whatsoever ye shall loose on earth shall be loosed in heaven."* This promise was not just made to Peter; it was made to the Christian community standing together in faith. This was the basis of the unfolding of the astonishing miracle we read of in Acts 12. Peter was arrested and put in prison after James had been assassinated by King Herod. And the Bible says, *"Peter therefore was kept in prison: but **prayer was made without ceasing of the church unto God for him**"* (Acts 12:5 emphases added). God's people were praying in earnest for Peter. They were having a round the clock prayer meeting, praying for the one they loved. The people of God were united in prayer. Many times we might say it is not the length of the prayer, but the quality of the prayer, that sounds good. The saints here were spending quality time in prayer. As they prayed and called upon God, deliverance came. Let us summarise the events that unfolded as a result of the prayer of these believers:

1. An angel was dispatched to the prison: united prayer causes heaven's intervention in the affairs of men.

2. Light shone in the prison: united prayer delivers God's people from confusion and indecision. Light in scriptures stands for illumination, wisdom, understanding, knowledge, inspired idea. Would not the Church of God be a far better place if everyone operates under the spotlight of the Holy Spirit?

3. The angel said, "*Arise up quickly…*" The corporate prayer of God's people would cause God to lead His people by His prophetic voice.

4. Chains were broken off Peter's life: The power of united prayer will break iron chains. Iron chains will fall off when God's people are united in prayer.

5. Iron Gate opened on its own accord: Impossibilities give way when the Church is united in prayer.

THE NAME OF JESUS: THE ESSENTIAL INGREDIENT OF CORPORATE PRAYER

Jesus declares:

> *For where two or three are gathered together **in my name**, there am I in the midst of them* (Matt.18:20KJV, emphasis added).

However, the later translations also give us something to think about:

> For where two or three are gathered together **unto my name**, there am I in the midst of them (Darby's English Translation, emphasis added).

> For where there are two or three gathered together **to my name**, there am I in the midst of them (Young's Literal Translation, emphasis added).

As already indicated in this book, the Bible gives an unequivocal impression that the name of Jesus Christ is the basis, in fact, the focal point around which His people gather. Here, our Lord teaches us that 'the Name' must be the centre of union to which believers gather, the bond or cord of unity that makes *them* one, just as a home contains and unites all who are in it. The love and unity of His disciples have great attraction to Jesus." *Where two or three are gathered in My name, there am I in the midst of them."* It is the living presence of Jesus, in the fellowship of His loving, praying disciples that gives united prayer its power.

> What therefore, makes the gathering of two or three believers God's powerhouse, guaranteeing the promises as earlier discussed in Matthew 18:18-20, is the common denominator they all share together that gives them a unified identity – the name of Jesus!

What therefore, makes the gathering of two or three believers God's powerhouse, guaranteeing the promises as earlier discussed in Matthew 18:18-20, is the common denominator they all share together that gives them a unified identity – the name of Jesus! Two or more believers who are filled with the Holy Spirit, gathered together in the name of Jesus, and pray according to God's will and not their own, will have their requests granted. It is fitting to conclude that the sincere agreement of two people, in Christ, gathered in Jesus name, is more powerful and result oriented than the superficial agreement of a multitude of people.

Chapter 36

ALL KINDS OF PRAYER

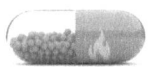

The book of Ephesians gives the clear indication that there are different kinds of prayer. In Ephesians 6:18, Paul writes:

> *Praying always with all prayer and supplication in the Spirit, and watching thereunto with all perseverance and supplication for all saints."* Also in 1 Timothy 2:1, he teaches, *"I exhort therefore, that, first of all, supplications, prayers, intercessions, and giving of thanks, be made for all men.*

Prayer is the all-encompassing way to describe the overall range or spectrum of expressions we offer to God. Accordingly, prayer includes supplication, intercession, praise, thanksgiving, adoration, repentance, warfare etc.

Understanding prayer from this broad perspective is of great importance, and will not only revolutionise the believer's prayer life, but will answer the crucial question as to the reason some, if not most prayers of God's children are not receiving answers as they should.

Sadly, most Christians are not aware that there are several types of prayers detailed in the word of God, and that if you use one type when you should be using another, it would not work. You would be applying the wrong spiritual tool to your needs or requests. God intends for each of the different forms of prayer mentioned in the Bible to have different functions, as described below. In essence, one should never pray just for the sake of it.

Like most things in life, the different types of prayer are governed by different rules. A misunderstanding or misapplication of these rules could render your prayers of non-effect.

If any of the above types of prayers are absent in your life then you should seek God's face about it. Ask Him to fill you with more of His love and make your prayer life richer.

In practise, however, we all use different types of prayer during our prayer times. What may start out as a prayer of faith can soon develop into prayer of intercession or supplication.

If any of the above types of prayers are absent in your life then you should seek God's face about it. Ask Him to fill you with more of His love and make your prayer life richer. There is no reason why your prayer-life should be narrowed to one or few of the different prayers discussed in this book. On occasions, God places a demand on His saint to engage in any of the prayers outlined here, hence it is very important to develop a prayer-life that is extensive and all embracing.

The following two scriptures would act as a springboard to set out our study:

> *Praying always with all prayer and supplication in the Spirit, and watching thereunto with all perseverance and supplication for all saints* (Eph. 6:18).

> *I exhort therefore, that, first of all, supplications, prayers, intercessions, and giving of thanks, be made for all men; For kings, and for all that are in authority; that we may lead a quiet and peaceable life in all godliness and honesty* (1 Tim. 2:1-2).

The different types of prayers there are in scriptures are well identified in the above Bible passages:

Here are the main types of prayers in the Bible:

PRAYER OF SUPPLICATION OR PETITION

Supplication means to petition or entreat someone for something. It is an entreaty for God to grant one's request. In His model prayer, Jesus taught, *"Give us this day our daily bread..."* which is an indication that the Father expects to be asked to meet our needs. A passionate zeal or hunger fuels the prayer of supplication. Supplications are requests that come from a heart, crying out to God for help. It is a very serious business between the supplicant and God. A splendid example is recorded about Jesus in Hebrews

5:7, *"who, in the days of His flesh, when He had offered up prayers and supplications, with vehement cries and tears to Him who was able to save Him from death, and was heard because of His godly fear"* (NKJV). Faced with the anguish of Gethsemane, the Bible says that Jesus, *"And being in an agony he prayed more earnestly:* **and his sweat was as it were great drops of blood falling down to the ground"** (Luke 22:44). At times, we are driven to praying the prayer of supplication because of imminent danger. The prayer of supplication can sometimes lead us into fasting (Neh. 1: 1-6). In 11 Chronicles 20: 4,14, we read,

"And Judah gathered themselves together, to ask help of the Lord: even out of all the cities of Judah **they came to seek the Lord***. O our God, wilt thou not judge them? for we have no might against this great company that cometh against us; neither know we what to do: but our eyes are upon thee"* (emphasis added).

Faced with the threat of invasion from armies of neighbouring nations, Judah assembled to pray to ask for God's intervention.

We are admonished in Philippians 4:6,

"Do not be anxious about anything, but in everything by prayer and supplication with thanksgiving let your requests be made known to God." Part of winning spiritual battle is to be *"praying at all times in the Spirit, with all prayer and supplication"* (Eph. 6:18).

A common characteristic of prayer of supplication is importunity. This is unequivocally emphasised in the teachings of Jesus:

> *And he said unto them, Which of you shall have a friend, and shall go unto him at midnight, and say unto him, Friend, lend me three loaves; For a friend of mine in his journey is come to me, and I have nothing to set before him? And he from within shall answer and say, Trouble me not: the door is now shut, and my children are with me in bed; I cannot rise and give thee. I say unto you, Though he will not rise and give him, because he is his friend, yet because of his importunity he will rise and give him as many as he needeth* (Luke 11:5-8).

In yet another parable, Jesus highlights the connection between the prayer of supplication and importunity.

> *In a certain town there was a judge who neither feared God nor cared what people thought. And there was a widow in that town who kept coming to him with the plea, 'Grant me justice against my adversary.'* "*For some time he refused. But finally he said to himself, 'Even though I don't fear God or care what people think, yet because this widow keeps bothering me, I will see that she gets justice, so that she would not eventually come and attack me!'" And the Lord said, "Listen to what the unjust judge says. And will not God bring about justice for his chosen ones, who cry out to him day and night? Will he keep putting them off? I tell you, he will see that they get justice, and quickly. However, when the Son of Man comes, will he find faith on the earth?* (Luke 18: 1-6).

Examples of prayer of supplication abound in scripture. Hannah, the mother of Samuel the prophet could attest to the power of prayer of petition, when against all odds, she had a child after a long and desperate wait. (1 Sam. 1:17). Jabez had a total life *makeover* after he blasted heaven with a destiny-altering prayer (1 Chr. 4:9-11). Jacob, whose desperate need for God's intervention in what was an imminent and specific danger, was another person that knew the power of petition prayer.

The prayer of Nehemiah offers a stunning portrait of the prayer of supplication, delineating the basic scriptural elements of this form of prayer.

The supplication of Nehemiah

"And I asked them concerning the Jews that had escaped, which were left of the captivity, and concerning Jerusalem. And they said unto me, Theremnant that are left of the captivity there in the province are in great affliction and reproach: the wall of Jerusalem also is broken down, and the gates thereof are burned with fire. And it came to pass, when I heard these words, that I sat down and wept, and mourned certain days, and fasted, and prayed before the God of heaven, And said, I beseech thee, O Lord God of heaven, the great and terrible God, that keepeth covenant and mercy for them that love him and observe his commandments: Let thine ear now be attentive, and thine eyes open, that thou mayest hear the prayer of thy servant, which I pray before thee now, day and night, for the children of Israel thy

servants, and confess the sins of the children of Israel, which we have sinned against thee: both I and my father's house have sinned. We have dealt very corruptly against thee, and have not kept the commandments, nor the statutes, nor the judgments, which thou commandedst thy servant Moses. Remember, I beseech thee, the word that thou commandedst thy servant Moses, saying, If ye transgress, I will scatter you abroad among the nations: But if ye turn unto me, and keep my commandments, and do them; though there were of you cast out unto the uttermost part of the heaven, yet will I gather them from thence, and will bring them unto the place that I have chosen to set my name there. Now these are thy servants and thy people, whom thou hast redeemed by thy great power, and by thy strong hand. O Lord, I beseech thee, let now thine ear be attentive to the prayer of thy servant, and to the prayer of thy servants, who desire to fear thy name: and prosper, I pray thee, thy servant this day, and grant him mercy in the sight of this man" (Neh. 1:2-11)

Here was no ordinary praying. He received the bad news about the condition of his city Jerusalem. He wept and mourned. Yes, people who supplicate have the situation so much at heart that they can weep. He did not only weep. He mourned for days! It is as though his whole being was breaking. He fasted and then he supplicated. His prayer was peculiar - he was before God day and night. He was burdened that he would take no rest and would give God no rest at all. He could not have prayed for a short time and given up. How could he give up? The burden of Jerusalem weighed heavily on his whole being. He knew that sin would block access to the Lord so he pleaded for the forgiveness of his sins and the sins of his people. He did not disguise their sin but truly opened up before the Lord in deep confession. He pleaded with God's promises to forgive his people if they repented. Having thus pleaded, he asked that God would grant him mercy before the king.

Nehemiah was going to ask the king for favours which would normally not be granted unless God touched the King's heart in a special way. He, desperately, supplicated with fervour, and how could God turn a deaf ear to such prayer? He answered! Glory be to His Holy name! May we too, supplicate, knowing that we will not depart empty handed. Paul assures the believer that our labour in the Lord attracts His due reward (1 Cor. 15:58).

INTERCESSION

> *The church that is not jealously protected by mighty intercession and sacrificial labors will before long become the abode of every evil bird and the hiding place for unsuspected corruption. The creeping wilderness will soon take over that church that trusts in its own strength and forgets to watch and pray* - **A. W. Tozer**

The Bible declares in John 15:13, *"Greater love has no one than this, than to lay down one's life for his friends"*. In God's kingdom, there are many ways to lay down your life for others. One of such ways is to actively pray for them; and when we pray for others, it is called the prayer of intercession.

Intercession is born out of the heart of God. It is born out of love. With this kind of prayer, there is a sacrifice of our very being; our lifestyle, time and energy. There is giving of ourselves to pray for other people and for God's will, plan, and purpose to be done in earth. Undoubtedly, the highest form of Christian service is intercession! The high water mark of spiritual experience is a life given to intercession. A church that is not given to intercessory prayer lacks power and recognition before God.

In God's kingdom, there are many ways to lay down your life for others. One of them is to pray; and when we pray for others, it is called the prayer of intercession.

God is looking for people who care enough to pray, for people who love enough to give of themselves to him and to the needs of others in the Prayer of Intercession.

Webster defines intercession as: the action of pleading on somebody's behalf- attempt to resolve conflict: the action of attempting to settle a dispute- prayer or petition: a prayer to God on behalf of somebody or something. Simply put, an intercessor is a person who goes before God in prayer on behalf of another person, situation or circumstance.

Intercession involves praying for others. It may involve praying in a general sense for such subject-matter as the church or the government, or praying for another, based on your knowledge of the person's needs; it means to plead or mediate on behalf of another person.

Heb. 7:24-25, referring to Jesus, says:

> But He, because He continues forever, has an unchangeable priesthood Therefore He is also able to save to the uttermost those who come to God through Him, since He always lives to make intercession for them.

Jesus, an unchangeable Priest is functioning right now in priestly ministry before the father, making intercession. Jesus is praying for us!

We stand in the priestly ministry of our Lord Jesus as His saints. Revelation 1:6 tells us that you and I have been made kings and priest unto God because of the New Birth. In our kingly ministry, we walk in our God given authority, and minister before the Lord, with the sacrifice of praise and worship - the fruit of our lips giving Him pleasure.

As part of our priestly ministry we also, like Jesus, make intercession. God has called us to be intercessors. Jesus is the intercessor in heaven; we, by the Holy Spirit, are the intercessors in the earth. In the words of Oswald Chambers, "Jesus Christ carries on intercession for us in heaven; the Holy Ghost carries on intercession in us on earth; and we the saints have to carry on intercession for all men."

Jesus' prayers are ringing out in heaven; our prayers are ringing out in the earth. We join together with His plan as we intercede.

The scripture references above show specific circumstances where intercession was being made. Intercession will involve various degrees of supplication. Intercession is not normally a one-off prayer. We are told to make intercession "for everyone" in 1 Timothy 2:1. Jesus serves as our example in this area. The whole of John 17 is a prayer of Jesus on behalf of His disciples and all believers.

A hallmark of prayer of intercession, like prayer of supplication, is that it requires persistence. Abraham demonstrated this clearly in the following scripture:

"And the men turned their faces from thence, and went toward Sodom: but Abraham stood yet before the Lord. And Abraham drew near, and said, Wilt thou also destroy the righteous with the wicked? Peradventure there be fifty righteous within the city: wilt thou also destroy and not spare the place for the fifty righteous that are therein? That be far from thee to do after this manner, to slay the righteous with the wicked: and that the righteous should be as the wicked, that be far from thee: Shall not the Judge of all the earth do right? And the Lord said, If I find in Sodom fifty righteous within the city, then I will spare

all the place for their sakes. And Abraham answered and said, Behold now, I have taken upon me to speak unto the Lord, which am but dust and ashes: Peradventure there shall lack five of the fifty righteous: wilt thou destroy all the city for lack of five? And he said, If I find there forty and five, I will not destroy it. And he spake unto him yet again, and said, Peradventure there shall be forty found there. And he said, I will not do it for forty's sake. And he said unto him, Oh let not the Lord be angry, and I will speak: Peradventure there shall thirty be found there. And he said, I will not do it, if I find thirty there. And he said, Behold now, I have taken upon me to speak unto the Lord: Peradventure there shall be twenty found there. And he said, I will not destroy it for twenty's sake. And he said, Oh let not the Lord be angry, and I will speak yet but this once: Peradventure ten shall be found there. And he said, I will not destroy it for ten's sake. And the Lord went his way, as soon as he had left communing with Abraham: and Abraham returned unto his place" (Gen. 18: 22-33).

In Ephesians 1:15-18, Paul writes: *"Therefore I also, after I heard of your faith in the Lord Jesus and your love for all the saints, do not cease to give thanks for you, making mention of you in my prayers; that the God of our Lord Jesus Christ, the Father of glory, may give to you the spirit of wisdom and revelation in the knowledge of Him, the eyes of your understanding being enlightened; that you may know what is the hope of His calling, what are the riches of the glory of His inheritance in the saints."*

Here, Paul wrote that he prayed regularly for the church in Ephesus and for the individuals there to receive these blessings.

Likewise, in his greeting to the Philippians, he affirms, *"I thank my God upon every remembrance of you, always in every prayer of mine making request for you all with joy"* (Phil. 1:3-4). The fact that Paul said he made requests for these saints suggests that this also was an example of intercessory prayer.

You can see that not appreciating the different types of prayer can hinder our prayer life, as said. If you only recognise the prayer of supplication, for instance, you may fail to intercede for another believer who is in trouble of any kind, or needs God to intervene in his or her life. Did you notice that Elijah had to keep praying - seven times - before the rain that God had already promised came down? (1 Kings 18:41-46).

When we take it upon ourselves to pray earnestly for other people, we enter into the realm of intercession. To enter into intercession, however, we must have a heart that really loves the Lord and cares about the things of God.

Chapter 37

PRAYER OF FAITH

> And Jesus answering saith unto them, Have Faith in God. For verily I say unto you, That whosoever shall say unto the mountain, be thou removed and be thou cast into the sea; and shall not doubt in his heart, but shall believe that those things which he saith shall come to pass; he shall have whatsoever he saith. Therefore I unto you, what things soever ye desire, when ye pray, believe that ye receive them, and ye shall have them (Mark11:22-24).

James 5:15 admonishes that, *"... the prayer of faith shall save the sick..."*

All prayers rely on our faith in God. In fact, prayer is faith in action. In the word of another, "Faith is the power line, but prayer switches it on." Although the phrase 'prayer of faith' is commonly used, the reality is that all prayers require faith in God to work. The prayer of faith is rooted in our confidence in God's Word. The woman with the issue of blood (Matt. 9:18-30) knew that touching Jesus would get her healed. Her faith made way for her healing. When you are sure that what you are praying for is God's will, the prayer of faith should be utilised.

If you are praying the prayer of consecration, for example surrendering yourself to the will of God, you must believe that God hears your prayer and responds to it. You may not know specifically what the will of God is for you at that the moment. But you must trust that He will receive your surrender and guide you into the knowledge of that will.

The prayer of faith, however, requires a different kind of believing. It requires us not just to trust that God hears and receives our prayer, but that He will respond in a specific way. To pray the prayer of faith, we must know without doubt what the will of God is about the particular issue we are addressing in prayer. The easiest way to know the will of God in this respect is to ascertain the coverage of the word of God on the matter. If the word of God makes provision for it, then, at least in a general sense, the will of God is known. We must be so certain He will give it to us. Note the size of your success here is determined by the size of your faith!

Rooted in Mark 11:22-24 are many rules to consider:

PRAYING AND SAYING:

It must be stressed that the profession of faith has much to do with praying and saying things (declarations). The praying part we are much conversant with. But very little is known about the 'saying' aspect. Unless we come to grip with the invaluable power that is embedded in our words as believers, we will never attain to the full level of authority and power Christ has invested us with. Christianity is much a profession of 'words.' As believers words are our means of exchange in the spirit realm. They are the divine currencies in God's kingdom. The words we speak either act as a rocket-buster to our desired haven or as surface-to-air missiles landing us in the swamp of defeat and despair. Words are powerful! We are enjoined in several portions of scripture to use the power of words (saying), which goes beyond the threshold of ordinary confession. I rather call it declaration or command! For instance, the Bible says, "**Let the redeemed of the Lord say so**, *whom he hath redeemed from the hand of the enemy*" (Psalm 107:2, emphasis added). Also in Isaiah 3:10, Prophet Isaiah instructs, "*Say you to the righteous, that it shall be well with him: for they shall eat the fruit of their deeds.*" Accordingly, Mark 11:22-24 establishes a principle that, in prayer of faith, apart from there being the praying part and the saying side, prayer must precede the 'saying' aspect, otherwise known as declaration or command. The reasoning behind the principle is quite clear. From a personal perspective, there needs to be an accumulation of power through long prayer, to make the process work. It is the power that is accumulated through a lifestyle of prayer that makes short prayers or declarations potent! In essence, verses 22 and 23 of Mark 11 draw their strength from verse 24: "*Therefore I say unto you, What things soever ye desire, when ye pray, believe that ye receive them, and ye shall have* *them."* This is where a lot of people misunderstand the concept behind these verses of scripture. Without doubt, verse 24 makes a ground preparation for the commanding limb of the scripture covered in verses 22 and 23. Without such spiritual preparation in the place of prayer, it is totally at odd with common sense to begin to 'dish' out commands to 'mountains' and expect there to be impact. In the words of Apostle James, it is *"…effectual fervent prayer…"* not command, that avails much (James 5:16). The Amplified Bible says such prayer *"…makes tremendous power available [dynamic in its working]"*. Indeed, prayer is a power generator, and such power is dynamic in its working! This is the power at work when we issue command while praying the prayer of faith. The proposition so far established points to one valid conclusion: the fact that a great deal of spiritual preparation is required before praying the prayer of faith.

There is a general approach that seeks to obscure the treasure of these scriptures, even though the scriptures are being appealed to. Very often, believers, without any preparations whatsoever, start speaking to situations in their lives, ordering them to be removed or changed. When their words do not seem to have the intended effect, they get discouraged and give up on the prayer of faith altogether. It is the power that is gained in the hour of preparations that brings the desired result into fruition. Time should be spent in the word of God, meditating on relevant scriptures. The Bible says, *"Search the scriptures; for in them ye think ye have eternal life: and they are they which testify of me"* (John 5: 39). Remember that the prayer of faith requires you to be acquainted with the will of God concerning the purpose of your prayer. You discover this as you search the scriptures. Furthermore, John 15:7 says, *"If ye abide in me, and my words abide in you, ye shall ask what ye will,* **and it shall be done unto you***"* (emphasis added). We need to draw power from the word of God in our hour of preparation before praying the prayer of faith. Notice in spiritual things that time spent in preparation is never wasted! We are told in scripture that Jotham became great because he prepared his ways before the Lord his God (2 Chr. 27:6). Remember, diligence is the mother of good fortune. So, for its efficiency and effectiveness, the prayer of faith requires a great deal of spiritual preparation. It is this degree of preparations in the spirit that gives the command of faith its result. It is all about purpose! Great minds pursue purpose, while others live at the threshold of wishes. To get accurate result in prayer, especially prayer of faith, you must pray accurately. It is never a guess work!

So, there is prayer of faith and there is the command of faith.

COMMAND OF FAITH... OR PRAYER OF DECLARATION

Now that we have studied the prayer of faith, let us look at Mark 11 again and examine the command of faith. Jesus Himself sets the example for us. In that chapter, we see Him on the way home from a long day in Jerusalem. He was tired and hungry.

> *And seeing a fig tree afar off having leaves, he came, if haply he might find anything theron: and when he came to it, he found nothing but leaves; for the time of figs was not yet. And Jesus answered and said unto it, No man eat fruit of thee hereafter forever. And his disciples heard it... And in the morning, as they passed by, they saw the fig tree dried up from the roots. And Peter calling into remembrance saith unto him, Master, behold, the fig tree which thou cursedest is withered way. And Jesus answering saith unto them, Have faith in God. For verily I say unto you, That whosoever shall say unto this mountain, Be thou removed, and be thou cast into the sea; and shall not doubt in his heart, but shall believe that those things which he saith shall come to pass; he shall have whatsoever he saith.* (Mark 11:13-14, 20-23).

As you can see from the above scripture, the command of faith is quite different from the prayer of faith. When you give the command of faith, you are not asking God for anything. You are not giving thanks to God. You are not speaking to God at all. You are speaking to the situation that needs to be changed. You are ordering it to obey the word of the Lord which is being spoken to it.

The command of faith can be given effectively only by a person who has a conscious revelation of the authority God has given to him. He is operating from the sphere of that authority, nothing else! It works only when you know who you are in Christ Jesus and you are absolutely certain the situation you are speaking to must obey you just as surely as it would have to obey Him if He spoke to it Himself.

The command of faith is not a request. It is not a prayer. It is not a plea. You do not beg mountain to be removed. You order them to be removed. Ezekiel 37 is an accurate portrait of the prayer of faith, delineating the scriptural principles that underscore its operation.

"So I prophesied... and as I prophesied, there was a noise, and behold a shaking, and the bones came together, bone to his bone...So I prophesied... and the breath came into them, and they lived, and stood up upon their feet, an exceeding great army" (verses 7, 10).

Spiritually speaking, that is what you do when you draw near to God and begin meditating on His word in a situation of the kind. When you abide in His word and let His word abide in you, you assume your God-given position, and you can speak authoritatively, and mountains move.

Spend some time waiting on the Lord and getting things straight in your heart and mind before you try to deal with the situation. In Isaiah 40:31 we are assured, *"But they that wait upon the LORD shall renew their strength; they shall mount up with wings as eagles; they shall run, and not be weary; and they shall walk, and not faint."* When you wait on the Lord, you actually entwine yourself with God and braid His word into your being so thoroughly that nothing can separate you from his promise.

When you wait on the Lord, you exchange your strength for His strength. So when you step out to deal with the situation, you are using His power, not your own.

The guiding principle of praying the prayer of faith is: Pray first, and make declaration of faith afterwards.

The Bible reveals that there were times when Jesus prayed about a situation before He gave the command of faith. One of such instances was when He raised Lazarus from death.

"Jesus therefore again groaning in himself cometh to the grave. It was a cave, and a stone lay upon it. Jesus said, Take ye away the stone. Martha, the sister of him that was dead, saith unto him, Lord, by this time he stinketh: for he hath been dead four days. Jesus saith unto her, Said I not unto thee, that, if thou wouldest believe, thou shouldest see the glory of God? Then they took away the stone from the place where the dead was laid. And Jesus lifted up his eyes, and said, Father, I thank thee that thou hast heard me. And I knew that thou hearest me always: but because of the people which stand by I said it, that they may believe that thou hast sent me. And when he thus had spoken, he cried with a loud voice, Lazarus, come forth. And he that was dead came forth, bound hand and foot with graveclothes: and his face was bound about with a napkin. Jesus saith unto them, Loose him, and let him go" (John 11:38-44).

The prayer of Jesus at the tomb of Lazarus before He raised Lazarus from the grave was insightful. *"Father, I thank thee that thou hast heard me"* (v.41). Those were the first words of His Jesus' prayer at the tomb of Lazarus, which gives the indication that Jesus had prayed extensively about the situation before He got there.

Clearly, Jesus had already talked to God about this mountain of death that had set itself before Him. Now He was ready to speak to the mountain itself. The Bible says, *"...and He cried with a loud voice, Lazarus, come forth"* (v.43).

When He did, what was the outcome?

"And he that was dead came forth, bound hand and foot with graveclothes: and his face was bound about with a napkin. Jesus saith unto them, Loose him, and let him go" (v. 44).

In Acts 9, we see Peter following the same pattern. The new believers in Joppa sent for him because their beloved sister in the Lord, Dorcas had died. When they brought him into the room where her body was laid, Peter sent them all out and, turning his back on the body of Dorcas, he prayed.

Then Peter "turning him to the body said, Tabitha, arise. And she opened her eyes; and when she saw Peter, she sat up" (v.40).

Peter prayed. Then he gave the faith commands. Once again, the mountain was removed and cast into the sea.

The rule to consider here is laid out in Mark 11:24:

"Therefore I say unto you, What things soever ye desire, when ye pray, believe that ye receive them, and ye shall have them."

Notice that the above scripture does not say when you will actually see the result of your prayer. It does not tell you how long it will take for that prayer result to appear. All it says is that believe that you have your needs met. This is often where most believers give up.

When you pray in faith, God immediately gives you what you prayed for—in the spirit realm. But in the natural world, due to a number of factors, it may take time for the answer to manifest itself. Remember Daniel's prayer in Daniel 10.

God answers prayers, and He will answer your specific prayer in line with His Word, but it is your faith that brings that answer out of the spirit realm into the physical world. How many times in Scripture does Jesus say to someone, "According to your faith"?

He referred to peoples' faith constantly, and even though it was His power that healed them, He always credited their faith with being the catalyst. In fact, when Jesus went to His hometown, we are told that "He did not do many mighty works there because of their unbelief" (Matt. 13:58).

Did Jesus suddenly lose His power on that visit to Nazareth? No!

His power never changed. What changed? It was the people's level of faith mixed with His power.

There is a simple spiritual explanation for this. God will not do something against your will. God cannot violate free will. If you do not have faith to do something, He would not arbitrarily override your lack of faith.

James 1:6-8 tells us how to get our faith to work for us:

> *But let him ask in faith, nothing wavering. For he that wavereth is like a wave of the sea driven with the wind and tossed. For let not that man think that he shall receive any thing of the Lord. A double minded man is unstable in all his ways.*

Given that faith is required in all kinds of prayer, especially the prayer of faith, undoubtedly, one must first spend time in the word of God to know what the will of God is concerning the subject matter of the prayer. But more importantly, given that the word of God is the source of faith, quality time must be spent in the word to build one's faith to the level required to achieve the desired result.

So, before making declarations or commands as required in Mark 11:22 -23, a whole range of preparations must be put in place. The following should be borne in mind, as stated:

- Ascertain the will of God concerning the matter
- Study the word to build up your faith
- Pray
- Make declarations or command.

Chapter 38

PRAYER OF AGREEMENT

In Matthew 18:19, 20, Jesus introduced the prayer of agreement when He said,

> *Again I say to you that if two of you agree on earth concerning anything that they ask, it will be done for them by My Father in heaven For where two or three are gathered together in My name, I am there in the midst of them.*

This is the bedrock of the prayer of agreement. Prayer of agreement is where two or more people are praying on the same issue together. These could be members of a church, two or more friends, or even more powerfully, a husband and wife; who stand on their pre-existing covenant relationship of marriage to agree together in prayer on specific issues before God.

God has given power and authority to the Church and when we stand together in unity, we can see more of God's power released (Matt. 28: 16-20). Unity is standing together with one purpose, sharing a joint vision and trusting God's Word to be fulfilled. We need to appreciate the power of unity if we are to see God's power released. Why is corporate prayer so powerful?

The Bible says, *"How should one chase a thousand, and two put ten thousand to flight, except their Rock had sold them, and the LORD had shut them up?"* (Deut. 32:30). In the words of Charles G. Finney, "Nothing tends more to cement the hearts of Christians than praying together. Never do they love one another so well as when they witness the outpouring of each other's hearts in prayer."

The elements of true, united prayers are contained in the words of Jesus in Matthew 18: 19-20. We shall examine some of them under the next heading.

CONDITIONS FOR PRAYER OF AGREEMENT

There Must Be Agreement

For prayer of agreement to achieve its desired objective, there must be agreement as to the thing asked. There must be actual, not implied agreement. It is not enough to generally consent to agree with anything another may ask. The agreement must centre round a distinct, united desire. If someone asks me to pray in agreement with them, I ask, "What specifically do you want me to pray for?" You absolutely must make sure you are in perfect agreement about what your prayer request is before you join with another believer in the prayer of agreement. Jesus says, *"If any two of you on earth agree."* You must make sure that the person you are praying with first, understands the purpose of the prayer, and second, does agree with you on the subject matter of your prayer. It is vitally important to find someone who will agree with you in the spirit. Please test the spirit! It has to be someone who believes in your vision.

Ask Together

Another important consideration about prayer of agreement, as seeing from the teaching of Jesus on the subject, is that the people praying must ask together about the situation.

We find a striking example of this in the book of Acts.

> *Peter therefore was kept in prison: but prayer was made without ceasing of the church unto God for him. And when he had considered the thing, he came to the house of Mary the mother of John, whose surname was Mark; where many were gathered together praying* (Acts 12: 5, 12).

Jesus says, "For where two or three are gathered together in my name, there am I in the midst of them (Matt. 28: 20). There is power in agreement!

When we agree together in prayer, power is released from heaven to bring about results on earth.

It may not be possible to always meet at the same location to pray together. But where it is possible, meeting together to pray should be the rule. What is of utmost importance, however, is the need for agreement.

The Name of Jesus – The Focal Point of the Gathering

Here the Lord emphasises that His name must be the centre and the bond of the union: *"For where two or three are gathered together in my name, there am I in the midst of them"* (v 20). The name of Jesus must be the centrepiece and focal point of the gathering. According to Henry Morris, in context, this statement of Christ indicates that even two or three members, meeting in His name, can constitute a church.

Assurance of Answered prayer

The last element of united prayer is the assurance of receiving the answer. Jesus says, *"...it shall be done for them of my Father which is in heaven"* (v 20). Jesus meant this statement as a means of securing special answer to prayer. Andrew Murray emphasises that a prayer meeting without recognised answer to prayer ought to be the exception to the rule. In the unity of faith, love, and the Spirit, the power of the name and the presence of Jesus acts more freely, and the answer comes unhindered. What a powerhouse united prayer is!

Chapter 39

PRAYER OF DEDICATION OR CONSECRATION

Jesus shows us example of prayer of consecration in Luke 22:39-42:

> Coming out, He went to the Mount of Olives, as He was accustomed, and His disciples also followed Him. When He came to the place, He said to them, "Pray that you may not enter into temptation. And He was withdrawn from them about a stone's throw, and He knelt down and prayed, saying, "Father, if it is Your will, take this cup away from Me; nevertheless not My will, but Yours, be done.

Sometimes, prayer is a time of setting ourselves apart to follow God's will. Jesus prayed such a prayer the night before His crucifixion: *"And going a little farther he fell on his face and prayed, saying, 'My Father, if it be possible, let this cup pass from me; nevertheless, not as I will, but as you will'"* (Matt. 26:39).

The prayer of consecration is a humble submission to the will of God. This is not always easy. After the Apostles had just been whipped for their faith, they immediately rededicated themselves to the will of God with prayer (Acts 4:29-31).

If God leads you into an area of ministry or work that is difficult it will take the prayer of consecration for you to fulfil it. The same is true of living a holy life. The prayer of consecration is asking for the strength to accomplish His will with His power.

As said, in Luke 22:41-42 we see a clear example of the prayer of consecration and dedication:

> *And He [Jesus] was withdrawn from them [Peter, James and John] about a stone's throw, and He knelt down and prayed, saying, 'Father, if it is Your will, take this cup away from Me; nevertheless not My will, but Yours, be done.*

He was praying, in effect, "If there is any other way to do this, let us do it that way." But the key for Jesus, and for us is, "Nevertheless not My will, but Yours, be done."

You pray that God's will would be done when you do not know His perfect will concerning a crucial matter. For instance, in such important matters as to who to marry, you need the clear leading of the Lord. Significant matters as to what city or nation to settle in, God's will must be ascertained, and this you do through the prayer of consecration or dedication. In the absence of direct instructions, the prayer of consecration and dedication says you will allow God to set your direction or make your decisions.

The prayer of consecration and dedication works when you have two (or more) godly alternatives before you, and you are not getting a clear sense at that time about which option God wants you to take. When the direction is unclear — but any of the options appear to be legitimate, righteous options — that is the perfect time to say, *"Lord, if it be your will..."* In the other forms of prayer covered in the word of God, the use of such phrase as "Lord, if it be your will" shows an apparent lack of faith in the petitioner and renders your prayer impotent.

Chapter 40

THE PRAYER OF PRAISE, WORSHIP AND THANKSGIVING

> *Let the high praises of God be in their mouth, and a two-edged sword in their hand; To execute vengeance upon the heathen, and punishments upon the people; To bind their kings with chains, and their nobles with fetters of iron; To execute upon them the judgment written: this honour have all his saints. Praise ye the Lord* (Psalm 149:6-9).

The prayer of biblical praise is a formidable weapon in warfare; it brought down the walls of Jericho. It was what gave Jehoshaphat and Judah victory over their enemies:

"And they rose early in the morning, and went forth into the wilderness of Tekoa: and as they went forth, Jehoshaphat stood and said, Hear me, O Judah, and you inhabitants of Jerusalem; Believe in the LORD your God, so shall you be established; believe his prophets, so shall you prosper. 21And when he had consulted with the people, he appointed singers to the LORD, and that should praise the beauty of holiness, as they went out before the army, and to say, Praise the LORD; for his mercy endures for ever. 22And when they began to sing and to praise, the LORD set ambushes against the children of Ammon, Moab, and

mount Seir, which were come against Judah; and they were smitten" (2 Chr. 20:20-22).

THE PRINCIPLES OF PRAISE

> O LORD, our Lord, how excellent is thy name in all the earth! who hast set thy glory above the heavens. Out of the mouth of babes and sucklings hast thou ordained strength because of thine enemies, that thou mightest still the enemy and the avenger (Psalm 8:1-2)

This is one of the most deadly weapons the believer is armed with. Praise functions most effectively where prayer fails. Praise disarms and silences the devil. It is a formidable weapon of warfare that activates the other warfare weapons.

In the scripture above, David started off by saying, "*O LORD, our Lord, how excellent is thy name*" (verse 1). The name of the Lord is the weapon David is using here. The name of the Lord is the rocket launcher of the weapon of praise. Any other weapon David might resort to is being busted and empowered by the formidable, almighty name of the Lord – the name at the mention of which, "*···every knee should bow, of those in heaven, and of those on earth, and of those under the earth, and that every tongue should confess that Jesus Christ is Lord, to the glory of God the Father*" (Phil.2: 10-11). And Jesus affirms, "*For it is written, As I live, saith the Lord, every knee shall bow to me, and every tongue shall confess to God*" (Rom. 14:11).

As we progress into this psalm, we see David using praise as a lunching vehicle to engage in warfare. He says, "...*Out of the mouth of babes and sucklings hast thou ordained strength because of thine enemies.*" God is always mindful of our position of victory over the enemies. Further he says, "*that thou mightest still the enemy and the avenger.*" God has ordained a method to silence the devil, and that is praise. Praise disarms the devil and renders him and his host of demons impotent.

Finally, notice the word 'mouth' in this scripture. According to Law, "All Spiritual weapons have one launching pad, and that is the mouth. The mouth is the springboard of all spiritual warfare weapons; here the weapons of God are lunched out of the month of babes and sucklings. Have you noticed that all, but one gifts of the spirit are exercised through the mouth? Your words are like spear, bows, arrows and rocket launcher in the spirit real. Learn to us this formidable weapon God has blessed you with, correctly.

WORSHIP

Man is essentially a worshipping creature. It is part of his nature. His choice is not whether he will worship, but only whom he will worship. In Scripture God demands His worship. He will not share our worship with anyone or anything else.

Worship is very central to man's relationship with his creator. Throughout the Scriptures, expressions of prayer and worship are inextricably linked. We see David exhibits an exuberance of free-flowing mixture of praise, rejoicing and prayer to God. In the New Testament, those who made requests of Jesus often came by way of worship. More specifically, Paul mentioned both prayer and expressions of worship as integral elements in the assemblies of the saints. Our understanding of the connection between prayer and worship will significantly affect the depth of our experience in the secret place. While prayer is a way of speaking with God and making requests and supplication, worship is an act of humbling our spirit to give God glory for what He has done and will do. God deserves our praise, just as He loves us, He wants to know that we love Him, and we can do this by worshiping Him.

Worship is a force that pulls a man's heart towards God; it is the all-inclusive expression of the heart, mind, and the body towards God. It is impossible to understand true worship without relating it to an attitude of the body.

It includes the stretching out of our hands towards God, sometimes a bending of our knee, indicating an attitude of submission to the supremacy and superiority of God. Scriptures are inundated with thrilling examples of this kind of worship. *"And there came a fire out from before the* LORD, *and consumed upon the altar the burnt offering and the fat: which when all the people saw, they shouted, and fell on their faces"* (Lev. 9:24).

"The four and twenty elders fall down before him that sat on the throne, and worship him that liveth for ever and ever, and cast their crowns before the throne, saying, Thou art worthy, O Lord, to receive glory and honour and power: for thou hast created all things, and for thy pleasure they are and were created" (Rev. 4:10-11).

WORSHIP FROM THE LORD'S PERSPECTIVE

A great deal of understanding of worship is gained when recourse is made to the temptation of Jesus in the wilderness. The devil said, *"All these kingdoms of the world will I give you if you bow down and worship me,"* Jesus responded and said, *"Get thee hence, Satan: for it is written, thou shalt worship the Lord thy God, and him only shalt thou serve"* (Mat. 4:10).

This highlights a great principle of worship. Whatever you worship you will ultimately and invariably serve. The more you worship a thing or a person, the more your commitment increases. You cannot worship a thing and refuse to serve it. Your right of choice is lost to whoever you serve.

The prayer of worship is similar to the prayer of thanksgiving. The difference is that worship focuses on who God is; thanksgiving focuses on what God has done. Church leaders in Antioch prayed in this manner with fasting: *"While they were worshiping the Lord and fasting, the Holy Spirit said, 'Set apart for me Barnabas and Saul for the work to which I have called them.' Then after fasting and praying they laid their hands on them and sent them off"* (Acts 13:2-3).

Praise and worship bring us into the presence of God. When we praise God in the midst of seemingly negative situations, we are affirming our faith in Him. This pleases God and helps our faith. Thanking God in the good times also keeps our eyes focused on the source of our strength.

Worship is shaped by your estimation of the greatness of God. The degree of worship that flows from your life to God is an indication of your estimation of God – His greatness, His attributes and His goodness.

This was exactly what David was doing in Psalm 8. As he ruminated on the greatness of God, His creation and all His attributes, he could not but give God extravagant worship.

"O LORD, our Lord, How excellent is Your name in all the earth, Who have set Your glory above the heavens! Out of the mouth of babes and nursing infants. You have ordained strength, Because of Your enemies. That You may silence the enemy and the avenger. When I consider Your heavens, the work of Your fingers. The moon and the stars, which You have ordained, What is man that You are mindful of him, And the son of man that you visit him?" (Ps.8:1-4).

To worship God acceptably:

- You must worship Him with all your heart. It is not a half-hearted business. God deserves and demands whole-hearted worship. The Bible says, *"Bless the LORD, O my soul: **and all that is within me**, bless his holy name"* (Psalm 103:1, emphasis added).

- You must worship God in spirit and in truth. Worship is a product of the spirit. It must be done in the spirit and by the Holy Spirit's inspiration, *"God is a Spirit: and they that worship him must worship him in spirit and in truth"* (John 4:24).

THANKSGIVING

> *Be careful for nothing; but in everything by prayer and supplication with thanksgiving let your requests be made known unto God. And the peace of God, which passeth all understanding, shall keep your hearts and minds through Christ Jesus* (Phil. 4:6-7).

The above scripture says that even when we pray the prayer of faith, we should always intersperse worship and praise.

Thanksgiving should be a regular part of our talking to God. Thanksgiving is an all-inclusive act that involves praise, worship and honour of God.

In this prayer, you are not asking God to do something for you or to give you something in particular. You are not asking for divine direction either; neither are you dedicating your life to whatever it is God has called you to do. Rather, you are appreciating Him for His many blessings (2 Cor. 9:15).

In the words of another, the "attitude of gratitude" is a wonderful anecdote to grief, self-pity, hopelessness, anger, and pride...we must approach Him in a manner worthy of who He is. This truth comes into perspective when we decide to humble ourselves... and acknowledge Him through thanksgiving and praise"

Chapter 41

THE PRAYER OF BINDING AND LOOSING

> God intends for the Body of Christ to police the evil forces of this world. We are to change circumstances to line up with God's will and put Satan under our feet through the power of God. We are to spoil his plans, plots and manoeuvres against God's people! The prayer of binding and loosing halts Satan's activities – Kenneth Copeland.

Jesus teaches, *"Assuredly, I say to you, whatever you bind on earth will be bound in heaven, and whatever you loose on earth will be loosed in heaven. Again I say to you that if two of you agree on earth concerning anything that they ask, it will be done for them by My Father in heaven"* (Matt. 18: 18-19).

Things do not begin in heaven and come to earth, but rather the action starts here on earth and flows to heaven.

There are several important lessons in Jesus' statements here, the first being that we have authority on earth by virtue of our covenant rights through Jesus. The second thing we notice is the direction of the action. Things do not begin in heaven and come to earth, but rather, actions start here on earth and flow to heaven.

Notice it says, *"Whatever you bind on earth will be bound in heaven, and whatever you loose on earth will be loosed in heaven."* We have been given unrestricted authority over the devil and his demons.

The Bible says, *"Behold, I give unto you power to tread on serpents and scorpions, and over all the power of the enemy: and nothing shall by any means hurt you"* (Luke 10:19).

In Matthew 12:29 Jesus says, *"Or else how can one enter into a strong man's house, and spoil his goods, except he first bind the strong man? and then he will spoil his house."* All the scriptures above point to one conclusion, and that is the fact that all satanic fortresses or strongholds can be utterly demolished through prayer.

This type of prayer is particularly useful in warfare! You bind satanic or demonic forces that are hindering people's progress, causing sicknesses, diseases, and an outright wreckage of peoples' destiny.

As you enforce the authority vested in the Church, speak directly to Satan. Exercise your faith in Jesus' work at Calvary. When Jesus was raised from the dead, He stripped Satan of his authority over mankind. That authority has been delegated to the Body of Christ in the earth.

When you pray in this manner, God affirms it in heaven and puts His seal of approval on your prayer. Binding and loosing have to be based on the authority

God has granted you in Scripture, not on some desires you have. It is to be noted, however, that there are times when the stronghold or satanic siege is deeply entrenched and the nature of the warfare will require more than just prayer to overcome and prevail over it. Very often, fasting proves to be a formidable weapon in such situations. It was in a situation of the kind that Jesus said to the disciples, *"Howbeit this kind goeth not out but by prayer and fasting"* (Matt. 17:21). Prayer and fasting make the enemy very uncomfortable. A combination of both weapons of warfare is God's atomic bomb for demolishing satanic strongholds (2 Cor. 10:4).

Do not give Satan any place by talking about the problem after you have agreed and bound him. Instead of talking the problem, talk the answer — God's Word.

In sum, God has provided each type of prayer for a specific purpose. Though you may use more than one at any given time, it is important to be clear about which type you are using and why, and to be aware of its limitations. If you follow the examples in the Bible, you will be sure to use them properly and have the desired results.

PART 9

UNDERSTANDING THE PURPOSE AND POTENCY OF BIBLICAL FASTING

Chapter 42

WHEN PRAYER IS NOT ENOUGH

INCREASING YOUR PRAYER LIFE THROUGH FASTING

> *And the fire upon the altar shall be burning in it; it shall not be put out: and the priest **shall burn wood on it every morning**, and lay the burnt offering in order upon it; and he shall burn thereon the fat of the peace offerings. The fire shall ever be burning upon the altar; it shall never go out* (Lev. 6:12-13, emphasis added).

One of the ways of reinforcing fervency in prayer, in essence, 'adding wood to your altar' is by biblical fasting. Jesus gave a clear indication of the fact that prayer is limited in some circumstances.

> *Then came the disciples to Jesus apart, and said, 'Why could not we cast him out?' And Jesus said unto them, 'Because of your unbelief: for verily I say unto you, If ye have faith as a grain of mustard seed, nothing shall be impossible to you. Howbeit this kind goeth not out but by prayer and fasting* (Matt. 17: 19-21).

Jesus had given the disciples power and authority over the devil and to cure all diseases: *"Behold, I give unto you power to tread on serpents and scorpions, and over all the power of the enemy: and nothing shall by any means hurt you"* (Luke 10:19). They had often exercised that power with tremendous results. But on this occasion, the disciples appeared to have failed. They went to Jesus to enquire reasons for the apparent failure to cure the lunatic boy. From the expression, *"Why could not we cast him out?"* it is evident that the disciples had made frantic efforts to deal with the situation, but to no avail. Jesus' answer was forthright, *"…because of your unbelief …"* (v.20). *Howbeit this kind goeth not out but by prayer and fasting"* (v. 21). These statements taken together give the indication that fasting is an antidote for unbelief, which still goes to prove that, had the disciples fasted, unbelief would not have been a contributory factor to their failure in this regard. It should also be noted, however, that there are "ranks" of demonic powers (Eph. 6:12), and evidently, some demons are stronger (more stubborn, resistant) than others. It is fitting to suggest that since the disciples had been given authority to cast out demons (Matt. 10:8), apparently, this demon was more difficult than most.

However, according to Andrew Murray, "...prayer needs fasting for its full growth. Prayer is the one hand with which we grasp the invisible; fasting, the other, with which we let loose and cast away the visible. In nothing is man more closely connected with the world of sense than in his need of food, and his enjoyment of it. It was the fruit, good for food, with which man was tempted and fell in Paradise. It was with bread to be made of stones that Jesus, when an hungered, was tempted in the wilderness, and in fasting that He triumphed."

To this Blumhardt adds, "Inasmuch as the fasting is before God, a practical proof that the thing we ask is to us a matter of true and pressing interest, and inasmuch as in a high degree it strengthens the intensity and power of the prayer, and becomes the unceasing practical expression of a prayer without words, I could believe that it would not be without efficacy..." Fasting is a tool that guarantees a life of notable miracles. Fasting knows no limit in its operation; even the most impossible circumstances receive God's attention through fasting. Very succinctly, Bill Bright concludes "... fasting as it relates to prayer is the spiritual atomic bomb that our Lord has given us to destroy the strongholds [of Satan]..."

WHAT IS FASTING?

Given the much misconceptions surrounding the discipline of biblical fasting, it is imperative to have a working definition as to what true biblical fasting is. Throughout Scriptures, fasting refers to abstaining from food for spiritual purposes. It stands in distinction to hunger strike, the purpose of which is to gain political power or attract attention to a good cause. It is also different from health dieting which stresses abstinence from food for physical, not spiritual purposes.

Fasting is aimed at withdrawing from food in order to concentrate or focus on God, His holiness, His will and purposes. Biblical fasting always centres on God and His purposes, not on man or the person observing the fast.

In Scripture, the normal means of fasting involves abstaining from all food, but not always from fluid. After Jesus' 40 days and nights fasting, the Bible says, *"... he was afterward an hungred"* (Matt. 4:2,), which gives a clear indication that His fast involved an abstention from food, and not from fluid. There were, however, occasions in the Bible where people fasted without food and water for different periods of time. For example, Queen Esther fasted without food and water for three days:

> *Go, gather together all the Jews that are present in Shushan, and fast for me, and neither eat nor drink three days, night or day: I also and my maidens will fast likewise; and so will I go in unto the king, which is not according to the law: and if I perish, I perish* (Esther 4:16).

Moses (Exod. 24:18 & 34:28), Elijah (1 Kings 19:8) both fasted 40 days. On two different occasions, Moses fasted for 40 days, when he abstained from both food and drink. The same holds true for Elijah. It must be noted, however, that these were supernatural fasts spent in the presence of God. Many people have undergone fasts of this duration without harming themselves, but it should not be done without being certain or convinced that you are in good health and have the assurance that God has called you to undertake a fast of this nature. As a matter of fact, fasts of this length should be the exception rather than the rule. God would not call any of us to do something that is harmful to ourselves.

So far we have seen that biblical fasting has to do with restraining oneself from food for a given period of time in order to engage in specific spiritual exercises.

We shall see that there were three main forms that fasting took in Bible time, but each involved literal abstinence. If at times the word may be widened to include other forms of self-denial, this does not alter the fact of its basic meaning.

In some quarters, fasting is regarded as a last resort in times of great crisis. This is a major misconception about fasting and its objective.

In some quarters, fasting is regarded as a last resort in times of great crisis. This is a major misconception about fasting and its objectives. The implication of such notion is that fasting outside times of crisis is both unbiblical and unprofitable. Such believes as these, are particularly erroneous and manifestly dangerous.

Fasting is as important a Christian discipline as prayer! Just as it could not be said that Christian should resort to prayer only in times of great crisis, reserving fasting observance for challenging times only is, in all ramifications, wrong and misleading.

"WHEN YE FAST..."

In the teaching of Jesus, there is an apparent assumption that Christians would fast as indicated by the phrase, "**'when'** you fast"… in Matthew 6:16. We can arrive at a logical conclusion that the fact that Jesus chose such a phrase and not the opposite – "'If you fast", indicates that the discipline of fasting has not been left at the discretion of the believer as to whether to fast or not. This could be due to the invaluable benefits of fasting. Fasting is no doubt, the duty of today's believer.

In His response to the seeming accusation levied by the Pharisees against His disciples' refusal to fast - an apparent violation of the Jewish custom - Jesus referred to a time when, after the departure of the Bridegroom (referring to the post - ascension era), the disciples would see fasting as a divine obligation placed on them. Jesus said to them:

> … *Can the children of the bridal chamber fast, while the bridegroom is with them? As long as they have the bridegroom with them, they cannot fast.* ***But the days will come, when the bridegroom shall be taken away from them, and then shall they fast in those days*** *(Mark 2: 19, 20 emphasis added).*

Accordingly, after the Lord's death, His disciples frequently fasted as of necessity, and went through much deprivation and trial. In essence, this prophetic word, as it were, has found fulfilment in the lives of His 'immediate disciples'; and should also for the His present day 'disciples', until He returns to take to Himself His bride, when there will be a glad and everlasting feasting.

Fasting is to be a natural outcome of discipleship. We are to fast for the same reason we pray. This does not, by any means, indicate that we are to fast every time we pray!

Jesus addressed fasting in association with both prayer and almsgiving. Jesus declared "when you give alms" (Matt. 6:2), "when you pray" (Matt. 6:6), and "when you fast" (Matt. 6:16). The logical conclusions from these texts are: though the Bible is silent as to how often we should fast, Jesus intends fasting to be undertaken by the believer as a discipline. Just as He expects us to pray and give alms, Jesus expects us to fast.

In addition, in the Sermon on the Mount, when Jesus spoke about prayer and fasting, He used similar language in addressing both subjects. The main difference, however, is that in relation to prayer; he included a structure of prayer we often refer to as 'the Lord's Prayer'.

PROCLAIMED AND PERSONAL FAST

"On a fast day...you shall read the words of the Lord" – Jeremiah 36:6

"Sanctify a fast; call a solemn assembly"... Joel 2:15

Usually, fasting is undertaken occasionally as the believer deems it necessary, as a matter between him and God. Public fast is an exception of this notion. Sometimes situations arise in which a church, a group of people or, a nation needs God's divine direction or intervention and, as a result, resort to fasting. This is a proclaimed fast.

PROCLAIMED FAST

There is generally a connection between public and regular fasts in that, almost all the regular fasts of the Bible were also public fasts, but not all the public fasts were necessarily, regular.

Regular fasts were those prescribed by God to be observed at specific times of the year. A good example is the Day of Atonement, prescribed by the Mosaic Law. On this day, God required the Israelites to afflict their souls (Lev. 23:27, Psalm 35:13).

In addition to "a fast day" (Jer. 36:6), associated with the Day of Atonement, the book of Zechariah contains four other regular fast days:

> *Thus saith the LORD of hosts; The fast of the fourth month, and the fast of the fifth, and the fast of the seventh, and the fast of the tenth, shall be to the house of Judah joy and gladness, and cheerful feasts; therefore love the truth and peace* (Zech. 8:19).

We have an indication of the observance of the regular fast (Day of Atonement) in the New Testament:

> *Now when much time was spent, and when sailing was now dangerous, because the fast was now already past, Paul admonished them...* (Acts 27:9).

This was no doubt, in reference to the Day of Atonement. During the earthly ministry of Jesus, the Pharisees made an empty religious ritual out of this practice as typified by the story of Jesus in Luke 18:11, 12:

> *The Pharisee stood and prayed thus with himself, God, I thank thee, that I am not as other men are, extortioners, unjust, adulterers, or even as this publican. I fast twice in the week, I give tithes of all that I possess.*

Notice Jesus' teaching in verse 9:

"Also He spoke this parable to some who trusted in themselves that they were righteous, and despised others"

The paramount purpose of a regular fasting is to provide a regular opportunity for spiritual examination and orientation. It is like a spiritual medicine for the soul and body.

This is a clear example of religious egotism; the Pharisees were known to despise others, even with their fasts. Fasting was used by the Pharisees at this period of time, as an instrument of oppression against the poor, the needy, and the meek. They despised the very people they ought to be caring for in their seasons of fast (Isaiah 58:7). This was a prototype of the manner and spirit with which the Pharisees held regular fasts in the days of Jesus.

Arthur Wallis, however, remarks that while caution needs to be taken not to allow regular fasting to become religious rituals, devoid of its spiritual intent, the practice should not be abandoned altogether. "It needs to be stressed", he continues, "that fasting, whether regular or occasional, is a matter between individual and God. Making it a requirement may lead to the same bondage in which the Pharisees were ensnared."

The paramount purpose of a regular fasting is to provide a regular opportunity for spiritual examination and orientation. It is like a spiritual medicine for the soul and body.

Generally, a proclaimed fast is for the purpose of bringing believers together for a special session of collective fasting and prayer. Proclaimed fast operates on the principle of spiritual agreement as taught by Jesus in Matthew 18:18:

> *Again I say unto you, that if two of you shall agree on earth as touching anything that they shall ask, it shall be done for them of my Father which is in heaven.*

However, greater power is released in fasting combined with prayer than in prayer alone. Proclaimed fast offers the believers the opportunity to move in the same direction of faith in one accord.

A wonderful, practical example of a proclaimed fast is found in 2 Chronicles 20:1-6.

> *It came to pass after this also, that the children of Moab, and the children of Ammon, and with them other beside the Ammonites, came against Jehoshaphat to battle. Then there came some that told Jehoshaphat, saying, There cometh a great multitude against thee from beyond the sea on this side Syria; and, behold, they be in Hazazontamar, which is Engedi. And Jehoshaphat feared, and set himself to seek the Lord, and proclaimed a fast throughout all Judah. And Judah gathered themselves together, to ask help of the Lord: even out of all the cities of Judah they came to seek the Lord. And Jehoshaphat stood in the congregation of Judah and Jerusalem, in the house of the Lord, before the new court, And said, O Lord God of our fathers, art not thou God in heaven? Andrulest not thou over all the kingdoms of the heathen? and in thine hand is there not power and might, so that none is able to withstand thee?*

During the reign of King Jehoshaphat, King of Judah, enemies from neighbouring nations invaded Judah. As stated, the Bible says "Jehoshaphat feared and set himself to seek the Lord, and proclaimed a fast throughout Judah."

This incident brought the people of Judah together to seek help of the Lord through prayer and fasting. Jehoshaphat prayed, relying on the covenant of protection and deliverance God had given to Abraham and his descendants. King Jehoshaphat's prayer as recorded in verse 12 is noteworthy:

"O our God, wilt thou not judge them? For we have no might against this great company that cometh against us; neither know we what to do: but our eyes are upon thee" (emphasis added).

There are definitely valuable lessons to be learnt in the nation's reaction to this imminent threat. Jesus was very succinct when He said that certain situations could not be dealt with otherwise, but with prayer and fasting:

"Howbeit this kind goeth not out but by prayer and fasting" (Matt. 17:21).

And the Bible says:

"He will keep the feet of his saints, and the wicked shall be silent in darkness; for by strength shall no man prevail" (1 Sam. 2:9, emphasis added).

Another translation puts it very beautifully thus:

"He guards the steps of his faithful ones, while the wicked are made silent in darkness. He grants the request of the

one who prays. He blesses the year of the righteous. Indeed it is not by strength that a person prevails" (1 Sam. 2:9 International Standard Version).

While these believers were all in agreement, praying and fasting, the Bible records, "Then upon Jahaziel the son of Zechariah, the son of Benaiah, the son of Jeiel, the son of Mattaniah, a Levite of the sons of Asaph, came the Spirit of the LORD in the midst of the congregation..." (verse14). This is the tremendous power of a proclaimed fast. The spirit of God did not come upon Jehoshaphat – the leader, but on another person in the congregation – how beautiful!

"And he said, Hearken ye, all Judah, and ye inhabitants of Jerusalem, and thou king Jehoshaphat, Thus saith the LORD unto you, Be not afraid nor dismayed by reason of this great multitude; for the battle is not yours, but God's" (verse 15).

You can imagine how good that sounded to them. The Holy Ghost spoke to them! This was the very purpose of their meeting. The effectiveness of a proclaimed fast rests on the unity and singleness of purpose it creates.

Ezra likewise, exhorted the Jews to conduct a public (proclaimed) fast before their journey back to Jerusalem, with the precious things for the temple. They were returning from their 70 years Babylonian captivity to rebuild the temple (Ezra 8. 21-22); the result? "So we fasted and besought our God for this: and he was intreated of us" (verse 23).

Esther also proclaimed a fast among the Jews in order to avert an imminent danger – the total annihilation of the Jewish race being orchestrated by Haman- the Prime Minister of the Land. Esther gave the following instructions:

"Go, gather together all the Jews that are present in Shushan, and fast ye for me, and neither eat nor drink three days, night or day: I also and my maidens will fast likewise; and so will I go in unto the king, which is not according to the law: and if I perish, I perish" (Esther 4:16)

After this fast, God did not only turn the situation that warranted the fasting around, the king ordered Haman to be hanged *"on the gallows that he had prepared for Mordecai"* (Esther 7:10).

The New Testament example is found in Acts 13:1-2:

> *Now there were in the church that was at Antioch certain prophets and teachers; as Barnabas, and Simeon that was called Niger, and Lucius of Cyrene, and Manaen, which had been brought up with Herod the tetrarch, and Saul. As they ministered to the Lord, and fasted, the Holy Ghost said, Separate me Barnabas and Saul for the work whereunto I have called them. And when they had fasted and prayed, and laid their hands on them, they sent them away.*

The Holy Ghost spoke in the midst of ordinary men, as they were fasting and ministering to the Lord. This set in motion a great move of God that literally changed the world."That assignment brought into being two-third of the New Testament…" Kenneth Copeland observed. As instructed, they laid their hands on Saul and Barnabas and sent them forth. The result of their exploits was overwhelming.

PERSONAL FAST

The other type of fast is the personal fast. The general purpose of this type of fast is self-affliction and repentance. It may be observed in times of personal or communal calamity in order to seek God's divine intervention or, more commonly, as penitence for personal wrongdoing. It could also be resorted to as a means of establishing a fasted-life i.e. taking on fasting as a way of life.

It must be stressed, however, that you do not fast to impress God. Fasting changes you, not God. Sometimes, fasting is viewed as an attempt to twist God's arm or to win His approval. But God does not respond to pressure.

One group of people in the book of Acts tried to get God on their side by manipulative fasting:

"In the morning some of the Jews made a plan to kill Paul, and they took an oath not to eat or drink anything until they had killed him. They went to the leading priests and the older Jewish leaders and said, 'We have taken an oath not to eat or drink until we have killed Paul" (Acts 23:12,14).

But God did not hear their prayer and their plan did not work. In essence, they fasted in vain.

Using fasting in a manipulative way was done by the people in Jeremiah's day too. God said,

"Although they fast, I will not listen to their cry; though they offer burn offerings and grain offering, I will not accept them. I will destroy them with the sword, famine, and plague" (Jer. 14:12).

Generally, personal fast is done in secret; a matter between the individual and God. However, this rule might be very difficult to observe in a household setting, where, for example, a wife is undertaking a fast but the husband is not.

In the first place, arrangements need to be made for the family meals. Secondly, as between husband and wife, where only one of them is fasting, it is perfectly in order to let the other party be aware of your intention to observe a fast, and for what duration well ahead of time, as this could mean an abstention from marital relationship for the duration of the fast (1 Cor. 7:5).

It is also highly recommended for husband and wife to mutually agree to engage in the act of fasting together towards achieving a common goal; that then becomes a proclaimed fast.

In Matthew 6:16-18, in the Sermon on the Mount, Jesus devoted a great deal of time teaching on how to engage on a personal fast:

"Moreover when ye fast, be not, as the hypocrites, of a sad countenance: for they disfigure their faces, that they may appear unto men to fast. Verily I say unto you, they have their reward. But thou, when thou fastest, anoint thine head, and wash thy face; That thou appear not unto men to fast, but unto thy Father which is in secret: and thy Father, which seeth in secret, shall reward thee openly."

There are valuable lessons to be learnt from the above scripture:

1. It is to be noted again that Jesus did not say 'if you fast' but "when you fast"; which places a responsibility on the believer to fast.

2. Jesus warned against using fasting as a hypocritical religious exercise. During the Lord's earthly ministry, fasting had become a very important part of the Jewish life.

Jesus condemned the "look-at-how-spiritual-I-am" attitude associated with fasting, as depicted by the attitude and motive of the Pharisee spoken of by Jesus in Luke 18: 10-14.

Let us now examine the story in some depth.

"Two men went up into the temple to pray; the one a Pharisee, and the other a publican. The Pharisee stood and prayed thus with himself, God, I thank thee, that I am not as other men are, extortioners, unjust, adulterers, or even as this publican. I fast twice in the week, I give tithes of all

that I possess. And the publican, standing afar off, would not lift up so much as his eyes unto heaven, but smote upon his breast, saying, God be merciful to me a sinner. I tell you, this man went down to his house justified rather than the other: for every one that exaltethhimself shall be abased; and he that humbleth himself shall be exalted."

Hypocritical piety will always defeat the purpose and power of a fast. If you publicise your spirituality in order to gain the praise of men, you would have succeeded in exchanging the reward of God for the praise of men.

The verdict of Jesus on fasting conducted with the wrong motive is swift and well delivered: *"...verily I say unto you, They have their reward"*(Matt. 6: 16).*"But thou"*, continues Jesus, *"when thou fastest, anoint thine head, and wash thy face; That thou appear not unto men to fast, but unto thy Father which is in secret: **and thy Father, which seeth in secret, shall reward thee openly**"* (vv17-18, emphasis added).

3. Jesus spoke of rewards for fasting. Rewards for personal fasting are on two different levels: You have rewards from the admiration of men, as described above, and an open reward that comes from God when you fast in secret. Believe God for this reward as you go into a fast. Focusing on the reward lessens the pressure fasting has on you.

Chapter 43

GOD'S PURPOSE FOR FASTING

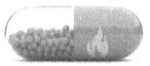

Fasting should always have a special object in view. No one should fast just for fasting sake. Whatever aims at nothing will achieve nothing! Every true fast should be purpose-driven. Our objectives need to be well defined before we take up a fast.

Fasting is not to be some religious ritual we go through. When we fast, we should have a specific purpose in view, a reason for it, something we want to accomplish as a result of our fast. It can be for something very simple as well as something complex and desperate. The question for our consideration under this heading is: why fast? Why should a person set apart a specific time when he denies himself the basic necessities of life for the purpose of seeking God? Since fasts in the Old Testament were in response to calamities and were to demonstrate humility and repentance. It would seem that the same purpose and attitudes would hold true for New Testament believers. Jesus hinted that this should be the purpose for fasting among His disciples. His disciples would fast after the bridegroom was taken away (Matt. 9:14-15; Mark 2:18-20; Luke 5:33-35). The departure of the bridegroom from His bride would normally be looked on as a tragedy that would evoke a felt need. In times of tragedy and heartaches, Jesus' disciples would fast. Fasting then is a legitimate response to dangers, trials, heartaches, or sorrows. In times of physical or spiritual needs, the believer realises his inadequacy, and in humility and repentance looks up to the Lord.

Let us examine some specific purposes of fasting:

Fasting as a Means of Self-Humbling

As human, we are prone towards pride, unless we deal with our hearts. Pride is the default mode of the human heart. It is a besetting sin and the root of all sin that we must continually seek to be conscious and repentant of. Pride is dealt with throughout the Bible in the sternest of terms. In the words of another, God's emotion towards pride is "hate" (Pro. 8:13). His action toward the proud is punishment (Pro. 16:5), that includes "destruction" and a "fall" (Prov. 16:18). Humility enables us to gain access to God. God's grace is only available to the humble; and fasting is God-ordained means of self-humbling. This is particularly so in the life of David. He says *"I humble myself soul with fasting"* (Psalm 35:13). Humility is not a transcendent experience, or a vague emotional experience. Humility is a way of life that becomes part of our 'being' as we make conscious, determined effort to incorporate it as part of the qualities that define us. We must bear in mind that God will not humble us, because He has given us the responsibility to work out humility for ourselves. David, in the scripture just quoted, has shown us the way to achieve humility. The Bible is inundated with teachings on the value of humility. It is an established principle of God that whoever goes the way of humility receives the Master's lifting.

"Humble yourselves, therefore, under God's mighty hand, that he may lift you up in due time" (1 Pet. 5:6).

Further, in Matthew 23: 12, the Bible says,

"And whoever shall exalt himself shall be abased; and he that shall humble himself shall be exalted."

From these two passages, it is very appropriate to conclude that in life, the 'way up' is 'down'. The choice, therefore, is whether to be exalted or abased.

It was the choice of John the Baptist to humble himself before the Master.

"He must increase, but I must decrease" (John 3:30).

John was saying in essence, 'This is the assigned moment for the Master to take the centre stage, while I slip off to the side-line'.

Since John's mission was to go before Jesus and prepare the way for Him (Mark 1:2-3), the time came when John needed to fade into the background of the Jesus' era and allow Jesus His place. It is with considerable grace and humility that John says, *"He must increase, but I must decrease"* (John 3:30). What can we learn from this statement? The answer is found in a similar statement made by John, *"I indeed baptise you with water unto repentance, but He who is coming after me is mightier than I, whose sandals I am not worthy to carry. He will baptize you with the Holy Spirit and fire"* (Matt 3:11). John had no pretensions about the superiority of Jesus' mission to his. The Pharisees sent a list of questions to John—whether he was the prophet, or the Christ, or Elijah resurrected—and John never rashly agreed to any inaccurate designation (John 1:19-26). John knew who he was—and that he was inferior to Jesus—and that did not bother him. Instead, "He must increase, but I must decrease" reflects a mindset of complete humility in the face of one greater.

John shows us that passing the torch is natural—yet still requires humility. "He must increase, but I must decrease" is the thought of each passing generation of God's leaders who are looking to the future of Christ's cause. It was the thought of Moses preparing Joshua, and David preparing Solomon, and Paul preparing Timothy and Titus. Yet we should never think that the need for a new generation to take the reins of leadership in God's work means that relinquishing those reins is easy for a generation accustomed to them! We desperately need the humility to say that we are not as important as the fate of a local church, or the development of leaders in worship and preaching, or the confidence of young believers. Let us promote and encourage them; acknowledging that they must increase, and we must decrease.

John reminds us that God's word is more important than any one person. Surely his followers warned him to be quiet about Herod's adulterous marriage (Matt 14:4) so that he could stay out of trouble and keep preaching — yet the word of God was more important than what happened to John. Further, consider what might have happened had John not stepped aside for Jesus — a power struggle, competing teachers and disciples, and a prevention of many disciples from coming to Jesus. Yet John conceding to Him enabled Jesus to say, *"Assuredly, I say to you, among those born of women there has not risen one greater than John the Baptist..."* (Matt. 11:11). Why? Because God gives us more grace when we humble ourselves before Him. The Scripture says: *"God opposes the proud but gives grace to the humble"* (James 4:6). We may advance the gospel, or detract from its advancement yet, it remains far bigger than we are, individually! We must guard against an inflated sense of self in spiritual matters! "He must increase, but I must decrease" is a distillation of a humble heart. Are we pursuing this humility? Having examined the inestimable worth or benefit of humility in our lives, whatever facilitates it must be appreciated tremendously.

Fasting as a Means of Subduing the Flesh

Eating is something we must do for survival – we have to eat. If we can, on a periodic basis deny ourselves what is a necessity of life, then we surely will be able to train our flesh in other areas. Paul said, *"I discipline my body and bring it into subjection, lest, when I have preached to others, I myself should become disqualified"* (1 Cor. 9:27 NKJV). He said all those who are able to train the flesh would be granted an incorruptible crown as reward for their discipline. Fasting is a way of mastering our flesh. It is an exercise of self-denial. Jesus said, *"If any man will come after me, let him deny himself, and take up his cross daily, and follow me"* (Luke 9:23 KJV).

If we can deny ourselves food and drink for a period of time, we should be able to deny our flesh in the realm of sinful desires and in the disciplines of the Christian life such as prayer. When the disciples were asked by Jesus to stand with Him in prayer, they fell asleep and Jesus said, *"Could you not watch with Me one hour? Watch and pray, lest you enter into temptation. The spirit indeed is willing, but the flesh is weak"* (Matt. 26:40-41 NKJV). If we can take control over the flesh in the area of eating then, we can control it in every other area of life.

Fasting is an Effective Tool for Repentance

Examples of this are found in Deuteronomy 9:18; 1 Samuel 7:6; 1 Kings 21:27; Ezra 10:6; Jonah 3:5; and Acts 9:3-9. In the Old Testament, when people wished to demonstrate that they were serious about repenting from their sin, they fasted. Our willingness to sacrifice shows the depth of our commitment and in this case, fasting is a pictorial way of saying to the Lord, "I care more about getting right with You, God, than I do about even my own life." Fasting is, therefore, self-chastisement, and will prevent many chastisement of the Lord from coming upon us.

Fasting Enhances Intimacy With God.

God wants us to become one with Him. The Scripture says that if you *"draw near to God… He will draw near to you"* (James 4:8). Fasting draws you closer to God, and gives you such a profound hunger for His presence that overcomes struggle in prayer, and leaves a lasting impact of the anointing upon your life.

Fasting is Instrumental For Interceding For those Who Are Sick.

There are two examples in Scripture of fasting on behalf of those who are sick: 2 Samuel 12:15-23; Psalm 35:13. Both of these examples come from the life of David. In Psalm 35:13 David says, "Yet when they were sick, I put on clothes of sadness and showed my sorrow by going without food." David saw fasting as a means of asking God for physical healing in the lives of other people.

Fasting is Instrumental In Averting Crises

There are occasions when death or danger threatens us. We see from the Scripture that it is certainly appropriate to employ fasting as a means of receiving God's protection during these times. When Ezra was carrying a large consignment of gold and silver to the temple in Jerusalem along a route infested with bandits, he records: *"I proclaimed a fast...that we might humble ourselves before our God, to seek from him a straight way for ourselves, our children, and all our goods"* (Ezra 8:21,23,31). Other examples of fasting for protection are found in the following scriptures:

> *And it came to pass in the fifth year of Jehoiakim the son of Josiah king of Judah, in the ninth month, that they proclaimed a fast before the* LORD *to all the people in Jerusalem, and to all the people that came from the cities of Judah unto Jerusalem* (Jer. 36:9).
>
> *When Mordecai perceived all that was done, Mordecai rent his clothes, and put on sackcloth with ashes, and went out into the midst of the city, and cried with a loud and a bitter cry; And came even before the king's gate: for none might enter into the king's gate clothed with sackcloth. And in every province, whithersoever the king's commandment and his decree came, there was great mourning among the Jews, and fasting, and weeping, and wailing; and many lay in sackcloth and ashes* (Esther 4:1-3).

Fasting Helps Us Discover God's Will.

If we expect God to reveal His direction for our lives, we must put Him first. Often this means putting aside the fulfilment of our physical appetites, so that we can focus our attention on Him. We find an example of fasting for direction, as stated, in 2 Chronicles 20:1-30. Three nations were coming against Judah to destroy them. King Jehoshaphat, the king of Judah, proclaimed a fast for the whole nation and they asked the Lord what they should do. God moved as a result of their prayer and fasting, and gave the people prophetic direction! God told them what to do.

Acts 13:2 is another example of direction being given by God during a fast. Here we find the leaders of the church of Antioch worshipping and fasting. The Holy Spirit used this occasion to tell the church leaders to choose Paul and Barnabas from among their group and send them out to spread the gospel among the Gentiles. So fasting is one of the ways we seek God's guidance and direction in our lives.

Fasting Intensifies the Power of Prayer

> *Fasting is designed to make prayer mount up as on eagles' wings. It is intended to usher the supplicant into the audience chamber of the King and to drive back the oppressing powers of darkness, thereby loosening their hold on those being prayed for. Fasting definitely will give an edge to (a person's) intercession and power ... petition* - Leonard Le Sourd remarks

Fasting ignites and enables the believer to pray with greater fervency, focus and intensity. Fasting is an effective aid to meaningful prayer. Through fasting, prayer is intensified, spirituality is sensitised, and ministry is more powerfully effective. If prayer is the fire, fasting is the high-octane fuel that makes that fire rage! Fasting deepens and strengthens your prayer life.

Fasting makes you a better intercessor. It enables you to engage in more serious, heart-felt intercessory prayer. (Neh.1:3-4).

In the words of Hallesby:

Fasting gives us that inner sense of spiritual penetration by means of which we can discern clearly, the reasons why the spirit of God would have us pray in exceptionally difficult circumstances.

Unceasing, incessant prayer is essential to the vitality of your relationship with the Lord, and your ability to function in the world.

In the Old Testament, God said:

"Command Aaron and his sons, saying, This is the law of the burnt offering: It is the burnt offering, because of the burning upon the altar all night unto the morning, and the fire of the altar shall be burning in it" (Lev. 6:9).

Further, we read in the law that the fire on the altar should burn always and ever. After God has lighted the fire, the priest was to ensure that the fire burned always, and never extinguished. How did the priest discharge this onerous responsibility? He was to *"... burn wood on [the altar] every morning, and lay the burnt offering in order upon it; and he shall burn thereon the fat of the peace offerings.* ***The fire shall ever be burning upon the altar, it shall never go out"*** (Lev. 6:12-13, emphasis added).

When your prayer life needs revitalisation, embrace the grace of fasting. Your heart will be touched more easily, your spirit will soar higher, and your awareness of His presence will increase.

In the words of Oswald Sanders, "... many who practice [fasting] from right motives and in order to give themselves more unreservedly to prayer testify that the mind becomes unusually clear and vigorous. There are a noticeable spiritual quickening and increased power of concentration on the things of the spirit."

This means that spiritual reality is more easily discernible through fasting. In a long fast, you are so overwhelmed with His presence that the desires of the flesh are significantly reduced and the spirit rises and soars, controlling the soul. In fact, the things of the world become absolutely meaningless. One cannot but agree with Oswald Sanders obvious view that one of the values of fasting lies in the fact that its discipline "helps us keep the body in its place. It is a practical acknowledgment of the supremacy of the spiritual.

Fasting is still God's chosen way to deepen and strengthen prayer. Without it, your prayer life will lack the requisite vitality and 'fire' to confront the gate of hell, and put the enemy on the run. Answers to prayer, guidance, direction, insight – all flow more freely when fasting is freely and willingly embraced with grace in the heart. Fasting will remove roadblocks and distractions in your prayer life and thus will intensify your prayer life, drawing you closer to God, to hear Him clearly. Fasting has established a new spiritual dimension in my life, lifting me to a higher plane of spiritual authority.

Fasting Strengthens Our Faith

The faith that we must have is a faith that has more to do with what kind of faith it is than with how much faith there is. Small amount of faith, as small as a mustard seed, can accomplish great things, if it is placed on a great and mighty God. Charles Spurgeon gives a fascinating analogy of the working of faith thus: "The eye cannot see itself. Did you ever see your own eye? In a mirror you may have done so, but that was only a reflection of it. And you may, in like manner, see the evidence of your faith, but you cannot look at the faith itself. Faith looks away to itself to the object of faith, even to Christ."

Fasting is an Effective Tool to Dealing With Demonic Forces.

Specifically, Jesus recommends fasting in dealing with satanic forces. He said, *"But this kind goes not out but by prayer and fasting"* (Matt. 17:21). Fasting breaks through satanic siege and deals with the force behind a particular situation. Usually, the enemy cannot resist the power of a fasting believer.

Fasting Mortifies the Flesh

Fasting mortifies and enables our members to break free from bondage (Col. 3:5). Our strongholds for the flesh are pulled down, so that faith has no real barriers (2 Cor. 10:3:5). Fasting casts down reasoning, so that we will not listen to the evidence that our senses may bring forth, but sets faith loose.

As you live a fasted life, you will not be flesh-ruled, and, the power to commit sin is broken! Why? Because when you fast, you are bringing our body into submission.

In 1 Corinthians 9:27, Paul asserts:

> *But I keep under my body, and bring it into subjection: lest that by any means, when I have preached to others, I myself should be a castaway.*

This has the consequent effect of causing the believer to develop and produce the fruit of the Spirit, according to Galatians 5:22.

Fasting was a regular part of the ordination of church leaders and missionaries.

As seen in Acts 13:3, after the church had received direction from the Lord to commission Barnabas and

Paul for missionary service, they prayed and fasted for them.

We find the same thing later on in the same book of Acts - Paul and Barnabas fasted prior to the selection of the first elders for the new churches they planted (Acts 14:23). It would appear that fasting in these cases is a way of seriously seeking God's blessing, anointing, and power upon the leaders of the church.

Fasting Helps Sustain the Anointing

Fasting plays a vital role in releasing and sustaining the anointing. Fasting has a direct link with the measure of the grace of God that operates in a believer's life. This is because fasting helps the believer to tune into the spirit realm where his inheritance already exists. When the believer feels dry spiritually or needs a fresh release of the unction of God, fasting is the secret key that unlocks the flood-gate of heaven and releases such level of grace that nothing else can. Fasting is for spiritual empowerment; without fail, it culminates in the release of astonishing power for outstanding achievements.

This is the secret of excelling in the work of the kingdom. The surpassing power of God is available to everyone who desires it and can pay the price for it; fasting is one infallible instrument for obtaining it. As said, Jesus the son of God fasted for forty days and nights. If Jesus could have accomplished all His earthly assignment without fasting, why should He fast?

The son of God fasted because He knew there were supernatural blessings, indeed, unction for exploits that could not be released any other way. How much more should fasting be a common practice in our lives? Fasting takes the believer from the ordinary realm to the extraordinary. Walking in favour is not a product of luck and coincidence! Breaking free from satanic forces, and life full of miseries, agony, mischief, shame and reproach, to the high life God has destined for you take more than prayer. This was the lesson the Master conveyed to the disciples who could not heal a demon possessed boy, when He said "...*this kind goeth not but by prayer and fasting*" (Matt. 17:20-21). Jesus says, "*If you will lose your life for my sake you will find it*" (Matt. 10:39). The Greek text says, "If you will up that low life, you will find the high life." Fasting is one of the tools that help you shed the low life. As you begin to live a fasted life, the spirit of God begins to change your taste in life, urging you to reach out to 'that' high life in God; the place of excellence, perfection, abundance, and uncommon breakthrough! How does it work? You see, prayer and fasting will cause you to be much more spiritually sensitive to the Lord and His direction in your life.

Fasting Deepens Your Understanding of the Word of God

In Isaiah 33:6, the prophet declared, "And wisdom and knowledge shall be the stability of thy times..."

This scripture is as applicable today as it was when Isaiah first spoke it concerning the sins that plagued Judah centuries ago. The situation is even worse now!

Today, the threat of murder, acts of terrorism (beheadings) and nuclear mishaps dominates our media headlines and tries to instil fear in our hearts. It is comforting to know that God has promised to provide stability in these precarious times through knowledge and wisdom.

One of the personal rewards of fasting as promised by God is: "Then [after you have fasted] shall thy light break forth as the morning…" (Isaiah 58:8).

The Bible says,

> *The entrance of thy word giveth light, and giveth understanding to the simple* (Psalm 119:130).

Bible revelation comes as a result of a conscious 'downloading' from the source – God, through His word. Fasting gives an edge, 'bigger' entrance, and weight to the word of God. As you get intimate with God through fasting, your spirit-man is ignited to receive deep insight, and such profound revelation from God that you would not receive otherwise. It was while Moses was settling the destiny of Israel with God, through fasting that God gave him a powerful revelation that became known as – the Ten Commandments. Fasting lightens up your inner-man to hear and receive from God with clarity. I am always amazed at the depth of revelations I receive when undergoing a fast.

> ...one of the greatest spiritual benefits of fasting" according to Elmer Towns, "is becoming more attentive to God – becoming more aware of our own inadequacies and His adequacy, our own contingencies and His self-sufficiency – and listening to what He wants us to be and do...

This impacts, not only your ability to receive revelations from God, but your ability in the delivery of God's word. Fasting puts you in the realm where you practically "rightly divide the word of God" (2 Tim. 2:15).

In Ecclesiastes 10:10, the Bible says,

"If an axe is dull, And one does not sharpen the edge, then he must use more strength; But wisdom brings success."

Fasting gives you that cutting edge of the anointing for kingdom service.

Fasting is a catalyst for Spiritual Growth

When you fast, you feed your spirit-man to grow. If you must operate in power, fasting must be a common practice in your life. Indeed, those who seek God through the discipline of fasting are open to reservoir of God's power because, fasting creates a deep hunger after God. When you get hungry for God, He gets closer. Spiritual hunger will move God, and open doors. The question is: how hungry are you for God? Notice, I did not ask, how hungry you are for blessings and His provision, but how hungry are you for Him? His face, not just His hands! Does your soul long, even faint, for the presence of the Lord? We very much need to be hungry if we are going to see God move in our lives. Again, how hungry are you for God's presence in your life? David expressed deep hunger for God with the following words:

> *How lovely are Your tabernacles, O Lord of hosts! My soul yearns, yes, even pines and is homesick for the courts of the Lord; my heart and my flesh cry out and sing for joy to the living God... For a day in Your courts is better than a thousand [anywhere else]; I would rather be a doorkeeper and stand at the threshold in the house of my God than to dwell [at ease] in the tents of wickedness* (Psalm 84:1,2,10; Amp.).

Deep hunger for God shuts down the influence of the flesh, so that the spirit man can take dominance.

EPILOGUE

In the thrilling and insightful words of Leonard Ravenhill, "*No man is greater than his prayer life. The pastor who is not praying is playing; the people who are not praying are straying. We have many organizers, but few agonizers; many players and payers, few pray-ers; many singers, few clingers; lots of pastors, few wrestlers; many fears, few tears; much fashion, little passion; many interferers, few intercessors; many writers, but few fighters. Failing here, we fail everywhere.*"

The plethora of materials and individual cases contained in this book point to one incontestable conclusion: prayer is the key to breakthrough in life! For everyone that desires a significant and enviable leap in life, for everyone that passionately and desperately needs a 'turn around' in life, for those who, like Jabez, are fed up of the status quo and urgently and intently hunger for a change, for the individuals who have come to the end of themselves and are badly desirous of heaven's intervention, for the many of God's wonderful children who had once tasted of the goodness of the Lord and are now singing the Lord's song in a 'strange land', and desperately desire restoration, prayer is the answer!

The power of prayer should not be underestimated. We have seen that God's help through the power of prayer is available for all kind of situations and circumstances. Philippians 4:6-7 admonishes, *"Be careful for nothing; but **in everything** by prayer and supplication with thanksgiving let your requests be made known unto God. And the peace of God, which passeth all understanding, shall keep your hearts and minds through Christ Jesus"* (emphasis added).

James 5:16-18 declares, *"...The effectual fervent prayer of a righteous man availeth much. Elias was a man subject to like passions as we are, and he prayed earnestly that it might not rain: and it rained not on the earth by the space of three years and six months. And he prayed again, and the heaven gave rain, and the earth brought forth her fruit."*

The only force on earth that moves God is prayer. The only link between heaven and earth is prayer. Prayer is the conveyor of God's blessings to mankind. God most definitely answers prayer!

The Word of God is full of accounts describing the power of prayer in various situations. The power of prayer has overcome enemies (2 Chr. 20:1-29), conquered death (2 Isaiah 38: 1-6), brought healing (James 5:14-15), and defeated demons (Mark 9:29). God, through prayer, opens eyes, changes hearts, heals wounds, and grants wisdom (James 1:5).

The power of prayer should never be underestimated because it draws on the glory and might of the infinitely powerful God of the universe into every situation! Daniel 4:35 proclaims, "*All the people of the earth are nothing compared to him. He has the power to do as he pleases among the angels of heaven and with those who live on earth. No one can stop him or challenge him, saying, 'What do you mean by doing these things?'*" (NLT).

God is Omnipotent. As seen, His great power is made manifest through prayer. So, no matter the situation you are in today, call upon Him! Remember He has promised: "*Call unto me, and I will answer thee, and show thee great and mighty things, which thou knowest not.*"

Child of God, answers await you in the presence of God, no matter the situation!

BIBLIOGRAPHY

1. Burck J.L., *Prayer therapy* , (Pub 1996)
2. Cho P.Y.*Prayer: Key to Revival,* (Pub.1984)
3. Cymbala J.*The Life God Blesses,* (Pub.2001)
4. Fomum Z.T.*Waiting on the Lord in Prayer,* (Pub.1996)
5. Hagee J.*The Power of the Prophetic Blessing,* (Pub.2012)
6. Hagin K.E.*The Interceding Christian,* 9th Edition (Pub.1979)
7. Hagin. K.E.*Classic Sermons* , (Pub. 1992)
8. Hammond L. and Cameneti P.*Secrets to Powerful Prayer,* (Pub.2000)
9. Hawkins O.S.*Nelson's Annual Preacher's Sourcebook,* (Pub.2013)
10. Hinn B.*Prayer that Gets Results,* (Pub.2005)
11. Jakes T.D.*Life Overflowing* , (Pub.2000, 2008)
12. Law T.*The Power of Praise and Worship,* (Pub.1985)

13. Lunstrom L. *How You Can Pray with Power* , (Pub. 1981)

14. Macintrye D. *The Hidden Life of Prayer,*

15. Morris. H *The Henry Morris Study Bible,* Master Edition (Pub.1995,2006,2012)

16. Munroe M. *Understanding the Purpose and Power of Prayer,* (Pub. 2002)

17. Murray A. *With Christ in the School of Prayer,* (Pub.2013)

18. Prince D. *Living as Salt and Light,* (Pub.2013)

19. Sorge. B., *Glory When Heaven invades Earth,* (Pub.2000)

20. Tozer A.W. *The Warfare of The Spirit,* (Pub. 1993)

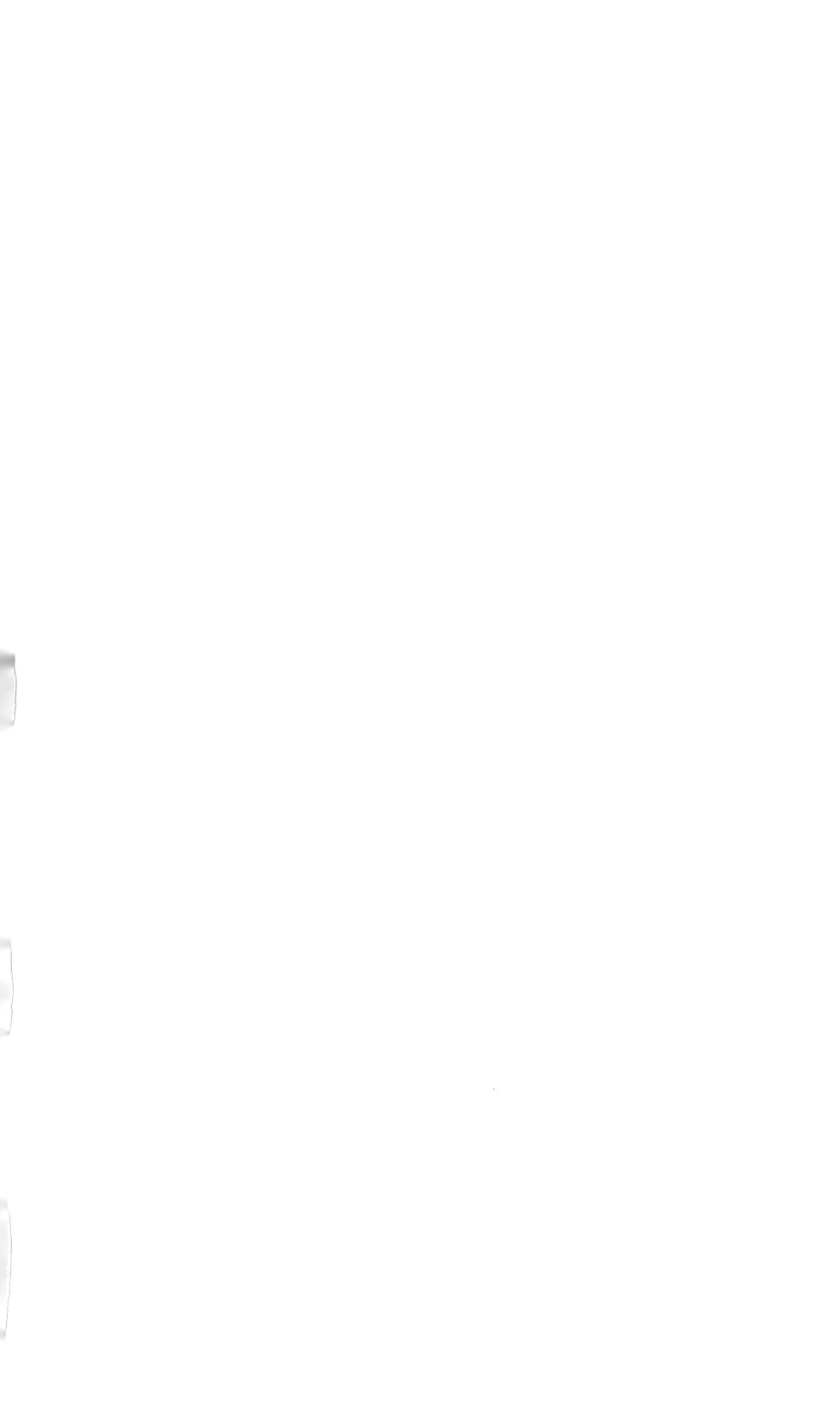

www.ingramcontent.com/pod-product-compliance
Lightning Source LLC
Chambersburg PA
CBHW032358100526
44587CB00010BA/190